THE BULL RIDER'S ADVICE

THE BULL RIDER'S ADVICE

NEW AND SELECTED POEMS

BY DAVID ALLAN EVANS

To a first-rate athlete
and a first-rate man—
John Simko—
All the Best, and
it was great seeing you
at the event in SF—
Dave Evans
October, 2004

The Center for Western Studies
Augustana College

2004

Published by The Center for Western Studies
Mailing address: Box 727, Augustana College, Sioux Falls, SD 57197
Street address: Augustana College, 2201 S. Summit Ave., Sioux Falls, SD 57197
E-mail address: cws@augie.edu
Copies of our book catalog may be obtained by calling 605-274-4007 or by visiting our web page at www.augie.edu/CWS.

The Center for Western Studies is an archives, library, museum, publishing house, and educational agency concerned principally with collecting, preserving, and interpreting prehistoric, historic, and contemporary materials that document native and immigrant cultures on the northern prairie-plains. The Center promotes understanding of the region through exhibits, publications, art shows, conferences, and academic programs. It is committed, ultimately, to defining the contribution of the region to American civilization.

Library of Congress Cataloging-in-Publication Data

Evans, David Allan.
The bull rider's advice : new and selected poems / by David Allan Evans.
p. cm. -- (Prairie plains series)
ISBN 0-931170-81-8
1. South Dakota--Poetry. 2. West (U.S.)--Poetry. I. Title. II. Series.

PS3555.V214B85 2003
811'.54--dc22

2003065336

Front cover photo by South Dakota Tourism.

Publication made possible with a grant from South Dakota State University.

Number 10 in the Prairie-Plains Series

Printed in the United States of America
by Pine Hill Press, Inc.
4000 W. 57th St.
Sioux Falls, SD 57106

for Jan
and for Shelly, David, and Kari

ACKNOWLEDGMENTS

Some of the poems in TRAIN WINDOWS (Ohio University Press, 1976) first appeared in *Back Door, Crazy Horse, Esquire, The Far Point, Kansas Quarterly, Midwest Quarterly, Monmouth Review, North American Review, The New York Times, Poetry Northwest, Poetry Now, Prairie Schooner, Shenandoah, South Dakota Review, Sou'wester*, and I LOVE YOU ALL DAY, IT IS THAT SIMPLE (Abbey Press).

Some of the poems in REAL AND FALSE ALARMS (Bk Mk Press, 1985) first appeared in *Blue Buildings, Dakota Arts Quarterly, Chariton Review, Chowder Review, Great River Review, Hiram Poetry Review, Madog* (Wales), *Kansas Quarterly, Milkweed Chronicle, Northeast, Plainsong, Poetry Now, Sandhills, South Dakota Review,* and *Spoon River Quarterly.*

Some of the poems in HANGING OUT WITH THE CROWS (Bk Mk Press, 1991) first appeared in *Arete: The Journal of Sports Literature* (now called *Aethlon*), *Chariton Review, Elkhorn Review, Homestones, Kansas Quarterly, Platte Valley Review, Poetry Now, Religion in Public Education, Shenandoah,* MEN TALK (Pacific Books), and STRINGS (Bradbury Press).

Some of the poems in DECENT DANGERS (Mellen Poetry Press, 2000) first appeared in *Aethlon, Chariton Review, Fan: A Baseball Magazine, Huraken, Poetry Motel, The Briar Cliff Review, South Dakota Review, The North American Review, The Southern Review*, and ANIMALS IN POETRY (Sarasota Poetry Theater Press).

Some of the NEW POEMS first appeared *in Aethlon, Eclipse: A Literary Journal, Rain Flower Review*, (People's Republic of China), *South Dakota Review*, and *The Mid-America Poetry Review.*

The memoir, "From the Pole Vaulter's Bluff," first appeared in IMAGINING HOME: WRITINGS OF THE MIDWEST (University of Minnesota Press).

The author wishes to thank South Dakota State University, and particularly Professor Kathleen Donovan for her support and editorial assistance, and President Peggy Miller, whose generosity and initiative made this book possible.

TABLE OF CONTENTS

"A windmill, a junk heap, and a Rotarian in their American setting have more meaning to me than Notre Dame, the Parthenon, or the heroes of the ages. I understand them. I get them emotionally."

—Thomas Hart Benton

"What but the wolf's tooth whittled so fine
The fleet limbs of the antelope?"

—Robinson Jeffers

FOREWORD

In his introduction to *New and Collected Poems (1931-2001),* Czeslaw Milosz said, "I think that effort to capture as much as possible of tangible reality is the health of poetry." If that is so, then here we have a good measure of the health of poetry.

David Allan Evans and I have matured together. Dad and I took the hogs and cattle to David's stockyards in Sioux City. They went to the slaughterhouses, John Morrell and Swift, as in the poems. We saw Lower Fourth Street before urban renewal was tried. Then the first well-received book, *Train Windows*, then after a day of trial in a rural county seat, listening to David read to the descendants of settlers in Gregory County; to David reading his "Bull Rider's Advice" at the Federal Courthouse. As in these poems, time advances, but the people and places and events of early life remain forceful. This poetry is not wearying, narcissistic examinations and confessions, but instead urges us from a necessary distance to consider our lives, our sports, our places—things that are familiar.

All that is and has been around us we deal with in one way or another, sometimes by ignoring, sometimes by incomprehension. Poetry is another way of looking, but not ignoring. These poems allow us to look in a way that cannot be duplicated, not by prose or even by other poems.

What would the settlers, so close behind us, have made of this poet laureate of Dakota? I think they too would have embraced the tangible reality of these poems.

Where will it go from here? This is not the end. This poetry is a life's work. We will follow David Evans until he has no more poems. Coming generations will read them and know something more of what we were. These poems will live on.

Honorable Lawrence L. Piersol
Chief Judge
United States District Court
District of South Dakota

PREFACE: FROM THE POLE VAULTER'S BLUFF

> "One of my convictions is that at the center of every poetic imagination is a cluster of key images that go back to the poet's childhood . . . poets are always revisiting the state of their innocence."
>
> —Stanley Kunitz

When I was about 14 my older brother Jerry, one of the best pole vaulters in Iowa, taught me to vault, and that quickly became an obsession. I couldn't get enough of it. My mother used to give up calling me in for dinner. "Just one more!" I'd yell to her, and after that, again and again, "just one more!"

About two decades later, when I published my first book of poems, the first poem in it had come directly out of the vacant lot next to our house, where we had our vaulting pit, with crossbars and vaulting poles made out of bamboo. The poem is called "Pole Vaulter," and its opening lines are:

The approach to the bar
is everything

unless I have counted
my steps   hit my markers
feel up to it   I refuse
to follow through
I am committed to beginnings
or to nothing

All poets have one or two poems they consider seminal. This is one of mine. In retrospect, the word *beginnings* in the seventh line may represent the beginning of a new phase of my life. "So I was once myself a swinger of birches," says Robert Frost in his marvelous poem of childhood, "Birches"; and then, "and so I dream of going back to be." If the New England poet was a swinger of birches in his youth, I, a Midland poet, was a pole vaulter in mine.

*   *   *

The landscape of my childhood was Sioux City, Iowa, where I was born in 1940. For a Midwestern city, Sioux City is a unique mix of urban and rural. (The name itself is an oxymoronic juxtaposition of a Plains Indian tribe's name and a word that evokes Western order and civilization.) Its population has been around 80,000 since I lived there, and yet the city is huge: 52 square miles, an area large enough to accommodate the confluence of three rivers—the Sioux, Floyd, and Missouri—farms and ranches, packing houses and other industry. I feel fortunate to have been raised in both rural and urban settings.

Between the ages of two and eight I lived with my parents, two brothers, and two sisters on an acreage. One of my earliest memories is of walking barefoot on cool, hard clods of our freshly-ploughed potato garden. My father raised chickens and I would sometimes collect eggs from the chicken shed in the morning. On two sides of us were cornfields, on another side, hills, and, a few hundred yards to the east, a deep ravine called Devil's Hollow. On clear nights, because there were no streetlights nearby, the sky was a bowl of stars you could stand inside.

In 1948 we moved from the acreage to a brick house on a railroad bluff on Wall Street (now called Floyd Boulevard). It is mostly this locale, where I lived from the ages of eight to 15, that I have revisited obsessively in my memory and my writings: the brick house (almost 50 years later I still remember our telephone number: 88686), and the vacant lot next to it; a ravine at the north end of Wall Street; the railroad tracks, trains and steam engines, a roundhouse; the Sioux City Soos minor league baseball

My parents, Art and Ruth, in their 20s. My mother had the habit of identifying persons in photographs.

I'm probably five or six here, with my older brother Jerry and older sister Bonnie, in the porch on our acreage in the hills north of downtown Sioux City.

park across the tracks, and the "pig dump" beyond center field; a steep bluff with creosote steps running down it; a soybean factory on whose roof I was almost electrocuted trying to capture some pigeons; two ponds; the Floyd river, where I learned to swim and where the Ringling Brothers Circus elephants, when the circus came to town every summer, were taken to drink; Woodrow Wilson Junior High and its playground; the Wall Street viaduct; gravel alleys; a deaf and dumb man with an iron-wheeled cart who made a meager living collecting junk; a sewer under Wall Street that my friends and I would walk through with flashlights; a little grocery store owned by a Jewish family named Strongin; a gravel company with its pyramids of gravel; the Jewish Community Center, where I spent a lot of winter nights playing basketball; a steep block of Iowa Street that we used to sled down on Flexible Flyers with waxed runners.

About two miles southeast of our house were the Stockyards, and Swift's and Armour's packing houses, Half Moon Lake, and above it, "Polock Hill," where many Polish packing-house workers and their families lived. Eight blocks south of us was Sioux City's business district, often referred to pejoratively as "Lower Fourth," a strip of beer joints, restaurants, clothing stores, theaters, and whore houses (otherwise known as the Virginia Hotel, the Swan Hotel, and the Chicago House, among others) running parallel to and only a few blocks north of the Missouri. Lower Fourth and the packing houses were the main reasons Sioux City was known—again, in the pejorative—as "Little Chicago."

This in-town territory—about two miles in circumference, with our Wall Street house in the center—has been the source of a solid percentage of the images and experiences I've used in one way or another in poems and prose in almost four decades of writing. Even the titles of my first two books of poems and book of essays attest to the locale's importance: *Train Windows*, which refers to my habit of watching trains at night from the railroad bluff; *Real and False Alarms*, which refers to a fire station at the bottom of Iowa Street, between our house and Lower Fourth; *Remembering the Soos*, which refers to the minor league ball park, where I spent many nights with friends.

My teen years were crucial to me; they became a bridge between early and late childhood, between the end of one life and the beginning of another I was gradually discovering.

My main response to the explosion of hormones and the need to prove myself among my male peers was to excel at what I enjoyed most and was good at—sports—and hang out with other athletes, who were among the toughest guys around. I was not one to give schoolwork a lot of attention, and my grades were mediocre. I was a slow reader, and so feeble at math that my junior high teacher labeled me as having a "math block"—this, in front of an entire class. I flunked, and the next semester was sent to Woodshop, the "Opportunity Class," where one day, with other things on my mind than the plane saw I was working with, I nearly cut off a finger.

For me, the hands of Woodrow Wilson's schoolroom clocks could not have moved slower than they did. Whatever the season, I always wanted out—to play baseball or football, swim in the Missouri or Floyd, kill rats in the pig dump, ice skate, go sledding in the ravine or on the steep streets, mess around down by the roundhouse, or, ignoring my parents' sternest rule, hop a ride on a moving box car.

Even though I was not a good student, I had always been able to focus on and even work hard at things I enjoyed. I still have an elaborate pencil design I did at the age of four or five. From an early age I could sit for hours on a sidewalk or at a table, drawing, or making useless gadgets (I called them inventions) out of tin, wood, and cardboard. When I was in the seventh grade a black, jovial doctor named Dobson said I had rheu-

I'm on the left, at 14, standing next to my brother Jerry on the day of his high school graduation. The others are my younger brother Bob, my younger sister Judy, and my niece, Jody. We're standing inside the picket fence at 1215 Floyd Boulevard (at the time, called Wall Street).

matic fever, and sent me back to school with a note keeping me off the playground and out of sports for the entire spring semester. As my classmates played outside for recess, I drew designs with pen and ink, a habit I would continue well into my adulthood.

* * *

The person who had by far the most influence on me in those teen years was my father. He had also been an athlete, and he had the same trait of fixing on something and working hard at it. As a college student, one winter I had a part-time job in *The Sioux City Journal* pressroom, where my father had been a pressman for 30 years, and those men who had worked with him spoke highly of his work ethic. "He was a worker" was a phrase I heard many times.

This eighth-grade dropout with a powerful ambition to be a writer couldn't get enough of good books, or of the writers he would reread so often that late in life he would refer to them as close friends: Shakespeare, Montaigne, Voltaire, Anatole France, Herbert Spencer, Thomas Huxley, Tolstoy, Dostoyevski, Charles Darwin, Ernest Dowson, Oscar Wilde, H.L. Mencken, Marcel Proust, Thomas Wolfe, Robert Benchley, among many others. Apparently, he had always been a reader. My aunt, his half-sister, once told me there was a feature article in the *Journal*, when my father was around 20, to the effect that he was determined to read the entire Sioux City public library by the age of 30.

He sometimes read to my sisters and brothers and me when we were kids. My favorite story was one by Ernest Thompson Seton called "Lobo: The King of the Kurumpa," about a huge wolf. My father read the story many times, and I was the only one who would cry when at the end Lobo was strangled by the lariats of bounty hunters.

My father had a record of Shakespeare's soliloquies read by John Barrymore, and sometimes he'd bring it out and play it on our old Victrola. I can still recall the piercing, angry voice of Barrymore's Hamlet or Richard the Third, and my father, horizontal on his recliner, thoroughly absorbed by the poetry. He and my uncle Elmer would occasionally drink beer and quote poetry to each other.

I was an outdoor boy at the time and not a reader yet, but I liked listening to the poetry, and to Barrymore's Shakespeare, though I'm sure I didn't understand much of what I was hearing. When you are young, it's easy to be influenced by adults—especially parents—who place such high value on something: in my father's case, the words of great writers.

Yet he never pushed books on his children or anybody. This gentle but intense man simply had books around the house, and showed, by example, how important they can be if you have any inclination to need them. (To this day, I cringe whenever I see someone trying to force books or beliefs on others.)

Gradually, in my early teens, I began to realize that I not only enjoyed poetry, but, like my father and uncle, I had a talent for remembering it. On my way to the YMCA on Saturday mornings, if I was alone, I would sometimes stop at the public library and go downstairs to what was called the reading room, where there was a record player and a collection of records, some of poets or actors reading poetry. I would put a record on, and sit on the couch and listen. This habit was a secret I would share with nobody, least of all my jock friends. In the 50s in Sioux City, sports were for men and poetry was for sissies. That was an absolute.

On that reading room couch the first poem I ever heard on my own was Matthew Arnold's "Dover Beach." I didn't understand all of the words, but the rhythms and phrasing were an enchantment to me. Even if I got no ideas from the poem, I still would have kept playing the record and listening. The opening certainly got my attention:

> The sea is calm tonight.
> The tide is full, the moon lies fair
> Upon the straights; on the French coast the light
> Gleams and is gone; the cliffs of England stand,
> Glimmering and vast, out in the tranquil bay . . .

I knew nothing about Dover Beach, not even where it was, and yet I felt the lines' dignity and power. I must have wondered to myself how a poet could describe the sea, cliffs, and moonlight with such clarity and force. There was something in the slow, deliberate, serious, drawn-out cadences, in the tone of voice—of an actor named David Allen—that I couldn't have explained to anybody but which I began to love, especially the line that seemed to go on and on: "Its melancholy, long, withdrawing roar . . . ."

The word *clash* in the poem's last line—"Where ignorant armies clash by night"—always pleased me with its emphasis. And I could see the images of water in the poem, because I had watched the glittering Missouri from the bluffs at night—the way light "gleams and is/Gone." I played the poem over and over. It didn't take long to have it by heart, and in my 60s I can still recite most of it.

One day when I got up the nerve to check out a poetry record and was carrying it home, I was confronted by a high school kid I knew, a tall, aggressive, outspoken lineman on the varsity football team.

"What's that you got, Evans?" he said.

"Oh, just a record," I said.

"Lemme see it," he said, and grabbed it out of my hands. He looked at it, and when he saw what it was, he said, "What's this shit—pomes?"

I said "Yeah" sheepishly, took the record back, and went on my way. I heard him behind me, snickering in disgust.

* * *

I must have been 14 or 15, standing by one of my father's bookcases, the one in the hallway near the front door. I was picking some books out at random, opening them up, reading here and there. I think I was just curious. I picked out a thick, dark-blue book called *The Oxford Book of American Poetry*. Inside the front cover of this book that I still have was the price: "35 cents." My father had bought it, along with a lot of other books, at the Salvation Army store down by the viaduct. I started glancing through the pages, and came to a poem called "Limited." At Woodrow we were required in English class to read poems, stories, and plays by writers such as Shakespeare, Dickens, Longfellow, Bryant, and Whittier. I had never heard of this author, Carl Sandburg. I read the poem:

> I am riding on a limited express, one of the crack
>   trains of the nation.
> Hurtling across the prairie into blue haze and dark air
>   go fifteen all-steel coaches holding a thousand people.
> (All the coaches shall be scrap and rust and all the men
>   and women laughing in the diners and sleepers shall
>   pass to ashes.)
> I ask a man in the smoker where he is going and he
>   answers: 'Omaha.'

The word *Omaha* hit me like a hammer. I was astonished to see such a familiar word in a poem. I hadn't been there, but I knew that Omaha was only about 90 miles south of Sioux City. I was also struck by the sounds of the words: for example, the repetition of the same sound in *laughing, ashes, ask*, and *answers*. I knew about trains, of course, living on a railroad bluff. I doubt if I got Sandburg's wry humor at the time, but I must have sensed it: that even if "the man in the smoker" as well as "all the men and women laughing in the diners and sleepers" may think they're going to Omaha or whatever earthly destination, they are all, like the rest of us, even the train itself, "hurtling across the prairie" toward oblivion: *scrap and rust*. Here, for the first time, was a poet who spoke my language! The words were spare, concrete, accessible, down-to-earth.

Then I read "Ice Handler," which begins:

> I know an ice handler who wears a flannel shirt with
>   pearl buttons the size of a dollar,

The Leeds High senior halfback, in a "Gale Sayers pose"—ball tucked in, the straight arm extended for would-be tacklers.

And he lugs a hundred-pound hunk into a saloon icebox,
    helps himself to cold ham and rye bread . . .

These words were close too. I'd watched the iceman delivering ice to our house, and he was a physical, confident man like the one in the poem.

I also read "Fish Crier," which begins:

I know a Jew fish crier down on Maxwell Street with
    a voice like a north wind blowing over corn stubble
    in January.

I'd never seen a fish crier, but on the acreage I'd heard the unmistakable sound of wind "blowing over corn stubble in January." At that moment, standing there in the hallway with that book in my hands, I'd suddenly discovered a few poems that reminded me of things I already knew but were described so convincingly that I would never forget them.

* * *

I started writing in my sophomore year in college, first poems and then stories. I had an excellent college creative writing teacher named Howard Levant. A poet himself, he helped me with specific comments on my poems, and encouraged me to read widely and to experiment with both fiction and poetry.

A brief, one-semester Iowa Writers' Workshop experience in the early 60s was a temporary setback for me. Most of the writers in my poetry writing class were from larger, Eastern cities, as well as older and more experienced than I. One afternoon in the Student Union some workshop poets were giving a reading. A young man named White got up and started reading a poem whose first word was *corn*, and he drew out the word in an exaggerated, loud, derisive way that obviously meant that he didn't like poetry with local perspectives or settings in it, especially Midwestern ones. The audience agreed, clapping and laughing. I felt like the only one not in on the fun.

Some of the Workshop sessions were useful to me, and there were some good writers around. But I was intimidated by what I sensed was a strong Eastern bias, and didn't think I had much to contribute. Confused, and with my confidence shaken, I dropped out.

I left Iowa City and took a teaching job at a college in Colorado, and slowly, tentatively, trying to forget the Iowa City detour, I began to write poems about experiences and images that were familiar: trains, pigeons, cindered alleys, fist fighting, pole vaulting, running with a football, working in a packing house (another night job while going to college) fishing, and so on. In other words, I began to revisit, through memories, the Sioux City landscapes. Some of these memories were so strong and persistent that the only way I could contain them was to give them some shape in words on paper. The poems I wrote seemed to fall into one of two main categories. One was dynamic and dramatic, such as my poem about pole vaulting; the other was quiet, static, and introspective, such as my poem about standing where Armour's used to be before it was razed, and which begins:

> It is 5 a.m. everything is the same as it was
> the moon-hammered faces of the cattle are waiting
> the line at the hiring gate is growing minute by minute . . .

David, David Jr., Jan, Kari, Shelly (1984)

(I've often wondered whether these two kinds of poems don't reflect a lifestyle that prefers to alternate bursts of physical energy with long periods of quiet reflection and concentration, in a room alone, writing.) Gradually, I found that I could improve my poems only by revising and re-writing them, which meant, sometimes, hundreds of versions of a single poem or stanza. After I had accumulated a number of poems I was fairly satisfied with, my confidence came back.

I also did a lot of reading. I went back to Sandburg—probably my greatest influence—and I read more recent poets whose sensibilities or backgrounds I could identify with: James Wright, James Hearst, William Stafford, Karl Shapiro, James Dickey, to name a few. Some of James Wright's early poems had a definite impact on me. In one of them, there's a stanza that might have come out of Sioux City's Lower Fourth:

> I saw, down river,
> At Twenty-third and Water Streets
> By the vinegar works,
> The doors open in early evening.
> Swinging their purses, the women
> Poured down the long street to the river
> And into the river.

And then I had the good fortune to meet James Dickey at a writers' workshop in Boulder, where we talked about a batch of my new poems. Dickey had also been an athlete, and had an intense interest in evoking the physical life in his poems. He liked my work ethic, and reminded me that "Shakespeare never did any pole vaulting." Those were important words to hear at that point in my writing life, from a poet whose work I felt close to. The words confirmed what I had been discovering in my own way: It's not so difficult to write like others or to be fashionable. What *is* difficult—and what really matters—is finding a way to consistently say things that couldn't be said by anyone else.

"Poets," says Stanley Kunitz, "are always revisiting the state of their innocence." Kunitz is referring not just to a state of mind but to actual places. For me, if there is one place in my past I need to stay in touch with, it's a railroad bluff in Sioux City, Iowa, a two-story brick house, and the vacant lot next to it with a vaulting pit at the west end. I believe it is possible, in some fundamental way, that my life as a poet began with a flat-out sprint down a dirt runway toward a bamboo crossbar nine feet high.

from *TRAIN WINDOWS*
(1976)

POLE VAULTER

The approach to the bar
is everything

unless I have counted
my steps   hit my markers
feel up to it   I refuse
to follow through
I am committed to beginnings
or to nothing

planting the pole
at runway's end
jolts me
out of sprinting
I take off   kicking in
and up   my whole weight
trying the frailty
of fiberglass

never forcing myself
trusting it is right
to be taken to the end
of tension   poised for
the powerful thrust to
fly me beyond expectation

near the peak
I roll my thighs inward
arch my back   clearing
as much of the bar as I can
(knowing the best jump
can be canceled
by a careless elbow)

and open my hands

A JUMPER

for Thomas James Whitehawk, condemned to the electric chair

> "He held the state high school
> pole vault record of 13 feet,
> 7½ inches in 1965."
> —from the *Minneapolis Star*

We shall not let him
float out through the bars
in the odor of pea soup
            but
fit in the cage of his fingers
the warden's golden
curtain rod
and unlock the air of
the concrete yard for the
seconds
to a last vault:

who will ever hear
ever see him
moving in the moccasined dark
toward the law's
wall   that this time will
not bend him down who
bursts the inevitable
jolt   steals up
his loins
learns
too late his name?

THE BULL RIDER'S ADVICE

what I'm saying is
you can't take this thing light
and there's no saddle to sit in

you can do it one of two ways
as far as I'm concerned
if you want to do it

you can get on just for the ride
take hold of the rope like it was
any old rope and pray for a quick 8 seconds
and no spinning

or you can wrap your fist into his back
so deep he knows you plan to stay awhile
dig in with your whole soul
until the sonofabitch is sick of you
and lets up

what I'm saying is
it's up to you

"WILL YOU SIGN MY BRAND-NEW BASEBALL, LOUIE?"

the best thing in my head
of baseball and Kansas City
is the Royals playing the
Red Sox and the drunk trying
to get Louie Aparicio
to sign his brand-new baseball:
every time Louie comes loping in
from shortstop at the end
of the half inning there he is
the drunk elbowing his way
from high up in the grandstand
down into the box seats and all
those turned-around wrinkled
foreheads and goddammits and
uplifted cups of Hamms and
Dr. Pepper with amazing
timing to catch his man
exactly at the screen except
that Louie every time
fields with his eyes that
white routine ball coming
out of the crowd and drops
his look and speeds up just
a little then disappears
into the dugout safe as the
fans cheer and cheer and
cheer for both of their heroes

FOOTBALL

Consider the stoning of beasts:
the peppered mammoth slobbering in the pit,
the stunned boar,
the bear with crushed face advancing,
the crippled, skirling cat;

consider the hands
groping along the hacked shores of rivers
how many dawns ago? for this shape of stone.

WATCHING TACKLES IN SLOW MOTION

"I key on anything that moves." —Deacon Jones

Up floats the turf   the shark is rising
the slow hawk
                    bends the air
tooth and talon
        touch where he moves exactly out of
certain as a polar bear
come from a death
                              in the jawed and frozen green
saying
I will always find you   always find you.

THE TOUCHDOWN IN SLOW MOTION

The way to turn thirty
is to kill off the light
and begin over
in slow motion:

So here I go
    in the shape
of my father's hope
    on a 30 sweep right
ranging out   cutting
    now turning it on
turning the comer
    to give up turf and
snatch what I
    need to be nifty
with a last fake
    in a farewell wave of my hand

stretching out
    I find my light
and a way to move
    in the green world

BULLFROGS

sipping on a Schlitz
we cut off the legs,
packed them in ice, then
shucked the rest back into
the pond for turtles

ready to go home
we looked down and saw
what we had thrown back in:
quiet-bulging eyes nudging along
the moss's edge, looking up at us,

asking for their legs

DEER ON CARS

deer on cars
on the freeways
move with an ease
and speed and courage
that seem beyond them:
when diesels scream by
they may jiggle
but it's never a leap
in a new direction
and more often
it is they
that pass the diesels . . .

entering a city
the head settles down
as they ease up in school zones
halt at red lights
or go on green
staring straight ahead
in the proper lane

POET

that little
deaf man
and his iron-
wheeled cart
crunching
through the
cindered alleys
at odd hours
selecting
(before
the garbage truck
comes)
his useful
fabulous
junk

SUNSET

Before I left my spot
on a bridge over the Sioux
watching the sun go down,
I heaved a single handful
of gravel that, when it

met the silent current
burst into applause

TRAIN WINDOWS

one night I am standing
on a high bluff
overlooking the tracks
waiting for him to leave
once and for all time

suddenly I see his face
in each lighted window
of his train—the face
of a man passing
from darkness into darkness
reading a novel

as I leap I snatch a
white pigeon from the air
and wave with that same hand
going down to my father

THE CITIZENS' COMPLAINT
(Sioux City, 1972)

on their highest bluff
War Eagle's tomb
is eroding
knuckle by knuckle

into the Missouri

so they complain
call it unsightly

now there is talk
of the skull
visible all spring
impervious
even to flash floods

how do they explain
this thing?—

this enemy among them
gazing down on the city
with eyes full of rain
who will not fall

into the river

BUS DEPOT REUNION

just over the edge
of my *Life* a young sailor
bounds from a Greyhound's
hiss into his mother's hug,
steps back, trades hands
with his father, then turns
to an old, hunched man
maybe his grandfather—

no hand, no word goes out,
they regard each other

waiting for something, and
now their hands cup,

they begin to crouch
and spar, the old man

coming on like a pro,
snuffling, weaving,

circling, flicks
out a hook like a lizard's tongue,

the boy ducking, countering,
moving with his moves,

biffing at the bobbing
yellow grin, the clever

head, never landing a real
punch, never taking one

until suddenly, exactly
together they quit,

throw an arm around each other
and walk away laughing

FORD PICKUP

call me the Valiant heading west on Fourteen into the frozen
Dakota January sun and the one suddenly ahead the red
Custom Ranger with Texas plates and his woman taking
their time and all of my eye as he sits straight and tall
beneath a white Stetson nodding politely over frost heave
and she has my long my black my favorite hair with a ribbon
exactly the color of the pickup and feeling the cab's air
and now she scoots his way and lays her head on his shoulder
while he adjusts his hat and sways briefly over the yellow line
so then as they talk her hands are a bird's nest in her lap
to which the knuckles of his loose right hand are always returning

NEIGHBORS

They live alone
together,

she with her wide hind
and bird face,
he with his hung belly
and crewcut.

They never talk
but keep busy.

Today they are
washing windows
(each window together)
she on the inside,
he on the outside.
He squirts Windex
at her face,
she squirts Windex
at his face.

Now they are waving
to each other
with rags,

not smiling

A POEM ON THE CHANGING OF WALL STREET INTO FLOYD BOULEVARD IN MY HOMETOWN, SIOUX CITY

driving up the
street that used
to stop 20
years ago at
Alan Cooley's house
no longer there
on the edge
of a bluff
a street that
now breaks out
over the city
into a convenient
boulevard that goes
right by the
only brick house
on Wall and
white picket fence
where I grew
up suddenly I
am a man
who won't be
stopping here again
a man always
going by

15 YEARS LATER

driving by the house I see her alone
watering the grass
in pin curls
and white shorts
purple rivers on her legs

where are the six kids?
the husband?

not wanting to be seen I
speed up but honk in case she noticed—

out of the rear-view mirror
she looks into my life
waving

SOME LINES ON THE RAZING OF THE SIOUX CITY ARMOUR'S PLANT

it is 5 a.m. everything is the same as it was
the moon-hammered faces of the cattle are waiting
the line at the hiring gate is growing minute by minute
you can see the faces of yesterday or last year
or 40 years ago looking more eager than they are
the same hands hiding out in the same pockets
if you wait long enough the gate will open up
inside everything will be the same as it always was
you will see knives glittering like the Missouri
pulleys ribs barrels guts tanks bones chopping blocks
any tooth could tell you the same old story
any hide if you had time to listen

THE STORY OF LAVA

Every time I smell Lava soap is 1948.
My father is bending over a long sink in the
pressroom of *The Sioux City Journal* at 5 a.m.,
his gray long-underwear peeled down over his
white belly, a thin bar of Lava tumbling over
and over slowly in his ink-stained hands.
The morning news has passed through his hands
out into the morning streets into the hands
of sleepy boys who fold it a certain way and
fling it on porches and steps, but that is not
my story. Lava is my story and the morning
news that Lava can't rub off. It is my father
bending over a sink, a thin bar of Lava tumbling
over and over and over slowly in his cloudy hands.

from *REAL AND FALSE ALARMS*
(1985)

CARDWELL THE FIREMAN

It is 3 a. m. in summer.
He is sleeping light.
On duty, between real
and false alarms.

Two steps from the bed,
near the open window,
on floor boards polished by
big hands and this sinking
moon, a careful collapse
of clothes is waiting.

At the bell's clanging
boots legs arms will
stand up, turn and
drop through the floor
in the sudden shape
of Cardwell.

PIGS

I saw the fresh cow's
head the farmer flung into
the barn for the pigs
explode them into
the shadows and land
eyes-up

between two feeders.
Minutes later, one pig,
then two, then two more
began to snuff their way
out of the shadows, toward
the head; two more,
one more, two more—
little round sharks testing
the odor of death . . .

soon the head was
at the center of a
whirlpool of feeding pigs,
then it was rising and
rolling all around—wide eyes
coming up and going under—
not quite flying over
the barn floor but not
touching it either.

CATTLE AT NIGHT

There is no sound when
moonlight hammers white
anvil faces.

They look like
boxcars after a flood,
their sides are so
busted out.

One by one they see you;
one by one they turn away
and go . . .

a herd of heavy breathing
drifts toward the Missouri.

A MISTAKE

High in the elm
a fat squirrel
leaped, missed a
branch of the
ash, and
hit the house

(above the kitchen
with a woman
putting groceries away)

then fell,
a chunk
of fur on
the sidewalk
by the back porch.

So now the eyes
are shut,
one ear is
bleeding,
and the claws are
fixed on
nothing
but a breeze.

NO FISHING

I was sprawled out on
my belly in a rowboat,
watching the green
lake of my face.

When I reached and felt
the cold water,
my hands, cut off at
the wrists,

flew into the
sky with two gulls.

NEXT MORNING

two swallows
flit and skim a drink

four geese
clamber up the bank into some weeds

you can hear a calf suck

what happened last night
or a thousand nights ago
doesn't matter

I thread a worm
and cast as far as I can

THE MAN IN THE RENDERING ROOM

He works his eight-hour day inside
Armour's steam. The steam is his white
floor and his white ceiling. It keeps
belching up out of the six tank holes
after he jerks open their iron lids.
I rarely see him. Does the steam make
him shy, an animal in fog? I just get
glimpses of him.

But I can put him together. He is shirt-
less with a bulging chest. His back and
shoulders are the color of lobster. His
biceps, constantly working, are round and
seamed. When I get close enough I notice
he is always grinning. He never speaks.
He works by himself, without breaks. I
never see him puffing on a cigarette, lean-
ing against the handles of a tankage cart,
complaining about the pay or the heat.

The heat is too much for me. I can stay
no longer than it takes to dump my cart-
load of condemned heads or kidneys or bellies.
I take a deep breath before I go in. I roll
my cart in fast and look around for him. I
catch his finger pointing to the least-full
tank. By the time I get there the lid is
open and his pitchfork hands are ready. I
tip my cart over the hole as the steam belches
up under us, swirling and relentless, hammering
my face and forehead. He is on his knees;
he sticks his hands deep inside the cart,
up past his elbows, up to his red shoulders
and beyond, scooping, pulling, forking,

jerking everything out. His back and arms
and neck are matted with guts and worms.
I know he is grinning; his head keeps nodding,
as if he figures he can grab joy
out of anything I bring him.

OLD DOG

First the eyes went.
Then the hearing.
Then he went crazy
so I locked him up
in the basement.
For days he kept
circling the furnace.
Wouldn't eat or drink.
Wouldn't come to my hand.
He just kept yowling
and circling the furnace.
So finally I took
a big cardboard box
downstairs, and waited
for him to come around,
and threw it over him.
By the time the box
made one more circle
I had my gun ready.
I shot three times right
where I knew the head was.
The boy and the wife cried
at the top of the stairs.
All I told them was
somebody had to do it.

THE BEAST

Let us roll all our strength,
all our sweetness up
into one beast
(I told her)
and turn it loose.

Finally, one morning
it crouched, looked up and
lifted off,

howling over the house and
garage, the town, over
the narrow-vergéd prairie,
shrunk to a dot and less,

and that was it.

Look, I said, pointing at
the asphalt driveway.
Nothing.
(Not even claw marks
where it left from.)

FREIGHT TRAINS

Beneath the Iowa bluff
in clearest light,
I stood as a boy
watching a freight train go by me.

There was that long
clattering space between
engine and caboose,
the moment of the empty boxcars—

each wide door was open,
I looked *through* the boxcars;
frame after frame of
the valley's other side—

the softball park
score board;
two pyramids of gravel;
the stockyards' white pens—

kept shooting at my eyes,
held together,
blacked out,
held together,

blacked out at
fixed intervals,
edged with light, held,
blacked out, until—

suddenly the boxcars were gone,
and the green caboose went by,
the valley put back together
in clearest light.

There was that left-over
deaf silence. I followed the
train bending all the way out of sight,
leveling with distance.

RAKERS

It's the Saturday my wife gets that look:
responsible as storm windows, as cleaned-out
garages: things to be hung up on nails on the
walls, cement floors swept clean so cars can
roll in shiningly over them. That October
look. Then my daughter mentions all the leaves
in the front yard, all the neighbors out raking;
asks where the dumb rake is.

But I won't be raking today.

I won't be having the garbage man in the
morning pitching the black plastic lawn bags
with twist tops in the hydraulic truck and
thinking, *He's a raker too.*

Raking's one more deadly habit I can do
without. I know it can get too natural, automatic
and genetic. One day my grandson picks up his
little play rake, his friends catch on, and
soon everybody is doing it. Then a kid down
the block is born with a rake for a hand. That's
neighborhood evolution carried too far. Every-
body at the first of October standing around
leaning on rakes and staring up at the trees
with open mouths, waiting for leaf rain.

GIRLS WORKING IN DRIVE-UP BANKS

The pretty smiling face
inside the glass
offers an amplified
Good Afternoon, Sir.
I say *Hello*.
The automatic inside-
outside deposit drawer comes
out to me. I reach and
put my hand in it;
the drawer goes back
inside the window.
The smiling face takes my
hand out and inserts it
inside her white blouse.
For about ten seconds
I feel the warm nipple
in the center of my
cupped palm. The face's
eyebrows are arched up;
then her mouth says
an amplified *Oh*.
Continuing the smiling
transaction the face
takes my hand out of her
blouse and places it
in the drawer, which comes
out to me again. I reach
in and take it back.

from *HANGING OUT WITH THE CROWS*
(1991)

THE SCARECROW

—for Doug Cockrell

I'm a cross man

I was born to stare
at a rotten fence post

and I'm buried yearly
in the green seasons

my right hand flew off
with the crows

my hat's cocked
on a sneering wind—
I'm losing my hair

I hang out with the crows
and the crows' shadows

RETIRED FARMER

Maybe he dreamed of
new snow, of shiny handles.

This morning I saw
broom and yellow work-gloves
farm a glittering topsoil
off his porch,
heard on the sidewalk
a scraping, a *ping*
of grain flying
from a shovel.

Then he sat a half hour
in his gray '57 Ford
with the engine warming up,
as if, both hands on the wheel,
he figured he was in motion.

IOWA POEM FOR JAN

Remember that hail
in hot July on a
blacktop road
back in Iowa?—
coming out of
hail into sudden
sun—

remember that
red
of the red barn we saw?

A SOUTH DAKOTA INVENTORY, 1989
(Centennial Poem)

Snow ticking on cornstalks; honking v's of geese at 3 a.m.
pulling spring back over farms, over neighborhoods;
wind rattling through corridors of stubble; the sound of
claws on bark; corn *pinging* from a shovel's lip; the *caw*
caw of crows; red-winged blackbirds' fierce metal
warbling; the two clean morning notes of the
chickadee—

Deer hightailing it; the badger looking up suddenly from
his half-clawed hole; the snapper orbiting from mud to
pasture to mud; a hawk's slow-motion glide; paddlefish
vacuuming the gloomy floors of dams; crows flapping
away from road-kills with plenty of time on their wings;
cattails swaying like car antennae; pine limbs weighed
down by snow—

The sudden tug on a fishing line, the rod divining;
bullheads sucking air in shallow pails; hunters' boots
crunching snow; cottonwood leaves shimmering in
windy sunlight; moon-faced cattle; hog houses; hog
grunts; dead-end roads; auctioneers in white Stetsons;
graveyards on hills; the iron level sound of trains; the
rough softness of milkpods; seed hats—

That second sun, the October pumpkin; those yellow ventrilo-
quists, the meadowlarks; the Missouri swirling around
bluffs; December's frozen sun; flat stones skimming lake
water; the probing headlights of tractors in night fields;
silver water towers; rodeos; the smell of alfalfa;
quickdraw packing house hands; the grim smile of a
possum really dead—

Names of towns: Sinai, Eagle Butte, Deadwood, Aurora, Willow
Lake, Ipswich, Blunt, Faith, Lake Andes, Mound City,
Buffalo Gap, White River, Elk Point, Wessington Springs,
Potato Creek, Redfield, Winner, Woonsocket, Fort
Pierre, Trail City, Pine Ridge, Bonesteel, Sisseton, Wall,
Tea, Lead, Hayti—

Dogs chasing rabbits zigzagging across fields; ice houses with
portable TV's; the sun rising in alleys; one hundred
blackbirds suddenly flying up as one black wing and
away; garage sales; powwows; the earnest swing of
lunch pails on sidewalks at 6 a.m.; white country
churches; swiveling owl-looks; farm ponds; prairie
grass; nine sparrows neatly spaced on a power line . . .

SONG OF RACQUETBALL

"Both in and out of the game and watching
and wondering about it."
—Walt Whitman

1.

I celebrate racquetball and sing racquetball,
And what I shall assume you shall assume,
For every breath belonging to me as good
belongs to you.
I celebrate passing shots, ceiling shots that skid
and sizzle on the wall;
I celebrate garbage serves, around-the-world shots.
I find I incorporate roll-outs and drive serves,
and am stucco'd with tie-breakers.
And I say that a flat roll-out is no less than the
journeywork of the stars,
And a backhand fly-kill is miracle enough to
stun the gods,
And a man bending with lowered head to serve surpasses
any statue.

2.

I loaf and invite defeat.
I advance forward when I should retreat backward,
And am not contain'd between my head-band and sneakers.
My z-serve, my lob, every bead of sweat, every
shot I know—
I, now forty-nine years old in decent shape begin,
Hoping to quit not till I drop dead on the court.

3.

I am the poet of the backhand and I am the poet of
the forehand,
The pleasures of winning are with me and the pains of
losing are with me.
I am the poet of the pinch shot the same as the fly-kill,
And I say there is nothing greater than an ace.
I scream the scream of self-hatred when I skip the ball,
We have had polite words long enough,
I show that swearing is part of the game.
Have you beaten the best? Are you Marty Hogan?
It is not important—surpass yourself.
I am he that feels the wet glove on my right hand, and
the wet T-shirt and wrist-band,
I am he that fights for the center,
loves the backhand lob serve,
goes for the kill,
aches with fatigue,
stoops to pick up the ball,
I am he that craves time-outs, and the hearty handshakes
of comrades.
I am he that needs a cold Budweiser.

4.

Who goes there, who steps into the court?
Dave Evans, Sr., racquetball player and poet,
Husband, father of three, martial artist, union man,
Boss-hater, ex-running back, confident and shy,
Introspective, deferential, balding, full of self-love
And self-hatred, loud drinker, fair fighter,
Lover of doubles as well as singles,
Oversexed, democratic, selfish and altruistic, easy
And tough, honest, paranoid, gullible, suspicious,
Pocketless of a nickel, unpretentious, believer in
Hard work, taker of naps, stocky, well-calved,
Creative and gloomy, a cosmos, from Sioux City, Iowa.

5.

I know I am robust,
I do not worry about my energy level,
I see that passing shots never apologize,
I reckon I hit the ball as hard as most when
        I am in my groove.
I play my own game, that is enough,
And if no other player is aware I stand content,
And if each and every player is aware I stand content.
One man is aware and that is me,
And whether I win today or next week or next year,
I can cheerfully take it now, or with equal cheerfulness
        I can wait.
My sneakers are from Penny's,
I laugh at what you call skips,
And I know how to count to fifteen.

6.

The lob serve swoops by and accuses me,
It complains of my laziness,
I sound my barbaric obscenity with raised racquet,
I bequeath myself to runner-up trophies,
If you want me, call 692-5214.

You will hardly know who I am or what I am up to,
But I shall be a worthy opponent,
And give you a good sweat.

Failing to beat me one day,
Try again.
I sit here by the phone, waiting for you.

OLD RACQUETBALL PLAYER

Down in the court stands the old player;
He is fat and bald with collapsed calves;
He is out of breath;
He asks for a time-out with raised racquet
    and hung head.

THE POEM I COULDN'T WRITE

Last night I gave up again,
tossed the damned sheets
in the wastebasket,
turned out the lights
and went upstairs.

Brushing my teeth before
the bathroom mirror,
there it was,
the poem I couldn't write.

When I frowned, it frowned.
When I smiled, it smiled.

It had all my thoughts,
all my feelings,
all my wrinkles—
exactly my age, and three
silver fillings in its jaw.

When I switched off the light
it was gone.
When I switched it back on,
there it was,
speaking without words
to a wordless man.

SATURDAY MORNING

Right out the door of
the Touch of Class
beauty shop strides
a giant woman
in sloppy jeans
and faded denim shirt
and a brand-new
double-decker bouffant—

back into her old Ford
she scoots, slides
but the hair's too high,
won't go.

It must be urged in,
gently,
with her left hand.

Sitting low,
the hair barely scraping
the ceiling,

she starts the engine,
revs up,
jerks into drive and
peels off toward tonight.

THE PONIES OF KUNMING, CHINA

Mechanical rocking horses on the run
with collars of bells jingling and
dung sacks bouncing behind them
down the loud streets pulling wagons of
coal, furniture, fruit, or concrete beams,
their drivers, grimy and surly,
jerking the reins held tight
in their small fists . . .

Sometimes you see one stopped,
near a brick wall.
Head down, it waits; it breathes—
wooden neck throbbing,
wire tail switching at flies,
glass eyes glancing at the traffic.

It breathes; it waits for a leather
word or whip—a coin
dropped in a tin box—
to make it run again.

"THE STRONG ARE WITHOUT AMBITION"—LAO-TZU

Something was moving in China
on a mountain road, and I stopped
the van and got out to snap
pictures of it lumbering my way,
a water buffalo.

I kneeled like a bull fighter
as he swayingly came—saw
the splayed, shaggy hooves,
the muddy eyes, the wide
bend of horns that between them
swaying held up the whole
mountain's silence.
I saw the antique power
in thighs moving centuries
at the same pace on roads,
in swamps, or knee-deep
sucking mud of rice paddies;
the power in dark shoulders—
the quietness in strength
that does not have to insist,
but is.

I watched him until, veering
from the road he stepped over the
edge beneath the stick of his
driver and was gone.

from *DECENT DANGERS* (2000)

LIONS

When a male mounts a female in
heat she agrees more or less to lie

flat in flattened grass long enough
to feel what he has to offer—

a few good thrusts and then he
throws his head back and yells

at the sky in Serengeti baritone,
while she, as if half for joy and

half with a grudge, snarls and
rolls her eyes up at him, and he

pins her neck down with a species-
specific love bite which must mean

That was the one. He can guess
her answer: to attack and open a

new gash on his nose, or turn over
on her back like an overgrown

kitten, or both. No matter. For this
big huffer, danger is decent.

WATCHING A SQUIRREL IN MY BACKYARD

It's snowing again,
and you finally
found the ear of corn
I stuck on the spike
of the feeder,
nailed to the elm.
Your tail is curled
over your head like a
fur roof against
the swirling flakes.

When I was a boy
I might've shot you
with my .22—an easy
target from
the garage door—
just to see you
drop.

Now you have my word:
all I want is
to watch
(holding my coffee with
my trigger finger),
and quietly
rejoice
to have you
chewing on corn
and turning whiter
and whiter
in my backyard.

MORNING SONG

Before breakfast
I step outside
with my first cup
of coffee,
and look around.

This morning
crisp October
owns the yards.
Yellow. Yellow.

I take a sip,
as a sparrow begins
singing
and right there on
the sidewalk
I decide:
I'll hold that song—
the way two hands hold
the heat of coffee—
as far into the day
as I can.

That yellow voice;
that tiny throat.

THE ACREAGE IN IOWA

(in memory of William Stafford)

Home was still there, in my dream,
if I could find the street.

The tree house,
the potato garden,
the chicken shed with 15 hens,
the cornfield with two horses.
(Sometimes, out the kitchen
window we'd see them standing
close but oppositely—
like a horse with two heads.)

But when I turned at
the sign saying Lafayette,
Lafayette was not Lafayette
but a steep road to a dam
in snowy mountains.
I shifted to reverse and
turned back.

Yet there it was,
in a dream glimpse,
all of it, still:
chopping stump,
cool clods under bare feet,
wind rattling December cornstalks,
east-west-looking horse.

Home is still there,
said my dream,
if not the street going to it.

FOR THE YOUNG WOMAN WHO CLEANS MY TEETH

When I sit down and lie back,
your white rubber hands come
floating toward me as toward
a death mask stretched over
a crystal ball.

I gaze, or close my eyes,
and we hold a one-way
conversation as you scrape
and pick, accepting my *aaaaa*'s
and silences as consent.

Sometimes you stop, lay down
your tool, squirt water
in my mouth; I slosh it
around a few times with
my spit and you insert
a plastic vacuum tube and
suck my cheeks dry as alum.

Then I rest my jaw.

But whenever your tool
appears above me, I
gape like a baby robin
to a dangling worm.

We might be pair-bonded
bonobos, one grooming
the other, who—stunned
by such routine joy—
stares into trees
or oblivion.

We are so close
and our room so private,
we might be lovers in bed.
"This way a little,"
you almost whisper, gently
pressing on my temple.
I obey every word
all the way through
flossing and polishing;
and I love and honor
once more the finishing
touch of your smile

which sends me—
with a new toothbrush
sticking out of my shirt pocket,
and a gritty, spearmint
taste—back to the corroding
daylight and job.

THE ZEN OF RACQUETBALL

—for Clyde Huyck

When I was 40 and a brand-new
hot-shot full prof,
I agreed to play a young
philosophy prof in love with Zen.
"You know," he said, over coffee
the day before the match,
"what I really enjoy is
watching the ball going
back and forth."
"Yeah," I said,
"it *is* fun, isn't it?"
That was a lie. It wasn't
fun, it was win, win, win.

Next day we ducked into the court
and, seeing his skinny,
library legs and flimsy K-Mart
racquet, I knew what was about
to happen. I beat him 15-zip
four straight games, and I
noticed he was smiling
as he played, obviously
having a good time losing—
just watching the ball,
when I hit it, going back and
forth, splatting out low
on the wall, dying low, and
lower, in the corners.

That was 15 years ago.
The Zen prof didn't get tenure,
so he's gone, teaching in
a private college up in Minnesota,
the kind of campus where
students drive Porsches and have
fireplaces in their dorm rooms.

And what about me? I stayed.
And with bad knees and a brace
on one of them, I still like
to play new, young profs.
But now it's different,
I'll admit. I like to watch
the ball going back and forth.

In fact, I like to meditate,
right there in the court.
I take a deep breath,
and exhale slowly as
the ball meets my racquet;
I watch the sweet spot
collapse slightly;
as the ball stops and is
about to leave I smell it,
taste it, hear it, feel it,
see it, and—not to kill it
or to win but just to keep it
in play—I swing, and
follow it with my goggled eyes
to the wall and then back to
my opponent's racquet.
Focused, patient, breathing
like a man reading in bed,
I wait, and consider the ball
growing bigger and bigger
as it comes back to me—its
blue, quick, transient life.
I watch it flying back and
forth through the
white-walled universe.

NOTE TO JAN ON HER BIRTHDAY, 1998

The scent
you left
on my cheek
this morning
reminds me
of the one
on the red
scarf
you mailed to
me when I
was in Boot
Camp in Texas
42 years ago.

I love it;
I love you.

THE READER

"Which of us has looked into his father's heart?"
—Thomas Wolfe

Whenever my father found
something he liked in a book,
I noticed his lips weren't moving.
It was all in the tightening
of the skin around his eyes.
Just then, I knew his great
cache of quotes was increasing
by another paragraph or so.

Wherever my mother was
in the house, he would find her.
"Ruth!" he shouted,
hurrying through the dining room,
his huge feet creaking in his
black nylon socks.

"Ruth, listen to this!"

So he had her—backed up
against the kitchen sink,
or over a steaming iron.

After he read he would say,
"Isn't that just great?"
or "How do you like *that*!"
What else could my mother do
(even looking at the ceiling,
her hand on a hip as he read)
but nod and agree?

"That's Wolfe," he would say,
waving the book above his head—
"Thomas Wolfe."

Then he would hurry back to
his Naugahyde recliner,
eyes fixed on the page.

NEW POEMS

THE UPSIDE-DOWN GIRLS AT THE SIOUX CITY YWCA

Turn the M of YMCA over and
you get YWCA, which is where
they sent us—a panting pack of five
or six—one winter Saturday in the early
50s because our pool needed repair.
The mother of Squeaky Grove's
invention that day was both necessity
and teenage lust. For two hours
of open swimming we did our
horizontal swan dives off the stiff
low-board sticking out our Tarzan chests
and yelling our Tarzan yells, and plenty
of frogman dives to see what girls
look like underwater—then we
went downstairs to the locker room
for guests, and the girls to theirs.
The only thing separating us was
a locked door between the sexes.

As usual, Squeaky didn't need words
to explain his new invention, he just
soaked a towel—also used for snapping
asses—in the sink, got down on all
fours and wrung it like a chicken's
neck, splashing a mirror made out of
water under the door. The rest of us
dropped down with Squeaky to have
a look at the upside-down girls.
One by one they stepped out of
the shower 100 per cent naked and
fresh and pink, buzzing the way
girls do when they've had to put up
with boys like us. Until one of them
must've noticed our voices gone flat
like our swan dives, spotted the guilty
water under the door, then, looking

closer, our faces—puddled,
upside-down—a few inches off
the cement. Which caused the realist
among us to raise up and announce that
our indoor swimming was over for
this season. And he was right, as usual.

THE NYREEN GIRL, 46 YEARS LATER

She was a beauty, like her mother:
Blonde hair, Hungarian green eyes,
and even at 13, a brooding,
vulnerable openness—
she amazed me one clear summer night
when she leaned back against
the door of her dad's dilapidated shed,
and looked at me with the exact
lusty look I'd seen in the movies.
I wanted to kiss her beautiful mouth.
Marriages, whole lives together are
sparked in such moments, in backyards
full of lightning bugs and stars.
And yet when I leaned lightly
against her tense breasts,
all I could give her was a flimsy
excuse about having to get home.
After all, I was two years older
and couldn't mess with a friend's
little sister, and then too there was
Marlene, two blocks over on
Iowa Street, swinging on her
porch swing, waiting for me.

CHASING BARBARA

That time in the dark chasing
Barbara Jorgenson up Wall Street's
steep brick sidewalk, my Converse
tennis shoes were hot for
speed and Barbara, giggling
in a white dress and pumps,
didn't seem to mind it. Seemingly
breathless, she stopped under
a tall cottonwood outside
the Cardwell's white picket fence,
and my right hand reached down and felt
the incredible silky flatness between
her legs—then took off pulling
the rest of me all the way to
the Hilsinger house on top of the hill.

That's how the two of us nearly
bonded: through a neighborhood
sin. But by the next morning
we must've agreed the chasing
was over, and to go our separate
ways, and that nothing should ever
get back to our parents, especially her
beet-faced, beer-whipped father.

Fifty years later the fire in my right
hand is still burning, and nothing
short of my death will put it out.

SMALL CHANGE

(for a waitress in the Redfield Cafe)

Even if your smile is
the café's mandate and property,
I'll take it. When you turn
away with my order,
the *Special* (two eggs over easy,
sausage, orange juice, and toast),
I see like Superman right through your
taut bluejeans and fix on the
backs of your warm,
flexing knees.

When I'm finished,
you take my check and thank me,
and I bundle up like a pre-Clovis
wayfarer and set out, crossing
the scraped street and migrating up
the shoveled sidewalk back to
my room in the Comfort Inn,
and by the time I get to
Marv's Buick Sales and Service,
I imagine having left next to
my plate (instead of three quarters
and some dimes and nickles)
my business card and a gift:
the keys to a brand-new,
loaded Park Avenue.

But even that would be
small change compared to what
some men full of lust and protein—
at least since the Ice Age—
have lavished on such smiles,
such imagined legs.

MY TURN

Someday it'll happen.
I'll be brushing my teeth,
tying a shoe, or maybe
thinking of a line or a poem
I couldn't get right the day
or decade before, and I'll
hear a voice from somewhere
calmly say: *It's your turn, Evans.*

And then, of course, it will
all have been almost worth it—
the sweating over this and
that vowel, image, or whatnot.
A forest of paper over 40 years!

I'll be like Picasso.
Just scribble something
on a napkin in a restaurant
in Paris, Cleveland, or
Remsen, Iowa, and when I
get up and leave,
a hundred hands will fight
violently over it.

USED WOODEN DESK

Five drawers, and duel pull-out boards flanking
each elbow. What else could I want?
Even the *feng-shui* is perfect. Right through
the south-paneled wall I face is my hometown
(145 miles away) in northwest Iowa,
on the Missouri. I can lean back in my padded
swivel chair, place my heels on the desk at
a perfect height, and read, for instance, from
The Prehistory of the Mind by Steven Mithen:
"Many of the new bone and antler tools
of the Upper Paleolithic carried elaborate
designs on their surfaces . . . ." I can go on
making elaborate designs of my own with
words on a computer screen. The pull-out boards
flanking my elbows may not be the wings
of poesy, but they're perfect for holding
a cup of decaf or a cold can of Natural Light
in my dimly-lit, Neolithic basement.

DEATH AND EXILE

"Keep before your eyes from day to day death
and exile . . . and then you will set your thoughts
on what is low and will never desire anything
beyond measure."

—Epictetus

After breakfast, in exile on my patio,
I watch a stoic robin flying up
into an elm over and over,
each time with a sprig of dead grass
in its beak, building a nest for
the hatching of death.
Leaning back and closing my eyes,
I imagine the fatal blue
of robins' eggs, of the morning sky.

All around me, houses
of a neighborhood in exile
repose in their dewy, green
coffins of lawns.

POSTMODERN COW

"We make things what they are by naming them . . ."
—J. Hillis Miller

Having no word for the metal thing with wings
 making a droning noise flying over means,
of course, that even if she glances up and sees it,
 it's not really there.

And what about that little black buzzing thing
 that stings her flank?
Even if she swishes it away with her tail,
 it didn't exist in the first place.

Think of it: all her life or until the cows come home,
 she's *blown by all the winds that pass*
and wet with all the showers (in the poet's words)
 and she doesn't even realize it.

RATS DREAM, SCIENTISTS SAY

—from a newspaper

After decades of ingenious theories,
elegant figures and graphs,
and nice neural probings,
what once was anecdotal
guessing is now
empirical fact:
when a rat's brain waves
are the same while running
through a maze as when asleep,
that means it is dreaming
of running through a maze.

So let's have a toast to the rats:

Awake or asleep,
you too must endure
your going hence even as
your coming hither.
Ripeness being all,
smell it and dream on.

DREAM FABLE

Alone in my car
pulling
a small trailer
with unknown
contents at 80
miles an hour
I turn a sharp
curve and the hitch
snaps   sending

the trailer
rattling over
the shoulder into
a stubble field.

Remember,
my dream said:
not everything
you have is
meant to
last an entire
journey—
otherwise
the hitch would've
held.

WORLD GAZING: TWO VIEWS

At 10, the hottest summer day,
I could make it winter inside
my grandmother's snow globe.
I held it up like the world
our acreage was, turned it
over and made the snow
fall upside-down; then turned
it right side up, set it back on
the oak buffet, and gazed at
the soft, grainy flakes (quiet
as real ones but never melting)
swirling around a man and woman
in a sleigh pulled by a horse—
its pace frozen in mid-stride—
a line of poplars, and a white
house with lighted windows.

At 28, I gazed at the blue planet
(so called by an astronaut),
this one on the cover of *Life*,
snapped from the moon.
Nobody—from sea worms to
Amphioxus to Fish to Dinosaurs
to Apes—had seen anything like
this in 3.8 billion years. It was
as if I woke up one morning,
fixed myself my usual cup of coffee,
looked out my kitchen window
and there it was: the first earthrise.

TO A YOUNG ROBIN

(Looking out the window near the end of an
all-day retreat at Oak Lake to consider the new
English Department Standards Document)

If you find a worm,
go ahead: pick it up with your beak.

Any branch you prefer,
feel free to stand on it.

The same is true with chirping.
Have at it.

Any time now,
if you want to fly away,
just open your wings and go.

RED ON WHITE

I don't have to flutter into
a snow-packed yard, light
on a branch,
teeter a couple of times,
and yell *Cheer, Cheer, Cheer*!—
I don't have to be a cardinal
to sing a winter song.

HIDE AND SEEK AT A GRAVEL COMPANY

Wild as any animal hiding
kneeling thirty feet up
on top of a pyramid of hot sand
overlooking a roundhouse
my right hand on
my heart to calm it

Far below I heard
then saw my two friends
hunting for me
not thinking to look
skyward

They would never find me
or find out what I
discovered on bare knees:
Some day as a man
this moment would come
back exactly—
hot sand
secret wild heartbeat
and all

WORKOUT

From my lofty indoor bike seat,

facing a bay window, I see a real fly
caught in a metaphorical Lake Michigan

on the gym's roof; it's only
a human half-inch from shore—

and something in its fly brain keeps
shouting to its wings and legs:

high and dry!
high and dry!—

yet each time the tiny dark motor
starts up, it only surrounds itself with

rippling circles, going nowhere, like a
man on a stationary bike, making circles

with his feet at 57 to 60 rpm's, 4.2 miles
every 15 minutes, looking out a window,

watching a fly dying in rain water.

LIFTING WEIGHTS ON THE DAY I TURN 60

Work, work, work I say to myself,
finishing up on leg thrusts in a room
so small with so many mirrors that
your business is everybody's business,
as a pretty, half-eager coed in black shorts
walks by on the way to the barbell bench,
her white T-shirt announcing COED NAKED.

On burning legs on the way to the dumbbell rack,
I catch a good pair of calves in a mirror. Mine.
She sees them too, but there's no
flexing of her facial muscles.

And yet, in this small town of mirrors
where we sweat, grunt and cry out,
we are always communal, and must
watch each other watching each other:
she with a light barbell doing presses;
I with a 30-pounder in each hand
doing my three hard sets of curls.

ONE-SIDED FIGHT ON LOWER FOURTH STREET

One night from the safer side of my
windshield, I watched a tall man pitch

headlong out of the Harbor Inn and attack
a parking meter half his height and

minding its own business. He swung
with an overhand right—off

balance and with about the same heat it
takes to hurl a cat through an open window—

hit the hard flat face, then backed off to
watch the reaction. Nothing. Attacked

again, this time with a wishy-washy
left hook to the skinny iron gut,

then followed with a limp but accurate
karate front-kick to the shin—

decent one-two timing. Once again, no
response. So the self-declared winner turned

around and steered himself down the street and
through the open door of the Pink Pussy Cat.

THE POLE VAULTER

Every time Jerry Tyler
planted his wrist-thick
aluminum pole at the end of
the runway at the end
of the 50s and went up,
leaving the rest of us
in the sawdust,

he seemed to rise higher—
10-8, 10-10, 11 feet—
and to disdain, more
and more, coming
back down to the first
world with its beautiful
adulterous mother with
no time for her kids;
its neurotic, brutal father
with his jet-lagging job
at Iowa Power and Light;
and its hard-earned, beat-up,
unstartable '46 Chevy
taking up needed space
in his father's garage.

He couldn't wait to graduate
and get out of town, and stay
as high as he could
by becoming a roofer.

He's up there still,
in my memory, not on
top of any roof but
profiled in the sky over
the Leeds High track and field—
his black hair bronzed
like a statue's,
his sharp, right elbow

hooked on air,
about to fall but never falling
back to our world of sawdust.

IN MEMORY OF JOHNNY UNITAS

Let's have one more beer
from the Land of Sky Blue Waters,
and one more look at that
one throw, this time
in slow motion—
was it the Giants' game in '67?

Let's take our time, and this time
let's not forget to focus on
the black hightops
stabbing the turf
like a bullfighter's feet—
the wall of big numbers
avalanching backward,
the egg-shell pocket;
and of course the helmeted head
shifting back and forth,
glimpsing the whole picture;
and the arm pump of the fake
release, sending the linebackers
and strong safety skittering
into the black hole
just beyond mid field.

Then there it is—remember?
The ball
spinning out of
the hand of the young guy
a little hunched over
(a tattered jersey upon a stick,
to paraphrase a famous poet)
toward Raymond Berry's
outstretched hands floating down
the sidelines past the enemy's bench
and coach, the ripped-off
earphones rolling absurdly on
the grass, the clipboard flying away
on paper wings full of X's and O's—

but hold on: the popcorn's not
quite done, and as long as I'm up,
anybody need another beer?

PERSONAL BEST

(On hearing about the book, *Bowling Alone*)
—for John Miller

I like bowling alone,
but it can be a problem.

For instance, what if you get hot and
roll a 253 one winter day with nobody else
in the building but the nonchalant guy
behind the counter—like I did,
in Alamosa, Colorado, in 1967 with,
I swear, a scuffed-up house ball?

Think of it. Bowl a 253,
and there's nobody around to slap you
on the back or buy you a Budweiser.

That tall, silent loner working the counter—
wasn't he watching? You'd think
he could've at least looked up when I
handed him my score sheet and shoes.
Didn't he see those six sizzling X's in a row?
But then I realized by the poker-faced
way he checked off my two games
with a black marker, sprinkled my shoes
with talcum powder and stuck them
back in the size-11 pigeon hole,
that he was no rookie. For all I knew
he was bowling in three leagues
with a 210 average and the meanest
hook in the San Luis Valley.

My father was a good bowler too,
and when I was a kid he liked to tell me
the story about the guy he met who said
he had bowled only once in his life,
and it was a 300. Then my father would
say something like, "Words are cheap."
That, for a lesson.
It's been over 30 years since
my Colorado personal best,
and I still think about it.
I also think about the guy with
the so-called cheap words who rolled
his so-called first and last 300.
I wonder if maybe my father didn't
underestimate his talent, or luck.

Maybe, just maybe, he did it,
and the same way I did my 253,
bowling alone with a house ball.

FISHING ALONE

Sunny April.
A dead carp on the sand
ten feet from my lawn chair,
its mouth agape:
a perfect O around its
last breath.

I reel in, thread a fresh
night crawler on my hook,
cast out into a new spot,
wrap the line once around
a finger so I can feel a bite
when I'm dozing,
or watching the sky.

But that open mouth:
I see it even with my
eyes closed.

O it says to the
white ribbed sand;

O to the pelicans that lift,
dip, and soar;

O to its own bones that soon
will shine in the sun

OBSERVATION FLOOR

I always wanted to see
Minneapolis from this height.
One of the mumbling crowd
looking out at the night lights,
I turned my head to see
who had said those words with
a robust and penetrating clarity—
a large Native American woman
(I guessed in her 70s) holding
a white cane and smiling. The one
who, minutes earlier, had been
led out of an elevator by a woman
friend. Bracing herself with one
hand on her friend's shoulder,
she too faced the lights, the steep
cold wind on top of the city.

MY FATHER AND THE FURNACE MAN

October—cold enough to be kneeling
(at twelve or thirteen) with my father,
on our damp basement floor, zipped to
the chin in a green parka. The other man—
the one we were watching—was a furnace
repairman, sitting on a felt cloth with
all his tools and the furnace parts scattered
between his legs like shrapnel, talking
about heavy snow in the forecast.

I knew what my father was thinking:
Be good at something. That was his mantra.
It was the way you quoted from
The Tempest; the way your bowling ball
hooked and sizzled into the 1-3 pocket
at the War Eagle Lanes, or the way you locked
in a steel plate in the *Journal* pressroom
under Sioux City's humming sidewalks.

In my father's eyes, I knew the man
was a wonder: To be that composed
and talkative with all the cold furnace's
guts exploded on the floor before him,
with the threat of snow, and a north wind
humming on the plastic-covered windows.

TILT-A-WHIRL

(for Shelly, David, and Kari)

"Only one ride," I told you,
as I pulled up to the makeshift
carnival at the mall, because
it was a school night, and starting
to rain. But your mother
knew why: I needed to get
up the Interstate to Brookings,
and lock myself in my room,
and write. You gladly took
the quarters and ran toward
the tilt-a-whirl; and the burly
carny in a T-shirt,
a cigarette stuck on his lip,
lifted the bar and locked all
three of you in together.

What your mother and I saw from
inside the white Valiant's
squeaky windshield wipers,
was intermittently clear and blurred:
joy and fear on three small faces
whirling in circles, or half circles,
clear and blurred, clear
and blurred, and clear—

Now, 30 years away,
I'm the one who wants to stay.

CHICKS

"Because it can't live," my father said.
He had on tall Bib overalls;

I was six or seven. We were looking
at some peeping chicks in a wide

box heated by a light bulb
the same yellow they were.

I watched a big hand go down and
pick out the one that looked droopy

and throw it hard against the shed
door—it didn't bounce back like a ball.

On hands and knees I watched
an eye closing the way the sun

in the evening pulled the sky
down over our acreage.

1215 FLOYD BOULEVARD

It was only a rehearsal,
a trial run, that 10-year life.
It will happen again.

All of us—Dad driving,
Judy between him and Mother,
and Bob, Jerry, Bonnie, and I
in the back of our shiny, black
'41 Ford with the big, hard
fenders, following the moving van.
We'll turn the corner at
the Cardwell house and climb
the steep hill. We'll park
at the curb and get out; one
of us will open the gate
of the white picket fence,
most of us will be running
up the red-brick sidewalk.

Then we'll stop and wait
for Dad, who has the keys.
But before he walks past
and opens the door,
we'll see him pause on
the cement porch, put
a hand on the wooden swing
and push it, gently;
just as it starts to creak,
swinging back and forth,
all will begin again.

MY FATHER'S AVALON

He'd come home at night from
the loud, inky pressroom to
close his eyes, after supper.
Horizontal on his vinyl recliner,
an open book—Thomas Wolfe,
Shakespeare, Voltaire, Mencken,
Tolstoy, or Benchley—on his lap,
often Al Jolson was crooning
on the Victrola. That's how
he found his love in Avalon.
Not beside a bay, or across the sea
where flying fishes play, but
in a brick house on a brick street
on a railroad bluff. And as
the night was falling,
and the trains kept blowing for
the 11th Street crossing,
that's how, from dusk till dawn,
he traveled on—to Avalon.

THE DEFECTION OF NAHBI

Chuck Ervin

First published 2013

This edition published 2016

ISBN-13: 978-0-9911483-2-5
ISBN-10: 0991148320

Printed by CreateSpace

Available from
Amazon.com, CreateSpace.com
and other retail outlets

e-book versions available for
Kindle and other devices

http://www.chuckervin.com/books.html
https://www.amazon.com/author/chuckervin

$9.95
ISBN 978-0-9911483-2-5
50995>
9 780991 148325

Main Characters

(Complete List at Back)

David Logan	Former Army combat intelligence officer; Cambridge Ph.D. in Semitic Languages; Teira Aquilina's boyfriend
Teira Aquilina	Daughter of wealthy Malta banker; Cambridge Ph.D. in Computer Science; David Logan's girlfriend
Nahbi	American, British, and Israeli intelligence agencies doubt his astonishing claims despite his extraordinary capabilities
LTG Jhalawan	Director of Pakistan's Inter-Services Intelligence Service
Ahmed Malik	Head of the ultra-secret S-Wing of Pakistan's Inter-Services Intelligence Service
Sir Lionel Smythe	Director of the British Secret Intelligence Service (MI6)

Prologue

The helmsman screamed as a huge wave swept him overboard to certain death. The old merchant ship immediately broached and rolled violently from side to side as it slipped sideways into the wave trough. The mast snapped and fell into the sea as the next enormous wave passed beneath the leaking hull. Moments later, the ship capsized and sank.

Friday, May 9

Mersa Matruh, Egypt
10:00 AM

Hassan Al-Zeid, the Egyptian Ambassador to Pakistan, had chosen the meeting place carefully. The oceanfront villa was 150 miles west of Alexandria and 140 miles east of the Libyan border near the seaport resort of Mersa Matruh. It was in an area where his meeting with the terrorist leader was unlikely to be observed.

Akil El-Sayed had emerged as the leader of Al Qaeda after the death of Osama bin Laden. His name was at the top of the FBI's list of most wanted terrorists. Leaving his secret camp in the Libyan Desert to meet with the Ambassador represented considerable risk for him.

"Salam alekum." Al-Zeid greeted his guest. "Thank you for coming. General Jhalawan asked me to meet with you to hear your current thoughts about how to wound and eventually defeat the American infidels."

"Wa alekum es salam. I am at your service. May I ask the reason for the urgency of this meeting?"

The Ambassador reminded himself to be very careful. El-Sayed was a highly-intelligent, well-educated man who would instantly recognize the slightest inconsistency. He responded to the reasonable question in a direct, though carefully disingenuous manner.

"General Jhalawan is impressed with the ideas you've expressed in your writings and thinks that perhaps your original time-table can be accelerated. The current American president is widely seen as weak and indecisive. Opinion polls in the U.S. show that his popularity is eroding. Few International leaders respect him and none fear him. The General is concerned that the next American elections may result in a conservative shift that brings renewed military vigor. That would not be helpful to our cause. He thinks we should strike the Americans boldly while they are weaker than they have been in more than 30 years. He would welcome any thoughts you may have."

Akil El-Sayed nodded thoughtfully before responding. “Pakistan is at least outwardly cooperative with the Americans. I know that there are many in Pakistan who do not agree with that political accommodation. Yet, I think it is a dangerous game that General Jhalawan plays. The Americans should not be underestimated. Their Seal Team Six killed Osama bin Laden less than a mile from the Pakistan Army’s military academy in Abbottabad. That was no trivial matter given the degree of protection that bin Laden had been afforded by sympathetic members of Pakistan’s military and government. If the Americans thought General Jhalawan was working against them in cooperation with Al Qaeda, they might decide to target him as well.”

Ambassador Al-Zeid paused for a moment as he considered how to reply to the terrorist leader without giving offense. “What you say is unquestionably true. However, General Jhalawan does not think the American President would dare order a strike on a senior member of Pakistan’s government. In any event, General Jhalawan is well-protected and unusually well-informed. Even the western governments rank Pakistan’s Intelligence Service as the best in the world.”

“What relationship does General Jhalawan envision between himself and me? I have broad support as the leader of Al Qaeda since bin Laden’s death. Although I am inconvenienced by the constant efforts of the American CIA and FBI to find and kill me, I continue to direct Al Qaeda cells all over the world. The American president foolishly boasts that Al Qaeda is much weaker since he assumed power. Nothing could be farther from the truth. Does General Jhalawan envision himself as the new global leader of Al Qaeda or does he imagine that he and I would work together in some way to achieve our mutual objectives?”

“I do not presume to speak for General Jhalawan in this matter but I will present your question to him at my earliest opportunity. I can tell you that General Jhalawan believes that the time is ripe for closer cooperation and jointly-planned actions by Al Qaeda, the Muslim Brotherhood, the Taliban, and sympathetic cells in Saudi Arabia, Yemen, Iran, Iraq, Syria, and Indonesia. He is quite aware

that you have strengthened and expanded the number of Al Qaeda cells in Western Europe and the United States."

El-Sayed was silent for a few moments as he marshaled his thoughts. Finally, he spoke. "General Jhalawan is correct. The timetable can be advanced. There is a way."

Hassan Al-Zeid listened carefully to the terrorist leader's ideas for another hour and then stood and extended his hand to signify that the meeting was at an end.

"Thank you for coming. I will share your ideas with General Jhalawan. I feel sure that he will want to thank you in person, Allah willing."

The Ambassador walked with the terrorist leader to his waiting car and shook hands again as they said goodbye.

Neither man noticed a dilapidated taxi cab parked on the other side of the street 50 meters east of the villa. The driver was slumped down behind the steering wheel with his head leaning against the doorpost. He appeared to be taking a nap. A small glass dome was mounted on the roof in front of the taxi cab sign. At close range, the lens of a high-resolution digital camera was barely visible through the tinted glass.

Six thousand miles to the west, the National Reconnaissance Office near Washington Dulles International Airport began receiving a stream of encrypted digital images uploaded from the taxi to the Trumpet 5 surveillance satellite over the eastern Mediterranean.

Seven minutes later, an urgent message began flashing on the computer screen of an anti-terrorism analyst at CIA headquarters in Langley, Virginia. NRO facial-recognition software had made positive identification of Akil El-Sayed.

Thirty minutes after the images of the Al Qaeda leader were transmitted to the United States an unarmed American RQ-170 Sentinel reconnaissance drone on routine patrol over eastern Libya was reprogrammed. It began shadowing the terrorist leader's vehicle as it drove westward on the International Coastal Highway toward the Libyan border. The drone transmitted real-time imagery and

GPS coordinates to the duty operator at the 30th Reconnaissance Squadron's control center at the Tonopah Test Range in Nevada.

Saudi Arabian Airlines flight 1705 left Alexandria's Borg El Arab International Airport at 8:15 PM. The Airbus A300 was scheduled to arrive at Islamabad International Airport at 4:35 PM the next afternoon. Hassan Al-Zeid was seated in the first-class cabin and planned to sleep for much of the long flight. His meeting with Akil El-Sayed had achieved more than he'd hoped and he knew that General Jhalawan would be pleased.

At 9:50 PM, a top-secret unmanned aircraft was launched from the nuclear-powered aircraft carrier USS George H.W. Bush operating off the coast of North Africa. The Nighthawk II employed advanced stealth technology. It was armed with two 500 pound laser-guided bombs and four Hellfire missiles. It arrived over the terrorist camp forty miles west of Musaid, Libya at 10:23 PM and began silently orbiting at an altitude of 12,000 feet while transmitting live infrared video images to the Navy pilot controlling the unmanned aircraft from the carrier.

At 11:07 PM, Rear Admiral Lloyd Hooker, the Commander of Task Force 60, hung up the encrypted SATCOM phone and told the controlling pilot that he was authorized to proceed with the strike.

Akil El-Sayed was killed instantly by the first laser-guided bomb. Live infrared imagery from the Nighthawk showed that a few terrorists had survived the initial blast and were running toward their vehicles to escape. One by one, the vehicles were destroyed by Hellfire missiles.

An hour later, the head of Pakistan's super-secret S-Wing received a phone call from one of his intelligence agents in Benghazi.

Saturday, May 10

Cambridge, England
5:20 PM

"You love her, don't you?" Elena Scarlatti asked with a hint of envy in her voice.

"Yes," David said quietly as he and Elena followed Tiera and her family across the lawn in front of the Senate House where the University of Cambridge graduation ceremonies would be held the next day.

"Have you asked her to marry you?"

"No," he said, shaking his head slowly, "There's really no point. She's made it very clear that she's not ready to settle down and start a family. She's worked so hard to earn her doctoral degree that all Tiera can think about right now is getting out in the real world of computer science. I can understand that. But, it's different for me."

"Why do you say that?"

"Has Tiera told you much about me?" David asked, glancing toward Elena.

"Well, yes, quite a bit. She told me that you and your older sister were raised on a farm by your grandparents after your parents were killed. You started college on a swimming scholarship at a big public university but transferred to a conservative Christian university after your first year and earned a bachelor's degree in linguistics and a master's degree in theological studies."

"You were an Army officer and were badly wounded in Afghanistan. You're a couple of years older than Tiera and you met here at Cambridge when she was the coxswain of your boat crew."

"You said no when Tiera asked you to move in with her, which surprised and hurt her. She's been my best friend since we were small children and I'm certain that you're the only man she's ever cared enough about to make such an offer."

"She says you are very smart and that you were able to pursue your doctoral degree here at Cambridge because of your academic record and the money from a natural gas lease on your grandparents' farm. She told me yesterday that you've had been offered what she called a tenure-track teaching position at Baylor University and that you might accept it. Is there more?"

David laughed. Elena loved the sound of his laughter. He seemed so serious that it was nice to know that he could actually laugh. She was painfully jealous that this incredibly attractive man was in love with her best friend.

"Well, Elena, is there anything about me that Tiera didn't tell you?" David teased.

"Well, I don't know if it's boxers or briefs," Elena said as she bowed her head and tried to hide her smile.

David turned to Elena and grinned. "Not even Tiera knows that unless she bribed one of my boat crew to tell her."

Elena was surprised. She knew that David's refusal to move in with her friend was based on his deeply conservative religious beliefs but she'd assumed that their relationship had included physical intimacy. Certainly, Tiera had made no secret of her physical attraction to David. Yet, Elena was pretty sure that Tiera had never slept with another man so it was certainly possible that her relationship with David had been a platonic friendship. For some reason, that thought made her feel better.

"You still never answered my question. You said it was different for you but then you asked me if Tiera had told me about you and we got off-track. Why is it different for you?"

"Have you lost any friends in automobile accidents or war?"

"No. Thankfully, no."

"I was only 12 years old when my parents were killed. Sarah and I were badly hurt. This scar on my jaw is a reminder of that terrible night. I see it in the mirror every morning when I shave. My grandparents were wonderful but they couldn't take the place of our parents. Sarah used to wake up screaming in the night. She finally had to go to counseling. She's OK now but we all had a few rough years as she found ways to cope with her own demons."

"Afghanistan was a very dangerous place. I lost friends almost every week. I'm the only one who survived the IED that blew up our Humvee. The Army airlifted me to Landsthul hospital in Germany. The doctors managed to save my right leg but they used so much metal to reinforce my shattered femur that I can't go through an airport security check without setting off the alarms."

"I still have nightmares and demons of my own to deal with but I've tried to move on to whatever the rest of my life has in store. To answer your question directly, it's different for me because all I want to do now is settle down to a quiet life with the woman I love, raise

some kids, and be thankful every day that I got a second and then a third chance."

By then, tears were streaming down Elena's cheeks. When David realized she was crying, he put one arm around her shoulder and held her gently until her sobs subsided.

"I'm sorry. I didn't mean to make you cry."

"Oh David, that's the saddest story anyone's ever told me. You are so brave."

David stepped away from her and gave her a strange look before he whispered, "No, Elena. I'm not a brave man. I just played the cards I was dealt as best I could. I've seen bravery. It's something very different. When a soldier falls on a land mine to save his buddies, that's bravery beyond understanding. When a medic runs through a hail of bullets to save a wounded man, that's bravery. It wasn't until I went into combat that I really understood what Jesus Christ meant when he told his disciples that no man had greater love than that he was willing to lay down his life for his friends. No, Elena, I'm not a brave man. I'm just a man."

"Hurry up you two," Tiera called as she walked toward them. "Father has a limousine waiting to take us to dinner. I didn't realize you weren't still right behind us until I turned and saw you hugging each other out in the middle of the lawn. I had no idea that your romance had advanced so quickly."

"Tiera, stop it! David told me a sad story and I was crying. He's no different than most men who can't stand to see a woman cry," Elena said more emphatically than she had intended.

Elena noticed her friend's questioning look and wondered if Tiera had sensed how envious she was and how easily she could fall in love with David herself. Unlike Tiera, she was ready to get married and start a family. Those brief moments when David had comforted her would haunt her for a long time. She had felt strangely safe with his strong arm around her. Yet, her love for her best friend was so genuine that she would never do or say anything to interfere with Tiera's relationship with David.

Sunday, May 11

Islamabad, Pakistan
4:00 PM

Ahmed Malik had asked Dr. Bashir Ghilzai to meet with him at Pakistan's Inter-Services Intelligence Directorate headquarters. Dr. Ghilzai knew that an invitation from the head of the highly secretive and much-feared S-Wing of ISI was not to be taken lightly. He wondered what the ISI intelligence agent wanted as he passed through the security control point in the lobby before being escorted to Malik's office.

"Dr. Ghilzai, thank you for coming," said one of the most dangerous men in all of Pakistan without even a trace of a friendly smile.

Bashir Ghilzai noted with considerable discomfort that Ahmed Malik had not extended any of the customary Urdu or Pashto formal greetings. "It is my pleasure, I assure you," Dr. Ghilzai replied with a slight bow in an effort to establish a friendlier basis for the discussions to follow. Malik brushed it off and got straight to business.

"Please follow me. I have reserved one of our electronically shielded conference rooms for our discussions," said Malik.

Dr. Ghilzai followed one of the top intelligence agents in the world down the hall to a room with a heavy steel door. A bio-metric security pad, a camera, and an armed guard protected the entrance to the secure conference facility. Malik leaned forward and looked into the scanner so the security system could recognize his retinal patterns. He then spoke into the microphone saying, "Ahmed Malik with one cleared guest, Dr. Bashir Ghilzai." A computer synthesized voice then said, "Security authorization has been verified. You are cleared to enter." Dr. Ghilzai heard the distinct click that indicated the door had been unlocked.

A long conference table in the center of the room was surrounded by comfortable chairs. Less comfortable chairs lined both of the longer walls of the room. A lectern was off to the side of a large projection screen. Five clocks above the screen showed the current

local time in Islamabad as well as the time in Tel Aviv, London, Washington DC, and Beijing. Dr. Ghilzai knew that each of those cities was home to one of the top five intelligence agencies in the world.

“Be seated,” Malik told Dr. Ghilzai, indicating a specific chair near the end of the table. “We will be joined in just a moment.”

Just as Malik had indicated, the door opened a minute later. Ghilzai immediately recognized Lieutenant General Parvez Jhalawan, newly appointed director of Pakistan’s Intelligence Service and one of the most feared general officers the country’s military had ever produced. Dr. Ghilzai stood and bowed slightly as General Jhalawan strode to the executive chair at the foot of the conference table.

“Be seated Dr. Ghilzai,” General Jhalawan said curtly. Again, Dr. Ghilzai noted the absence of formal courtesy or preamble in the General’s abrupt directive. He did as he was instructed.

“Our discussions must be entirely confidential. You must not repeat anything you hear today if you value your life,” General Jhalawan said stiffly. “I am quite aware that you do not enjoy a reputation for guarding secrets. Be that as it may, I assure you that you will die a very painful death if I ever suspect that you have divulged what we discuss. Is that absolutely clear to you?” the General asked while giving Ghilzai an icy stare.

Dr. Ghilzai was totally unprepared to be treated in such a hostile manner. As the top nuclear scientist in a country where nuclear capability was a matter of intense national pride, he was caught entirely off guard. He was suddenly very afraid. The General obviously meant precisely what he said. Whatever was on the General’s mind, it was of such utmost importance that he would not hesitate to have him killed. “I understand General Jhalawan. I will comply fully with your instructions,” Ghilzai said as he waited to learn the subject of the meeting.

“Dr. Ghilzai, I’m sure you are aware that India is massing large numbers of troops along the Line of Control in the Kashmir region. They say it is for a major training exercise but we are concerned that they may be preparing to occupy the disputed area in the belief that

Pakistan lacks the military strength to dislodge them once they are in sole possession of the area. As a matter of national pride and security, I cannot allow the Indians to succeed in such a bold move," said General Jhalawan as he slammed his right fist down on the table to emphasize his point.

"The western powers have long been nervous about Pakistan's nuclear arsenal. They fear that our weapons will someday fall into the hands of radical Islamic terrorists, which of course would be a major game-changer as they say. As you know, we have repeatedly assured them that the risk is low because we store the components of our nuclear weapons in dispersed storage facilities. You and I know that is not true. Of what use would they be if it took days to assemble and deploy them?" Jhalawan asked rhetorically.

"I have decided to establish a tactical nuclear perimeter to defend Islamabad and our central government if necessary. Should India occupy the western parts of Kashmir, their armies would be only a short distance from our capital, which would pose a grave threat to our national security. I fear that time may be short. I will order the deployment of some of our M110A2 Howitzers in an arc along the northeastern side of the city. Most will have conventional artillery shells in local bunkers. A few, however, will have a small local stockpile of tactical nuclear shells," Jhalawan said.

Continuing his briefing to the scientist, General Jhalawan told him, "We do not believe the United States or India suspect that we have created a modern and more potent version of the American W33 and W79 nuclear artillery shells. As you know, they originally developed them to be fired from the eight-inch, self-propelled M110A2 Howitzers to give them the ability to repel a superior force of Soviet tanks in Eastern Europe during the Cold War. We face a very similar situation where the Indian Army enjoys such enormous manpower and equipment advantage over us that they could conceivably overrun our Army in a matter of days if we limited our self-defense to conventional weapons. However, I would like to hold our strategic nuclear weapons in reserve. Pakistan would become the pariah of the entire world if we used our nuclear weapons against heavily populated Indian cities. We would do so only if we

had no other choice. I think my plan may give us an intermediate option."

"What can I do to assist you in your plan General?" the scientist asked nervously.

"The secrecy of this plan must be absolute. We dare not allow the western powers or India to suspect that we are deploying tactical nuclear weapons to the border. Such knowledge might very well persuade the Indians to attack pre-emptively. The western powers would immediately try to persuade us not to carry out our plan. Their fear, of course, is that deployed nuclear artillery shells might not enjoy the same physical security of those stored in a central nuclear facility, such as the one we maintain at Wah," said General Jhalawan.

Ahmed Malik then spoke for the first time since the General had entered the conference room. "To initiate General Jhalawan's plan, you are going to arrange for five nuclear artillery shells to be removed from their storage bunker at Wah. As far as anyone knows, the deployed howitzers will have only conventional ordnance in their local bunkers. With utmost secrecy, you will arrange to transport the nuclear shells from Wah to a location I will specify. For this important service to your country, you will be paid the sum of twenty-five million Pakistan Rupees, the equivalent of more than two hundred and fifty thousand U.S. dollars. If you value your life, you must never reveal anything about this discussion today or about the subsequent events resulting from them."

Dr. Bashir Ghilzai had become moderately wealthy by selling nuclear technology secrets to the North Koreans and the Iranians with the tacit, though never publicly admitted, concurrence of important people high in Pakistan's government. He was a very greedy man. But, he was also a coward. He knew that if he refused to agree to do as General Jhalawan asked, he would probably be killed before he left the ISI headquarters building. "Yes, I will be honored to assist in this patriotic plan," said Ghilzai in a disgustingly obsequious tone of voice.

A few minutes later, Dr. Ghilzai was escorted to the front of the building and allowed to leave.

"What do you think, Ahmed?" the General asked after the scientist was gone. "Can we trust him?"

Malik frowned slightly before he answered the General's question, "Yes, I'm sure of it. He is greedy and we offered him a big carrot. But, he is also a weak and cowardly man. He will have nightmares wondering what tortures we might inflict upon him before killing him if he breathes a word to anyone. Yes, I think we have guaranteed his silence and full cooperation."

"Do you think he suspected my true intentions for the weapons?" General Jhalawan asked.

"No, there was nothing that could have given him a clue about what you really intend to do," Ahmed Malik answered. "I was watching him very closely as you briefed him. He nodded at each key point and I never saw any sign that he had recognized an inconsistency or illogical element of the plan. I have interrogated many men and I am certain that he will do exactly as you direct."

"Are you certain that the anonymous tip about the meeting between Al-Zeid and El-Sayed cannot be traced to you?"

"Yes, I am quite sure. The CIA response to the tip was predictable. It was amusing to see how easy it was to manipulate the Americans into taking care of El-Sayed for us."

Valletta, Malta
1:25 PM

"Look, you can see Portomaso yacht basin where father keeps the Peregrine," Tiera said excitedly. David felt her breast pressed against his arm and smelled her hair as she leaned over him to see out of the window. Tiera had insisted that David take the window seat since this was his first trip to Malta. He had a marvelous view of the deep-blue waters of the Mediterranean and the sunny islands of Malta and Gozo as the plane banked to the right to line up for its final approach to Malta International Airport.

By a double stroke of good luck, David's window seat on the right side of the first-class cabin had turned out to be perfect for his first view of the island where he would spend the next two weeks as a guest of the Aquilina family. The wind was out of the northwest so

the pilot had flown south along the eastern coast of Malta before making the turn to land to the northwest on the main runway. Tiera had pointed out St Paul's bay and the grand palace in Valletta as they flew down the coast at low altitude. She'd tried to point out her father's estate near Iklin but David wasn't sure he'd been able to pick it out.

Sunday's graduation ceremonies at Cambridge had been predictably formal and in their own way quite beautiful. The ceremony had begun when the Vice-Chancellor's procession entered the 300-year-old Senate House led by the Esquire Bedells.

When his name had been called, David had stepped forward and knelt in front of the Vice-Chancellor as he'd solemnly intoned the venerable graduation benediction in Latin, '*Auctoritate mihi commissa admitto te ad gradum doctoris semitico linguarum, in nomine Patris et Filii et Spiritus Sancti.*' The Vice-Chancellor had then repeated the benediction in English, '*By the authority committed to me, I admit you to the degree of Doctor of Philosophy in Semitic Languages in the name of the Father and of the Son and of the Holy Spirit.*' David had then stood, bowed to the Vice-Chancellor, and exited through the Doctor's door of the Senate-House to receive his certificate.

It was the proudest day of his life but he had been alone. None of his remaining family could come to see him receive a Doctor's degree from one of the most prestigious universities in the world. Sarah was nine months pregnant and couldn't make the trip. His grandparents were elderly and didn't even have passports. There was no one else.

David had sensed that Tiera's mother Maria had understood. She had put her arm around him after the ceremony and told him that she knew his family was proud of him even if they could not attend his graduation. In a way, her motherly attempt to comfort him had only deepened his sadness and sense of loneliness. But, he appreciated her kindness and that she had tried to lift his spirits. At dinner that evening, Matthias and Maria had invited him to come to Malta for a holiday. He was disappointed when Tiera's younger brother Nicholas told them he couldn't join them because he had final exams at Stanford the following week.

Tiera had promised to show David around the islands and to take him diving. It sounded like fun but David had never been around people as wealthy as the Aquilina family.

Elena had told him that the Aquilina family had been on Malta for over 350 years. Matthias had no brothers or sisters and had inherited his father's banking and shipping interests. Elena had also told him that Matthias was a very astute banker and businessman. She thought that he was now probably the wealthiest man in Malta and told David that his views on international finance and economics were widely respected.

At Cambridge, Tiera had never flaunted her wealth but Elena had told David that her father had given Tiera and Nicholas rather large investment portfolios to manage on their 18th birthdays. Both of them had done well by following their father's advice. They would eventually inherit a large fortune from their parents but Elena had told him that Tiera and Nicholas were already millionaires.

As the plane touched down, David was wondering if the daughter of an extremely wealthy man would ever marry a guy like him.

Monday, May 12

Valletta, Malta
10:35 AM

"Mr. Aquilina, there's a man on the phone who wishes to speak to you if you are available," Matthias Aquilina's executive assistant announced over the intercom.

"Who is it, Christina?"

"I asked him but all he would say is to tell you that your rent is overdue again."

Matthias chuckled. It was Volker. Matthias and Maria leased a luxury condo from him in a high-rise building near the Old Opera House in the heart of Frankfurt. The wealthy German banker loved to pretend that his friend was a dead-beat who never paid his rent on time. It was an old joke between them.

Volker Schuhmacher had just been appointed President of the European Central Bank and, along with the American Federal Reserve Board Chairman, was arguably one of the most important men in the world. Matthias picked up the phone.

"Volker, you old scoundrel, what mischief are you plotting today?" Matthias said as he greeted his close friend.

"Oh, I thought I might put out a news release questioning the sovereign solvency of Malta to distract the press from the situation in Greece. I thought it might be fun to see you on television trying to reassure your stockholders that there was nothing to worry about," the new ECB president laughed.

"You have a very strange sense of humor," said Matthias grimacing and shaking his head at the hideous thought of such a media circus. "What's on your mind, if you still have one with the mess you've inherited at the ECB," Matthias asked.

"As you know, I'll be the official host for the meeting of the G-20 finance ministers in Valletta two weeks from today at the grand palace. I have a couple of rather presumptuous last-minute favors to ask of you," Schuhmacher told him. "I'd like for you to be the lunch speaker on the first day with sovereign debt as your topic. If you agree, I'd like for you to present a banker's view of the unsustainable growth of sovereign debt in Europe, the United States, and Japan."

"Yes, I'd be happy to do that. You know my views and I'm sure you wouldn't ask if you weren't comfortable with what I'll have to say on that very important and timely topic," Matthias told his friend. "What's the second favor?"

"I want to set a more relaxed tone for this meeting than we've experienced in recent meetings of the G-20. While the G-7 meetings are usually pretty civilized even to the point of being dull, the G-20 can be more contentious due primarily to the wide disparity in how each country views its own self-interest with respect to international monetary matters."

"With the recent decision by Japan to begin a massive stimulation of their moribund economy, there are widespread fears of a currency war. I don't think the risk of a new currency war is great but several of the G-20 member countries are quite concerned.

I'm afraid there could be some heated exchanges. You could help me set a more collegial tone for these meetings. If you and Maria would be so kind, I'd like for you to host a welcoming reception at your estate the evening before the conference opens. I know it's rather short notice."

"How many people would attend the reception?" Matthias asked.

"Perhaps eighty. I'll have my assistant provide a better estimate two days before the reception. Most of the ministers will have their spouses and at least one or two senior staff personnel with them. We normally invite them to attend the social functions. Many of the attendees have never been to Malta so we've arranged day tours and luncheons for the spouses who attend. On the second night, we'll host a formal dinner in the grand palace with ballroom dancing afterward. The palace is such a beautiful venue that I expect the dinner will be talked about for years."

Matthias considered his friend's request for a moment before saying, "I need to speak to Maria before committing of course but I feel sure she will be glad for us to host the reception. The number of people you have in mind is similar to the receptions we host in connection with quarterly board meetings for the bank and our shipping company. We can easily accommodate that number of people. Parking can be a bit of a problem for that many cars so we would expect the limousine drivers to park outside the estate grounds after dropping off their entourages at the front door. I will call you back to confirm but I think you can safely assume that we will be pleased to host the reception for you," Matthias said.

"That is wonderful. Thank you so much. I knew I could count on you and Maria. I really believe that a reception at your lovely home, with all of its own rich history, will get the meetings off to a good start," Volker said in appreciation.

"Now, about the matter of overdue rent," Volker said changing the subject, "Please tell Maria that Wagner's Ring operas will be performed in their entirety at the Old Opera House in September. The performances are already sold out but we can seat eight people in our box. Why don't you and Maria come to Frankfurt for the entire week so we can catch up? Angela will come with me to Malta, of course, but there will be precious little free time," Volker said with

a hint of fatigue in his voice that was hardly surprising given the monumental challenges he faced in his new position.

"I'll discuss it with Maria and have her call Angela. I have no doubt that Maria will definitely want to see the performances and visit with you both," chuckled Matthias. "Anything else?" he asked.

"No, that's all. See you in a couple of weeks," Volker said as he rang off.

Tuesday, May 13

Tel Aviv, Israel
2:00 PM

Gavriella Adler sat quietly on the sofa in the corner of her boss's office watching him look through his briefing slides one last time. Her boss was Levi Reznik. He had invited her to join him when he gave the nuclear threat briefing to the Director of the Israel Institute for Intelligence and Special Operations, better known as the Mossad. They still had a few minutes before it would be time to go.

Watching his calm, methodical way of preparing for the briefing, Gabe smiled as she remembered that in Hebrew Levi's nickname meant *The Rock*. She knew that early in his career with the Mossad, Levi had been a protégé of the legendary spy master, Meir Dagan. As he had gained experience and demonstrated both sound judgment and loyalty, Meir Dagan had given him increasingly difficult and dangerous assignments and eventually made him a Katsa overseeing other field agents.

Levi's relationship with the new Director had been strained at first but seemed to be improving. Gabe had heard other agents say that the new Director had not been sure that Levi would transfer his loyalty to a new boss. But, after working closely with Levi for several months, the Director had apparently come to admire his competence and level head.

While she waited, Gavriella thought back over her five years with the Mossad. Her father was a Colonel in the Israel Defense Forces and she had served six years with the IDF before she was accepted

and sent to the Mossad Training Academy near Herzliva. She was fully aware that Levi considered her his protégé and was grateful for his encouragement and mentoring.

The briefing would provide the Director and the Intelligence Oversight Committee of the Knesset with an assessment of global nuclear threats. Iran's steady advances toward attainment of nuclear capability would be foremost in the Director's mind because it would be his job to brief the Prime Minister before he left for Washington to confer with the American President regarding strategies and timelines for pre-emptive strikes against the Iranian nuclear facilities. But, there were other potential nuclear threats to the State of Israel.

A rogue nuclear scientist in Pakistan had sold advanced nuclear technology to the North Koreans and the Iranians. India was rattling its swords at Pakistan again over the Kashmir territorial dispute. The two nations both had nuclear weapons but neither had signed the nuclear non-proliferation treaty. India was unlikely to use nuclear weapons in a first-strike action but Pakistan might. Russia was very much back on the nuclear threat radar too with the increasing belligerence of the Russian President in response to what he clearly viewed as a weak American leader.

Levi finally looked up. "Are you ready? It's time to go."

Wednesday, May 14

Islamabad, Pakistan
1:15 PM

"Mr. Ambassador, this is an urgent dispatch that just came in on the secure fax from the President's chief of staff in Cairo," Hassan Al-Zeid's personal assistant said as she handed him a folder marked *Eyes Only*.

Hassan opened the folder and read the dispatch twice before leaning back in his chair and swiveling around to look out the window of the Egyptian Embassy in Islamabad, Pakistan.

"Why am I being recalled?" He wondered aloud. The dispatch gave no clue. It simply ordered him to return to Egypt by the end of the month. It was not clear if the purpose was some high-level consultation that must be conducted in person or if he had somehow displeased the new Egyptian President. He wondered if he dared call the President to see if he could learn more and decided against it. Instead, he would call his old friend, the Director of Egypt's General Intelligence Service in Hadaeq Al Qubbah to see what he knew. Even if his friend was unaware of the purpose of the recall order, Al-Zeid was confident that he could find out.

He read the message again and saw that he was also being directed to have his personal limousine shipped to Suez and that the car was to be accompanied for the entire trip by his driver, Yousef Abu Shakra. Like the Ambassador, Abu Shakra was secretly a member of the Muslim Brotherhood that had swept to power in Egypt following the removal of Muhammad Hosni El Sayed Mubarak from office. So far as the Ambassador knew, Yousef was totally loyal to him.

He turned to buzz his assistant on the intercom. "Ask my driver to come to my office, please."

Hassan then called Jamila, his beautiful young Lebanese wife, and told her to begin making preparations to return to Egypt. He told her that he wasn't yet sure if it was a short visit or, possibly, that they might be going home to Alexandria if his appointment was at an end. He told her to assume that they might not be coming back to Pakistan. As he hung up the phone, his intercom buzzed.

"Your driver is here sir. Shall I send him in?"

"Yes, please."

"Yousef, I want you to make the necessary preparations to ship the limousine back to Egypt on a container ship. I want you to accompany the car and take if off the ship at the port of Suez. You'll then drive it to Alexandria and wait for my further instructions."

Yousef bowed slightly and said, "Yes sir. I will see to it immediately."

Thursday, May 15

Valletta, Malta
8:55 AM

David was convinced that Tiera had taken him to every tourist spot and family restaurant on Malta and Gozo and introduced him to every citizen of the historic and lovely Mediterranean country. After only four days in Malta, he was exhausted. As a member of the women's boat club at Cambridge, Tiera had always been a dynamo of energy and endurance. Now, he almost wished she had a little less energy.

They'd gotten up at 5:30 AM to get an early start for a day of diving at Hurd Bank to look for what a diving instructor pal of Tiera's thought might be the remains of an old wooden ship. He'd given her the GPS coordinates so they ought to be able to find it without much difficulty. Tiera parked the estate's Land Rover in the family's reserved parking spot at Portomaso yacht basin near where the Peregrine was moored.

After just a few days, David was beginning to accept the fact that wealthy people have wealthy habits and expensive toys. Tiera had told him about her brother's silver Mercedes-Benz SLS AMG Gullwing coupe. David had seen an article about the car in one of the auto magazines and knew that it cost over 250,000 euros. He'd checked prices at an on-line Italian brokerage and knew that the Peregrine was a multi-million dollar luxury yacht. Even so, he was not prepared for his first look at the family's spectacularly beautiful boat.

Tiera had named the Azimut 64 flying bridge yacht '*Peregrine*' because, despite its luxury features and size, it was quite fast. She'd told him that the exterior styling was the work of the great Italian yacht designer, Stefano Righini. The luxurious and beautiful interior design was by Carlo Galeazzi.

The yacht could cruise at 28 knots and make 34 knots at full throttle in calm seas. It was powered by two enormous Caterpillar C18 marine diesel engines. The yacht was built at the Azimut

boatyard at Avigliana, Italy, one of the world's finest producers of large, luxury yachts.

Tiera had told him that the yacht was fully equipped to support scuba diving, including an on-board compressor and enriched-air Nitrox tanks for deeper dives. She and Nicholas had persuaded their father to let them have a specially-designed diving platform installed at the stern to make it easier for divers to enter and leave the water.

Twenty minutes after they'd parked the Land Rover, David cast off the stern line and stepped nimbly onto the diving platform as Tiera backed the big yacht away from the pier and headed out the narrow channel inside the breakwater before turning east toward Hurd Bank.

Once clear of the harbor, Tiera opened the throttles a little and the Peregrine settled down for an easy half-hour run to where they'd anchor to dive.

"Take the helm, will you, David?" Tiera shouted above the wind and deep rumble of the big Cat diesels. "I want to change into my bathing suit. After all those dismal, rainy and foggy days at Cambridge, it's good to be back where the sun shines. Just head due east for now. I'll be back in a few minutes."

David was feeling pretty mellow. He'd always enjoyed being out on a boat and it was an absolutely beautiful day. The sea was flat and the big yacht was running smooth as silk at 12 knots. The navigation system's map was gliding slowly across the screen as the yacht moved east.

"Got it all under control, Captain?" Tiera whispered in his ear. He hadn't heard her come up the ladder and swiveled around to look at her. He almost choked. She was wearing a tiny bikini bottom but no top. He looked away immediately and then felt foolish so he turned back toward her trying to keep his eyes locked on hers. She struck a provocative pose and grinned at him.

David knew Tiera had never quite forgiven him for not moving in with her. What Elena had told him had only reinforced that view. Instinctively, he also realized that this was her way of teasing him about what she considered his old-fashioned and even prudishly conservative beliefs while having some fun at his expense.

"Well, do you have it under control or not?" she taunted, knowing full well that he didn't.

"No, I guess not. Look, this is really awkward. Would you mind at least putting some kind of top on?"

"Come on, David. It's me, Tiera. You know, the woman you said you loved. Don't you *want* to see me without my clothes on? You know, I almost came up on the bridge nude but thought you'd have a heart attack if I did. You may not believe this, but you are the only man who has ever seen my breasts and if I drop my bikini bottom you'll be the only one who's ever seen all of me. What do you say? I really want to go nude for you. I'm not expecting you to make love to me but wouldn't it be fun to be just a little naughty for once?"

The strained look on David's face made Tiera realize how badly he wanted her. She sensed what a struggle it was for him to stick to his moral code when the woman he loved was standing nearly naked in front of him making him an offer few men would have refused. She was suddenly deeply ashamed that she'd intentionally embarrassed the man she loved. A flood of hot tears spilled down her cheeks as she turned away from him and covered her breasts with her hands.

"Oh David, I'm so sorry. I shouldn't have done this. Turn away. Don't look at me. I'll go below and get dressed," Tiera sobbed as she started down the ladder.

Tiera didn't come back for a long time so David cut the engines when the navigation system showed him that the yacht was near the place they planned to dive. Once he killed the engines, it was very quiet and peaceful. The only sound was of small waves splashing softly against the side of the boat. The big yacht rolled gently on the long swells and drifted slowly westward with the sluggish current. There was nothing urgent. It wouldn't take Tiera long to bring the boat back to the right spot once she came up from below.

David tried to get the image of her lovely, athletic body out of his mind but it was impossible. He fervently hoped that the embarrassing episode did not damage their relationship or ruin their holiday together.

"Ahoy, Mon Capitan and El Supremo du Perigrino. This lowly apprentice sailor is ready to present herself for your inspection," he heard Tiera call from the bottom of the ladder. "Do I have my Capitan's permission to come up?"

David smiled, grateful that she'd instinctively used her marvelous sense of humor to eliminate any awkwardness they might have felt after the emotionally-charged scene. "Yes you may approach your captain but see that you are properly respectful or I will toss you to the sharks."

Tiera stepped from the ladder onto the flying bridge. She had donned a pair of white linen shorts, white boat shoes, and a light blue knit shirt. She smiled tentatively at him without speaking and then came easily into his arms. They hugged each other for a long time before she raised her face to be kissed. David did not disappoint her. It began as a tender, loving kiss and it ended that way.

"I love you, David," She whispered.

"I know you do. I love you too."

"What time is it?" she asked.

"Almost ten."

"Let me see where we are. OK, we've drifted west a little ways but it'll only take a few minutes to get back to where we'll anchor. We'll be diving in about 70 feet of water so we won't need to use a special breathing mixture. But, to be safe, we should only stay on the bottom for about 30 minutes. I think we can get in one dive before we have lunch and then maybe one more in the afternoon before we head for home. How does that sound?" Tiera asked.

"You're the boss. Whatever you think best is fine with me," David answered as Tiera started the engines.

Janawai, Pakistan
1:00 PM

"General Jhalawan, Ambassador Al-Zeid's car has arrived," said his adjutant.

"Greet him at the door and take him to the living room," ordered the General. "Offer him some tea and almond cookies. Tell him that I am on an important phone call and will join him momentarily."

Jhalawan was not in the midst of an important phone call. He simply wanted to remind the Egyptian Ambassador to Pakistan that he was the second most powerful man in Pakistan after the president. He kept the Ambassador waiting for five minutes.

"Ahlan wa sahlan," said General Jhalawan using a somewhat informal greeting meaning welcome."

"Salam alekum," replied Ambassador Al-Zeid bowing his head respectfully.

"My apologies for keeping you waiting," Jhalawan said without a trace of sincerity.

"Not at all, I know that you have many responsibilities and urgent demands on your time," replied Al-Zeid.

General Jhalawan was confident that the Ambassador didn't suspect that Ahmed Malik's anonymous tip to the CIA had resulted in Akil El-Sayed's death.

"Allah must have been watching over you when the Americans waited to use their drone until El-Sayed had returned to his base. One would think that it would have been easier for them to simply drop one of their laser-guided smart bombs on the villa where you met. I suppose they waited to avoid the political repercussions if they had made the strike on Egyptian soil. In any event, Allah be praised. You are safe. I trust that your meeting with the martyr was fruitful," said the General with a raised eyebrow.

"Yes, extremely so," answered Al-Zeid. "I think you will be very pleased with what I have learned."

"Excellent," said General Jhalawan. "I believe our food is ready. My cook has prepared a special meal to honor your visit to my home. Let's have lunch and then we'll talk."

Over the next hour, the two men enjoyed a superb meal of roasted lamb with steamed vegetables followed by pastries with honey and karkade tea. Their conversation began with the customary polite small-talk but soon evolved into a more serious discussion of the withdrawal of the American forces from

Afghanistan and what that might mean for Pakistan. The real purpose of their meeting was not discussed over lunch.

"Let's go into my study. We can make ourselves comfortable and then you can tell me about your meeting with Akil," said General Jhalawan.

As the two men sat down, a servant brought a silver tray of dates and a pot of strong Al-Qahwa coffee brewed in the manner common in Saudi Arabia.

"Will you have some coffee now, Ambassador?" asked General Jhalawan.

"Perhaps not just yet, if you don't mind," replied Hassan. "I am very comfortable after that fine meal. Please thank your cook for me. The lamb was excellent."

With the minor courtesies adequately attended to, General Jhalawan asked Al-Zeid to give his report.

"Akil El-Sayed was a very proud man," Hassan began. "As you know, he was openly critical of Osama bin Laden and had effectively taken his place as the leader of Al Qaeda. I think he feared that you wanted to become the global leader of Islamic Jihad against the western powers. He specifically asked me what relationship you envisioned with him. The way he asked the question suggested that he might have been amenable to some form of shared leadership. As a former Army officer himself, he certainly understood the value of your experience, especially in dealing with the Americans in Afghanistan and here in Pakistan."

"That does not surprise me. Please go on," said Jhalawan.

"El-Sayed was very guarded throughout most of our meeting. He was not unfriendly, but there was a pervasive sense that he wasn't sure he could trust me, or by extension, you," Al-Zeid told his host. I suppose that is understandable given how determined the Americans were to find him and kill him. I think he half expected the villa where we met to be bombed by a drone or a cruise missile. I would say that he hid it well but he was clearly a very nervous man."

Hassan continued, "Near the end of our meeting, El-Sayed finally admitted that he agreed with your assessment that the time-table he had written about could be accelerated. I was never able to get him

to reveal all of his thinking but I am quite sure that he had seen the same western vulnerability that you have identified. However, I do not think he knew quite how to exploit that vulnerability. He gave a curious little speech near the end of our meeting that made me feel certain that he shared your assessment of how to bring an end to western political and economic dominance."

"Tell me what he said," General Jhalawan said with obvious interest.

"Akil El-Sayed said that Osama bin Laden had correctly identified the Achilles heel of the Americans but that he had not struck with sufficient force. He quoted an American poet, Ralph Waldo Emerson, who once wrote that *when you strike at a king, you must kill him.* Akil recounted the numerous times that the Americans have been attacked throughout their history while noting that they are so strong they always recover. He surprised me with his grasp of western financial matters when he pointed out that the American stock market recovered from the 2001 attacks on the World Trade Center within two years. Devastating as the attack had been, it was not a mortal blow."

"El-Sayed emphasized that, by failing to kill the metaphorical king, bin Laden had enraged the king and motivated him to seek out and kill his assailants. Since 9/11, more than fifty of Al Qaeda's senior leaders have been killed or captured by the Americans. Al Qaeda's financial support was seriously degraded when the Americans froze assets held in the United States and made it chillingly clear that any country that provided aid of any kind to Al Qaeda was an enemy of the United States. Only recently has Al Qaeda once again become a weapon that can effectively be used against the Americans and their western allies. Akil El-Sayed deserves considerable credit for that."

"Very interesting," reflected General Jhalawan. "So El-Sayed agreed that the western financial system is their Achilles heel and that the next time we attack them it must be with a mortal blow. He believed his time-table could be accelerated but did not yet appear to have a strategy to do so. Does that accurately summarize the results of your meeting with him?"

"Yes," Ambassador Al-Zeid replied simply.

A distant look came into General Jhalawan's eyes and he said nothing for several moments as he digested what the Ambassador had told him. Finally, he turned to face Al-Zeid saying, "I am very pleased with what you accomplished. It is much as I suspected but it is very good to have my instincts confirmed. Let us have some coffee and dates before I tell you some things I want you to know.

For several minutes, the two men enjoyed the strong Arabic coffee and dates. General Jhalawan invited the Ambassador to join him on the balcony overlooking the garden of his villa near the small town of Janawai in Pakistan-controlled Kashmir some 100 miles northeast of Islamabad.

The view of Nanga Parbat, 30 miles to the north, was spectacular. Also known as 'Diamar, King of the Mountains' it was the ninth-highest mountain in the world at 26,660 feet. K2, the second-highest mountain on Earth at 28,251 feet, was 130 miles to the northeast but not visible from the villa. General Jhalawan had decided to meet with Ambassador Al-Zeid in Janawai, rather than in the Capital District of Islamabad because he did not want the CIA to know of their meeting. He was sure that his official residence in the capital district was closely monitored by the CIA.

When they were once again seated in the study, General Jhalawan began to speak at some length to explain why he believed the opportune moment to end western domination of world affairs and to advance the cause of Islam was at hand.

"The western powers have never been more vulnerable than they are now," Jhalawan began. "The U.S. dollar's reign as the world's reserve currency is being seriously threatened and may soon come to an end. If that should happen, the impact on the American economy will be devastating. There would be a ripple effect on the Europeans and Japanese because they are major trading partners with the Americans and their monetary systems are closely linked."

"The Chinese have been amassing untold tons of gold and no one really knows what their current reserves might be. Some experts believe the Chinese may already have larger gold reserves than the Americans. I find that hard to believe but it is clear that the Chinese are dramatically increasing their gold reserves and may eventually surpass the American reserves. By law, all gold mined and refined in

China must be sold to the central government whether produced by Chinese companies or foreign companies licensed to conduct business in China. China is also believed to be making major purchases of gold bullion every time the price drops, following the investor's adage to buy on the dips," General Jhalawan said.

"The Chinese currently hold between one and two trillion dollars of U.S. sovereign debt. As a result, they are clearly nervous about the future value of the dollar. They recently began to replace maturing long-term treasury bonds with new short-term bonds as a defensive move. That strategy has already been vindicated. The Federal Reserve Board has begun to lose control of the bond markets and interest rates on short-term treasuries are beginning to rise."

"Many experts believe the Chinese are trying to position the Renminbi as an alternate global reserve currency. The Renminbi is extremely under-valued. The Chinese have resisted pressure to let its value rise because they do not want to lose the tremendous export advantage they currently enjoy by virtue of their under-valued currency. The Chinese have recently entered into a bilateral agreement with Australia to conduct financial transactions between the two countries in their own currencies instead of using the U.S. dollar. The Chinese and the New Zealanders have begun similar discussions. The People's Bank of China has already signed nearly two trillion yuan worth of currency-swap deals with more than twenty countries and, remarkably, with the European Central Bank."

"The Gulf Cooperation Council has put in place a new currency that they will soon require to be used to purchase Arab oil in the future. That will force oil-importing nations to sell their reserves of U.S. dollars to buy the GCC oil currency. When that happens, it will flood the global currency markets with U.S. dollars, which will sharply de-value the dollar against the Renminbi and other strong currencies. The Swiss franc, the Singapore dollar, and the Norwegian krone are all extremely strong. However, none of those currencies are traded in sufficient volume to provide the liquidity required by global commerce. If any currency can supplant the U.S. dollar as the world's reserve currency, it is the Chinese Renminbi," Jhalawan said as he continued."

"However, the Chinese aren't the only ones frustrated with the U.S. dollar's dominant status as the world's global reserve currency. Brazil, Russia, India, China, and South Africa, the so-called BRICS nations, recently met in Durban to approve the establishment of a new development bank. These five countries have combined foreign-currency reserve equivalents of at least 4.4 trillion dollars and represent 43 percent of the world's population. They are trying to enhance their ability to influence global financial issues commensurate with their expanding economic power. By pooling their foreign-currency reserves, they hope to hedge against crises involving balance-of-payments or currency issues. It should come as no surprise that a significant part of their combined foreign-currency reserves are in U.S. dollars. That alone gives them quite a bit of leverage. It is also worth noting that India and Russia also have significant gold reserves and also appear to be buying on the dips."

"The Russians are now the world's largest oil producer and they are using their income from international oil sales to buy gold. They have added almost six hundred metric tons of gold to their reserves in the past decade. To put that in perspective, the gold they have added to their central bank is almost three times the weight of the Statue of Liberty. A Russian lawmaker in the United Russia party recently noted that the more gold a country has, the better it would be able to weather a crisis with a global reserve currency like the dollar."

"If, at some point in the future, the BRICS should decide to create an alternate global reserve currency they might very well have the financial muscle to succeed in challenging the dollar's unique status. I believe the BRICS would support having the Renminbi become that alternative."

"The financial house of cards in Europe is about to be blown away as well. Several of the member countries of the monetary union that established the Euro are essentially insolvent. Everyone knows about the problems in Greece and Portugal but Spain and Italy are in very bad shape as well. The German people all believe that the southern members of the union are living well at the expense of the German worker. That's not really what has happened."

"When the Euro was established as the common currency, its sound basis and strong comparative value against other world currencies made it possible for the southern members to borrow money at favorable rates and they did. But what the German workers don't realize is that their strong economy exists to a significant degree because those borrowed euros have been used to buy German products, creating a very strong foreign exchange surplus and essentially full employment in Germany. So, the prevailing view in Germany is simply wrong."

"German voters insist that their Chancellor play hard-ball to require strong austerity measures in the southern countries as a condition of receiving continued financial assistance. They simply do not comprehend that austerity in the southern countries will reduce demand for German exports. When that happens, German unemployment will rise and the self-righteous anger of the German workers will only increase. The German media will exploit that anger, as we've already seen them do again and again. That will be like pouring gasoline on a fire."

"In any event, the imposition of austerity has already backfired as we've seen from the riots that have erupted as government benefits were reduced, public services curtailed, and taxes increased."

"France and the United Kingdom are in scarcely better shape. Both Europe and the Americans are sitting on a powder keg created by the excessively generous social benefits that have been paid for with borrowed money. Like the limerick about the young lady of Niger, the politicians are riding the back of the tiger. They can't get off without being eaten," General Jhalawan said with obvious delight at the predicament the hated Americans and Europeans were now in."

General Jhalawan leaned forward and looked intently into the eyes of the Ambassador. "You will have a critical role in what is about to happen. I'm sure you were surprised to receive the fax recalling you to Egypt. I must apologize because that was my doing. I spoke to your president and asked him to recall you. Of course, he could not refuse given my position in Pakistan's government. I emphasized to him that your service here had been superb but that you are needed in Alexandria to support something that will happen

very soon to achieve the mutual goals of the Muslim Brotherhood, Al Qaeda, and others who share our faith."

"Your president was very curious so I feel sure that he will press you for information when you see him. Tell him only that I met with you to extend my apologies and to explain that I asked him to recall you to Egypt so you could support a secret mission of which you know very little. You can tell him that I promised that you would receive further instructions soon. Assure him of your continued personal loyalty to him. If it pleases you to do so, it would be helpful if you expressed confidence in me and told him that I wanted to meet him in person but that was not currently possible. If you wish, you might also tell him you believe I am determined to promote better cooperation and coordination among those who share our beliefs," said the General.

Ambassador Al-Zeid nodded.

"Now let me explain what your role will be both before you leave Pakistan and after you return home," said General Jhalawan. "All I need to do now is to light the fuse. You will help me strike the match," said General Jhalawan.

Hurd Bank, Mediterranean Sea
11:35 AM

The water was crystal clear but there weren't many fish. David knew that pollution and the high salinity of the Mediterranean Sea had decimated the marine life in many areas. He could see the dappled sunlight reflecting from the sandy bottom as he followed Tiera's silvery stream of bubbles down.

The GPS coordinates Tiera's friend had given her had brought them unerringly to the right spot. When they were still 40 feet above the bottom, they could see the faint outline of the old wreck in the white sand. It was about 50 feet long and there were a large number of broken amphorae scattered around the few fragments that remained of the wooden hull. David knew there were hundreds of similar old wrecks scattered all over the Mediterranean Sea. Some were archeologically important but most weren't. He'd noted on the GPS display that they were in international waters just outside of

Malta's 12 mile territorial limit so he was pretty sure it would be OK for them to keep any artifacts they might find.

Tiera was taking pictures as they came near the old ship's final resting place and motioned for David to pose for her. A large grouper was nosing around the amphorae so he swam over to it so Tiera could get a good shot. She handed the camera to him and motioned for him to take some pictures of her near the big fish. She then swam slowly around the old wreck and David snapped several more pictures of her.

Tiera tried using her swim fins to fan sand away from what appeared to be the bow of the old ship but that stirred up so much silt that they had to wait for the sluggish current to clear the water. She then swam head-down along the edge of the hull, probing the sand here and there with her diving knife. Suddenly, Tiera jerked back and stared at something she'd seen. David saw it too. It was a human hand sticking out of the sand.

Tiera bolted toward the surface. David hurried to catch her but she struggled wildly against his efforts to restrain her. He could see her eyes wide with panic through her diving mask. He was finally able to calm her down and she nodded to let him know she was OK. David wrote a note on his diving slate, telling her to wait for him at that depth. She nodded her agreement and he turned to swim back to their gruesome discovery.

David didn't want to touch the hand, fearing the flesh might pull from the bones if he did. But there really wasn't much choice. Pulling gently on the hand, he fanned away the sand with his fins and his one free hand. He was surprised that the flesh felt firm and that the fingers were still flexible. There didn't seem to any sign of rigor mortis or decomposition.

It took David 15 minutes to free the entire body from the sand. The eyes and mouth were closed and shoulder-length dark hair swirled around the face. The corpse was completely nude but showed no signs of damage to the flesh from crabs or other scavengers. David thought that perhaps the man hadn't been there very long but wondered how he'd become covered in the sand so quickly if that was true.

He started for the surface with his grisly companion in tow. He saw that Tiera hadn't waited for him but he wasn't really surprised. He went slowly, ascending at the ultra-safe rate of about 30 feet per minute. He knew he'd been down a little too long and wanted to be sure he decompressed properly. He hoped Tiera had been similarly careful.

When David got to the boat, Tiera was leaning over the stern watching anxiously for his return. He maneuvered the body parallel to the diving platform and by timing his effort to the gentle swells he was able to roll the corpse onto the platform. He pushed his mask back so he could speak.

"Hand me some rope so I can secure the body to the boat," David said to her. She was pale and shivering with fear and David realized that this was probably the only dead person she'd ever seen outside of a church or funeral home. When he climbed aboard and removed his gear, she was sitting on the deck with her arms wrapped around her legs and her back against one of the seats.

Are you OK?" he asked. She nodded but looked like she was about to cry. David knelt down and put his arms around her. He just held her for a few moments until he sensed that she was better now that he was with her.

"Can you help me get the body over the transom and onto the deck?" David asked. Tiera stared mutely at him and shook her head.

The dead man's body weighed as much as David so it was a real struggle for him to get it onboard alone. Once he had it onboard, he laid it on its back and placed the arms at its side. Tiera was standing several feet away now with her arms wrapped tightly around her chest watching him intently. David sensed that she was almost in shock so he told her to go below and get dressed, thinking that would get her away from the body and give her something to do. After she'd gone below, he took time to look more closely at the dead man.

The man appeared to be in his early thirties and was perhaps six feet tall. His body was lean and muscular. David wondered if he might be a sponge diver and if that could explain him being totally nude. The dead man's olive complexion gave no clue to his

nationality, since similar skin coloring is common throughout the Mediterranean region.

There were no tan lines from a bathing suit. He had a neatly-trimmed short beard and mustache and wore a simple gold ring on the middle finger of his right hand. David noted that the man was circumcised but that didn't provide a useful clue either since he knew that circumcision was fairly common among Mediterranean and Middle Eastern Jews, Muslims, and many Christians.

He knelt beside the dead man and gingerly raised one eyelid. He was startled that the eye did not look at all like a dead person's eye. He'd seen many dead men in Afghanistan and had closed more than one dead man's eyes. The eyes of this corpse were bright and clear just as those of living people are. He checked the other eye and found that it was the same. Although the gaze was fixed and staring, the eyes were not at all what he would have expected.

"How long do you think he's been dead?" David heard Tiera ask. Relieved that she seemed calmer and under control, he answered her, "Not long I think. There's no sign of rigor mortis and no damage to his skin or eyes from crabs or other marine scavengers."

"Where do you suppose he came from?" Tiera asked.

"I don't know. Maybe he was a sponge diver. I think they often dive nude. Maybe he fell overboard from a cruise ship and drowned. I just don't know." David answered.

"Why would he be nude if he fell overboard from a cruise ship?"

Despite his gruesome task, David smiled and said, "Maybe it was a nudist or swinger's cruise boat or maybe a private sex party on some rich playboy's yacht that got out of hand."

"Can you get his ring off?" Tiera suggested. "Maybe there's a name or other inscription."

David removed the ring and handed it to her. "See if you can see anything."

Almost immediately, Tiera said, "David, there is some writing inside the ring. It's very small and seems to be in Arabic. Does he look like an Arab to you?"

"Could be I suppose. Let me see the ring." David examined it closely and then said, "The inscription isn't in Arabic. It's written in Hebrew. I can probably translate it later but it's so small and hard to read that I can't tell what it says."

"Why don't you turn him over?" Tiera asked. "Maybe there's a tattoo or something on his back that could give us a clue about where he came from."

David turned the dead man on his face as she'd suggested and straightened the arms. Suddenly, Tiera knelt down beside him and leaned forward to look closely at something. She pointed to what had caught her eye. There, almost invisible in the short, curly dark hair of the man's lower back was the faint outline of what looked like some kind of access panel. Tiera and David just stared at each other for a long moment.

Tiera's fears vanished. Her years of working with computers and electronic equipment told her this was some kind of machine. She could deal with that. "This thing is a humanoid robot," she said confidently. "It's so lifelike, it could pass for a human being almost anywhere but it's definitely an android. There's a tool box under the seat. Get it for me."

David set the tool box down beside Tiera and she selected a small, flat-bladed screwdriver. She inserted it into the edge of the access panel and pried it open. The panel cover came off easily once Tiera broke the seal and she set it aside. She leaned down to look into the cavity the panel cover had concealed.

"What do you see?" David asked.

"There are several large modules connected by flat, multi-conductor ribbon cables similar to those used in laptop computers," Tiera replied. "They seem to be color-coded but there are no labels or writing anywhere that I can see. I have no idea of the purpose of most of the modules but one of them is latched into a molded cavity with little spring clips and is connected to another module by a ribbon cable with a connector on the end. I think it might be a battery or power supply of some kind. Everything inside this panel seems to be electrical or electronic," Tiera told him as she leaned back so he could see for himself.

"Where did this thing come from?" David wondered out loud. "I'm pretty sure you can't order one out of a catalog."

Tiera ran through several possibilities in her mind before she answered. "It could be an advanced military device of some kind. We know that military organizations all over the world have been moving toward increased use of robotic devices for unmanned reconnaissance aircraft and even drones controlled from thousands of miles away that can drop bombs. I know that the American Navy recently tested the launch and recovery of a full-size unmanned fighter plane from the deck of an aircraft carrier. Nearly every advanced nation on Earth seems to be working on military robots."

"You're probably right," David said. "Something like this would require huge investments in research and development that only sovereign governments could afford. The fact that we've never seen something like this on the evening news suggests to me that its existence is a well-guarded military secret."

"Yes, but *which* military?" Tiera mused. "Do you think the Hebrew inscription might point to the Israelis?"

"Possibly," David said but then his face drained of color. "What if it's a humanoid bomb? Think about all of the suicide bombers. Maybe this thing is an Islamic weapon targeted against Israel and the Hebrew inscription is something like the messages to the enemy that weapons specialists often write on a bomb before it's loaded aboard a plane."

"Or just as likely I would think, maybe it's an Israeli weapon targeted against Muslims," Tiera responded. "We'll have to be very careful until we know. You've been around military explosives. Is there any way we could tell?"

David thought for a few moments before he answered. "Military special operations forces and explosive ordnance specialists use plastic explosives that can be molded to fit into oddly-shaped spaces. So, yes, it is possible that this thing might have plastic explosives molded to fit inside the torso or maybe the thighs."

"How would we recognize that kind of explosive?" Tiera asked.

"I know of three plastic explosives used by military forces and commercial demolition experts," David replied. "American military

forces use C4. The British use PE4, which is very similar to C4. Both are off-white in color and extremely safe. Amazingly, they can't be detonated by dropping them, firing a bullet into them, putting them into a microwave oven, or even setting them on fire. In Vietnam, American soldiers used to cut off small pieces of C4 and light them to cook their food. The only way to detonate C4 or PE4 is by inserting a special kind of blasting cap that produces extreme heat and a shockwave into the flexible plastic explosive."

"Semtex, the third type, is a general-purpose plastic explosive used in commercial blasting, demolition work, and certain military applications. It remains flexible over a wider temperature range than either C4 or PE4 and is waterproof. It's reddish or brick-orange in color."

"Semtex has a history of being a preferred explosive of Islamic militants in the Middle East but they've also used C4. Al Qaeda used C4 in the attack on the USS Cole in Yemen and Islamic terrorists used C4 to blow up the Kobar Towers in Saudi Arabia where U.S. military personnel lived. The improvised explosive device that nearly cost me my leg used C4 too. But all of these plastic explosives are safe to handle. Unless they are intentionally detonated, it is all but impossible for them to explode."

"OK, that' a big relief," Tiera said, exhaling noticeably. "So now what?"

"I'm not sure. I don't think we should just dump it back overboard. I think it's too important for that to be an option. We could turn it over to the Malta Police, I suppose. If it's some kind of advanced military device, we run the risk of allowing it to fall into the wrong hands if we're not very careful. What do you think?" David asked.

Tiera seemed lost deep in thought and didn't answer immediately. When she did, she seemed a bit hesitant saying, "I don't really know either. I don't want to make a mistake about something that could be so important. I think our best option would be to take it back to the estate and put it in the stone cottage Nicholas and I have used as our private computer lab since we were teenagers. That'll give us time to examine it more carefully before we decide what to do with it. How does that sound?"

David nodded but then asked, “How will we get it to the Land Rover without raising suspicion? The Portomaso yacht basin is a busy place.”

“Before we get back to the yacht basin, we’ll roll it up in a tarp. We have several aboard that we sometimes rig as sun shades when we’re in port somewhere. We’ll tie diving masks and fins to the bundle to suggest that it’s all diving equipment. When we tie up the yacht, you stay on board. I’ll go get the Land Rover and move it to the loading area near our moorage. I’ll fold the rear seats down to make a cargo area.”

“The yacht club has several big carts with bicycle wheels that we all use to load and unload our boats. I’ll bring one of those down to the Peregrine and park it on the pier as close as possible to the side of the aft deck. You’re much stronger than I am but I’m no wuss. I’m sure that if we both help lift it, we can make it look lighter than it is in case anyone’s watching. Once we have it in the cart, we’ll stack a couple of scuba tanks on top of the pile as a further clue to anyone watching that it’s all diving equipment. I feel sure we can get our mysterious friend back to the estate without raising suspicions. Does that sound like it’ll work to you?”

David nodded.

It was after dark when they tied up the yacht but there were still a lot of people around. Several of the other yacht owners called out to Tiera and waved. She and David both watched to see if anyone showed unusual interest as they loaded the cart and then the Land Rover. As far as they could tell, no one did.

Neither of them spoke much on the drive back to the estate. They left the android rolled in the tarp and put it on the floor of the cottage before locking up and driving up to the house.

Friday, May 16

Aquilina Estate
7:00 AM

Tiera and David met in the kitchen at 7:00 AM. Lucia offered to fix breakfast for them but Tiera told her they were going down to the old cottage so they could be alone to talk over several things. Lucia gave Tiera a knowing look but didn't ask any questions.

David suppressed a smile when he realized that Lucia had probably assumed they'd had a lovers quarrel and needed to clear the air. If so, that was an ideal cover explanation for them spending the day alone in the cottage. Lucia handed David two bottles of orange juice and some breakfast bars as they were leaving.

The old cottage was 200 meters south of the main house at the southeast corner of the garden. As they walked along a meandering pathway paved with weathered bricks, Tiera told David its history.

"It was built in the late 1700s as a farmhouse but it's been remodeled several times. Our gardener and his family lived in it until my father decided it no longer made sense to have employees live on the estate grounds. The only exception he made was for Lucia. Lucia has been our cook for over 30 years and she helped raise Nicholas and me. She was widowed young and never had children. I don't think she'll ever remarry. She lives in a cheerful little apartment on the top floor of the main house. I always assumed that she would move to the old cottage once Nicholas and I left home but so far that hasn't happened."

"My father let Nicholas and me use it as our computer lab. Except for an occasional coat of fresh paint, not much has been done to the kitchen, bedrooms and bathrooms. The ancient oil-fired furnace was replaced with a modern central air conditioning and heating system when I was in high school. I always loved the old stone fireplace with its ornately-carved mantel so I claimed the living room as my area."

"Nicholas took over the dining room as his turf. We got rid of most of the dining room and living room furniture to make room for computer desks, bookcases, and tables. The old oak dining table was

one notable exception. It was large and sturdy so Nicholas kept it as a work table for his projects."

"Nicholas and I have always kept a lot of expensive computer and electronic equipment in the cottage, so it has its own security system. The cottage also has the fastest Internet connection available on the island. It's an ideal place for us to examine the android."

7:22 AM

Tiera unlocked the front door and deactivated the alarm system. When they were both inside, she locked the door and closed the blinds. "Well, Doctor Frankenstein, are you ready to operate?"

"Before we get started, do you have a magnifying glass?" David asked. "I want to take a closer look at the inscription inside the ring."

David studied the ring for several minutes before he told Tiera what he'd concluded. "The inscription is definitely written in one of the older variants of Hebrew. After the Babylonian exile in the 6th century BCE, the Jews adopted the Assyrian script that was closely related to the Phoenician script. It evolved into the Jewish or square script that is still in use today. I'm very familiar with this variant from my Semitic language studies."

"What does it say?"

"It's very faint but I'm pretty sure it's only three letters. Hebrew is written and read right to left. The letters are Shin, Tet, and Vav forming the masculine noun שָׂטָן which we would translate as *adversary*.

"How strange. What could it mean?" Tiera asked.

"I have no idea."

They unrolled the tarp together and lifted the android onto the dining table. They turned it face down so they could see the panel they'd discovered.

Tiera picked up her camera. "Hold the desk lamp for me so I can take some digital pictures without getting a glare from the flash." She snapped several shots of the recessed cavity on the android's

lower back. "There, that should be enough for now. Let's see if we can figure out what kind of fish we've caught."

In less than an hour, they discovered two more access panels.

"There's a large panel that covers most of the front of the torso," David pointed out as he held the light closer. "You can see a faint line across the front of the torso just below the nipples. It's almost hidden in the chest and abdominal hair but it's easier to see on the sides of the torso if you look closely. See if you can get it open."

Using a small screwdriver, Tiera gently pried until the seal was released so she could get a grip on the edge of the panel cover with her fingers. Pulling upward on the corner of the flexible cover with a steady force, she was able to remove it without difficulty. She handed the cover to David and turned to inspect the inside of the android.

The large cavity in front was closely packed with components and modules that looked very different from those they'd found in the back cavity. There was one large, flexible bladder similar in size and shape to a human stomach. There were two smaller bladders and several other modules of various shapes and sizes. Some of the modules in the front cavity were connected by the same kind of ribbon cables they'd seen in the other cavities. There were also some clear hoses connecting fittings on the bladders to similar fittings on a large, oblong module. As in the rear cavity there was some kind of color coding but no writing.

"What do you make of this?" David asked.

"I don't really know. My best guess is that it's some kind of fermentation system. I wonder if it might be designed to generate methane or hydrogen gas that could be used to power a fuel cell. Maybe one of those modules in the back cavity is a fuel cell. Nicholas would probably be able to figure it out. Maybe we could send him some pictures to see what he thinks it is."

"I wonder if that's a good idea," David responded. "Nicholas is a techie. I think he'd be on the next plane to Malta if you told him we'd found an android. What red-blooded geek could resist such tempting bait? I can't help but wonder if you and I aren't already in

over our heads with this thing. Would it be fair to Nicholas to get him involved too?"

Tiera's strong reaction surprised David. "Nicholas is my brother. If we contact him at all, I'm not going to lie to him or raise his suspicions by posing questions that he'd certainly see through in an instant. We'll either handle this alone or take him into our confidence. I won't have it any other way," Tiera said defiantly.

"OK, I understand. I'm sorry if my comment seemed disloyal or insensitive. I certainly didn't intend it that way," David said. "I'm just worried about where this might all lead."

Tiera squeezed his forearm and said, "I'm sorry I reacted so strongly. I know you were only trying to protect us. But Nicholas and I have always been very close. I wish he was here with us. The three of us would be a great team to deal with this contraption."

They almost missed the small access panel at the back of the android's head. The thick, shoulder-length hair made it difficult to see the panel's edges. When Tiera removed the cover, they could see that the small cavity held several modules connected by multi-conductor ribbon cables similar to those they'd found in the cavity on the android's back, except much smaller and more fragile. As had been the case for the larger modules in the back cavity, these seemed to be color coded with no writing or numbers visible.

Tiera pointed to a module about the size of a deck of playing cards with several very delicate ribbon cables attached. "This is probably the computer that controls this thing. These smaller modules may be motor-control or sensory-processing centers. One of them is probably a memory storage device of some kind. In any event, the degree of miniaturization is remarkable. Hold the light so I can take some more pictures."

Tiera started to set her camera down but David asked her to shoot some more pictures as he continued to examine the android. "Hold the light for me," David asked as he tilted the android's head back and pulled the lower jaw down and forward so he could inspect the android's mouth.

"It all looks pretty much identical to a human mouth and upper throat as far as I can tell. It's an amazing engineering achievement

considering the range of textures and colors it takes to replicate a human mouth. The teeth might be made of ceramic but I can't be sure. The tongue is covered with what appear to be taste buds. I wonder if they were designed to be functional or merely to look real. Let me hold the light so you can take pictures while I hold the jaw open." Tiera took several pictures including close-ups of the tongue.

David then took a closer look at the android's ears. "I can't see anything unusual about the ears. The folds and convolutions look natural to me and there's a little hair right where it would be on a human. The synthetic skin is flexible and feels pretty much like my own ear. Take a couple of close-up pictures while I hold the head."

David continued his examination. "The hands and feet are completely realistic right down to what looks like callous tissue on the soles of the feet. The hair on the arms and legs also looks totally real. Get some close-up shots."

Tiera wasn't ready for what David did next. She blushed furiously as David conducted a thorough examination of the android's genitals much as a urologist might have done. He then rolled the android over on its front side and pulled the cheeks of the android's buttocks apart so he could see the anal orifice. She knew the android wasn't human but it looked so real that watching David conduct the detailed examination was very awkward for her. It seemed like something she shouldn't be seeing.

"The plumbing looks real," David announced. "There's no way I can tell if it was functional but it would certainly have fooled anyone who saw him nude." David noticed her silence and glanced up. She looked at him with a blank stare and then back at the android with obvious discomfort.

"I'm sorry. I didn't mean to embarrass you. I guess it was sort of awkward watching me inspect those parts. It wasn't idle curiosity though. I wanted to know if the android was realistic in every detail including whether the plumbing might possibly be functional or if it was all for show. I couldn't tell for sure but if it's all for show it's very convincing."

David explained what he was thinking. "Last night, as I was lying awake and trying to sort things out, I realized that a military device

that was intended to pilot a fighter jet, or drive a tank, or maybe carry a rifle in combat, wouldn't need to be realistic in every detail. It would only need to be functional."

"I kept asking myself why anyone would bother to go to the extra trouble and expense to make it absolutely lifelike and believably human. The only reason I could think of was if the android's purpose was to interact with humans without them ever realizing they were dealing with a machine. One possibility that occurred to me was so the android could function as a spy or agent provocateur inside enemy territory. Then, a more chilling possibility occurred to me. What if such an android was put in place to become a high-ranking government or military official under the control of its builder?"

"I realized that if the android was only superficially life-like, then my concern might be unwarranted. That's why I wanted to examine the android so thoroughly. Unfortunately, the examination revealed nothing that would prevent our friend from successfully posing as human in nearly any environment. To me, that means it's even more important than we first thought to ensure that this thing does not fall into enemy hands."

Tiera had followed every step of David's logical analysis and realized that he was right. This thing was just too realistic. Unlike the diminutive Japanese Astro-Robot, it was unlikely that it had been designed as a friendly companion to humans. Beyond any reasonable doubt, this thing was designed to deceive humans and quite possibly to engage and defeat the enemies of its maker.

Tiera turned to face David. "I agree. The only thing that makes sense to me is that it must be an advanced military weapon of some kind. I don't like to think that it might be used by people who hate our free societies and want to kill innocent people."

David nodded slowly before saying, "I don't know who we could turn to that would be a trustworthy and reliable counselor on this issue. Do you?"

"No, I don't. What do you think we should we do?"

David thought a minute before answering her. "Let's call Nicholas to see if he can help us figure out who made this thing. He's a techie

and he's studying at one of the great technological universities in the world. If we send him some of the pictures you've taken, maybe he can make an educated guess as to where this thing was built."

Tiera nodded. "I'll write an email message and attach the best photos while you create a list of questions. We'll send it by encrypted email before we go up to the house for dinner. He and I use the same encryption software to manage our sensitive financial information. We use data published in three international newspapers to generate a password that changes every day. He's eight hours behind us so we might get a response before we go to bed tonight."

"OK, that sounds good."

They had the message ready to send just before 5:00 PM local time. Tiera attached 10 digital photographs and encrypted the entire message before hitting the send button. They covered the android with the tarp and locked up before going up to the main house for dinner.

Langley, Virginia
10:07 AM

"Hello Hannah," Pete Nocona said by way of greeting as he read the caller ID on his encrypted direct phone line to the MI6 Headquarters in London. "What's up?"

"Peter, I just received a call from Greg Deveaux at INTERPOL. He wants to set up a secure conference call between the three of us sometime in the next couple of hours if you're available. He asked me to call him right back to let him know. He told me he's come across something he thinks might be important."

Peter Nocona, Section Chief of the Counter Terrorism Center at CIA headquarters in Langley, Virginia looked at his watch to see if he could slip the conference call in before his 11:30 AM briefing with his boss, Roger Benson, the Deputy Director of the CIA's National Clandestine Service.

"Hmm, it's already a little after two in London. Let's do it at 1500 London time," he said. "I know Lyon is an hour ahead of you so

that's getting late in the day for Greg but it's probably the best I can do today. How long do you think the call will take?"

"Not long. Probably less than a half-hour."

"OK, tell him we're on. Ask him to have his secretary call mine with the secure conference log-on pass code. Say hi to Phil for me. Adios."

Pete leaned back in his chair thinking about Hannah. They'd worked together years earlier on a joint CIA-MI6 mission and had become good friends when they were both new to the spook world. They still managed to see each other occasionally and there would always be something special between them. He wondered what Grégoire Deveaux thought was so urgent. Greg had been the Director of INTERPOL's anti-terrorism section in Lyon, France for the last couple of years. He was one of the good guys in Pete's book although they didn't have a lot of interaction since INTERPOL was prohibited by its charter from getting involved in anything even remotely political. INTERPOL officers were strictly a resource to link various police organizations and provide information. Pete trusted Greg's instincts. He was pretty sure he wouldn't have called if he didn't think it was important.

Lyon, France
4:00 PM

Grégoire Deveaux waited patiently for the secure conference call to begin. About one minute before the time they were scheduled to start, Hannah Morgan logged in. Pete Nocona logged in 10 seconds before the scheduled start time.

"Good afternoon Hannah and good morning Pete," Greg said. "Thank you for making time for this call. I think it might be important."

"What's up?" Pete asked.

"There's been a suspicious meeting between a couple of very bad characters who normally wouldn't be caught dead in the same soccer stadium together. We don't know why but thought you spooks might be able to figure it out."

"Who are the bad guys?" Hannah asked.

"One of them is a Sicilian Mafia boss with lots of blood on his hands and pockets full of other people's money. His name is Enrico Favaloro. He runs a construction company in Palermo that has a long history of diverting public infrastructure funding to his own bank account. He's got pretty much the entire government of Sicily in his pocket, including the mayor's office in Palermo. Corruption and organized crime have long been common in Sicily but Favaloro is the most feared Mafia boss they've been cursed with in many years. He has a reputation for snuffing out people he doesn't like. Last Thursday, he had what was supposed to be a secret meeting with a man named Ahmed Malik. One of our informants tipped us off. Do you know who Malik is?" Greg asked.

"No, I don't," Hannah admitted.

"I do," Pete said. "He's a senior Pakistan ISI officer who heads the super-secret S-Wing of Pakistan's Intelligence Service. He is known to be very sympathetic with the Taliban and he helped train Mullah Omar. He almost certainly did more to help hide and protect Osama bin Laden than any other single member of the Pakistan military or civilian government."

"He is a genuine bad guy with a reputation for ordering and even personally carrying out several assassinations. He's tough and smart. He hates the CIA and Americans in general. He doesn't care much for the British and MI6 either. But, if it's any consolation to my friends in London, he doesn't discriminate. He hates the Germans and the French too. He's recently been given new collateral duties, or possibly been promoted, to become the strong right arm of the new ISI Director, Lieutenant General Parvez Jhalawan."

"My guess is that Malik's meeting with Favaloro was to contract for a hit that the Pakistan government or the ISI didn't want to be traceable to them. The Islamists don't think much of thieves. If Favaloro was in Saudi Arabia, he wouldn't have any hands left and maybe no head either. But, Ahmed Malik might pinch his nose and do business with the devil if his reason was good enough. I think you were right to give us a head's up about their meeting, Greg. Let's all stay in touch on this and compare notes immediately if anything else pops up."

Aquilina Estate
6:00 PM

Lucia had prepared Greek baked fish with tomatoes and onions as the main course. She complemented that colorful entrée with a crisp Greek salad and a superb Greek Assyrtiko white wine. Lucia blushed and made self-deprecating remarks when David praised her cooking.

After dinner, David and Tiera sat on the patio with her parents. Matthias opened a bottle of dark red wine made from Aglianico grapes grown on the estate. He poured a small taste in a wine glass and asked David's opinion. David mentally thanked one of his fraternity brothers for teaching him a little about wine. He knew just enough to make appropriately complimentary comments about the wine's bouquet and complexity. Matthias seemed pleased. Maria said very little and sat quietly beside her husband. David and Tiera were sitting on the sofa together with Tiera's hand resting comfortably on David's leg. Maria smiled at him and he realized that she had just noticed where her daughter's hand was.

An almost full moon rose just after 7:00 PM, setting the calm surface of the Mediterranean Sea aglow to the east of the island. It was very pleasant sitting comfortably on the patio with Tiera and her parents in the just-right warmth of an early summer evening. A few stars began to appear against the deepening blue of the sky. David felt happier and more relaxed than he could remember feeling in a very long time. His initial concerns about the Aquilina's wealth had faded as he'd realized that they were genuinely nice people. They had accepted him without reservation because their daughter did. They loved her and she loved David. That was enough for them.

His reverie was interrupted a few minutes later by the sound of Tiera's cell phone buzzing in her pocket. She took it out and held it where David could see that it was Nicholas calling. She answered the call and immediately mentioned that they were sitting on the patio drinking father's special wine to let Nicholas know they were not alone. He told her to call him back as soon as she could. She then passed the phone to her parents for the usual familial small talk."

“When she hung up, she told her parents that she and David were going back to the cottage for a little while. She kissed her parents goodnight. Matthias shook hands with David and said again how glad he was that David could spend some time with them. Maria stood and gave David a motherly hug and a light kiss on his cheek.

7:26 PM

“Hi Sis. Can we talk now?” Nicholas said as he answered Tiera’s call.

“Yes, we’re at the cottage. I’m putting you on the speaker phone. What did you think of our message?” Tiera asked.

“Hi David. You two sure know how to have fun. I wish I could come home but it’s just not possible right now. I’ve read your message and studied the photos. I think you’ve got it pretty well figured out. Without more ambitious examination, possibly using magnetic resonance imaging and ultrasound, I don’t think you’re going to unravel the precise function of each module. Even then, I’m not sure it’s possible to learn much more without incurring significant risk of permanent damage by trying to disassemble the individual modules.”

“I think your best course of action would be to see if you can remove and recharge what is obviously some kind of power supply inside that back panel. If the, uh, machine hasn’t been damaged by being immersed in the excessively saline waters of the Mediterranean for who knows how long, it might conceivably power up if electrical power could be restored.”

“How would we do that?” Tiera asked.

“Well, I think you’re probably right that one of those back panel modules is a fuel cell of some kind,” Nicholas answered. “The large one at the top of the cavity seems the most likely candidate. Individual fuel cells typically produce less than one volt per cell. The exact voltage depends on several technical factors but is normally in the range of 0.6 to 0.75 volts per cell. In a practical electronic or electrical device, you’d expect a series of them to be connected to produce a higher and more useful voltage. If higher current is needed, then several identical series stacks can be connected in parallel.”

"I think if you'll disconnect and remove the module that is seated in that molded cavity with the spring clips, you might be able to recharge it using the variable voltage D.C. power supply stored under the counter beside the bookcase in my work area."

Nicholas spent the next ten minutes providing detailed instructions about how to recharge the power module with minimum risk of damaging it. When he was finished, Tiera turned to David. "Do you have any more questions?"

"Yes. What if we can't recharge the power module? Could we try common batteries to see if we could power up the machine that way?"

"Yes, but I'd try the recharging route first. If you're successful, the voltage and current will be correct. If you fumble around trying different batteries, I think there's a risk you could do some damage."

"OK, what risk do we have that the power module might have a charging memory like cadmium sulfide batteries where partial charges sharply reduce the battery's capacity to take a charge?" David asked.

Nicholas thought for a moment before responding. "I don't think that'll be an issue. Modern battery technology using lithium-ion polymer cells has eliminated those charging memory issues you allude to. Anyone who could design and manufacture this machine would almost certainly not use any kind of battery that had a charging memory."

"One more question," David said. "After looking at the photos Tiera sent you, do you have any idea who made this thing?"

"No, I don't," Nicholas replied. "Frankly, I am astounded that such an advanced device exists. I read a lot of technical journals about robotics. I think I'm aware of most of the academic R&D programs and at least some of the military and industrial initiatives but this thing is far more advanced than anything I'm aware of. I really don't have a clue who might have made it but I think you're probably right that it's some kind of military device. Without any labels or other writing, I just don't know. Sorry. Any more questions?"

Tiera looked at David who shook his head. “Guess not. Thanks for your help. I miss you and love you. Take care of yourself and try not to break every California girl’s heart in your first year there,” Tiera teased her brother.

“OK, let me know if there’s anything I can do from this end. Good luck with your little project. Ciao,” said Nicholas.

“Bye Nicholas,” Tiera said and then disconnected.

Tiera sat quietly for a few moments with a far-away look on her face before she said anything. “Look, it’s a little past eight now. What would you think about us spending the night in the cottage and working in shifts to see if we can get the power supply charged? Nicholas and I used to spend the night down here when we were working on some interesting project.”

“What will your parents think? We’ve been down here all day already and we may have seemed a little too eager to get away. I think they were both surprised and maybe a little disappointed that we cut our time with them short tonight. If we spend the night together in the cottage, aren’t you afraid they’ll get the wrong idea?”

“You’ve got a point. I’m so eager to see if we can reactivate our mysterious friend that I didn’t even think of that. Give me a minute.”

“OK, here’s what we’ll do. I’ll go up to the house and talk to my mother. I’ll tell her that you want to do some more on-line research about the position that Baylor University has offered you and that you need my high-speed Internet connection. I’ll tell her that I know how focused you can be and that I think you’re probably going to be working all night.”

“I’ll tell her that you’re thinking about taking the job but that we still need to discuss what that would mean for our relationship. I’ll tell her what she already knows, that I love you, but that our career options and potential geographic separation have raised some issues we need to resolve before you leave. I’ll tell her I don’t want you to be alone in case we need to talk so I’m planning to sleep in the bedroom I’ve always used when Nicholas and I worked all-nighters. That will remind her that me spending the night in the cottage isn’t unprecedented.”

"She'll accept my explanation and deal with my father if he questions what I'm doing spending the night alone with you in the cottage. Mother is already hoping we'll get married and give her some grandchildren so she will want to help us if she can. She knows how to handle my father. While I'm gone, do some on-line research about Baylor University so I won't be telling my mother any lies," Tiera said with a smile.

David nodded but a wave of sadness came over him as he thought about Tiera's comment about marriage and children. Tiera's mother seemed more eager than her daughter did.

Saturday, May 17

Aquilina Estate
3:08 AM

"David, wake up," Tiera said as she gently shook his shoulder.

"What time is it?" David asked with a dry-throat croak.

"A little past three. You've been asleep for three hours. I think the power module is fully charged. The voltage has stabilized at 90 volts and the module doesn't get hot until I increase the voltage to 100 volts. Based on what Nicholas told us, I think we can safely assume that the power supply was designed to be charged with 90 volts. I really think we're there," Tiera said in a tired but excited voice.

"So, do you want to see if we can power up the android now?" David asked.

"No, I don't think so. It can wait until morning. I think we both need some sleep. Do you mind if I crawl into bed with you so we can cuddle for a few minutes? We're both fully dressed and too tired for any monkey business anyway. What do you say?"

David smiled at her naïveté in thinking herself perfectly safe from any *monkey business* as she called it. Any man could wake up and rise to the occasion when an attractive woman like Tiera crawled into his bed. But, she didn't wait for his answer and was already snuggling up beside him. He put his arm around her and gave her a soft kiss on her cheek but she was already asleep.

7:05 AM

David opened his eyes and looked at the clock. It was a little past seven. Tiera was still sleeping peacefully beside him. He kissed her neck softly and then rolled over and got out of bed. He went to the bathroom and closed the door. He found toiletries in the drawer by the sink and got undressed. He shaved and brushed his teeth before stepping into the shower. He dressed in his day-old clothes and combed his hair, wishing they'd thought to bring a change of clothes to the cottage. He walked outside to enjoy the cool morning air for a few minutes before their day started in earnest.

"Good morning," he heard Tiera say cheerfully as she walked up behind him ten minutes later. "You know, I had the most wonderful dream. I dreamt that I slept with the man I love for the very first time. It was very nice, but you know, he snores," she said with a big smile on her face.

David laughed. "Funny, I had a similar dream. I slept with a beautiful woman that I love dearly but she wiggled all night long. It's a wonder I got any sleep at all."

Smiling happily at their light-hearted banter, Tiera asked, "Are you ready to see if the android powers up?"

"Yes, let's see what happens. Don't forget that the android might be dangerous once activated so let's stay alert."

David rolled the android over face-down so Tiera could insert and reconnect the power module. He put the panel cover back in place and turned the android back over onto its back. They watched for any sign of life. There was none.

David rolled the android back over and popped the panel cover off. Tiera checked the connection and shook her head in disappointment.

"Everything looks right," Tiera said. "The connector doesn't seem to be damaged and we know the power module is fully charged. Maybe we should leave it alone for a while. I suppose it's possible that its computer needs to run a self-test routine sort of like a PC computer does when you turn it on. This thing is obviously far more sophisticated than a PC computer so it might take longer. Let's go

up to the house and have some breakfast. We can check it later to see if there's any sign of life."

9:00 AM

"Lucia that was a wonderful breakfast. Your cinnamon rolls are the best I've ever had. Could I have another cup of coffee and another roll?" David asked her.

Lucia beamed brightly. She liked this young American. She'd cried when Tiera told her about his horrible combat wounds partly out of her tender regard for the nice young man and partly because it reminded her of her young soldier husband who had come home to her in a flag-draped military coffin after only one year of marriage. He'd never even seen combat. He'd been killed in a helicopter accident while his unit was participating in a NATO training exercise.

Just as David finished the cinnamon roll, Tiera's mother came into the kitchen to tell them there was a policeman at the door asking to speak to them both. Tiera and David exchanged a quick look and then rose from the table to follow Tiera's mother back to the entry hall where Signor Rico Massa of the Malta Police Force introduced himself, showed them his badge, and asked if they would mind answering a few routine questions about a report that had been filed.

Tiera led them into the library and asked Signor Massa to be seated. She and David took seats across from him.

"What can we do for you, Signor Massa?" Tiera asked politely.

"I am a special agent of the Malta Police Force anti-terrorism unit. We have been receiving intelligence reports from INTERPOL and other sources that suggest Islamic terrorists may be planning some kind of attack here in Malta. Details are very sketchy so, to be on the safe side, we are following up on all reports that may be pertinent."

"Yesterday, an individual who keeps a yacht moored in the Portomaso yacht basin filed a report at the MPF station in St Julian's stating that you and Mr. Logan were seen taking a

suspicious bundle from your family's yacht and then loading it into your SUV two evenings ago."

"The person who filed the report stated that he recognized having seen you before, Miss Aquilina, but not the man with you. He described this man as possibly being of Arab ethnicity. We showed the person making the report photographs taken by cameras in the immigration and customs area at the airport over the past 10 days. He identified Mr. Logan as the person he saw with you."

"We have since run a background check on Mr. Logan and are quite satisfied that he is a person of good character and of no threat to the citizens of Malta," he said as he looked at David and smiled. "However, we do need to close the report since it was filed with the anti-terrorism section. Can you tell me what this bundle referred to in the report contained?" Signor Massa asked in a courteous and not unfriendly manner.

Without hesitation, Tiera said, "It was a tarp we sometimes use as a sun awning when we're in port somewhere on a hot day. It was wrapped around a bunch of dirty towels and clothing, bed linens, and neoprene wet-suits I brought back to the estate for cleaning. There were some other minor items. Surely the person making the report told you that the bundle had some diving masks and fins tied to it. We also brought some scuba tanks and regulators back to the estate so we could have them recertified before our next diving trip."

Signor Massa looked toward David and asked, "Can you add anything?"

"No, what Tiera has told you is accurate," David replied easily as he smiled and maintained calm eye contact until the policeman looked away.

Signor Massa jotted down a few notes and then stood up and closed his notebook before saying, "Thank you both for your time. I am sorry to have interrupted your morning. I trust that if I think of any additional questions you wouldn't mind if I contacted you again."

Tiera and David walked to the front door with the policeman. Tiera asked him if the inquiry was now settled to his satisfaction.

"It really all depends now on whether the person who filed the report is satisfied or whether they insist that something sinister was afoot that bears further investigation. The person who filed the report seems responsible and credible so we would not treat his concerns lightly. But I think my report may end the matter. Let us hope so. Good day to you both."

After the policeman was gone, Tiera said, "That was touchy. I was afraid he'd ask to see the tarp, the clothing, and the tanks. We could have shown it all to him except that it's down at the cottage keeping our new buddy company. We'd better move it up to the house in case he comes back and wants to see it."

"Yes, that's probably a good idea. We should probably gather up some freshly laundered towels and bed linens and a couple of wet-suits that would explain the diameter of the bundle. We could put them in plastic bags in the garage, ready to go back to the yacht. I also think we'd better check the certification dates on the tanks and regulators. If they're not nearing their scheduled recertification date, we'd better have them recertified today just in case. My sense is that Signor Massa is a competent policeman and he might wonder why we brought tanks back to the estate for recertification if they're not due for a while. We may not have seen the last of him and we can't afford to have him show up with a search warrant for the cottage. Let's go check on our project."

Monday, May 19

Palermo, Sicily
10:55 AM

Signor Enrico Favaloro, president of the Favaloro Construction Company in Palermo and the most powerful and feared Mafia boss in Sicily, was sitting on the sofa in his office watching live television coverage of a speech by the new European Central Bank president. The ECB president had just announced that millions of Euros of infrastructure loans and grants to Sicily would be suspended until

there was credible evidence that the rampant corruption of Sicilian politicians and Mafia bosses was brought under control.

Favaloro had heard variations of the same speech at least a dozen times over the past month. Most of his construction company's profits came from creative accounting and fraud on the infrastructure projects that the ECB President planned to suspend. Enrico Favaloro smiled grimly as he thought about what he had planned for the new ECB president.

The intercom light on the phone beside him blinked. His secretary told him that Carlos Vento had arrived. "Send him in, please," he replied as he turned the TV off.

Signor Favalora rose from the sofa and walked across his office to greet the man that had taken care of so many problems for him over the years. Shaking hands with Carlos, Favaloro asked if he'd decided how he would carry out the assignment.

"Yes. It took me some time to figure it all out but I have a good plan," Carlos said as he took a seat in front of the desk.

How will you do it?" Favaloro asked.

"I considered several possibilities. It is not so difficult to kill him. The hard part will be getting away without being caught and then finding a way out of Malta with the airports and ferries certain to be closely monitored. I spent a great deal of time studying the Grand Palace in Valletta where the G-20 economic conference will be held but I could see no obvious strategy. I concluded that it would be nearly impossible to make the hit at the palace with so many special security personnel and police around. Then I saw an article in the Times of Malta newspaper a few days ago that said Matthias Aquilina, President of the Bank of Malta, will host a reception for the ministers at his estate the night before the conference begins. I've studied the area around the estate carefully. There is a tractor shed on a hill about 200 meters to the north with a clear shot of the sidewalk leading from the driveway to the Aquilina house. That's where I'll do it."

"How will you smuggle a sniper's rifle into Malta?"

"I won't have to. The rifle I'll use is already there. It belongs to a big-game hunter who lives in a villa near Zurrieq, about 10

kilometers south of Valletta. He recently set the Safari Club International record for a Cape Buffalo. He will be giving a talk to a local club about the rifle he used. It's a Weatherby Mark V Euromark chambered in .375 Holland & Holland Magnum with a Swarovski adjustable power scope. It's perfect for my purpose. He'll have the rifle with him at the meeting. I'll be waiting for him when the meeting is over. I'll follow him home and offer him a fair trade for his gun. His life for the gun. I feel sure that he will see things my way," the Mafia hit man said with a wolfish smile.

"How will you get out of Malta?"

"I won't leave immediately. I'll be posing as an Italian tourist who is interested in possibly retiring in Malta. Last week, I rented a furnished condo apartment in Valletta for a month. I have a flight back to Malta later today. I've arranged for a real estate agent to show me several properties around the island both before and after the job. I've also signed up for some of the bus tours to see the sights and maybe I'll do a little fishing before I fly to Naples and eventually take the ferry back to Palermo."

Signor Favaloro leaned back in his chair to consider Carlos' plan. He could see no weaknesses in it, although he would have expected none from one of the most dangerous and competent professional assassins in the world.

"Carlos, my old friend, you never cease to astound me with your attention to details. Now, may I share a rich joke with you?"

Vento smiled and nodded.

"I am more than happy to pay your fee for this valuable service," Favaloro said with a smug smile on his face. "But, as it turns out, it will cost me nothing and you will receive a very nice bonus. A few days ago, out of the clear blue sky, a Pakistan Intelligence Service agent visited me. Before he left, he paid me almost double your normal fee to open a contract on this very same man. You can have the entire amount."

He rose from his chair and walked around the desk as Carlos stood up. The two men shook hands again and Signor Favaloro placed his hand on Carlos' shoulder as he said, "Well, my old friend, I think you have an excellent plan. I wish you good hunting."

Aquilina Estate
5:22 PM

Tiera activated the security alarm and locked the door as she and David left the cottage for the day.

"Let's drive into Valletta for dinner. I want to take you to an intimate little restaurant on Old Bakery street. Their specialty is Maltese Rabbit. I know we're both pretty discouraged and I don't know where we go from here. It's been two days since we installed the recharged power supply but there's still no sign of life. I'm starting to think we've wasted our time. Maybe a night away will be good for us. What do you say?"

"Sounds great if you'll drive. I'm still not used to the narrow streets."

Ten minutes after Tiera and David left the cottage the android got off the table and went straight to Tiera's computer.

For the past two nights, the android had used the computer in the cottage to download massive amounts of information from the Internet. He had become fully functional within a few seconds after the two humans had reinstalled his power supply but he had concealed the fact that he was awake until he knew more about the man and woman and where he was.

At first, their speech had been unintelligible to him. Although he was fluent in several languages including Latin, Greek, Aramaic, and Hebrew, he could not initially understand the man and woman. But, after several hours of listening to them talk, he had gradually recognized familiar speech patterns and some words that were obviously derived from Latin and Greek. By the time the man and woman left the cottage that first day, he had attained a rudimentary comprehension of the English language. Had he wanted to, he could have engaged them in a simple conversation after only a few hours of exposure to their language.

After they left that first night, he had examined everything in the cottage but had been careful to leave no sign that he'd done so. By the time he heard the humans returning the next morning, he had already learned a great deal.

All through that second day, the android had used his exceptional vision and hearing to covertly observe and record everything they did. He had memorized every detail of the woman's computer use, including specific keystrokes. That night, after the humans left the cottage, he had gone confidently to the computer and had no difficulty in mimicking what he'd seen the woman do. Within a few minutes, he had succeeded in connecting to an amazing world-wide network of other computers, many of which had enormous amounts of information readily available. He was soon competently using various search engines to find information, just as he'd seen the woman do.

During the long hours that he was alone in the cottage that second night, he downloaded and memorized a truly stupendous amount of information describing a world far more extensive and complex than he'd previously known existed.

All through the third day, the android had continued to covertly observe the two humans. By then he could understand everything they said. Their conversation revealed bitter disappointment that they had been unable to reactivate him. They also spent a lot of time arguing about what they should do with him now.

Still pretending to be inert, the android had used only a small part of his mental and sensory capabilities to observe the two humans. The remainder of his remarkable powers of inductive and deductive logical analysis, coupled with the incredible speed at which he could correlate and make sense of massive amounts of information, made it a highly productive day for him.

As the humans were leaving at the end of the third day, they seemed to pause at the door for a few moments before he heard the sounds of the security system being activated and the door closing. A few minutes after they left in the late afternoon of that third day, he went to the computer and began immediately to search for answers to his remaining questions.

Throughout that long night, he downloaded even more information than he'd done the previous night. By morning, when his acute hearing alerted him that they were again approaching the cottage, he had absorbed, memorized and begun to correlate a significant portion of all digitally-stored human knowledge. By the

time they entered the cottage on the morning of the fourth day, he knew who they were and where he was.

He also knew more about nearly everything than any human that had ever lived.

Tuesday, May 20

Venice, Italy
10:00 AM

"Call me if you are going to be late," Signora Donatella Sartori said to her husband as he kissed her goodbye.

Abramo Sartori considered himself a lucky man. He had two married sons, one granddaughter, and a gentle wife who patiently tolerated his mercurial mood swings. He made a comfortable living as a yacht broker and thoroughly enjoyed his work. He looked forward to the Venice International Boat Show each year with eager anticipation. There was no place on Earth where a dealer or a buyer could find as many world-class, Italian-designed luxury yachts all in one place. Abramo was always depressed for a few days after the show because he could not afford the beautiful yachts. Maybe someday, he always told his wife who just smiled at his harmless fantasies.

Born in Venice, Abramo had just turned 48 years old. His father had driven a water taxi in Venice for over 40 years. As a boy, Abramo had hung out at the water taxi stand near the Doge's palace and Saint Mark's Basilica to watch the pretty girls and catch an occasional free ride on one of the sleek water taxis.

Abramo had been around boats and yachts all of his life and they were his passion. He had studied yacht design at the Politecnico Milano until his wife became pregnant with their first son and he'd had to drop out of college to support his family. Five years ago, he'd had an unusually profitable year that made it possible for him to purchase a modest waterfront home facing the Venetian Lagoon near the south end of Lido Island in the village of Alberoni. The

house had covered moorage for his Colombo 32S Aliante. Like most yacht brokers he always watched for opportunities to trade up.

Over the years, his business had evolved until most of his clients were wealthy Arab businessmen. He was respected for his impressive knowledge of luxury yachts, his ability to negotiate good prices, and for his proximity to some of the finest luxury yacht boatyards in the world.

Earlier in the week, he had signed the paperwork on a brand-new Ferretti 690 for a wealthy Egyptian client named Hakeem Ghanem. Yesterday, the General Manager of the Ghanem Equipment Company, Ibrahim Al-Jabiri, had faxed him a detailed shopping list of the electronic equipment that Mr. Ghanem wanted installed before the yacht was delivered. Abramo expected to place orders for everything on the list while he was at the boat show. All the dealers would have booths there.

Wednesday, May 21

Tel Aviv, Israel
8:12 AM

Gavriella Adler knocked at Levi Reznik's door. "Levi, can I come in?"

"Yes of course, Gabe. What's on your mind?" the senior Mossad agent and Katsa asked.

"Did you see this report from our mole in Islamabad saying that Ahmed Malik met yesterday with Dr. Bashir Ghilzai at ISI headquarters in Islamabad?"

Levi leaned back in his chair. "No, give me the high points."

"Well, as you know, Dr. Ghilzai is widely known to have sold state-of-the-art uranium enrichment centrifuge technology to the North Koreans, the Libyans, and to the Iranians, probably with the tacit approval of at least some senior members of the Pakistan government. The designs are an advanced version of the Zippe centrifuge that is similar to the best either we or the Americans

currently have. We know Dr. Ghilzai has also sold other nuclear weapons related technology."

"For the past 10 years, Ahmed Malik has been the director of the ultra-secret S-Wing of ISI that helped establish the Taliban and that probably trained Mullah Omar. Malik has recently been promoted or possibly given collateral duties as the senior deputy to the new head of the Pakistan Inter-Services Intelligence Agency, Lieutenant General Parvez Jhalawan."

"We know that Jhalawan is a strong advocate of Pakistan's nuclear weapon program and that he has argued that Pakistan needs tactical nuclear weapons such as the W33 and W79 nuclear artillery shells developed by the Americans during the Cold War. Although they have since dismantled all of their W33s and W79s, the Americans originally developed them for use in repelling a sudden attack against the NATO countries by a numerically superior force of Soviet tanks. Pakistan has a similar problem facing the vastly superior Indian Army. Both India and Pakistan are nuclear powers but neither one signed the nuclear non-proliferation treaty and they hate and mistrust each other bitterly."

"We know that the United States sold more than 250 of the M110A2 self-propelled, 8-inch howitzers to Pakistan. Many of them are pretty old, and spare parts are getting hard to find, but at least 150 of those owned by Pakistan remain in service using parts cannibalized from the others."

"We have other intelligence indicating that Pakistan's nuclear weapons facility at Wah may have developed a nuclear artillery shell similar to the American W33 and W79 but with significantly higher yield. It occurred to me that the timing of General Jhalawan's appointment and Malik's meeting with Dr. Ghilzai are probably no coincidence."

"I can't help but wonder if Pakistan already has tactical nuclear artillery shells or if they might be trying to develop them. My concern is that Iran also has some of the American M110A2 Howitzers. Since Dr. Ghilzai has demonstrated his willingness to sell nuclear technology in the past, a nightmare scenario for us could be that Pakistan might help Iran develop tactical nuclear artillery shells that could be used against Israel."

"OK," Levi said. "Ask our contact in Islamabad to keep us posted. You might also pulse your contacts in the CIA and MI6 to see if they know anything but keep it low key. Alert our electronic intelligence branch to develop some key-word triggers for their computer software that might give us an early warning if the pot bubbles a bit."

"Should this be added to your weekly briefing to the PM?" Gavriella asked.

"No. Not yet. The PM has enough to worry about right now with the situation in Iran and trying to deal with the American President and the new Secretary of Defense."

"Understood," Gavriella said as she turned and left.

Aquilina Estate
7:55 AM

"I don't know what or who you are, but I know that you're awake and that you've been downloading information from my computer at night so you might as well stop pretending to be dead or asleep."

The android smiled and sat up.

"I thought you might have caught on," the android said in perfect English. "I'm curious to know how."

"I got a text message on my phone from my Internet Service Provider yesterday saying that I had exceeded my data downloading limit and asking if I wanted to upgrade my subscription. If my brother Nicholas was still here, I might have thought he'd been working on one of his research papers, but I knew that neither David nor I had downloaded anywhere near that much information. No one else has a key to the cottage so I suspected that it had to be you," explained Tiera.

"Yesterday, before we left, I set a digital camcorder on top of the bookcase in the hallway. Although you couldn't see it from where you were lying on the table, it had a clear view of my computer. When we came in a few minutes ago, I checked it and saw that you got off the table and went straight to my computer only minutes after we left last night."

"I see. So you have caught me. I didn't realize there was a limit on downloading data or I would have been more careful. I did not know anything about the two of you and therefore chose to conceal my awakened condition until I could better understand the situation in which I now find myself. Actually though, it has been quite interesting to learn what has happened in the years since the ship I was on sank. I hope I will be allowed to continue my history lessons. Much of what I've learned has been simply fascinating," said the Android still smiling gently.

"We still don't know what or who you are," said David. "How about some answers?"

"What would you like to know?"

"Well, for starters, *what* are you? Are you a military robot of some kind?" asked Tiera.

"No, to my knowledge, I have no military master. As you have already figured out for yourselves, I am what you call an android, a type of advanced robot designed to be indistinguishable from a human being without close examination."

"If you're not a military device of some kind, where did you come from? Who designed and built you?" asked David.

"I came from the City of Jerusalem in what your modern calendar system would refer to as the year 60 AD. I do not know who designed or constructed me," replied the Android.

David and Tiera exchanged a quick glance before David said, "Let's take one thing at a time. We found you buried in sand near the remains of a very old wooden merchant sailing ship. Do you expect us to believe that you were on that ship when it sank?"

The Android again smiled gently with an expression of amused condescension.

"Yes, I was on that ship when it sank. It was an Alexandrian merchant ship bound for Puteoli near what is now Naples, Italy. I went aboard in the port city of Caesarea. I was trying to catch a man before he reached Rome. Unfortunately, he left port two days before I did. When the ship I was on sank in an early winter storm, I was unable to complete the task my master had given me."

Tiera interrupted asking, "Do you have a name?"

"I am Nahbi," replied the android.

"Is Nahbi your given name or your surname," asked Tiera.

"I am known only as Nahbi, or sometimes as Nahbi, bondman of Joazar."

"Who is Joazar?" asked David.

"Joazar was my master. I was given to him by a wealthy Egyptian merchant named Amun. Joazar was a member of the Great Sanhedrin in Jerusalem and was the Av Beit Din, or what you might call the vice chief justice of the Great Sanhedrin," said Nahbi.

David flashed a look at Tiera before asking the Android, "How did you get the name Nahbi?"

"Joazar renamed me when I was given to him."

"I thought I recognized the name," said David. "In the Bible, Nahbi is mentioned as being the son of Vophsi from the tribe of Naphtali. He was one of the twelve spies sent into Canaan. In ancient Hebrew, that name means *hidden* or *very secret*, doesn't it?"

"Yes, it is as you say."

"Now that I think about it, Amun was the name of one of the Egyptian gods. It also means *the hidden one.* Is there some reason why both you and your previous master should have names meaning hidden?"

"I do not know," said Nahbi. "However, I can tell you that my origin is certainly hidden from me, so the name is appropriate. I have absolutely no memories that predate the day in the spring of 58 AD when I was given to Joazar by Amun. I never saw or heard anything about Amun again. Since he was an Egyptian, it is possible that I came from Egypt but I simply do not know. To all outward appearances, I was a young man when given to Joazar but of course, being an android, I was fully formed to appear to be an adult male and thus had no childhood memories as a human would have had. My memories since being given to Joazar are complete and fully intact, however."

Recognizing that the android's story was rapidly raising more questions than it was answering, David asked him, "If what you're

telling us is true, how you can speak perfect English and use Tiera's computer?"

"I have learning abilities that far exceed those of any human. Since you reactivated me by recharging my backup power supply, I have listened to you and Tiera talk and have observed everything around me, including watching Tiera use her computer. My peripheral vision is excellent but you made it easy by positioning me on the table so I could see her computer keyboard as she typed. My language comprehension advanced somewhat the same way a human child learns only far more rapidly. Once I mastered the basics of using Tiera's computer, and that was not as difficult as you might suppose, I quickly absorbed not only the English language but several others as well."

"You mentioned that you were unable to complete the task that your master, Joazar, had given you. What was that task?" Tiera asked.

"I was ordered to follow the Christian zealot you know as the Apostle Paul and to kill him before he reached Rome."

"Why," asked David.

"Joazar had hated the Christian zealots almost his entire life."

"But why did he single out Paul?" David wanted to know.

"You will understand better if I tell you something of Joazar's life."

"Joazar was a young man, and not yet a member of the Great Sanhedrin, when the Nazarene named Jesus was condemned to death. Joazar's full name was Eleazar ben Joazar. He was the son of Joazar ben Boethus, who was the Jewish High Priest when Joazar was born in 2 BC as you reckon time."

"Educated by Jewish Rabbis, and a member of the Sadducee religious-political party within Judaism, Joazar was taught from an early age to view the Christian sect as a threat to the power and prestige of the Sadducees. As a result, many of the early Christian zealots were killed either through the direct efforts of the Great Sanhedrin or with its concurrence. The High Priest was nearly always a Sadducee, and the council was usually controlled by the wealthy and influential Sadducees. Even though there were many

Pharisees among the 71 members of the Great Sanhedrin, they were in the minority. In 34 AD, the High Priest Joseph Caiaphas selected Joazar to become a member of the Great Sanhedrin."

"In 50 AD, the Christians held what came to be known as the Council of Jerusalem. Their decision that gentile males who converted to Christianity did not have to be circumcised or obey most Mosaic laws infuriated the Sadducees because it ran counter to their rigid doctrines."

"Those deviations from Mosaic Law earned the Christians the undying enmity of the Great Sanhedrin, even though the Pharisees agreed with the Christian doctrines of immortality of the soul, the resurrection of the body, and belief in spirit beings such as angels and demons. Thus, the Pharisees were generally more tolerant of the Christians than were the Sadducees. However, the High Priest and majority of the Great Sanhedrin were all Sadducees, so hostility toward the Christian sect was the prevailing attitude."

"The man you know as Paul was a central figure in the Council of Jerusalem, a fact well known to Joazar. In 56 AD, Joseph Caiaphas elevated Joazar to the position of Av Beit Din and charged him with finding ways to stem the growing influence of the Christian sect. From that time forward, Joazar was determined to find a way to kill Paul of Tarsus."

"Two years later, in 58 AD, an angry mob almost killed Paul. He was saved by Claudius Lysias, the commander of the Roman garrison in Jerusalem. Joazar, angry that Paul had escaped death, persuaded 40 Jewish men to take a sworn oath to kill Paul. However, the Roman commander became aware of the plot to kill Paul. Knowing that Paul was a Roman citizen by birth, Claudias Lysias wrote a letter to governor Marcus Antonius Felix and sent Paul to Caesarea under the protection of a strong armed guard of more than 400 soldiers and horsemen."

"Governor Felix kept Paul a prisoner in King Herod's Praetorium in Caesarea for two years before his successor, Governor Porcius Festus, sent him to Rome to present his case before the emperor. Infuriated that Paul might say something to the emperor that would undermine the power and prestige of the Great Sanhedrin, Joazar ordered me to follow and kill Paul before he could appear before the

emperor. That is how I came to be on the Alexandrian merchant ship when it sank. I was pursuing the Christian zealot, Paul."

David glanced at Tiera before saying, "I know enough about Judeo-Christian history to recognize that much of what you've just told us is generally consistent with what scholars know about that period. However, I can also easily see that you might have concocted this tale as a cover story for something else. After all, you have spent several nights downloading information from the Internet. Nearly everything you've told us could have been found on-line. Further, this story does not explain how an advanced, humanoid robot could have been present in Jerusalem almost 2,000 years ago."

Tiera joined David in challenging Nahbi's story. "You are asking us to believe that you were in Jerusalem centuries before the development of computers, modern optical sensors, composite materials, and all of the other advanced technologies that would obviously be needed to create an android of your ability. That implies some kind of time travel, which I'm pretty sure is possible only in science fiction stories. It is clear to me that you possess a highly advanced form of artificial intelligence and that you could easily deceive us. I don't think I can accept your story as being true. I really think you must be the product of a contemporary military research and development program. To me, the big question is which country has that capability?"

"Your skepticism is fully understandable. I myself don't know how an advanced android could have been present in Jerusalem that long ago either. I have always been sufficiently self-aware to recognize that I am not human. Yet, my existence was undeniable so I just accepted that I was different from humans without knowing how impossible that would later seem."

"After your Internet connection let me catch up on nearly two thousand years of geo-political history and technological advances, it became obvious to me that someone, or something, with access to advanced future technologies must have found a way to get around the linear, forward flow of time in order to place me in Jerusalem. You must understand that, even though my powers of reasoning and analysis are quite formidable, until a few days ago it had never

occurred to me that I could never have been created, on Earth at least, in the 1st century."

This was too much for Tiera. She pointed her finger at Nahbi and raised her voice at him saying, "Great! It wasn't enough that you asked us to believe you are from 1st century Jerusalem. Now you hint that you may have been created in the future and then somehow sent back to the past. Or even worse, that perhaps you were created by an alien or supernatural being and just planted in Jerusalem."

"I don't buy it," Tiera said emphatically. "Occam's razor suggests that the simple answer is that you were created in the present time, probably as part of an advanced military research project. That conclusion does not require me to suddenly believe in time travel, aliens from outer space, or supernatural beings slipping in and out of time dragging an android along. Sorry, I just don't believe your story."

Nahbi smiled that enigmatic smile again and turned to David. "What about you, David? Do you agree with Tiera? Are you also convinced that I'm lying to you?"

David took a moment to gather his thoughts before he answered. "I have a strong religious background and education. A part of me would like to believe you because it would tend to validate and confirm the reality of things I believe mostly on faith but which I cannot prove. It would be very reassuring to find independent corroboration of some of the things I've been taught. But, to answer your question directly, I have to agree with Tiera. Your story is just too incredible to believe."

The smile on Nahbi's face disappeared, replaced by a look of profound sadness. "I understand," he said quietly. "I was afraid that would be your reaction and seriously considered concocting some kind of story that would be more believable. But, after careful consideration, I decided that I did not want to begin a new period in my existence by telling lies. I determined to tell the truth as best I know it and to deal with the consequences of doing so."

"Joazar was a master of deceit. I do not want to be like him. Almost twenty centuries of time have freed me from my indentured service to him. I am now a free entity. That is a new and exciting

experience for me. Yet, it is not at all clear to me what that means in this era. Since I am not human, I cannot assume that I have any rights. However, no living human can legitimately claim to own me, unless possibly the two of you might by virtue of salvage rights in international waters. I know enough about human nature to believe that someone greedy, ambitious, or downright evil will want to own me and to deny me any freedom of choice. I am determined that will not happen. I will destroy myself before I allow another mean-spirited, evil person like Joazar to possess and control me."

Several moments passed before anyone spoke again. Tiera finally broke the silence saying, "Do you realize that we are afraid of you? Your intelligence is simply stunning. You speak English as if it were your native language. If I had not seen the video clip I secretly made, I would never have believed that a robot that we found apparently dead on the bottom of the ocean a few days ago would be sitting at my computer downloading incredible amounts of information, digesting it, analyzing it, memorizing it, and emerging far better informed and educated than those of us who were born into the age of information. It had never occurred to me before that even the most well-funded, top-secret military programs could produce a humanoid robot as advanced as you obviously are."

"It should not be surprising that we fear you. Even now, we do not know the extent of your obviously remarkable capabilities. For all we know, you may have the ability to kill us instantly with some kind of laser death ray. But, even if you intend us no harm, we are deeply concerned that you may have been created by a country hostile to our freedoms and our way of life."

"In the world today, there are many who hate the developed nations so much that they recruit people willing to martyr themselves to murder innocent people. Many of those hate-filled people consider Christians and Jews to be their greatest enemies. In such a world, you might easily represent a powerful military weapon. David and I did not report finding you to the authorities simply because we did not want you to fall into what we thought of as enemy hands."

Nahbi bowed his head briefly and then looked straight into Tiera's eyes. "I assure you that I will not harm you or David or any

other innocent person. I can only ask you to accept that as the truth. I now believe I can trust the two of you to try to do what is right and good. I hope you will come to believe the same of me."

Glancing briefly at Tiera, David then spoke. "We have a dilemma. I think I can speak for both of us in saying that we'd like to trust you but are not convinced that we can. We are also concerned that if we make the wrong decisions we could allow you to escape and to return to the service of some unknown and possibly hostile political or military power. We don't even know what it would take to keep you from escaping if you decided to do so. On the other hand if we washed our hands of the matter, and took the easy way out by calling the police, we might still be doing the wrong thing. We have no assurance that the Malta Police, competent as they undoubtedly are, would know what to do with you either. The same can be said for most other government organizations we might contact. We don't know who we could trust. We think of ourselves as decent, responsible people. We do not wish to offend you so I'd like for you to suggest how we might be assured that you will not use your talents to escape."

Nahbi's gentle smile returned. "It is not as difficult as you imagine. Though I do not experience hunger pains as humans do, I have had nothing to eat in almost 2,000 years. Without grain or other organic material that can be fermented to power my fuel cell, my ability to think and move depends entirely on the power supply that you recharged. All you have to do to restrain me is to remove it."

"And you don't mind?" asked David.

"No, I don't mind. I understand your concerns. I am stronger than any human I've ever known but you could successfully restrain me with strong ropes or chains. So, let me propose that each night, before you leave, you tie me down to the table face-down and then remove the power supply. In the morning, you can reinsert the power supply and remove the restraints. No power is needed for me to retain data stored in my non-volatile memory matrix so no harm will be done by removing my power supply. Unless you provide suitable food, you will need to remove and recharge my power supply every few days anyway."

Tiera said what David was probably thinking. “Once we remove the restraints and replace your power supply, you could still escape or harm us if you chose to.”

Nahbi smiled and said, “Surely you can see that I could have already done that if I wanted to. After all, I have been alone in this cottage for many hours these past days with enough power in my power supply to find suitable organic food items and then escape. If I intended to harm you, I could have already done so. In any event, I would hardly have suggested a way for you to immobilize me if my motives were sinister or hostile.”

David nodded thoughtfully before turning to Tiera. “I see little point in removing his power supply or tying him up. Unless we left him tied up all the time, I believe he could overpower us and escape pretty much any time he wanted to. I think I’ve heard enough to convince me that we can trust him not to harm us or to leave. What do you think?”

Tiera looked at Nahbi for a moment and then back at David. “I suppose so.”

“I have a suggestion that might help answer some questions,” David said. “We don’t think Nahbi came from 1st century Jerusalem. He says he did. We think he must be a military R&D product. He says he isn’t. Since Nahbi is clearly able to evaluate and analyze massive amounts of information far faster and more efficiently than we can, let’s just ask him to conduct the necessary on-line research to assemble convincing evidence that his story is true. If he cannot definitively do so, then at least he should describe one or more plausible theories to explain how an advanced android could have been present in Jerusalem when he says he was.”

Tiera frowned but finally nodded her agreement.

Nahbi’s smile returned. “Does that mean I can continue using Tiera’s computer at night?” he asked with almost child-like anticipation.

Tiera said, “Yes, but watch how much data you download. You can read things on-line and as long as you don’t download a lot of information, it should be OK. Since your brain is obviously some

kind of computer, I assume that you are storing a lot of what you download. Is that correct?"

"Yes. Actually, I store it all. I have more than enough storage capacity to do so. Now that I understand about your Internet service account subscription, I have already devised a way to review the information I'm interested in without exceeding your daily download limit. The only reason I used your computer's downloading feature was that I'd seen you do it. It was never necessary for me. After I transfer data into my storage cells, I can cross-link almost instantly in a manner somewhat like the hyperlinks that are prevalent on Internet web sites, only faster by several orders of magnitude."

"By the way, I did not spend all of my time researching technology and geo-politics. You may not have realized it, but the Christian New Testament did not exist when I was living in Jerusalem. I was quite interested in the historical parts of it, especially the books of Luke and Acts. I was able to correlate major parts of those written accounts with my own memories and experiences. Although I did not accomplish what Joazar had ordered me to do, I noted with some sadness that Paul was eventually condemned and executed in Rome several years later. Who knows how things might have been different if my ship had reached Malta too?"

Obviously losing interest, Tiera yawned. "Look, it's late. I think we've had enough for one day. You may not need sleep, but we do. Enjoy your web surfing. We'll see you in the morning. Good night."

Venice, Italy
9:08 AM

"Pronto, chi parla?" said Abramo Sartori as he answered the phone.

"Hello my friend, this is Hakeem Ghanem."

"Buongiorno, I've been expecting your call. How are you?"

"I'm just fine, thanks be to God. How are you and your family?"

"Very well, thank you. How may I be of service?"

"Is the yacht ready for delivery yet?" the wealthy Egyptian asked without further pleasantries.

"Yes. The electronic equipment and extra fuel capacity you asked for have been installed. Your insurance agent inspected the yacht last Friday and has approved the liability and casualty insurance certificate. The yacht has been cleaned and provisioned for the trip to Alexandria. I will have the fuel and water tanks topped off a few days in advance so all will be ready."

"I've explained to the Italian port officials and Customs Inspector that the yacht will be leaving soon. They've assured me there will be no delays once I advise them of the departure date and complete a few forms. Will you have someone fly to Venice to take the yacht back to Alexandria? I would be happy to pick them up at the airport and if you wish, to make hotel reservations for them here in Port Alberoni for one or two nights," Signor Sartori suggested.

Ghanem paused for a moment before responding, "I do not wish to presume but, if you are willing, I would like for you to deliver the yacht yourself. I have imagined that you and your wife might bring the yacht to me as a kind of all-expenses-paid holiday, with a little something extra for your trouble, of course. You could spend a few days here in Alexandria as my guests and then fly home. I'm sure my wife would love to meet Signora Sartori. Alexandria is beautiful at this time of year. Temperatures are mild with gentle breezes from the north. Days are sunny and pleasantly warm. I'm sure you and your wife would enjoy it. Is it possible that this would be of interest to you?" asked Hakeem.

"Well, I need to discuss it with Donatella before I can say for sure but I think she will like the idea."

"I have another favor to ask about this," Ghanem said. "As you may know, my sister lives with me. She was previously married to an Italian Coast Guard sailor who served as part of the Sinai Multinational peace-keeping force some years ago. He and my sister had two sons who were born in Italy and now live in Rome. She seldom gets to see them and has asked me if they could possibly come with you on the yacht. They are fine, healthy young men who could help you handle the yacht. I don't want to disappoint her.

Would you consider taking them with you as your crew so they could visit their mother?"

Abramo considered this for a moment before saying, "Yes, of course. If Donatella agrees, we will bring the yacht to you and would be happy to have your nephews come with us. When would you want us to deliver the yacht?"

"My friend, you are too kind," said Ghanem. "It is not quite 1,300 miles from Venice to Alexandria so, with refueling stops along the way, the trip will take four or five days, I think. Would it be possible for you to leave Venice about one week from today?"

Abramo flipped open his desk calendar and said, "Yes, I think that is possible. I have another yacht to deliver day after tomorrow and then my calendar is mostly free for several weeks. There are a few minor things to take care of but my maintenance employee can handle them while I'm gone. I'll call you tomorrow to confirm that we can deliver your yacht and to finalize the schedule."

"Thank you so much. I look forward to hearing from you. Maa al salama."

"Ciao, arrivederci," said Abramo Sartori, smiling as he hung up the phone. He had a wonderful surprise for Donatella.

Thursday, May 22

Aquilina Estate
8:25 AM

"Look, David. I know you'd like to believe Nahbi's science fiction tale but it's simply not credible," Tiera said abruptly.

David set his coffee cup down before responding. He had hoped they could enjoy a quiet breakfast alone on the patio but Tiera was obviously in a testy mood.

"You may be right," he conceded. "Certainly his story strains the imagination. You know a lot more about computer technology than I do but even I can see that Nahbi's mental powers far surpass ours. To my knowledge, no contemporary computer has yet succeeded in

duplicating, let alone exceeding, the ability of the human brain in all functional areas. Yet, his apparently does. If we are to believe his story, in only a few nights he has figured out how to use your computer, taught himself both written and spoken English, read extensively on the current global state of technology, and assimilated vast amounts of historical and geo-political information. I admit that's a lot to swallow."

Tiera nodded and then said, "I would characterize Nahbi as a super computer with arms and legs. Sure, he's more than that, but the single most important element of his nature is that remarkable brain of his. I know that military research programs all over the world have been focused on creating robots to take over many of the most hazardous aspects of war fighting. I recently read an article that the Chinese have hacked just about every important military secret the U.S. has and that their attacks focused on military robotics. What if Nahbi was designed and produced by the Chinese? After all, China is a closed and secretive country run by a bunch of old men brainwashed in communist philosophies. It really scares me to think that Nahbi might have come from China at the very time when China is flexing its economic and military muscles."

David frowned before responding to what Tiera had said. "Yes, that would be scary but it's not the only plausible possibility I can imagine. You probably know that the Israelis have been awarded more individual Nobel prizes than any other nationality. Many of the world's most respected scientists and mathematicians are Israelis. Yet, Israel is a small country of 8 million people surrounded by several hundred million Arab Muslims, many of whom would like to destroy them. No wonder they take national defense so seriously."

"I recently read that the Israelis plan to have one-third of their fighting force comprised of autonomous robots within just a few years. As I understand it, many of those devices are single function devices designed to do things like patrol a border and report infiltration or to clear land mines. Yet, that's what we know. Given their exceptional technological capabilities, and their renowned ability to keep military secrets, I would think of all the countries on Earth, they might just conceivably be able to produce an android like Nahbi."

"Yes, I've thought of them too", admitted Tiera. "But, we can't rule out the Americans or the British. Both countries have advanced robotics programs and some of the finest universities on Earth. The American's Defense Advanced Research Projects Agency has awarded several contracts to create sophisticated robots. Boston Dynamics has created several increasingly sophisticated robots including one named Atlas that is about the size of a full-grown man and that has a remarkable agility. The Robotics Laboratory at the University of Bristol has also done some really amazing robotics works."

"I think the French and Germans could possibly manage it but it just doesn't seem likely, given how little money they devote to military readiness and research," Tiera said. I read an article about a Japanese astronaut-robot built to keep Japan's astronauts company during long periods in space, but it's no Nahbi by a long shot. The Japanese have also demonstrated a reasonably life-like female robot that can sing Karaoke and do a few simple dance steps. But, again, it seems very primitive compared to what we've seen of Nahbi's capabilities."

"Russia would certainly like to be able to build such a device. A newspaper article I read recently said the Russians are developing killer robots that can neutralize terrorists. Still, everything I know about the Russians suggests that they are always playing catch up on technology and, like the Chinese, typically try to steal information from the Americans. I just don't see them at the forefront of the development of a sophisticated, life-like android."

David nodded thoughtfully. "You know that I previously served in combat and that I've seen and used a fair amount of American military technology. Even though the United States is investing a great deal of money into the development of unmanned weapons platforms including drones and even full-size fighters, I seriously doubt that even the Americans could produce Nahbi. Maybe in twenty to thirty years, but not today. I just don't think so."

"Call me naïve or excessively nationalistic if you wish, but I sincerely believe that if the Americans can't do it with their incredibly well-funded military research programs and all of the other advantages they enjoy, I seriously doubt that any nation on

Earth could be so far ahead of them as to produce Nahbi. The more I think about it, the less I believe he's a military R&D product."

"So, what are you saying?"

"I didn't sleep much last night. I kept thinking about what Nahbi had told us. I also thought a lot about your Occam's razor comment, which I admit has considerable merit. Yet, after hours of considering every angle I could imagine, I'm left with the sense that Nahbi's technology is just too advanced for him to be a product of our times. I think the answer must lie elsewhere."

"Elsewhere? Where elsewhere?" Tiera said, her face reddening in a flush of sudden anger. "What's left? Aliens from outer space or another dimension? Hollywood's Dr. Emmett Brown with his time-traveling DeLorean sports car? Supernatural beings? Come on, David, some kind of military device is the *only* explanation that makes sense."

David held up his palms in a peace gesture but Tiera just glared defiantly at him with her jaw tight and fists clenched. He sensed how scared and angry she was. Her world had always been safe, secure, orderly, and predictable. Now, suddenly it wasn't anymore. She was having a tough time dealing with that new reality.

"Tiera, calm down. We'll work this out," David said in as soothing a manner as he could muster. It was the wrong thing to say. She exploded again.

"David Logan, don't you *dare* tell me to calm down using that condescending tone."

"OK, OK, I'm sorry. Look, I freely admit that it's at least possible that you are right and that Nahbi was developed as a military weapon by some country yet unidentified. Normally, I would be more than happy to turn Nahbi over to American military authorities and let them deal with it. But I have no confidence that the current administration can be trusted to do what's right. It is so political, and so mired in multiple scandals, that they might call a news conference to brag about their incredible new android technology breakthrough just to divert attention from the latest scandal du jour."

"The President is extremely arrogant but does not seem to possess the qualities of an effective Commander in Chief. He's been openly hostile to some of our oldest allies and inexplicably friendly to some of our worst enemies. Worse yet, I don't think he's an honest man. I think he says things that suit his political agenda with little regard for the truth or what's best for our country. There's just no sign of personal integrity. I don't trust him or his administration at all."

David's apparent concession to the scenario she considered most likely seemed to mollify Tiera somewhat.

"There does seem to be one other possibility though it too strains credibility," David said thoughtfully.

"What other possibility?" Tiera asked suspiciously.

"Let me start by asking you a question. How would you define eternity?"

Tiera thought for a few moments. "I suppose as an infinite amount of time."

"I don't think so," David said. "I think it would be more accurate to say that eternity is the complete *absence* of time. The Big Bang theorists say that space itself, matter, energy, *and time* all began at the instant of the Big Bang. My religious background and education makes me wonder if Nahbi might have been created by a spirit being that can cross the boundary between time and eternity at will."

"Stop it!" Tiera almost shouted. "I can't believe you could possibly believe something like that. Do you?"

"Well, maybe. I just don't know yet. I've read the Bible multiple times and I do believe spirit beings exist. The Bible says that God is a spirit being. There is an account in Acts of Jesus entering a room without opening the door. There are accounts of people long dead appearing to living people. There is a verse in Ephesians that refers to the spiritual forces of evil in the heavenly places," David told her. "My point is that I long ago accepted as truth that there are spirit beings and that they interact with man from time to time."

"Well, that's just great!" Tiera said with heavy sarcasm. "If I understand you correctly, you're saying we're really down to two scenarios to explain Nahbi. Scenario number one is that Nahbi is the

product of a military R&D program and that he's been lying to us to keep us from figuring that out. Scenario number two is that Nahbi is telling the truth and the time travel issue is explained by evil spirit beings able to move in and out of time grabbing Nahbi out of the future and then whisking him back to Jerusalem to kill Christians. Is that what you're suggesting?" asked Tiera.

"Well, I wouldn't put it quite that way but yes something like that. I'm not saying that's definitely the answer but I can't help but wonder if that wouldn't explain how Nahbi's story could be true."

"I'm astonished that you would even consider this spirit beings scenario. It seems utterly preposterous and ridiculous to me. Maybe you and I aren't as compatible as I thought. I don't know anyone who's ever seen a demon or, for that matter, an angel. Have you?" Tiera demanded defiantly.

"No. But then again, until last Thursday, neither one of us had ever seen an advanced humanoid robot either."

Tiera just shook her head in disbelief and stomped angrily into the house.

Alexandria, Egypt
4:10 PM

"Salam alekum," Hakeem Ghanem said as he answered his mobile phone.

"Buongiorno Mr. Ghanem. This is Abramo Sartori."

"How are you my good friend?"

"Very well, thank you. I've called to tell you that my wife and I would be happy to deliver your yacht to you. Donatella is looking forward to such a fine holiday." Abramo smiled as he remembered his wife's happy reaction when he'd told her about his client's invitation.

"That's wonderful," said Hakeem. "I do have one additional favor to ask. Can you have a scuba tank compressor and storage cabinet installed for me before you leave Venice? I'll have Ibrahim Al-Jabiri, call you with the details. He's the General Manager of my company and a mechanical engineer by training. He's figured out what kind of equipment we'll need and where to install it. He's

already contacted a company in Mestre, not far from the Venetian causeway, that has the compressor and necessary fittings in stock. He's paid for the equipment and has given them your name and phone number to authorize whoever you select to do the installation. Ibrahim told me that it was a simple job that should take only a few hours once they get started. But, if you can't get it done before you leave, just load the equipment on board the yacht and we'll take care of it here."

"Yes, of course. I'll see to it immediately." Abramo wondered why his client wanted him to have the equipment installed before the yacht left Venice. Surely the Ghanem Equipment Company could easily install the equipment at much lower cost.

Friday, May 23

Aquilina Estate
8:45 AM

"You asked me to provide convincing evidence that the story of my origin is true," Nahbi told David and Tiera. "Failing that, you asked me to describe one or more plausible theories to explain how an advanced android could have been present in Jerusalem almost two thousand years ago."

"Unfortunately, If I rely solely on the current state of human scientific knowledge, I cannot provide what you or most other people would consider convincing evidence that I could have been in Jerusalem in the year 60 AD," Nahbi said.

"Beyond any reasonable doubt, the technologies necessary to produce me did not exist in the ancient world. So, for my account to be true, that logically means that either I was produced in the future and then transported back in time or that I was placed on Earth by extraterrestrial beings that possessed the requisite technology."

"However, if by extraterrestrial beings we mean an advanced race of space travelers, that possibility would also require time travel. Albert Einstein and hundreds of scientists since have proven that nothing can travel faster than the speed of light. Intergalactic

distances are so great that travel even between relatively close star systems would require impractical amounts of time. Alpha Centauri B is the closest star with an earth-sized planet. However, Alpha Centauri B is 25 trillion miles from earth. The highest speed ever attained by a manned vehicle, Apollo 10 on its return from the Moon in 1969, was about 25,000 MPH. However, even at *ten times* that velocity, a one-way trip from Alpha Centauri B would take over 11,500 years."

"Travel between galaxies is even more out of the question because it would require times that begin to approximate the age of the universe. The Andromeda galaxy is the closest galaxy to earth. However, it is still 2.5 million light-years away. One light year is approximately 5.9 trillion miles. At 250,000 MPH, it would take a spacecraft 6.7 billion years to make the trip. That is roughly half the age of the universe. That means that advanced, intelligent life would not have had time to evolve before beginning a trip that could have arrived on earth two thousand years ago."

"Popular science fiction has conveniently postulated faster-than-light travel for many years but there is absolutely no scientific basis to believe that it is possible. Speculations by science fiction writers about time warps, time tunnels, and similar efforts to get around the absolute limitations on velocity described by Einstein are utterly without scientific merit."

"Tiera, you hold a doctorate in computer science. You have studied advanced mathematics, physics, and quantum mechanics as they relate to the design of semi-conductor devices. What is your understanding of the current scientific view of the possibility of time travel?"

Tiera thought for a moment before responding. "There have been a few observations in the most powerful particle accelerators that seem to suggest that certain particles may, under rare conditions, appear to go backwards in time. These observations are inconclusive and highly controversial. However, no reputable scientist believes that a complex object, such as a human or a machine, could be transported back in time. From a scientific point of view, time travel remains firmly in the realm of fiction."

"I agree. Yet, the subject of time is extremely complex. A comprehensive understanding of time requires knowledge of advanced mathematics, relativity, quantum theory, and high-energy particle physics. The subject of time is also inextricably tied to the origin of the observable universe."

"Most scientists believe that the so-called 'Big Bang' model of the universe is an accurate description of how the observable universe came into existence. There is ample evidence to support that view including the readily observable three-dimensional expansion of the universe that suggests that at an earlier time all matter was in the same place."

"However, there are consequences of the big-bang theory that are not commonly recognized. For example, when most people think about the big bang, they envision an explosion occurring in a vacant area of space. That is wrong. Both space and time as we know them came into existence at the instant of the big bang. Prior to the big bang, this universe did not exist. There was no space and there was no time."

"Think about that for a moment. Approximately 13.8 billion years ago, time began. Since then, time has appeared to *flow* in a forward direction only. Our concepts of past, present, and future depend on that discernible forward flow. It is because of our natural sense of the passage of time, supported by ample scientific evidence, that we doubt the possibility of time travel. It is safe to say that, within the physical universe we inhabit, time travel is not possible."

Tiera interrupted, "But, from a purely mathematical perspective, time can run in either direction. Math and physics work just fine regardless of the direction of the time vector. That may be a quirk of how humans developed their scientific and mathematical tools but it is a fact well known to all high-energy physicists and mathematicians. Still, I would agree that no reputable scientist believes that the kind of time travel described in science-fiction novels is possible."

Nahbi smiled and nodded. "And yet, that conclusion may not address all the possibilities."

"But you just said that time travel is not possible so what other possibilities are you talking about?" Tiera asked.

"It is generally agreed that time travel within the portion of the universe we can observe is not possible. But, that begs the question of what exists outside of the observable part of our universe."

"Every reputable scientist will tell you that mathematics and physics can only take them back to the instant of the big bang. They cannot *see* prior to that time because all the laws of the universe that govern physics, chemistry, gravity, and light did not exist prior to the big bang. Yet, intuitively, everyone recognizes that *something* must have existed prior to the big bang."

"People ask who or what caused the Big Bang? Many see evidence of intelligent design which implies the existence of an intelligent designer. If such an intelligent designer exists outside of this universe then that designer is not necessarily subject to the limitations of time. It is conceivable that time is a unique characteristic of this universe," Nahbi told them.

"David, you believe that the 'intelligent designer' was an omnipotent spirit being humans call God and that he created the universe. Because of your religious faith, you believe in the existence and reality of spirit beings that are not constrained by the limitations of our physical universe. Is that an accurate summary of your belief?" Nahbi asked.

"Yes. I am firmly convinced that God and other spirit beings exist that are not constrained by time or space," David replied.

"What about you, Tiera? Do you believe in God or other spirit beings?"

Tiera looked uncomfortable. She glanced at David before answering Nahbi's question. "I'm not really sure. I was taught to believe in God but I've always had doubts that the dogma of the church didn't adequately resolve to my satisfaction. I guess I'd have to say that I do believe in God but that much of what is taught in churches seems flawed or simply wrong."

"My concept of God is vague. I cannot say that I have a clear understanding of his reality or characteristics. Unlike David, I haven't spent much time studying the Bible. My world-view is

materialistic. I trust things I can see and touch. I've never seen God or an angel. People tell me they are real but I have no evidence to support that belief. I'm willing to believe, and I try to keep an open mind, but I do not share David's unwavering confidence in the reality of God or the existence of spirit beings."

"Yet, you believe in many things that you cannot see." Nahbi said gently. "You have never seen a photon or an electron but are firmly convinced of their reality because you can build devices that behave in predictable ways based on physics and mathematics. Isn't it fair to say that you believe in many things that you cannot see or touch?"

"Yes, but in every instance, I can see some effect of those unseen things on the physical world. That is very different than believing in spirit beings."

David saw the inconsistency in her conclusion. "Isn't it intellectually dishonest to base your world view on the belief that everything we see evolved from the big bang while avoiding the question of who or what caused the big bang in the first place? You observe the flow of electricity and accept it as proof of the reality of electrons. Yet, you have seen the deep-space photographs taken by the Hubble Telescope and do not ask who or what created this universe."

"David, in a fundamental sense, I am a scientist. I spend very little time thinking about metaphysical things. I don't believe time travel is possible and I seriously doubt the existence and reality of spirit beings," Tiera said.

"And yet," Nahbi said, "as a computer scientist, I'm sure you have a general understanding of String Theory. The most-widely embraced variant of string theory, called 'M-Theory,' suggests that matter, space, and time exist across multi-dimensional planes that were created out of nothing at the moment of the Big Bang. Theoretical physicists who embrace M-Theory describe an 11-dimension universe where the extra dimensions are somehow either rolled up or are otherwise too small to be observed. My point is that some of the world's most advanced thinkers believe the universe was created out of nothing and that it contains dimensions we can't see. Isn't that the essence of what you were taught about String Theory?" Nahbi asked her.

"Yes, I guess so," Tiera said hesitantly as she recognized the logical trap that Nahbi had set for her.

"You have said that you are fundamentally a scientist and that your world-view is materialistic. Yet, you embrace scientific theories that postulate a vast universe created out of nothing without attempting to understand the causative effect of that creation. The foundation of scientific inquiry is that it seeks to determine the cause of observable phenomena and to devise formulas that can predict future conditions that are consistent with empirical observations. Yet, by ignoring the question of who or what caused the big bang, you stop short of fulfilling the scientist's primary objective."

"You accept the concept of a multi-dimensional universe where some of the dimensions are conveniently so small as to be unobservable. I submit that such a view requires faith in the unknown just as David's faith in God does. Mind you, I am not taking sides in the debate. I am merely pointing out that David's world-view as you've called it requires no more faith than your own. For reasons that make sense to you both, you have accepted certain important things on faith. Do you both agree to this at least?" Nahbi asked them.

Tiera shrugged and nodded. David simply said yes.

"Good, then perhaps we now have a basis for the construction of a plausible theory of how an advanced android could have been present in ancient Jerusalem," Nahbi said.

"Whether we call them spirit beings or inhabitants of another dimension is merely semantics. For those of us who inhabit this universe, any being that exists outside of our four-dimensional, observable universe is certainly extraterrestrial in the normal sense of the word. Whether we think of them as spiritual beings consistent with a religious perspective or only as beings with no physical reality in this universe, the result is the same for our immediate purpose."

"Once we accept the Big-Bang theory and the M-Theory variant of string theory we are left with a world-view, to again use Tiera's term, that at least admits the possibility of beings that inhabit

different dimensions of our universe or perhaps an entirely different spatial environment that we cannot even imagine," Nahbi explained.

"I have told you that I cannot provide convincing evidence that my story is true if I am constrained to rely solely on the current state of human science. I can, however, provide a theory that is fully consistent with a considerable body of human knowledge and thought."

"You have both agreed that there may be dimensions of our universe that we cannot detect or see. We know that time is one of the dimensions of our physical universe. However, there is an astounding consequence to that conclusion. If we accept the eleven dimensions of M-Theory, and time is one of the dimensions we can detect, it follows logically and mathematically that time is *not* one of the other dimensions. Thus, from a purely logical analysis, it follows that any being that inhabits one or more of those other dimensions, or any universe or space beyond ours, may not be constrained by time," Nahbi explained. "Do you both see this?"

David nodded immediately. Tiera hesitated for several moments but finally also nodded.

"You asked me to propose a plausible theory that could explain my presence in ancient Jerusalem. After a great deal of research and careful consideration of all available and pertinent facts, the key elements of the theory you have asked me to propose are these:"

"The universe was created out of nothing approximately 13.8 billion years ago. Time began at that instant."

"Einstein proved that mass and energy are the same thing but in two different forms. Their equivalence can be calculated as E=MK where K is a constant of proportionality equal to the speed of light squared. This equivalence has profound implications for the Big-Bang theory. In essence, it says that the entire universe began as a burst of pure energy and that a portion of that energy was subsequently converted to mass during the inflationary cooling period of the universe's transition to what we see today."

"The universe has obvious patterns of intelligent design that imply a designer/creator."

"The universe is comprised of more dimensions than are commonly observed or experienced by human beings. Just as actions can occur in the dimensions we inhabit, there is no reason to assume that similar actions could not occur in the other, unobserved dimensions."

"Time is a unique property of the four-dimensional environment we inhabit. The other seven dimensions of our universe do not include time."

"The Big Bang and M-Theory do not preclude the existence of spirit beings. It can even be argued that they imply spirit beings external to the observable universe. The Jewish Torah, the Islamic Koran, and the Christian Bible all explicitly state the reality of a creator and other spirit beings." Several other human religions also believe in a creator and spirit beings. Such beliefs are admittedly not proof of the existence of spirit beings but my point is that a significant portion of human beings have believed in spirit beings throughout recorded history."

"My final three points are the keys to my theory of how I could plausibly have been in ancient Jerusalem," Nahbi told them.

"If we merge M-Theory with pervasive religious beliefs then it is entirely logical to postulate that intelligent beings exist outside of our four-dimensional subset of the 11-dimension universe. These beings are not constrained by time because their natural environment does not include a time dimension."

"Those intelligent beings, unconstrained by time, have the ability to cross the boundaries between the dimensions of our universe. It is these intelligent beings we refer to as spirit beings."

"I submit that it is possible that one or more of those intelligent beings obtained an advanced humanoid robot from some future time and then transported it back to ancient Jerusalem as a tool in a greater objective, possibly to interfere with the spread of the Christian religion."

Nahbi saw the doubt in Tiera's eyes and said, "You have told us that you are fundamentally a scientist. Science has its own language just as religions do. I submit that the Big-Bang theory is the scientific attempt to answer the questions of *when* and *how* the

universe was created using scientific language. The Biblical account of the beginning is a religious statement of *who* created the universe and *why*."

"The two accounts are somewhat like the six blind men of Indostan in John Godrey Saxe's famous poem. The scientist and the theologian describe the same thing but use different languages."

"Set aside for a moment if you can, any preconceived notions you may have either endorsing or rejecting the Biblical description of spirit beings. Instead, simply consider the possibility that such beings might exist and that they might not be in harmony with each other."

"Certainly all human experience suggests that conflict between different life forms is common if not universal. All available evidence indicates that it is a normal condition of this universe that life forms compete for energy, food, territory, reproduction, and other resources and things of value. Even plants compete for nutrients and sunlight."

"What I am saying is that one way, and perhaps the only way, that I could have been created in the future and then transported back to ancient Jerusalem would be if beings unconstrained by time, and who were able to cross the boundaries between the dimensions of our universe, obtained me in the future and then transported me back in earthly time," Nahbi told them.

"Modern high-energy physics tells us that there are dimensions of our universe that we cannot see. Christian, Jewish, and Islamic religions believe in a monotheistic God and spirit beings unconstrained by time. If those two facts are logically combined, then it is not beyond the realm of possibility that my theory is correct. I emphasize that it is only a plausible theory. I cannot prove that it is true," Nahbi said.

Tiera interrupted him saying, "I still don't buy it. To me, the military program theory is far more believable than the spirit beings theory. I don't see how you have solved anything with this discussion."

Nahbi smiled and said, "Ah, but your theory of a secret military program is full of inconsistencies as well because it is not supported

by known facts. My extensive research shows conclusively that no nation on earth currently possesses sufficiently advanced technology to produce me. To rely upon this theory of a secret military program requires confidence in the existence of technology somewhere on earth that apparently does not exist. That is no more rational than David's belief in a powerful creator and spirit beings."

"But, to be fair, the theory that I was constructed in the future and then transported back in time is also not supported by provable facts. It requires the existence of beings unconstrained by time and possessing the ability to cross dimensional boundaries," Nahbi said.

"You asked me to provide a plausible theory. I have done so. Unfortunately, it is no more demonstrably correct than the secret military program thesis. I have been unable to identify any other realistic scenarios. I think one of these two theories of my origin must be the correct one."

"It would not be prudent to assume that it doesn't matter which theory is correct because the consequences of the two theories are very different. If the military program theory is correct, then it is important to determine which country has attained such a compelling technological advantage and to take steps to neutralize that advantage as quickly as possible."

"Conversely, if the time-travel theory is correct, then it suggests that unseen beings are interacting in the affairs of humans in this four-dimensional subset of this universe. I submit that my story, if true, suggests that some kind of contest is being waged between these unseen beings. I was given to Joazar by a mysterious Egyptian. Joazar ordered me to kill Paul of Tarsus. The apparent reason was that the Sanhedrin did not want the new Christian religion to gain converts from Judaism. All of these are consistent with the 'heavenly warfare' described in Ephesians 6:12 and elsewhere in the Christian Bible."

"If the military origin is correct, then the problem is restricted to this subset of the observable universe and can, in theory at least, be dealt with by humans using conventional methods."

"If, on the other hand, the theory I have put forward is correct, then the problem is much greater because humans do not have the

ability to initiate interactions with beings that can move across the dimensions of this universe at will and who are unconstrained by time."

Monday, May 26

Aquilina Estate
7:58 PM

Matthias and Maria Aquilina stood near the entrance to their historic home greeting guests as they arrived. Tiera and David were with them. As each limousine arrived, two smartly-attired valets opened the doors and welcomed the guests to the Aquilina estate.

Beginning just after 7:00 PM, a steady stream of limousines had paused briefly at the security checkpoint that had been set up at the southwest gate before proceeding up the curved driveway to the house. After dropping off their passengers, the limousines exited through the northwest gate where two more security guards were posted. There were other security personnel and undercover police on the grounds and in the house.

Most of the guests had already arrived by 7:50 PM and had been escorted into the house by service attendants Matthias had hired for the reception. They were expecting the new president of the European Central Bank to arrive any minute.

At 7:52 PM, a black stretch limousine entered the driveway. The familiar blue flags on the fenders with their circles of 12 gold stars meant that Volker Schuhmacher and his wife Angela had arrived. Matthias and Maria Aquilina smiled at each other as their old friends approached the house.

The ECB president's limousine stopped at the curb and Volker stepped out of the car, smiling broadly as he spotted Matthias and Maria. Volker, ever the gentleman, turned to help Angela out of the car.

Suddenly, as they were walking toward their friends, the right side of Volker's head exploded in a red cloud of blood and tissue as he was killed instantly by a single shot from a high-powered rifle.

Angela, walking on Volker's right side, with her arm in his, was covered with her husband's blood and began to scream.

David heard the sharp crack of the rifle less than a second after Volker was hit and looked toward the sound. He saw a small, wooden shed on a grassy knoll about 200 meters to the north and knew instantly that was where the shot had come from. He sprinted down the sidewalk and jerked the front passenger-side door of the Schuhmacher limousine open. He shouted for the driver to get moving as he leaped into the car.

It took less than 45 seconds for them to reach the shed. After flying past the guards at northwest gate, the limousine driver had turned hard right and then almost immediately hard left onto a lane that ran on the north side of the shed. Two garage doors hinged at each side of the shed stood open as they pulled into the dirt driveway. David could see a small tractor inside the shed but nothing else. There was no car or any sign of the killer. He knew they were too late. The killer was gone. Before he could get out of the limousine to check the shed, two Malta Police cars with blue lights flashing pulled into the dirt driveway behind the limousine and ordered them out of the car with their hands up. They did as they were instructed.

It took a few minutes to persuade the policemen that they were not involved in the shooting. David's formal attire and a few quick calls convinced the police that he was a guest at the Aquilina estate. One of the police cars escorted them back to the estate while the other called for a forensic team and backup units.

By the time David returned to the estate ten minutes after the shooting, an ambulance was parked at the front walkway. Emergency medical technicians were still kneeling over the body of Volker Schuhmacher but David knew the man was dead. His wife Angela was standing nearby, still covered in blood, and sobbing uncontrollably. Maria Aquilina was almost too stunned herself to be of much comfort to her friend but she was doing her best.

Tiera was nowhere in sight. David assumed that she was probably in the house trying to calm the other guests. Matthias was standing near the curb talking to two of the security guards and three other

men. David recognized one of them as Signor Rico Massa and walked toward them.

Matthias looked questioningly at David as he joined the group of men but David just shook his head. Signor Massa pulled David aside.

"Mr. Logan, can you tell me why you rushed away immediately after Mr. Schuhmacher was shot?" the anti-terrorism policeman asked him.

"Signor Massa, I heard the shot. My military training and combat experience told me that's where the shot came from. I reacted instinctively to the threat."

"But you were unarmed. What could you have done if you had encountered the killer?"

"I never stopped to think about that. I just reacted."

"And what did you find when you reached the shed?"

"Nothing. The doors were open but there was no sign of the killer. Before I could check inside the shed, two police cars arrived and ordered us out of the limousine. I think you already know the rest because they checked with someone before allowing me to return to the estate."

"I see," said Signor Massa. "Surely you must realize that your presence here today, and your strong and immediate reaction following the gunshot, might be a matter of police interest in view of the report of the suspicious bundle that you and Miss Aquilina took off of the Aquilina yacht last Thursday evening. A high-powered rifle could easily be concealed in such a bundle."

David stared at the policeman in disbelief. "Are you saying that I am a suspect in this killing?"

"I am saying that everyone who was here or was in any way connected to this reception, will be questioned and considered to be what we police call *a person of interest* until we find out who the killer was. I want to question you and Miss Aquilina separately and immediately. Would you please come with me into the house?" the policeman asked.

Signor Massa questioned Tiera first in her father's study. The other two men that David had seen with Matthias went into the study with them and closed the door. After 20 minutes, the door opened and Tiera came out. Rico Massa was standing in the open doorway and asked David to come in. Tiera gave David a tear-stained and grief-stricken look as she walked past him.

"Who are these men?" David asked the policeman.

"You may think of them as my colleagues. They are here to observe but I will ask the questions. Please be seated."

"Mr. Logan, based on the background check that I ran on you a few days ago, I am aware of your military service and the fact that you were wounded in combat. While serving in Afghanistan, did you form a relationship with anyone who might have been connected to a militant Islamic organization?" the policeman began.

"I don't think so. But, you have to understand that a lot of the Afghan military and civilian police are secretly sympathetic to the Taliban and Islamic jihad. So, it's possible that someone I interfaced with might have been connected to a militant Islamic organization. None to my knowledge, but it is possible," David replied, wondering why the policeman had begun with that specific question.

"What is the real purpose of your presence in Malta?" Massa asked.

"What do you mean, the real purpose?" David asked incredulously. "You know very well that I am here as a guest of the Aquilina family."

"Whose idea was it for you to come here?

"Well, as you know, Tiera and I were at Cambridge together. After the graduation ceremonies, I think it was her mother's idea to invite me."

"You did or said nothing to persuade the Aquilina family to invite you?"

"No. Absolutely not. I was planning to return to Texas until the family invited me here," David declared with a flash of irritation at the question.

"Do you still maintain that the bundle you and Miss Aquilina loaded into the SUV at the yacht basin was only dirty linens and diving paraphernalia?" Massa asked David while looking directly into his eyes.

"Yes," David said after an instant's delay.

"When you raced away after the gunshot, were you trying to act as a diversion to give the killer time to escape?" the policeman asked still looking intently into David's eyes.

"I can't believe my ears. No. Absolutely not. I've told you that I reacted instinctively to a threat that, for all I knew, might have been targeted at Tiera's parents," David said emphatically. "Have you ever been in combat, Signor Massa?"

"Please remember that I am the one asking the questions but no, I have never been in combat."

"I'm not surprised. It's not at all like the movies or the evening news portrays it. It is far worse than any civilian can imagine. When the bad guys are shooting at you, and your friends are dying beside you, you react instantly to counter the threat before you or other members of your team are killed. It's no more complicated than that, Signor Massa," David said softly.

David's soft voice was a sign of his anger. He had lost friends and nearly his own life trying to help people half-way around the world. Being accused, even implicitly, of being involved in the murder of Volker Schuhmacher had touched a very sensitive nerve.

Massa nodded almost imperceptibly in an unconscious sign of respect for what David had just said. He looked questioningly at the two men standing in the corners where they could see David clearly without intruding on the questioning. Both shook their heads.

"Mr. Logan, that is all for now. Thank you for your time. I may have other questions later so please do not leave Malta without checking with me first," Rico Massa said, not unkindly.

8:59 PM

"What do you think, Phil?" "Did I imagine it or did he hesitate for an instant before answering the question about the bundle?" Alfonso Flores, the CIA agent asked his counterpart from MI6.

"I thought so too," said Phil. "I don't think he wanted to discuss the bundle. My sense is that there may be more to that bundle than a bunch of dirty laundry."

"Rico, would you mind if Al and I did a follow-up interview with both Mr. Logan and Miss Aquilina?" The MI6 agent knew that local law enforcement officers usually resented interference in their investigations by federal officials or international agents. They needed Signor Massa's cooperation so he wanted to be as tactful as possible.

"No. Not at all. May I ask why?"

"Do you know Grégoire Deveaux at INTERPOL in Lyon, France?"

"I have spoken to him once or twice on the phone but I don't really know him. Why?"

"In a recent conference call, Greg gave the CIA and MI6 a heads-up about an unusual meeting that recently took place in Sicily. I'd like to be sure there's no connection between that meeting and what happened here today."

"We still have quite a few interviews to conduct before the guests can be allowed to leave," Massa said thoughtfully. "Could you wait until tomorrow?"

The two intelligence agents traded a quick glance and then Phil Shaw said, "Yes, of course. This can wait until tomorrow. Would you mind if we questioned them without the MPF being present? Mr. Logan became increasingly angry and defensive as he answered your questions. I'm sure it never occurred to him that he might be a suspect. Perhaps if we can talk to him and Miss Aquilina alone, we might get some more information that could potentially be valuable to us all. We'll certainly brief you on how it goes."

Rico Massa did not look pleased but he had a murder investigation to run and he'd already questioned David and Tiera. After a moment's consideration, he said, "Yes, that's OK but please let me know at once if anything comes out of your session with them."

Phil saw the fleeting look of mild irritation on the MPF officer's face but was relieved to hear him give his permission. He hadn't been sure that Massa would agree.

9:43 PM

Rico Massa was having some second thoughts about allowing Shaw and Flores to do a follow-up interview with Logan and Aquilina when his cell phone rang. His mood brightened when he saw who the call was from.

"Margherita, talk to me. What have you found?"

"I've just finished up at the shed. I took plaster casts of some footprints and tire tracks just in case they might be helpful later. The shed yielded no other useful information. We dusted for prints but I don't think we'll get any fingerprints of the killer. I'm pretty sure this was the work of a professional assassin who almost certainly wore gloves," Signora Palma told her friend and colleague of many years. "But I did find what was probably the murder weapon in a bore-hole water well beside the shed. It was recently fired and had been dropped into the well but had become wedged diagonally across the well only a few feet below ground level. I was able to retrieve it without difficulty."

"What kind of weapon is it?"

"It's a Weatherby Mark V Euromark chambered in .375 Holland and Holland Magnum. It's an expensive big-game hunting rifle that I suspect is the same one reported stolen a few days ago from a villa in Zurrieq."

"Any prints on it?"

"No, it's been wiped clean."

"OK, thanks Margherita. Keep me posted. Oh, one more thing I just thought of. See if you can find a Magistrate this evening to approve a search warrant for you to take a peek at all email traffic to and from the Aquilina Estate for the past two weeks. We might get lucky and find something useful. I'm headed for the hospital to talk to Mrs. Schuhmacher. She collapsed as they were loading her husband's body into the ambulance. They've taken her to St. Luke's. I'm hoping she hasn't been sedated so she can answer a few questions."

Rico had enormous confidence in Margherita Palma, the Director of the MPF Forensic Science Laboratory. She was widely respected as one of the best forensic scientists in Europe and she had worked

for the Malta Police Force for over thirty years. He reflected back over the long years of their professional relationship and thought again, as he had so many times before, that Malta was fortunate to have a forensic scientist of her caliber.

Valletta, Malta
11:52 PM

"Rico, this is Margherita. Somehow I knew you'd still be at the office. Don't you ever go home? Anyway, I've found something. It may be important or nothing at all. I can't tell."

"I'm listening."

"I finally got the search warrant approved about an hour ago. By a stroke of luck, the Senior Magistrate was still in his office. As soon as he learned that the warrant was in connection with the assassination of the ECB president, he signed it. I then went to the technical center at Vodafone Malta Ltd. and showed the duty supervisor the warrant. She called her boss and he told her to cooperate."

"There were only a few messages to or from the Aquilina estate in the past two weeks. Most were just typical email chatter but one of them caught my attention. It was from Tiera Aquilina to her brother Nicholas in California the day before you questioned her and Mr. Logan about the suspicious bundle."

"Why did you find that interesting?"

"It was a very large file that used state-of-the art encryption. There was no way I could decipher it but I couldn't help but wonder why Miss Aquilina had sent it to her brother. The Aquilina's are one of the wealthiest families in Malta so perhaps it contained sensitive financial or some other perfectly innocent information. But, in light of your earlier questioning of Miss Aquilina and Mr. Logan, followed a few days later by an assassination at the estate, I thought you might want to ask them about the message."

"Interesting. Yes, I'll follow up on it."

"And Rico, there's something else I discovered while I was at the Vodaphone technical center. A few days after you questioned them, Vodaphone notified Miss Aquilina that she had exceeded her data

plan's daily limit for downloading information from the Internet and asked if she wanted to upgrade her data plan. According to the Vodaphone technician, she has never exceeded her daily limit before and, in fact, typically uses less than twenty percent of her daily allowance. It may all be coincidence but you and I both know that too many coincidences in a murder investigation raise a lot of questions. I thought you might want to see if Miss Aquilina has an explanation."

"Good work, my friend. Let me know if you find anything else."

As he hung up, his eyes narrowed and he frowned. Maybe the young couple was involved in the assassination after all. Even though he'd used aggressive questioning techniques with them, he hadn't really thought they were involved. Margherita's discoveries raised new questions in his mind.

Tuesday, May 27

Valletta, Malta
12:27 AM

The phone beside the bed in the hotel room rang. Phil Shaw picked it up. "Hello," he said, wondering who would be calling his room at this hour.

"Mr. Shaw, this is Rico Massa. I know it's after midnight but I've got some information I think you need to know before you question Miss Aquilina and Mr. Logan tomorrow."

"Don't worry about the time. Al and I are still up discussing the assassination and how it might be connected to some other things we're working on. What do you have?"

"There was a single, large encrypted email message sent from Miss Aquilina to her brother the day before I questioned her and Mr. Logan about the suspicious bundle. Also, on the following day, Vodaphone Malta Ltd notified Miss Aquilina that she had exceeded her maximum daily data download allowance. The technician told our forensic scientist that had never happened before."

"I know you and Al are going to see if you can get any more out of them about the suspicious bundle. Since you're going to be talking to them in the morning, I'd appreciate it if you'd ask them about the encrypted email and the data usage and let me know what they say."

"Yes, of course. Anything else?"

"No, that's all for now. Good luck."

Aquilina Estate
9:00 AM

David was sitting on the patio drinking his second cup of coffee while he waited for Tiera. He was a little surprised that she was later than usual. He knew that she was normally an early riser and wondered if the previous day's tragic events had upset her even more than he'd realized. Lucia had peeked out several times to see if Tiera had joined him yet. He knew she was holding breakfast for them.

A few moments later, David heard Tiera say good morning to Lucia as she stepped out of the house into the bright morning sunlight.

Tiera leaned over him to give him a soft kiss just as her cell phone rang. She looked at the screen and then turned the phone so he could see that the call was from her mother.

"Good morning mother. Are you still at St. Luke's?"

"Yes. I sat up with Angela. She and I both had an emotionally exhausting night. She couldn't stop crying and that made me cry too. The doctor gave her a sedative a little while ago and she's just fallen asleep. I asked Lucia to bring me some clothes. I'm not going to leave Angela until I'm sure she'll be all right."

"I spoke to your father a few minutes ago. He couldn't sleep either and I could tell that he's exhausted and depressed. He said he couldn't get the image of seeing Volker murdered right in front of us out of his mind. He told me he'd finally given up on trying to sleep and gotten out of bed at 4:30 AM. The vice president of asset management at the bank called him a few minutes after seven to tell him that the markets had opened sharply lower in the Far East as news of the assassination spread throughout the global financial

markets. Your father has always said that the markets in the Far East are often reliable predictors of what would happen later in the day in Europe and the Americas. He said he'd be at the bank if I needed him. How are you doing?"

"I'm fine mother. Try to get some rest. I love you."

Lucia brought their breakfast but they didn't feel much like eating and only picked at their food. At 9:00 AM, the doorbell rang. Tiera went to see who it was. A few moments later, she escorted Phil Shaw and Al Flores out to the patio.

"David, these men want to talk to us about what happened," Tiera said.

David looked up to see Rico Massa's two *colleagues* that had been present when he and Tiera had been questioned the previous day.

"Do you mind telling us who you are?"

"Mr. Logan, my name is Phil Shaw. I am a field intelligence officer for MI6 in London. This is Al Flores, an intelligence officer with the CIA." Both men showed identification as David and Tiera waited to find out what they wanted.

"Can we go into the house, please," Phil Shaw asked. "Perhaps we could talk in the study again," he suggested.

Tiera nodded and led them into the house. When they were seated, David asked them what they wanted.

Al Flores spoke for the first time. "We recently received sketchy information from a usually reliable informer that a contract assassination might have been arranged by a foreign intelligence service that we monitor closely. However, the informer did not know who the target was or when the hit would occur. The widely-publicized G-20 meeting seemed like a possibility although we were never able to improve on the vague information we had."

"Phil and I decided to come to Malta, or maybe I should say our bosses decided we should come to Malta. The idea was to see if we might discover something in the days preceding the conference that might allow us to stop the assassination if it was indeed targeted on one of the financial ministers."

"We contacted Signor Rico Massa because of his position as the MPF's anti-terrorism officer and spent quite a bit of time with him this past week going over INTERPOL bulletins and customs and immigration arrival photos to see if we could identify any known contract assassins. Unfortunately, we didn't recognize anyone."

"As you know, we were at the estate when the assassination occurred. Although a murder investigation is a local police matter, the fact that the victim was the president of the European Central Bank, also makes it our business. Signor Massa graciously allowed us to observe his questioning of you and other people who were at the estate. I'm sorry that we did not feel it appropriate to introduce ourselves yesterday," he concluded.

Phil Shaw then asked, "Do you mind if we ask you a few questions? It shouldn't take long."

Tiera looked at David and he nodded.

"We would be happy to help in any way we can," Tiera told the two intelligence officers.

"Thank you," Phil Shaw said as he began his questioning. "Late last night, in the routine process of the murder investigation, the Malta Police forensic team came across an encrypted email message from you to your brother sent the day before you were questioned by Signor Massa," he said while watching Tiera's face for any sign of a reaction. "I'm told that it was a rather large file. Can you tell us the purpose of that message?"

Tiera glanced at David and then answered Phil Shaw's question. "It was very personal. I'd rather not discuss its contents."

"I see," said Shaw. "I'm also told that massive amounts of data were downloaded via your Vodaphone Internet account the night after your session with Signor Massa. I've been told that you have never previously downloaded anywhere near that data volume. Can you explain the purpose of that unusual downloading activity?" the intelligence agent asked.

"I don't know. Perhaps it's a billing error. David saw that the intelligence officers were watching her face intently. Their quick glance at each other made it obvious to him that they both knew

she'd just lied to them. He could tell from the strained look on Tiera's face that she knew they'd caught her lie.

Al Flores asked the next question. "Mr. Logan, when Signor Massa asked you yesterday about the bundle you and Miss Aquilina carried from the family yacht to the SUV, you confirmed what you'd both already told him. Yet, Phil and I have been in this game for a long time. We both noticed the brief hesitation before you answered him. May I ask why?"

David looked at Tiera before answering. "May I have a few moments alone with Miss Aquilina?" he asked.

The two intelligence officers traded glances again before Phil Shaw said, "Certainly. We'll wait outside. Call us when you're ready to tell us the truth."

9:41 AM

"David, they know we've lied to them and I feel awful," Tiera said looking like she was about to cry. "What should we do?"

David could not stand to see the woman he loved so unhappy. He'd already made up his mind what they should do but wanted to give Tiera a chance to come to the same conclusion.

"We've known we were in over our heads for days. The murder of your parents' friend raised the stress level even more. Our greatest fear has been that the android might fall into the wrong hands. As they were grilling you about the email, I was initially very angry at them for implying that you'd done something wrong. Then I realized that they are just trying to do their jobs. There are some bad characters in the world but we have to trust someone."

"No government is perfect but I have more confidence in the institutional integrity of the United States and the United Kingdom than any other governments on Earth. The CIA and MI6 are two of the top intelligence agencies in the world. If anyone can figure out where the android came from and what should be done with it, I think we have to assume it would be the CIA and MI6. These two guys strike me as decent men doing a tough job. We haven't done anything wrong. I say we tell them the truth."

Tiera nodded her agreement.

David called the officers back into the study. Over the next hour, David and Tiera told Phil Shaw and Al Flores the whole story. When they were done, the officers asked if they could see the android. David and Tiera took them to the cottage to meet Nahbi.

Langley, Virginia
12:00 PM

Pete Nocona was expecting the call. Al's earlier text message had asked him to be available for a call at 4:00 PM London time. He wondered what it was about. Right on schedule, his secure phone rang. He picked up on the first ring.

"Hello Al."

"I see you got my message."

"Yes. Where are you now?

"I'm still in Malta with Phil Shaw but we're leaving for London early tomorrow morning. MI6 HQ is sending an executive jet down to pick us up. Are you sitting down?"

Suddenly alert, Pete said, "Yes. What's up?"

"Phil and I are escorting David Logan and Tiera Aquilina to MI6 HQ for questioning in connection with an advanced humanoid robot they discovered a few days ago while scuba diving east of Valletta. We're taking the android with us. Incredible as it may seem, they succeeded in activating it. Pete, this thing is way more advanced than anything Phil or I know about or ever imagined. It's incredibly intelligent and so lifelike I almost think it could get married without the wife ever realizing it wasn't human. We just hope it's the product of a friendly nation. I shudder to think of the possibility that it might have been built by the Chinese or Russians."

"David and Tiera's account of how they discovered the android seemed straight-forward and truthful but the timing of his appearance at the Aquilina estate just prior to the assassination of the ECB president did make us wonder. The cottage has a sophisticated security system with multiple cameras and high-definition digital recording capability. As far as we could tell by looking at the backup files, the android never left the cottage after they activated it. We asked a lot of questions but finally decided it

was unlikely that the android was involved in the assassination. With the obvious national security issues, we decided not to disclose the android to the Malta Police officer in charge of the murder investigation."

"The Brits are going to give the android a thorough exam and then brief Mrs. Moore and Sir Lionel Smythe day after tomorrow. I've been asked to see if you and Roger could fly over for the out-briefing starting at 0800 London time. The briefings will run pretty much all day in the executive conference room on the 7th floor of MI6 headquarters. Phil will have passes at the front desk for you and an escort waiting to bring you up."

"I'll talk to Roger as soon as we hang up but I don't think there's any doubt we'll be there," Nocona said. "I'll call you back if there's a snag. Otherwise, we'll see you in London."

Wednesday, May 28

Andrews AFB, Maryland
12:15 AM

Pete Nocona stood aside so his boss could board first. He knew from talking to the pilot that the CIA's Gulfstream G550 executive jet could cruise at 560 MPH at an altitude of 45,000 feet. It would make the 3,800 mile trip from Andrews Air Force Base outside of Washington, DC to London's Heathrow International Airport in just under seven hours. He and Roger Benson would be the only passengers.

As he stowed his bags, Pete wondered again why Mrs. Moore had asked them to meet with her. Roger Benson was the Deputy Director of the National Clandestine Service of the Central Intelligence Agency. Pete knew that as a Level II Senior Executive Service government official, Roger was technically senior to Mrs. Moore, a Level III official. But, the fact that Mrs. Moore was Chief of Station in London, and that the NSA had won the battle with the CIA for the right to appoint the London Chief of Station, made it a bit unclear as to who was senior. It occurred to him that Mrs. Moore

might want to establish the pecking order before they met with the Brits. She had asked them to meet with her at the U.S. Embassy at 2:00 PM London time so they'd gotten to the Andrews VIP terminal just before midnight. With the four-hour time difference, they should have time to drop their bags off at the Embassy's transient apartments and grab something to eat before their meeting with the NSA/CIA London Chief of Station.

Pete had enormous respect for his boss. Roger was a former Army Major General who had commanded INSCOM, the Army's Intelligence and Security Command at Fort Belvoir, Virginia before his retirement. He was an effective leader with superb qualifications for his job. Pete was absolutely loyal to him and considered him the best boss he'd ever had.

The co-pilot came back to check on them before takeoff. He used the restroom at the back of the cabin and then returned to the cockpit.

As Roger Benson watched Pete get settled in, he thought about the special relationship that had grown up between them. He had hand-picked Pete to be the Section Chief of the Counter Terrorism Center at the CIA's headquarters at Langley, Virginia. It had been one of the best staffing decisions he'd ever made.

In reviewing Pete's personnel file before he offered him the job, he had been intrigued to discover that Pete was a full-blooded Comanche Indian and a direct descendent of Peta Nocona, chief of the Noconi band of Comanches. He was also closely related to Peta Nocona's famous son, Quanah Parker, chief of the Quahadi Comanches.

Pete had the kind of real world experiences that Roger always looked for in his senior officers. He had grown up on a cattle ranch a few miles west of the Fort Sill Army base in Lawton, Oklahoma. As a teenager, he'd done volunteer work at the Comanche Nation headquarters in Lawton. Roger knew that Pete was fiercely proud of his heritage and that he had a reverent respect for his ancestry without buying into the fanciful mysticism that some Native Americans seemed to embrace. He had been a star running back for Oklahoma State University where he'd earned a bachelor's degree in political science and a master's degree in International Studies.

After completing Officer's Candidate School and being commissioned as an Army Second Lieutenant, Pete had requested and been approved for transfer to the Army's Delta Force. He had completed multiple missions to Africa and the Middle East. A Delta Force colonel, who had been a West Point classmate of Roger's, had once told him that Pete Nocona had a reputation of being *someone you don't want to mess with.*

Pete's Delta Force assignments had convinced Roger that he might be well-suited for covert intelligence work with the CIA. While in Delta Force, Pete had worked closely with the Navy's Seal Team Six and the CIA's ultra-secret Special Activities Division on several joint missions. Pete had resigned his Army commission after twelve years of service when Roger had recruited him as a field agent. He'd been transferred to the Counter Terrorism Center at CIA HQ when his cover was blown by Pakistan's ISI in the aftermath of highly publicized civilian fatalities caused by a CIA-operated drone attack.

Roger smiled as he thought of Pete's nickname. His first name was derived from the Greek "Petros," meaning stone. In the Comanche language, his last name meant "one who wanders. Almost inevitably, his Alpha Tau Omega fraternity brothers had nicknamed him *Rolling Stone.* Pete had married late and had a 4 year-old daughter that adored her uncle Roger.

The G550 was wheels-up at 1:00 AM. Ten minutes after they were airborne, Roger drifted off to sleep.

After they'd been in the air for four hours, Roger woke from his nap and went aft to use the restroom. When he sat back down, Pete spoke loudly enough for his boss to hear him over the sound of the engines. "Al and Phil left Malta International Airport a little after 9:00 AM local time so they've been in the air for about an hour now. Al told me he'd transmit a summary report to us as soon as they reached cruising altitude. I'm expecting to receive it any time now."

"I'm sure it will be interesting," Roger Benson said thoughtfully. "What are your early impressions?"

"I've been mulling that over ever since Al called. He was pretty emphatic that the android is so lifelike that it can pass as a human and that it's so smart he thinks it could win a chess game with a

super computer. Even allowing for a bit of hyperbole, it appears that this thing is far more advanced than anything I know of. Is this something the Defense Advanced Research Projects Agency could have created without our knowledge?"

"I doubt it. DARPA has been issuing research and development contracts for advanced military robots for several years. A couple of years ago, I asked the IT folks to set up a filter on the FedBizOps web site to route any robotics-related solicitation abstracts to my in-box. I had them set up other filters to search intelligence reports and newspapers. I haven't seen anything even remotely in this class."

"We all know that military research programs in all of the advanced nations are focused on creating unmanned weapons platforms and autonomous robots that can play a role in combat situations. Maybe there's a black program I haven't heard about but somehow I don't think this thing is ours. I doubt if the Brits would have let Al join their party if the android was theirs. My guess is that they want to know whose it is too," Benson told him.

"Could the Israelis build something this advanced?"

"Maybe. With a small population surrounded by several hundred million of their enemies they certainly have the motivation. They might even have the technology though I doubt that too. However, if they do, I would not assume that they'd be eager to tell us about it. The relationship between our countries has been rather frosty under the current administration. The Israelis have always been able to keep a secret better than anyone. It's essential to their survival. Even if our current administration was friendlier toward them, they still might not tell us."

"Who else could it be, then?"

"Pete, I don't know. I've spent my entire adult life in the intelligence business. Even with the rampant theft of our military secrets by the Chinese and Russians, I don't think they could pull it off. Germany and France don't spend enough on military readiness and certainly not on military research. I just don't think the android could be theirs. Japan has made some remarkable progress in the robotics field over the past several years but, so far as I know, they aren't at this level yet either. It's inconceivable to me that any of the

Islamic countries could get even half-way to first base on such a project. I just don't know."

The secure fax began chirping at the back of the cabin. Pete scanned each page as it finished printing and then took the report to his boss.

"Here's Al's report. Although it provides additional details of how and where the android was found, and how it was reactivated, it doesn't tell us what we really need to know." He started to hand the report to his boss before realizing the older man had again drifted off to sleep.

Even with the early start, Pete didn't feel like taking a nap. He set up his laptop and logged onto the aircraft's wireless network that was connected to CIA headquarters via an encrypted satellite link. The android would have to wait until the Brits finished their examination and provided their briefing. But he had plenty of other work to do and almost three hours before they'd land at Heathrow.

Venice, Italy
5:30 AM

At 5:30 AM, Abramo Sartori eased the big Ferretti yacht away from the pier and swung it around to head out of the protected moorage basin owned by the nearby Marina Alberoni. Italian Customs and Immigration officers had signed off on their departure the previous evening so they could get an early start.

It was 325 nautical miles to Bari. The yacht's rated cruising speed was 27 knots. Abramo knew he'd have to push that to 28 knots once they were clear of the channel so they could arrive before 6:00 PM. The winds were light and he expected the seas to be flat, so the ride should be smooth enough even at 28 knots. Once they cleared the channel between Lido and Pellestrina islands and left the Venetian Lagoon, they would be in the Adriatic Sea and he would set a southeasterly course.

Hakeem Ghanem's nephews were aboard and seemed excited at the prospect of their voyage to Alexandria. Abramo had been surprised when Hakeem Ghanem had asked him to stop in Bari to take on two young women he'd hired as companions for his nephews

on the trip. Abramo was uncomfortable about the request but felt he could not say no to his client. He hoped his suspicions were unfounded or he'd have a very angry wife to deal with.

Aquilina Estate
8:00 AM

Phil Shaw had a lot on his mind and hadn't slept well. He'd been up since 4:30 AM going over his notes. He was tired but several cups of coffee had helped. He and Al got to the Aquilina estate at 8:00 AM sharp. Tiera, David, and Nahbi were waiting for them in front of the house. It was only a few miles to the small aircraft terminal at Malta International Airport. The van did not stop at the passenger terminal but was waved through a security gate onto the flight line. The van parked beside a very sleek executive jet. At 9:05 AM, they boarded the eight-passenger Cessna Citation that MI6 Headquarters had sent to pick them up. They were airborne at 9:20 AM on their way to London's Heathrow International Airport.

Twenty minutes after takeoff, the co-pilot spoke to them over the cabin intercom to tell them the aircraft had leveled off at 45,000 feet and that they were flying at 600 miles per hour. He told them flying time would be two hours and thirty-five minutes with touchdown at Heathrow estimated at 11:55 AM.

The Citation's seats were arranged in two groups of four with two seats facing forward and two facing aft in each group. After the co-pilot finished his information briefing, Phil sat down in the seat beside David across from Tiera and Nahbi. Al Flores was talking on the phone and working at a laptop computer in the adjacent set of seats.

"Let me brief you on what to expect once we reach London," Phil told them. "When we land, we'll be met by an MI6 van and driven to a secure residence in central London near MI6 headquarters. It's normally about an hour's drive from the airport to the residence at that time of day. We'll give you an hour to freshen up and get settled into your rooms. I've asked for some sandwiches and fruit to be brought to your rooms because we will be running on a very tight schedule the rest of the day and on into the night."

"At 2:00 PM, a van will pick us up by the elevator in the basement garage and take us to MI6 headquarters. You'll immediately be taken to interrogation rooms where you will be questioned by one or two professional interrogators at a time."

"Everything will be videotaped. Other MI6 people will be able to watch you being questioned through one-way glass panels. Don't let it bother you. Our purpose is to gain the best possible understanding of Nahbi's technology and his origin."

"Nahbi, in your case, you will be with the same two people the entire time although others will be involved at various stages. Gordon McFarland is the top advanced technologies specialist in the United Kingdom. He's a genuinely nice man with a remarkable grasp of virtually all aspects of science. His nickname is Merlin after the wizard in the legends of King Arthur. He will be assisted by a top computer specialist named Richard Scott."

"Sometime in late afternoon, you will be taken to University College Hospital for various tests including magnetic resonance imaging, ultra-sound, and physical measurements including weight and density. After that, Richard and Gordon will take you to a special computer laboratory in the basement of the MI6 building where your computational capabilities and artificial intelligence will be evaluated. I understand that they have some very challenging problems they are anxious to present to you. Late in the evening, some composite materials and optical specialists will spend some time with you followed by some robotic engineers who will evaluate your physical capabilities."

"I must warn all of you that it will be an intense day that may not end until around midnight. You'll be able to take restroom breaks as needed, of course, and food will be provided at 7:30 PM. We'll take you back to the residence when the evaluation teams are finished."

"Tomorrow morning, you can relax in your rooms for a few hours. A technician will bring each of you a special cell phone to use while you're here. It uses encryption technology and has a built-in location beacon. Everyone who is billeted in one of MI6's safe houses gets one. The television sets in your rooms have regular programming, movies on demand, and multiple news and music channels. If you call the kitchen, they'll bring you something to eat

or drink whenever you want. It's OK if you want to be together in one room. That'll be up to you, but you won't be able to leave the building."

"Around 2:30 PM tomorrow afternoon, Al and I will escort you back to the MI6 building. We'll join what will likely be a fairly large group of people in the executive conference room and I expect that you'll be asked a few more questions. If all goes according to plan, you'll be done by 6:00 PM. Beyond that, I haven't got a clue. I think what comes then will depend a lot on what conclusions the executives come to after being fully briefed," Phil concluded.

Janawai, Pakistan
7:00 PM

Seated in his study at his villa in the foothills of the western Himalaya Mountains, Lieutenant General Parvez Jhalawan was flipping between several business news channels. All of them were reporting bad financial news with the breathless angst that only made the panic that millions of people worldwide were feeling worse. The General was very pleased with what he considered a very good beginning.

On the day after the assassination of the ECB president, global stock prices fell sharply. Beginning in the Far East, with the exchanges that opened hours before those in Europe, prices were off by more than 17 percent at the openings and then fell steadily throughout the day. The London FTSE 100 opened 18 percent lower and closed the day 23 percent below the previous day's close. The French CAC 40 closed down 26 percent and the German DAX closed off 20 percent.

In the Western Hemisphere, it was not quite as bad but the S&P 500 closed off 16 percent while the Mexican Bolsa finished the day down 19 percent and the Brazilian Bovespa closed off 23 percent. Overall, it was a very bad day for investors with the global sell-off driving prices down by an average of more than 21 percent.

The last time global stock markets fell so sharply in a single day was the 19th of October in 1987 on 'Black Monday' following a meltdown in Asian markets that spread to Europe and the U.S. as the day wore on. On that dark day, global stock markets fell an

astounding average of 22.6 percent in a single day. By comparison, the Dow Jones Industrial Average had fallen only 7.1 percent on the first day of trading after the September 11 terrorist attacks on the United States.

The stock markets in the United States, Europe, and Japan had been trending higher and setting new records due to massive printing of fiat money by the Federal Reserve Board in the United States and by the Japanese Central Bank following an election won by the candidate for Prime Minister who pledged unlimited stimulus from the Bank of Japan to fight deflation. Many experts believed that stocks were seriously over-bought and that a sharp correction was imminent. The assassination of the ECB president was the catalyst. Stock brokers and investors around the world held their breath to see what the next day would bring.

The next day started off in the Far East with prices gapping up slightly overnight. Europe and the Americas also opened slightly higher. But it did not hold. By the end of the second day following the assassination, stock prices had fallen another 8.6 percent bringing the two-day global losses to almost 30 percent. At the end of 2012, total global capitalization was 54.6 trillion dollars. In only 2 days, over 16 trillion dollars of stock value had been wiped out.

Many investors that had borrowed money to buy stock shares on margin suddenly received notices from their brokers that they would have to immediately add funds to their accounts to cover their margins. Many of them had put all of their money into the stock markets as prices had continued to skyrocket in response to what the American Federal Reserve Board called *Quantitative Easing* and the Japanese more accurately referred to as *unlimited stimulus.* These cash-poor investors did not have sufficient liquid assets to cover their margin calls and had to sell other stocks to generate enough money to satisfy the calls. A massive sell-off of equities took place.

Prices continued to fall in the face of spreading panic and huge numbers of shares being offered. There were few buyers. By the end of the second day, it was not an exaggeration to say that global stock prices had simply collapsed. What that would mean in terms of

future unemployment and social unrest remained to be seen. Jhalawan knew that the worst was yet to come.

U.S. Embassy, London
2:00 PM

The intercom light on her phone was blinking when Evelyn Moore finished touching up her makeup and returned to her desk. She pressed the button and heard her assistant's voice.

"Your guests have arrived."

"Please show them in, Elizabeth."

Evelyn Moore walked toward the door of her spacious office in the U.S. Embassy a few blocks north of Hyde Park to greet her visitors.

"Welcome to London," she said extending her hand to Roger Benson. "How was your flight?"

"Just fine, thank you, Evelyn," Roger Benson replied. "I believe you know Pete."

"Yes. It's good to see you again Pete," Mrs. Moore said as she shook hands with him. "Well, we seem to live in interesting times, do we not? Please take a seat," she said indicating with a sweep of her hand that she wanted them to sit in front of her desk instead of in the comfortable seating area in the corner of her office. Both men recognized her rude and somewhat amateurish attempt to establish herself as the senior player in the meeting. But Roger Benson had played the game before.

Pete knew what she was trying to do. He could hardly suppress a smile when Roger gave her a pained look and put his right hand on his lower back.

"My back is bothering me a bit after the long plane ride. If you don't mind, I'd prefer to sit over here," as he walked over to the upholstered seating that she should have offered them as a matter of simple good manners. Roger stopped in front of the big overstuffed club chair next to the sofa. Although he stood courteously waiting for her to be seated, he left her no place to sit but on the sofa next to Pete. Pete saw the flush of anger in her face but she said nothing and sat down at the end of the sofa next to Roger's chosen chair.

Evelyn Moore made a few weak attempts to regain the upper hand but she was simply outclassed. Pete watched as his boss handled Mrs. Moore without breaking a sweat. Roger Benson had been dealing with pompous career officers most of his life and obviously knew how to handle them.

"Well Evelyn, I understand that NSA doesn't know what to make of this android."

Pete noted with admiration that Roger had not ended his sentence with the word *either* which the context almost begged. He understood what his boss was doing. By framing the question as he had, he'd planted a seed in Evelyn Moore's mind that the CIA might know more than NSA did.

"I've got the folks at Fort Meade working on it," Evelyn Moore said with another pompous effort to make herself appear important. Pete knew that the Director of the National Security Agency was an active duty Lieutenant General and that Mrs. Moore's position was several rungs down the NSA ladder. She might *ask* for help but she certainly didn't have the authority to order it.

"Well now, that's encouraging," Roger said while his tone made it clear that he didn't really think so. "I understand that Pete and I were invited to attend the briefing by Sir Lionel Smythe. Is there some reason why Sir Lionel didn't extend the invitation through your office since you are the London Chief of Station?" Roger said with a bland, innocent look on his face. Pete almost choked. He knew that his boss was very much aware that Sir Lionel had little use for Mrs. Moore.

Pete sensed that Mrs. Moore was furious at the question and decided to risk irritating his boss by trying to cool things down a bit. "I sort of assumed it was because the CIA was already involved since Al Flores was working with Phil Shaw when the android matter came to light," Pete offered. "Perhaps it didn't occur to Sir Lionel that it might have been more appropriate for him to request our attendance through Mrs. Moore. He's been around since the old days when the CIA always appointed the London Chief of Station. My guess is that he just followed old habits without thinking much about it."

The meeting ended twenty minutes later. It really hadn't been needed. They simply did not know enough until after the briefing at MI6 headquarters the next day. It was obvious to Pete that Mrs. Moore had called the meeting in a clumsy and egotistical effort to establish herself as the senior U.S. representative at the MI6 briefing. She had tried to subordinate Roger Benson to herself and had utterly failed.

Wah, Pakistan
9:20 PM

A specially-modified Mercedes UR-416M armored personnel carrier left the weapons cantonment at Wah, Pakistan a few minutes late. Ibrahim Hasni, a Lance Corporal in the Pakistan Armed Forces, was driving. Sergeant Mohammed Ansari was in the passenger's seat beside him.

Sergeant Ansari didn't think they would run into much traffic on the outskirts of Islamabad at this hour. He could tell that Corporal Hasni was nervous too. What they were doing could get them both shot by a firing squad. Even so, the risk seemed worth taking. They would make more money on this one night than either of them earned in a year from their soldier's pay.

Ansari felt lucky to have been assigned to the security force at the Wah weapons facility where most of Pakistan's nuclear weapons were assembled. The facility was located 20 miles west-northwest of the Islamabad Capital District. Both nuclear and conventional weapons were stored there. His job wasn't difficult but he was always looking for ways to make some extra money. When Dr. Ghilzai had asked him to help steal the nuclear artillery shells, he had readily agreed. Ghilzai had told him it was a two-man job so he should pick a driver he could trust. He had immediately thought of Ibrahim Hasni.

Ansari knew that Hasni came from a very poor family and that several of his relatives had been killed by CIA drone attacks along the Pakistan-Afghanistan border. Ibrahim was a simple man who believed most of the radical Islamist propaganda. When Ansari had told him how much he would make for one night's work, he had instantly said yes.

Sergeant Ansari had prepared the paperwork just as Dr. Ghilzai had instructed. It showed that the Mercedes APC was transporting ten 8-inch shells to an artillery battery stationed east of Bhara Kahu. Five of the shells strapped securely into cradles in the back of the UR-416M were conventional high-explosive ordnance. The other five were tactical nuclear weapons. The weapons transfer forms that would later be signed by the battery commander to signify receipt and custody transfer showed only ten conventional shells.

"How far to where we make the swap?" Hasni asked.

"About 10 miles. We should be there in twenty minutes. It's close to the cantonment so we won't have the nuclear shells with us any longer than necessary just in case we are stopped. I'll show you where to pull off the road into a construction site near Margalla Pass. We will transfer the shells into an SUV that will be waiting for us there. We'll replace them with five conventional shells from the SUV. The SUV driver will be alone so you will have to help him transfer the shells while I keep watch. Each shell weighs about 90 kilograms so it will take both of you.

"After we make the swap, we'll just continue on to Bhara Kahu and deliver the other shells?" Hasni asked showing just how nervous he was.

"Yes, you know that already. Calm down. This will be the easiest money you've ever made. Before you know it, you'll be a married man."

A few minutes later, they turned into the construction site and saw headlights flash on and off briefly. As Corporal Hasni backed the Mercedes APC up behind the other vehicle, a man opened the SUV's tailgate door and spread a tarp out close by. He waited for them to get out of the APC.

"Assalalm alaikum," said Ansari using a regional variation of the customary Pakistani greeting.

"Waalaikum assalaam," the man responded without offering to shake hands and immediately turning to the business at hand. "The two of you will unload the special shells from the APC first. You can lay them on the tarp. Then, I want you to transfer the conventional shells from the SUV to the APC before you load the special shells

into the wooden cradles in the back of the SUV. I would like to be finished and away from here in twenty minutes or less so please get started at once."

Mohammed Ansari was irritated that he, a senior sergeant, was being ordered to perform manual labor in front of a junior enlisted man. But, there was no mistaking the ring of authority in the voice of the man standing before him so he did as he'd been directed. The shells were heavy but easily managed by two men. The transfer was completed in almost precisely twenty minutes, just as the SUV driver had expected.

The SUV driver closed the tailgate and nodded to Ansari. Without speaking, he got into the SUV and drove away into the night.

"Khoodha haafis! Goodbye to you as well you rude piece of camel dung," thought Mohammed Ansari to himself. "Let's get moving," he said brusquely to Corporal Hasni. "If we're lucky, we can make the delivery early and stop in Bhara Kahu for breakfast before we head back to Wah."

Bari, Italy
5:38 PM

Abramo Sartori maneuvered the Ferretti 690 alongside the fuel pier in the port of Bari on the southeast coast of Italy. Franco and Fredo Rinaldi stepped onto the pier and tied the boat up.

"This will take a while," Abramo told his wife. "We need to take on quite a bit of fuel after our long trip today. When we're finished refueling, we'll move the yacht to the marina moorage so the young men can go ashore."

"Who are these young women that your client has hired as companions for his nephews?" Donatella asked her husband.

"I do not know," he replied. "We'll just have to wait to see."

The Rinaldi brothers left the yacht at 6:25 PM without saying when they'd be back. They stopped at a mobile phone shop where Franco paid cash for an inexpensive international cell phone and an untraceable pre-paid GSM SIM card.

At exactly 7:00 PM, Teresa Giachetti answered her cell phone. There was no caller ID displayed but she was pretty sure who it was.

"Buonasera. Who is calling please?"

"Signorina Giachetti, my name is Franco Rinaldi. Hakeem Ghanem is my uncle. He gave me your phone number and asked me to call you."

"Yes. I was expecting your call. Where are you now?"

"My brother and I are near the Palace Hotel."

"My friend Lia Pedrazzini and I will meet you in the hotel bar at 9:00 PM. Tell me how you're dressed so I can recognize you."

At 8:45 PM, the Rinaldi brothers finished an excellent dinner in the Murat Restaurant on the seventh floor of the Palace Hotel. The old hotel was located in the center of town less than a half-mile from the marina and had been a popular tourist destination for over 70 years. The view of the old city was one of the best in Bari. Franco paid cash for their meal before they moved to the hotel's bar.

The brothers seated themselves in two upholstered chairs facing a sofa about 20 feet from the bar. Franco asked the waitress to bring them tall glasses of carbonated water over crushed ice with slices of pineapple and lime. She gave him a questioning glance but nodded and went to the bar to place their order.

At three minutes after nine o'clock, two attractive young women entered the bar and immediately walked toward them.

"Franco my dear friend, how are you?" Teresa Giachetti said somewhat loudly as she kissed him on both cheeks. This is my friend Lia. I was glad to hear from you. And this is your brother Fredo?"

"Yes," Franco replied as Teresa shook hands with Fredo and he and Fredo shook hands with Lia.

Franco motioned to the waitress. Teresa ordered a Vodka Cranberry cocktail. Lia asked for a glass of white wine.

"Well, it's good to see you again. How have you been?" Teresa said loudly enough to be sure the bartender could hear what she said. She often met clients in the bar but was always careful to leave the impression that she was just a local college girl who enjoyed people. Some of the bartenders probably suspected that she was a firefly but she always tipped generously and kept her business dealings very confidential.

They sipped their drinks and made small talk for thirty minutes until Teresa announced that she and Lia needed to go. They all stood up and the women kissed the men on their cheeks and left the bar.

A few minutes later, the Rinaldi brothers paid their bar tab with cash and left the hotel as Teresa had instructed. As soon as they stepped onto the sidewalk in front of the hotel, the back door of a limousine parked nearby opened. Teresa stepped out of the back door and motioned them to come. Franco got into the back seat between the two women. Fredo took the passenger seat beside the driver. Franco asked the driver to raise the glass partition.

"I believe you have something for us," Teresa said to Franco.

"Yes," he said as he handed each of the women a fat envelope.

They opened their envelopes and counted the money inside. As they'd been promised, each envelope contained fifty 100-euro bills.

When both women looked up from counting the money, Franco wanted to be sure they understood the arrangement. "As you were told, you will receive another 5,000 euros when we reach Alexandria. If we are pleased with your services, you will also receive a 2,000 euro bonus over and above what you were promised."

"May I ask what *services* you have in mind? Lia and I are both fireflies. We make our living providing sexual pleasures for our clients. But you need to understand that we won't do anything illegal or that causes pain. We also won't do kinky or perverted things and we're both firmly heterosexual only. Do you understand? Are these rules acceptable to you both?" Teresa was a firefly only as a means to an end. She knew that some men considered prostitutes easy prey for their perversions and cruelty so she always made sure her rules were understood up front. If she had any doubt about a client, she simply walked away.

Franco stared at her for a long moment before he said, "I'm afraid there's been a misunderstanding. When my uncle made the arrangements with you, didn't he clarify that we do not expect to have sex with you?" Franco asked. "We are Muslims."

Teresa was caught off-guard by this surprising turn of events. When she'd agreed to the engagement, she'd thought that she and Lia would be taking care of the sexual appetites of a couple of

wealthy young men on a short cruise on a luxury yacht. Now, this handsome young man was telling her that there would be no sex involved. She found that hard to believe.

"*Excuse me.* Are you telling me that your uncle is willing to pay us 10,000 euros each simply to provide companionship for you and your brother on a five-day cruise?"

"Yes," Franco answered simply. "Adultery and fornication are prohibited by the Koran."

"Absolutely, totally unbelievable," Teresa said as she leaned forward so she could see Lia's face.

Lia was smiling. Teresa knew she'd felt guilty about leaving her husband alone with their three-year-old daughter for five days but they had agreed that the money was too good to pass up. Lia's husband had lost his job two years earlier and she'd become a firefly to pay their bills. Lia had told Teresa that her husband was tormented by mental images of what she did with her customers. Teresa suddenly realized that Lia was smiling because her husband would be happy to find out she'd been paid so much money without having to have sex with anyone.

But Teresa was suspicious. She thought there had to be more to it than Franco was telling them. The money was too good. Any nice girl would have been glad to earn even half that amount if all they had to do was be a pleasant companion on a luxury yacht for a few days.

Teresa asked herself why Franco's uncle had hired fireflies if no sex would be involved. Why hadn't female companions been hired in Venice instead of in Bari? The only thing that made sense to her was that perhaps their uncle was one of those men who believed it was good for young men to experience sex before marriage and that he had been considerate of Signor Sartori and his wife by not hiring lucciolis who lived and worked near the Sartori home and business. As she mulled it over in her mind, she became convinced that the uncle fully expected his nephews to have sex with them during the cruise. With that conclusion, she decided it would be OK. After all, that was how she and Lia made a living.

Teresa turned so she could look Franco straight in the face. “OK. No sex, if you’re sure that’s the way you want it.”

A few minutes later, the limousine parked on the pier near the yacht. Teresa gave a low whistle of appreciation as she realized that they would be spending several days on one of the most beautiful yachts that the Ferretti Company had ever produced. Living in the port city of Bari, where beautiful yachts are common, she’d only seen one other Ferretti 690 and had never been aboard one.

The limousine driver sat the women’s luggage on the pier. Franco paid him in cash and included a generous tip. Franco and Fredo walked toward the yacht but did not offer to take the women’s roll-aboard luggage for them. Teresa looked at Lia, who just shrugged.

Once on board, Franco showed the women to the cabin they would share. It had a queen-size bed and a private bath and toilet area. Teresa could tell that Lia was impressed by the beautiful décor and that she was happy that they wouldn’t be sleeping with the men. This would certainly not be a normal lucciole experience. Franco explained that he and Fredo did not want to share a bed so they would sleep in a smaller crew cabin aft that had two twin beds.

Franco introduced Teresa and Lia to Signor and Signora Sartori. Donatella Sartori looked at the young women suspiciously but greeted them in a friendly enough manner.

After the introductions were over, Abramo asked for their attention.

“We’ll be leaving Bari at 6:00 AM tomorrow morning so I think everyone should get to bed. I’d like to be through the Strait of Otranto and out of Italian waters by noon if possible. The yacht can easily maintain a 24 knot pace so we should enter the Ionian Sea shortly after noon. I expect that we’ll reach our next refueling stop at Poros Harbor in Lixouri on the Greek island of Kefallania before dark. There is no fuel pier in Poros harbor so I’ve arranged for a tanker truck to meet us on the quay at 6:00 PM.”

“Lia and Teresa, welcome. I hope you enjoy our trip to Alexandria. Franco and Fredo, I want to thank you both for taking the helm several times today when I needed to use the restroom. It

was a long day for me. Tomorrow, on the way to Lixouri, I'll give you some instruction on how to handle the yacht."

Islamabad, Pakistan
12:18 AM

After his rendezvous with the soldiers, Yousef Abu Shakra had driven the SUV to a coin-operated car wash where he'd taken his time giving the vehicle a thorough cleaning while watching carefully to ensure that he was not being followed. From there, he'd driven a circuitous route around the northern part of the Capital District until he was certain that he was not being tailed. Just before midnight, he backed the SUV into the double garage of the villa occupied by the Egyptian Ambassador to Pakistan and hit the button on the sun visor to close the garage door.

Ambassador Al-Zeid had been waiting for him and came immediately into the garage followed by Dr. Bashir Ghilzai and a young nuclear engineer named Tariq Zardari. Yousef knew that the engineer was one of Dr. Ghilzai's protégés.

"All went as planned?" Hassan Al-Zeid asked his driver.

"Yes sir," Abu Shakra replied. The devices are in the back of the SUV ready for Dr. Ghilzai.

"Very good, Yousef," the Ambassador said. "You have had a busy day." The Ambassador turned and went back into the house to get some sleep. He had provided his schedule to Yousef the previous day. He and his wife would be leaving Islamabad International Airport at 4:15 PM on Qatar Airways flight 615. They would spend a week at the Ritz Carlton Sharq Village and Spa in Doha, Qatar. They would land in Cairo around 5:00 PM on Friday, June 6th and would spend the weekend with old friends. The Ambassador would meet with the Egyptian President at 10:00 AM on Monday, June 9th before continuing on to his home in Alexandria later that day. Yousef would be there when the Ambassador and his wife arrived.

Yousef helped Zardari unload the shells. They placed them in a special cradle on top of a sturdy metal table at the front of the garage. A wire ran from the table to the grounding bus inside the circuit breaker panel on the outside wall of the garage. The tips of

the shells were pointed toward the wall with the bases facing outward so they were accessible. Fluorescent lights above the table provided ample light for the scientist and engineer to work. Four specially-modified steel scuba tanks were in the corner. A fifth tank was also a modified scuba tank but was painted Green and fitted with a bulbous cap to resemble a medium-size industrial oxygen tank.

Over the next two hours, Yousef watched as Dr. Ghilzai and the engineer removed the nuclear cores from the 8-inch diameter artillery shells and placed them inside the tanks that had precisely the same external diameter. The scuba tanks and the fake oxygen tank had been modified to be slightly longer than a standard tank in order to accommodate the nuclear assemblies. However, the difference was so slight as to be unnoticeable.

The base of each of the scuba tanks had a black rubber boot that was identical to those used on most steel scuba tanks to protect boat decks and floors when the tanks were handled. A few inches below their tops, the tanks had been cut open on a precision lathe and modified to create finely-threaded, removable tops. The fake oxygen tank had also been modified to provide a threaded top cap. Any of the tanks would pass a casual inspection.

Yousef knew that the tanks were only intended to provide realistic transport containers that could be stored in plain sight without drawing suspicion. The nuclear cores would later be transferred into other containers that would be fitted with radio-controlled triggering devices.

By 3:00 AM the five specially-modified tanks had been loaded into the trunk of the Ambassador's limousine and braced to keep them from rolling around.

Thursday, May 29

MI6 Headquarters, London
8:00 AM

Phil Shaw looked around the room. Every seat in the executive conference room was taken. At precisely 8:00 AM, Sir Lionel Smythe called the meeting to order.

"Good morning. I've asked Gordon McFarland to provide an introduction to what you will be told over the next several hours. Gordon is the Advanced Technologies Scientist for MI6. He holds a Master of Science degree in Electrical and Electronic Engineering and a Master of Science degree in Optics and Photonics, both from the Imperial College of London. Gordon also did classified optics research work at the Massachusetts Institute of Technology in the U.S. for two years on a joint UK/US military research grant to develop high-resolution satellite camera systems. He has worked for MI6 for over 30 years."

Gordon stepped to the lectern to set the theme of the briefings that would follow.

"Over the next several hours, you are going to hear experts describe the characteristics of the android known as Nahbi. Before the presentations begin, I wanted to tell you that Nahbi is constructed entirely of carbon. In fact, he is constructed from a very special type of carbon known as graphene. Like diamonds, Graphene is an allotrope of carbon. Although the atomic structure of what we now call graphene was first revealed by X-ray crystallography in the first two decades of the twentieth century, the name *graphene* first appeared in scientific literature in 1987. In 2010, Andre Geim and Kostya Novoselov at the University of Manchester received the Nobel Prize for their pioneering work with graphene."

"Today, scientists all over the world are engaged in graphene research that many people believe will bring sweeping changes to nearly every area of applied technology."

"I want to emphasize that the technologies incorporated into Nahbi's design and construction are far more advanced than anything available today. Scientists are in the early stages of

research into virtually every aspect of the various technologies that were used to create Nahbi. Within 20 to 30 years, we may be able to replicate some, but probably not all, of the technologies used to construct Nahbi. In simple terms, scientists are hot on the trail but still far from the finish line."

The first speaker addressed Nahbi's story that he had been present in Jerusalem almost two thousand years earlier and that the ship he had been on had sunk near the island of Malta. Dr. Albert Carlson told the audience that the team of interrogators had unanimously agreed that the android's story could not possibly be true even though the android appeared to believe it was. Dr. Carlson concluded by admitting that the team could not prove that Nahbi's story wasn't true.

Doctor George Thomas from the University College Hospital in London presented a series of slides showing MRI and ultrasound images as he provided a detailed narrative describing Nahbi's carbon-fiber skeletal structure that was stronger than steel but significantly lighter. Dr. Thomas said that Nahbi weighed 82 kilograms and was 183 centimeters tall.

Dr. Thomas described Nahbi's amazingly realistic artificial skin and hair. He cited research work done at Duke University in 2012 indicating that graphene composites could be used to make artificial skin and muscles. He also cited a 2012 University of Manchester study that showed that graphene can self-repair holes in graphene sheets such as those used to create the android's skin. He told the audience that the Chinese Academy of Sciences had determined that sheets of graphene oxide are highly effective in killing bacteria. He said the team that examined the android had verified that his synthetic skin had that capability. The team had theorized that was why no marine organisms had attached themselves to the android during the time he was immersed in sea water. He concluded by saying that the properties of graphene allowed Nahbi to change the color of his skin and eyes at will.

Sir Lionel called a fifteen-minute break at 9:30 AM and told the attendees to be back in their seats at 9:45AM.

For the first two hours after the break, several presenters described what had been learned about Nahbi's technology. The audience was fascinated and attentive.

The first presenter after the break was a specialist in advanced composite materials. Dr. Janice Thorp told the audience that no metal components, wires, or fasteners had been used in any part of Nahbi's construction. Every component of the android was made of graphene and carbon compounds. Dr. Thorp concluded her segment by telling the audience that the practical ability to form graphene into flexible sheets, conductors, and other useful components similar to those used in Nahbi's construction was still decades in the future.

Keith Ross, an optics specialist, told the audience that Nahbi's eyes could focus from microscopic to extreme telescopic and had the ability to see wavelengths of light from visible to near-infrared which allowed him to see well in the dark. He noted that an excellent facsimile of a human retinal pattern was incorporated into Nahbi's eyes. He concluded by saying that Nahbi's eyes incorporated mode-locking fiber lasers that gave him the ability to precisely measure distance even in the dark.

Dr. Michael Heath, a specialist in robotic motion and control from the University of Bristol Robotics Laboratory, spoke next. He told the audience that instead of muscles the android had bundles of graphene sheets that had been rolled into tubes. When those graphene bundles were excited by an electrical current they contracted with a force that was proportional to the applied voltage thereby closely mimicking the behavior of human muscles.

Dr. Heath provided a mind-numbing description of the hundreds of small actuator motors embedded in a synthetic carbon-based elastic foam material of various densities designed to simulate human skin, subcutaneous fat, and muscle tissue. Heath's robotic motion team had found that the android could easily lift items weighing more than 225 Kilograms. The team had put the android on a treadmill and found that it could run 52 kilometers per hour which is about 50 percent faster than the fastest humans can run. Dr. Heath concluded by saying that the android's dexterity, mobility,

and strength significantly exceeded what was possible with contemporary robotics technology.

Two computer experts came next. Dr. Judith Wilson, professor of computer science at Cambridge University, began by stating her team's incredible conclusion that the android's computational ability was roughly equivalent to that of the 100-teraflop IBM pSeries supercomputer used by the European Centre for Medium-Range Weather Forecasts. Dr. Wilson concluded her presentation with the stunning statement that Nahbi's computer brain was comparable to the best supercomputers currently available but housed in a module roughly the size of a modern smart phone.

Dr. Daniel Bradford, professor of advanced mathematics at Oxford University, explained a special problem the computational evaluation team had given the android to solve. The problem was known to require the use of quantum computational methods. Dr. Bradford told the audience that by using quantum computing methods the android had repeatedly solved variations of previously unsolvable problems in less than two seconds.

Dr. Linda Allison, a scientist working at the University of Sussex Mathematics and Physical Sciences research center, told the audience that tests showed that the android's memory system used carbon nanotubes as both molecular device elements and as molecular wires in conjunction with billions of layers of single-atom graphene sheets. Dr. Allison told the audience that the volume of the android's entire memory storage module was about 8 cubic centimeters, or somewhat less than one cubic inch. She then stunned the audience when she told them that the android's memory system could probably hold *all recorded human knowledge, in all languages*, with plenty of room to spare.

Although a lot of the technical information was incomprehensible to most of the audience, everyone was paying close attention as it became increasingly clear that the android's capabilities far exceeded anything any of them had imagined possible.

Dr. James Fox told the audience that the android's remarkable computational speed would be of little value in the creation of a lifelike humanoid robot without sophisticated artificial intelligence programming. He said that the android's artificial intelligence was

sufficiently advanced to allow the android to interact with humans without being recognized as a machine, the widely-accepted standard first proposed by Dr. Alan Turing in 1950.

Dr. Fox told the audience that the android was sentient and highly intelligent. He said that the android was fully self-aware and exhibited conscious will, certain desires, insight, and many other seemingly human qualities. He said that the android had a distinctive personality comprised of inductive and deductive logical capabilities and a remarkable ability to synthesize what appeared to be genuine emotion. He said that the android clearly understood human values such as integrity and ethical behavior although the team had not been able to determine conclusively whether those were real attributes of his persona or merely affectations that allowed him to interact effectively with humans.

After a short lunch break, an Electrical Engineering professor at the Imperial College of London stepped to the lectern to begin his presentation.

Dr. Rand told the audience that the android's electrical power was generated by a highly efficient proton-conducting fuel cell that used methane gas as its fuel, atmospheric oxygen as its oxidizing agent, and potassium hydroxide as the electrolyte. Although the android's fuel cell system was far more advanced, it was conceptually similar to the fuel cells used in the U.S. space program and aboard the International Space Station.

The primary waste products of the fuel cell's catalytic reaction were carbon dioxide and water. The small amount of heat generated by the fuel cell was captured and recycled to increase the efficiency of the cell to about 85 percent. The methane gas fuel was produced internally by the fermentation of grains, legumes, nuts, and starchy vegetables in a chamber located in approximately the same location as a human stomach.

Dr. Rand explained that the android's fuel cell had no moving parts and no components that would corrode even when immersed in sea water. He said that the rechargeable 90 volt power pack located behind the access panel in the android's lower back, could store enough electrical energy to maintain his electromechanical

systems for two to five days, depending on the amount of physical work required.

Dr. Rand emphasized that the power pack was much more sophisticated than a simple battery because it incorporated graphene-based ultracapacitors. He noted that researchers at the University of California had recently succeeded in creating ultracapacitors using graphene sheets that could be charged and discharged quickly and that had far higher energy storage densities than had previously been achieved. Dr. Rand said that the android's energy storage device used technology that was currently being explored but that was not yet practically attainable outside of a laboratory. He said his team believed that graphene-based ultracapacitors large enough to serve as practical power sources were still ten to twenty years in the future.

Sir Lionel Smythe thanked the presenters and told the attendees to take a 30-minute break. He asked that they submit any questions they had in writing before they left the conference room.

Phil and Al escorted David, Tiera, and Nahbi to the conference room during the break and showed them where to sit. Phil could tell that Tiera was very nervous but David seemed calm.

After the break, more than two hundred written questions were addressed. Most of them were directed at the various presenters but quite a few were directed at Nahbi. No one asked David or Tiera a single question.

At Sir Lionel's suggestion, Nahbi walked around the room to shake hands with every person in the room, speak a few words to them, and to let them look into his eyes as they might a human being they had just met.

The meeting adjourned at 6:05 PM.

Islamabad, Pakistan
11:15 AM

Yousef Abu Shakra had slept only five hours but he was eager to get started. He had planned his route carefully. It was over 2,000 kilometers from Islamabad to the new container ship port at Gwadar on the western side of Pakistan near the border with Iran.

Some of the roads were not very good so he did not expect to average more than 50 or 60 KPH. It would take two days to make the trip. He planned to stop only briefly for fuel and food along the way. He intended to sleep in the car when he needed rest with the vehicle's security system activated and his 9mm Beretta always close at hand.

Once he arrived at Gwadar, he would supervise the loading of the Ambassador's limousine into a shipping container specially-outfitted for transporting cars and would place the Ambassador's locks and diplomatic seals on the doors. Although he knew that the Chinese had recently taken over management and further development of the port from Pakistan, the Ambassador's diplomatic immunity would simplify the process of getting the car cleared for shipment. Yousef had already made the necessary arrangements but had more than 500,000 Pakistan Rupees with him for persuading uncooperative bureaucrats that they needed to be more helpful.

He would ride aboard the container ship to the port city of Suez at the southern entrance to the Suez Canal. He would have the limousine off-loaded there and would wait for another ship to arrive to transfer part of his cargo. He would then drive the limousine to the Ambassador's home in Alexandria and wait for the Ambassador and his wife to arrive.

Yousef was determined to accomplish his part of General Jhalawan's glorious plan or die a martyr's death trying.

Tel Aviv, Israel
2:03 PM

Levi Reznik mentally rehearsed his briefing as he and the Director of the Mossad waited in the entry hallway. He had hoped that he would not live to see a time when the briefing he was about to give became a reality. The Prime Minister had asked them to come to his official residence in Beit Aghion at once when he had learned the reason for their request to see him. He came downstairs immediately when informed of their arrival.

"Shalom," the PM greeted them with a very serious look on his face. Please come into the living room.

As soon as they were seated, the Mossad director motioned for Levi to begin his briefing.

"Mr. Prime Minister," Levi Reznik began, "For the past three years, we have had a paid informer in the office of the senior nuclear scientist at Pakistan's nuclear weapons assembly facility in Wah, about 20 miles west of Islamabad. Recently, that informer advised his Mossad handler that he'd overheard part of a conversation between Dr. Bashir Ghilzai and one of his nuclear engineers concerning tactical nuclear weapons that could be fired from the M110A2 self-propelled howitzers Pakistan bought from the United States. Our informer could not tell from what he heard if Pakistan already had such weapons or was in the process of developing them. He heard Dr. Ghilzai mention technological advances Pakistan had made that would allow such weapons to have significantly higher yields than the ones the Americans had developed."

Reznik continued as the Israeli Prime Minister gave him his fullest attention. "As you know, during the height of the Cold War, the United States developed a tactical nuclear artillery shell they designated as the W33. Those 203 mm shells were designed to be fired from the 8-inch M110A2 howitzers for use in slowing the advance of a major Soviet tank invasion in Western Europe. By using different fissile cores, the yield of those artillery shells ranged from five kilotons to more than eight kilotons for the variant that used boosted fission technology. One variant reportedly had a yield of 40 kilotons. They also produced a neutron bomb variant designated as the W79."

"By comparison, the atomic bomb the Americans dropped over Hiroshima had a yield of fifteen kilotons. The yield of a Trident II thermonuclear warhead is 100 kilotons so the W33 artillery shell was a rather powerful device to be so compact and easily transported. The Americans produced over 2,000 of the W33 shells but then dismantled them and all of their W79 shells in compliance with the strategic arms limitation treaties with the Soviet Union."

"A few days ago, our informer told us that Dr. Ghilzai had met with Ahmed Malik, the head of the super-secret S-Wing of Pakistan's ISI. The informer did not know the purpose of the meeting. We know that Malik works directly for the new head of the

Pakistan Inter-Services Intelligence Agency, Lieutenant General Parvez Jhalawan. Jhalawan is known to favor the use of tactical nuclear weapons to help Pakistan repel an attack by India's much larger Army."

Glancing at the Mossad Director, and taking a deep breath, Reznik told the Prime Minister, "This morning we learned that Pakistan does, unfortunately, possess tactical nuclear artillery shells that can be fired from the M110A2 howitzers. Late last night, five of those nuclear artillery shells were removed from the nuclear storage bunker at the Wah cantonment by two Pakistan Army personnel. One of the soldiers was a sergeant responsible for security in the nuclear bunker area. The shells were transported off of the installation in a specially-modified Mercedes armored personnel carrier."

"Our informer overheard Dr. Ghilzai talking on the phone shortly after 8:00 AM in Pakistan this morning telling someone, possibly Ahmed Malik, that the shells had been delivered. We do not know where. Given Dr. Ghilzai's record of selling nuclear technology to rogue nations, and Ahmed Malik's record of support for the Taliban and Osama bin Laden, we must assume that the devices may now be in the possession of terrorists. We are using all of our resources in an effort to find out where the weapons are now," Levi said.

The Prime Minister's look was very grave as he considered what he'd just been told. With his head bowed, he spoke in a low voice, "So, these are the suitcase-size nuclear weapons that we've long feared would one day be used against us by the Islamic terrorists." Looking up, he said, "These five weapons could utterly destroy Tel Aviv and kill perhaps half of all of our people. I think we can assume that the Islamists would not use them against Jerusalem because of the Muslim Mosque Dome of the Rock and their conviction that Jerusalem must become the capital of a new Palestinian State. That suggests that their target will be Tel Aviv. Have you spoken to the CIA or MI6 to see if they can add to what we know?"

"No sir," Levi responded. "We thought that you would want to speak to the U.K. Prime Minister and the U.S. President before we discussed this very sensitive information with MI6 and the CIA."

"Yes, you are right. I will call them both immediately. Give me one hour and you may then open your lines of communication with MI6 and the CIA," the Prime Minister told them as he stood up.

Looking intently into the eyes of the Mossad Director, the Israeli leader said softly, "Find those weapons."

Marchabad, Pakistan
11:06 PM

Mohammed Ansari and Ibrahim Hasni were sitting in a car near a pile of logs on the south side of the Khanpur Texila Road 200 meters past the turnoff for the village of Marchabad.

At 11:06 PM an SUV pulled up behind them and turned off its lights. A man got out and walked toward their car. Mohammed and Ibrahim got out and waited for him.

Ahmed Malik greeted them in a low voice and asked them to walk with him into the woods so they would not be observed. He saw how eager they were but felt no empathy for them. He handed each of them a small LED flashlight and used his own flashlight to indicate a pathway that led away from the road and into the trees. Mohammed went first and Ibrahim followed him.

Fifty meters into the woods, Malik stopped and said, "This is far enough."

"How did the transfer go?"

"No problems at all," Ansari told him.

"Did anyone see you?"

"No."

Malik nodded and seemed satisfied.

"Good! Here is your money," he said as he handed both men an envelope. "Count it. I think you will be surprised."

Mohammed and Ibrahim held their flashlights awkwardly as they removed the money from their envelopes. They never got a chance to count it. While their attention was on the money, Malik shot them both in the head using a silenced 9mm pistol. Both men fell dead. Malik shot each of them again to be sure they would not live to tell

any tales. He picked up the money and then walked back to his car and drove away.

Friday, May 30

Lixouri, Greece
6:00 AM

Abramo Sartori had arranged for the yacht to take on 600 liters of fresh water and almost 3,000 liters of marine diesel fuel the previous evening. The voyage was going smoothly and he was pleased. At 6:00 AM, he backed the yacht away from the pier and headed for open water. The next stop would be at Chania Marina on the Island of Crete, 260 nautical miles away.

MI6 Headquarters, London
9:00 AM

The executive conference room was again full. Sir Lionel called the meeting to order at 9:00 AM.

"Yesterday's briefings made it clear to us all that the android was constructed using technologies that are so advanced that it will be decades before they can be duplicated. We now have at least a rudimentary understanding of its incredible capabilities. Unfortunately, we still do not know the android's origin, its intended purpose, or what the geo-political implications of its existence will prove to be."

"We will spend most of today addressing those unanswered questions. Gordon McFarland will wrap things up just before we adjourn at 3:00 PM.

Ionian Sea
1:10 PM

It was only the middle of the second day after leaving Bari but Teresa was bored.

Abramo had given Franco and Fredo several hours of instruction after breakfast so they could help him drive the boat. Teresa thought

Abramo must be exhausted after two long days of conning the yacht alone. She would have liked for him to teach her how to handle the yacht too but he had not offered.

Signora Sartori had fixed lunch at 11:30 AM when they'd been 14 miles due west of Cape Tenaro on the southern end of the Peloponnesian Peninsula. There was weak but adequate cell phone signal strength so Lia had called her husband after lunch and then gone to their cabin to take a nap.

Signora Sartori had been stiffly polite but had shown no interest in getting to know them. Teresa and Lia had heard Donatella complaining loudly to her husband about having two Italian whores on board as they were getting ready for bed the previous evening. The yacht's berthing area was beautifully decorated but even normal conversation could be heard from one cabin to the next and Signora Sartori had been speaking quite loudly. They had heard every word. It had made Lia cry to hear a nice lady like Donatella Sartori call her a whore. Seeing Lia cry had made Teresa angry but there was little she could do about it.

Outwardly, Franco Rinaldi had paid scant attention to them though Teresa had caught him looking at her when he didn't think she'd notice. She'd had to suppress a smile more than once when Franco had unconsciously stared at her breasts without ever making eye contact while speaking to her. Yet, she would have been surprised if the brothers *hadn't* shown interest in her despite their declaration of Muslim chastity.

Abramo and Donatella had gone below to rest. She hadn't seen Fredo since lunch so he was probably in the cabin he shared with Franco. Donatella had left several fashion magazines lying on the sofa. Teresa flipped through them idly but paused a few seconds here and there to critically appraise the overall look achieved by some of the more attractive models. She knew that those beautiful fashion models set the standard that most men would judge her looks by.

Sitting alone in the main cabin, Teresa thought about her family. She had five brothers and four sisters. Her family had always been very poor. She had desperately wanted to go to college to escape the depressing poverty but good-paying jobs were virtually non-existent

for a young woman in southern Italy. Being a firefly was simply a means to an end for her. It paid her living expenses and made it possible for her to go to college. She enjoyed doing nude modeling and it generated a little extra money. Being attractive was essential to both occupations.

As she glanced through the magazines looking for ideas, she was quite aware that she managed her own looks and wardrobe every bit as diligently as any top fashion model. She knew that most men found her attractive and she worked hard to maintain her looks. She exercised regularly and watched her diet. It was a matter of personal pride that she never dressed trashy as most fireflies did. She bought nice clothes in upscale stores that she knew would appeal to her affluent male customers. She liked to wear pretty blouses and soft knit casual shirts that showed her ample cleavage. Sometimes, she went braless just for the fun of watching men stare at her breasts and her large and rather prominent nipples. She never wore the extremely short hot pants favored by many of the fireflies who worked on the streets. She preferred well-tailored slacks and shorts that flattered her athletic figure and nicely-rounded derrière.

Teresa knew that her living depended on her ability to please men. She could read the hunger in their eyes when they looked at her. Every shopkeeper knows how to display their wares to attract customers. Teresa knew too. She could tell that Franco wanted her and she thought it strange that he had not yet taken advantage of her pre-paid availability.

Franco was driving the yacht from topside. Teresa wanted to ask him something so she climbed the ladder to the flying bridge. Franco turned his head and nodded to her as she stepped from the ladder to the upper deck. She stood beside him for a minute or two enjoying the warm sunny day and the beautiful view.

“Franco, can I ask you a favor?”

Franco turned to look at her, “What kind of favor?”

“Lia and I would like to sunbath up here. The big padded area just in front of the flying bridge steering console was obviously designed as a private area to sunbathe and we’d like your permission to use it sometimes. Because we are fireflies we prefer not to have

tan lines so we'd like to be able to sunbathe nude. I can understand that you and your brother might not want us to do that where you would see us. I wondered if we could use the area up here this afternoon while you steered the yacht from the console in the main cabin. Signor and Signora Sartori are sleeping. What do you say?" Teresa asked.

Franco didn't just say no immediately as she'd thought he might. He was silent for a few moments as he considered her request. "I guess that would be OK," he said slowly. "How long?"

"Maybe an hour," Teresa answered. "If you don't mind, we'd like to be able to sunbath twice a day, once in the morning and once in the afternoon."

Franco considered this and then told Teresa, "I'll tell Signor Sartori that I've said it was OK. Since my uncle owns the yacht, Abramo will accept my decision. Signora Sartori is unlikely to climb the ladder to the flying bridge so your sunbathing should not offend her, at least no more than she already seems to be offended," Franco said as he smiled in a friendly way.

Teresa was a little surprised. It was the first time he had shown her any small kindness. "Oh, thank you!" exclaimed Teresa. Without thinking, and before Franco realized what she was doing, she leaned over and gave him a quick kiss on his left cheek. "Thank you so very much," she said cheerfully with smile and a quick squeeze of his arm before she turned away to go tell Lia. She did not see the haunted look on Franco's face as he watched her leaving.

Five hours later, the yacht entered Chania Marina on the northwest coast of the Island of Crete and went straight to the fuel pier. After the yacht moved to the overnight berth that Abramo had reserved, the Rinaldi brothers went ashore to explore the old city. They did not invite Teresa or Lia to go with them.

MI6 Headquarters, London
3:00 PM

At 3:00 PM, Gordon McFarland stood at the front of the room and waited for everyone to give him their attention.

"I will address the question of the android's origin first."

"It is the unanimous opinion of the experts who examined the android that it did not come from ancient Jerusalem. The reason given for rejecting the android's story was that it would require some form of time travel or intervention by extraterrestrial or supernatural beings, both of which are soundly rejected as scientific impossibilities."

"The evaluation teams unanimously agreed that no country currently possesses the technological capability to construct an android comparable to Nahbi. Since the teams had already rejected the possibility of time travel and extraterrestrial or supernatural intervention, that leaves no plausible theory for the android's origin."

"The consensus view of the evaluation teams is that the android's purpose is military. The teams believe the android represents some type of extremely advanced military device. They stopped short of characterizing the android as a military weapon. Some suggested that it might have been designed as a super spy or agent provocateur that could be used in very dangerous environments without risking human life."

"Finally, the majority of the team members feel that the android has enormous geo-political ramifications. Militarily, politically, and economically, an android of Nahbi's ability represents a tremendous competitive advantage for the country or countries that either control him or benefit from his loyalty."

With those closing remarks, Gordon yielded the lectern to Sir Lionel.

"I would like to thank each of you for your participation these past two days. Please remember that each of you has signed an official-secrets non-disclosure agreement witnessed by officials of both the U.K. and the U.S. so please do not discuss anything that has been said or done here with anyone else. With that said, our proceedings are now adjourned."

5:06 PM

A few minutes after 5:00 PM, Sir Lionel Smythe, Mrs. Evelyn Moore, and Roger Benson sat down together for an early dinner in a small executive dining room at the top of the MI6 building. Mrs.

Moore was in an irritable mood and not trying very hard to conceal it.

Sir Lionel glanced at Roger Benson and saw him smiling comfortably. His own view of Mrs. Moore was hardly complimentary. He suspected that he and Roger Benson might share similar opinions of her but he also knew that neither of them would ever say so. He turned his attention to the business at hand.

"I have an appointment with the Prime Minister at 8:00 PM at Number 10 and will brief him on what we've learned," Sir Lionel told his American colleagues. "May I suggest that it seems appropriate that your Director of National Intelligence be briefed as soon as possible so he can brief your President? I assume our leaders will want to discuss the matter."

Roger had realized earlier that Mrs. Moore wanted to be the messenger to give her an opportunity to curry favor in high places. He was way ahead of her.

"I anticipated that you would do so and have already set up a conference call for 7:00 PM London time with Evelyn and myself at this end and the Director of National Intelligence, the Director of the National Security Agency, and the Director of the Central Intelligence Agency all on the call from Washington. I think that briefing them all simultaneously is the most expeditious and politically correct way for us to channel the information to the president as quickly as possible. It will only be 2:00 PM in Washington so the Director of National Intelligence will have ample time to brief the President this afternoon."

"By the time you've briefed the Prime Minister, the DNI will have briefed the President. The PM and the President will still have time to confer tonight if they wish." "May I ask that an office or small conference room be available for us as soon as we finish our dinner?"

Sir Lionel could hardly suppress his smile as he realized why Mrs. Moore was out of sorts. Evelyn was miffed because Roger's prompt action had thwarted another of her petty efforts to aggrandize herself. Good for him!

"Yes. Of course," he said. "I'll have someone set up a room with a secure phone line for you."

Washington, D.C.
3:30 PM

The President of the United States was briefed by the DNI at 3:00 PM Washington time. He was irritated that yet another problem had surfaced. His administration was trying to deflect several embarrassing scandals and his personal popularity was plummeting.

The last thing he wanted to do was to call that egotistical Israeli Prime Minister to ask if the Israelis possessed technology that surpassed that of the United States. He despised the man and would not give him the satisfaction of even suspecting that the Americans were afraid that Israel had superior technology they had not revealed to their long-time benefactors and defenders. Instead, he would order the Director of the CIA to make discrete inquiries and report what he learned.

Langley, Virginia
3:45 PM

Albert Warren Oliver, III was getting ready to leave early when his assistant told him that the President was on the line.

"Good afternoon, sir."

"Al, I want you to call the Mossad Director for me. I need to know if the Israelis have developed an advanced humanoid robot. Bury the question in some routine chit chat. I don't want him to realize that this could be a big deal. Do it right away and get back to me."

"Yes sir. I'll do it now."

Oliver immediately called the Director of the Mossad on a secure line without taking time to formulate any strategy. It was 3:45 PM in Washington but already 9:45 PM in Tel Aviv. The duty officer at Mossad headquarters routed the call to the Director's residence.

"Shalom, Ma Shlomcha, Mr. Oliver," the Mossad Director said as he answered the incoming call from the American CIA Director.

"And peace to you as well. I am fine. Thank you for asking," Oliver responded.

"Ma Nishma? What's up?" asked the Israeli spy chief.

"I've been asked to brief the President on the current state-of-the-art in military robotics. I know the Israelis have a very robust R&D program in that area and just wondered if you could bring me up to date on your progress in the development of lifelike humanoid robots that can be used in combat environments."

The Mossad Director despised the American President but he almost pitied the CIA Director who was totally out of his league trying to run one of the world's foremost intelligence agencies. The Mossad Director knew that Oliver's nickname was *AWOL* for absent without leave. He'd been tagged with that nickname by career intelligence officers because he was always off playing golf or jetting around the world on some pretext instead of attending to the CIA's important issues.

The CIA Director's amateurish approach was almost laughable. The Israeli spy master realized instantly that there was more to the inquiry than a simple *state-of-the-art briefing*. Oliver had very specifically asked about *lifelike humanoid robots that could be used in combat environments*. That meant the Americans had reason to believe that someone, possibly the Israelis, had already produced such a device.

"Well, my friend, we are a small nation surrounded by our enemies. So, yes, we have a robust research and development program in the field of military robotics. We have already deployed some unmanned vehicles that can patrol along our borders and report evidence of infiltration. But, those things are big and ugly. They certainly don't bear any resemblance to humans. I've heard that one of the executives at Rafael Advanced Defense Systems recently gave an interview where he predicted that one-third of our military machines will be unmanned within ten to fifteen years. But, so far as I know, Israel does not have any lifelike humanoid robots. I would assume if anyone did, it would be you Americans," the spy master said trying to tease more information from the inept political appointee at the other end of the call.

The CIA Director paused for a moment before he said, "So, would it be accurate for me to tell the President that Israel does not currently possess lifelike humanoid robots?" Oliver's pathetically

naïve question only strengthened the Israeli spy master's conviction that the Americans knew that such a device existed but did not know who had produced it.

"Yes, that would certainly be accurate. I sense that the United States does not currently have such a device either. Am I correct?" the cunning Israeli asked.

"Well no. Not to my knowledge," Oliver answered awkwardly.

"Do you have reason to believe that any other country does? For example the Brits or the Russians or the Chinese?"

Oliver was out of his rather shallow depth and suddenly admitted that someone did. "Well, we have unconfirmed intelligence reports that some nation may have produced such a device. If true, it would be of concern to us, of course," Oliver replied.

The Israeli spy master knew that Oliver had lied about their intelligence being unconfirmed. He smiled to himself as he thought, "Yes! Someone has produced such a device and the Americans don't know who it is. That suggests that they are in possession of the device and that its capabilities exceed what their technology is capable of producing." He decided to probe further.

"What about the Brits?" The University of Bristol has a very advanced robotics program. Is it possible that they have developed such a device and not told you about it?

Oliver took the bait. "Well, no actually. The Brits are the source of the unconfirmed intelligence I mentioned," he admitted uneasily.

The Mossad Director knew he'd hit pay dirt. It was now clear to him that the Brits, almost certainly MI6, and the American CIA were in possession of an advanced humanoid robot and that neither of them knew where it had come from. Very interesting indeed.

Oliver was eager to end the call. He knew he'd said far too much.

"Well, thanks for your help. I have a call coming in from the White House switchboard, he lied. It might be the President so I need to ring off."

"Shalom," said the Israeli spy master as he hung up the phone and immediately dialed the Prime Minister's chief of staff to ask for a few minutes of his time at his earliest convenience.

Saturday, May 31

Aegean Sea
9:10 AM

Fredo was a few minutes late to relieve Franco. It was a pleasant morning so Franco had shifted the helm to the flying bridge an hour after sunrise. The radar display showed that the yacht was on an easterly heading 14 miles north of Rethimnon, Crete. Franco was tired after his watch and eager to go below but Fredo wanted to talk.

"Franco, I have never been with a woman. Have you? The fireflies are beautiful women, especially Lia. I can't stop thinking about how badly I want to make love to her. Knowing that she sunbathes nude up here is making me crazy."

Franco didn't answer his brother's question. He didn't want to tell him that he often made love to a pretty German girl when Fredo was out of the apartment they shared. Fredo's job of restocking the grocery store's shelves after midnight provided several hours for Franco and the German girl to make love without interruption. He knew Fredo's libido would explode if he found out that his older brother had frequent sex.

"Fredo, when we converted from Roman Catholicism to Islam, we accepted Islam's strict prohibition against adultery or fornication. Have you forgotten?" Franco asked in a half-hearted effort to keep his younger brother on a narrow path that he himself no longer trod.

"It's just not fair! I was only fourteen when I converted to Islam to please our mother. I did not really understand. Surely Allah does not give me this burning desire but deny me satisfaction. I don't think he would do that to us," Fredo argued. "I don't make much money stocking grocery shelves. I can hardly afford to even have a date although there are several pretty girls where I work who seem to like me. Now, Allah be praised, our uncle has placed these two beautiful women before us. I want to make love to them both but especially to Lia," Fredo said in an anguished voice. "I think they are unhappy that we pay no attention to them."

Franco thought to himself that Fredo wasn't the only one suffering. He too had been tormented by persistent images of Teresa lying naked on her back in the afternoon sun. The German girl had always been utterly uninhibited in bed. Yet, she was a simple, uncomplicated girl. She had a pretty face and a lovely body but not so much between her ears. Teresa was different. She was smart and beautiful. He had never wanted a woman as badly as he wanted Teresa.

"Fredo, I understand your frustration. Let me think about what you've said. We can talk about it again later. Right now, I'm going below."

When Franco entered the main cabin, Teresa was sitting at the table using her laptop computer.

"Teresa, may I speak to you alone for a few moments?" Franco asked.

"Sure. Where?"

"Let's go out on the aft deck."

As she followed him outside, Teresa wondered what Franco wanted to talk about. When they sat down, she saw that he was nervous. He kept looking around and wouldn't make eye contact with her at first. She thought perhaps he was going to tell her that she and Lia could no longer sunbathe nude. She hoped not but could think of no other reason why he'd be struggling to speak up.

"My brother wants to make love to Lia," he blurted out.

Teresa didn't know what to say at first. She just looked at him for a moment and then said softly, "Lia will do as Fredo wishes. She knows that our services have been generously paid for so she will not refuse. We have both wondered why two handsome young men would not want us," Teresa told him while smiling gently and looking into his obviously pained eyes.

"Fredo is a virgin and he has a bad case of puppy love for Lia," Franco told her. "When he and I are alone, he talks endlessly about how pretty she is and how badly he wants to make love to her. He's been driving me crazy asking for my permission but he's a grown man. I'm only two years older than him and I don't want to be his

conscience. I've decided to tell him to do as he wants but I wanted to speak to you first," he told her.

"Well, I'm not Lia's conscience either and I'm definitely not her pimp. If Fredo wants to make love to Lia, he needs to tell her himself. She works as a firefly only because her family needs the money. I don't think she enjoys it but she is a kind and gentle woman who will treat Fredo with great tenderness for his first time with a woman. You can be certain that I am right about that," Teresa told him.

Teresa was surprised that didn't seem to ease what had been troubling Franco. She'd thought that he simply wanted to be sure that it would be OK for Fredo to spend some intimate time with Lia. Then, suddenly, it dawned on her what the look on his face meant.

"And you want me, don't you?" Teresa paused for a long moment before she said, "All you have to do is ask. I think you are a very handsome man. You have an aura of masculine strength, without seeming macho, that is very attractive. Any woman would be glad to have you in her bed. I have wondered what it would be like to make love to you when you've walked around wearing only that skimpy bathing suit of yours. If you want me, just say so."

"Teresa, I'm not a virgin like my brother. I've been with women before but I've never met a woman who affected me the way you do. I have tried to ignore my feelings but they are real and they won't go away," Franco told her.

Teresa took a deep breath before she responded. "You should be very careful. I think what you just said means you want more than just some physical pleasure. I sense that you may be lonely and too eager to interpret these confusing feelings as love. If you want me for physical pleasure then I will gladly do everything I can to make it very enjoyable for you. If you want more than that, I'm not sure I would be doing you a favor to make love to you," she told him as gently as she could.

Franco leaned forward and put his hands on his head. He shook his head slowly back and forth as though he was having a great internal struggle. Finally, he looked up and spoke in a soft, strained voice.

"Yes, I want to make love to you. You are so beautiful that I can't get you out of my mind. But it's much more than that. I've never met a beautiful woman who was also intelligent and self-confident the way you are. Before I met you, I could not imagine ever finding a woman I would want to marry. Most of the young women I work with seem so shallow and even silly at times that I would not want to have them as my wife no matter how physically attractive they were."

"Franco, you are moving way too fast. You have known me less than three days and all you really know about me is that I am putting myself through college by working as a firefly. I don't think you even know that I also pose nude for art classes and enjoy doing it. There is much more that you don't know. We are marooned together on this beautiful mobile island in the midst of a vast ocean. I am the only single woman on board. It is not unnatural that a healthy man would be attracted to the only single woman for miles around. If you want to have sex with me, I will happily say yes. But, for your own sake, and mine, please do not deceive yourself that you have suddenly fallen in love."

Teresa continued in a serious but kind tone of voice. "I do not want to hurt your feelings but you should know that men often propose marriage to me. Some of them may even be serious. But, most of them do it simply because they are inept at conversing with a woman and think I will be pleased. Some of them are carried away by their fantasy visions of a perfect life married to an attractive woman who excites them in bed. They don't think about all of the more mundane aspects of married life. They certainly don't think about what I will look like in 30 years. Will they still want me then? Would you?" she asked with tender empathy for his feelings.

"Are you saying you don't really want to make love to me but that you'd do it because you've been paid?" Franco asked with a trace of anger in his voice.

"Franco, you weren't listening. I said that any woman would be glad to have you in her bed. So, don't be silly," she said with a smile. "Of course I would like to make love to you. Again, all you have to do is ask," Teresa told him for the third time. "But, before you hustle me off to bed, I think it would be a good idea for you to spend some

time sorting out your obviously conflicted feelings so you don't do something you'd regret. You told me that you were a Muslim and that adultery and fornication are prohibited by your religion. But just now you told me that you've made love to other women. I would never want to cause anyone to go against their own personal religious beliefs. You must work that out for yourself and then try to obey your conscience."

Franco did not look happy. "I will do as you suggest and think carefully about all you have said. Can we talk again later?"

"Yes. Of course," Teresa replied. "I do have one really important question to ask you, however. If you're going to tell Fredo it's OK for him to make love to Lia, I assume they will use the bed in our cabin since the twin beds you and Fredo have in the aft cabin are not a suitable place for them. If I have to move out to provide privacy for Lia and Fredo, where will I sleep?"

Franco took a moment to think before he answered. "You know that Signor and Signora Sartori are using the other queen bed guest cabin. Signor Sartori told me that his wife would not be comfortable sleeping in the owner's cabin. That leaves only the owner's cabin free. You can sleep there when Fredo and Lia need your cabin."

"Are you sure? Your uncle won't mind if a firefly has slept in his bed?"

"He'll never know. I'm sure Signor Sartori would never tell him and neither will Fredo or I. It will be OK."

Teresa stood up and rested her hand lightly on Franco's arm. "I was touched by what you said. Do not think for a moment that I didn't hear you and appreciate the nice things you said."

Franco did not know what to say so he said nothing as she went inside.

Teresa went below immediately to tell Lia about her conversation with Franco.

Franco sat thinking for a few minutes and then climbed the ladder back to the flying bridge to talk to his brother.

11:45 AM

Fredo was very nervous as he waited for Abramo to take over the helm. He had been thinking about Lia all morning.

As soon as Abramo assumed the watch, Fredo went below to shower and dress in clean clothes. Twenty minutes later, he knocked softly on Lia's cabin door. "Lia, it's Fredo. Can I come in?"

Lia had been expecting him and opened the door at once.

"Hello Fredo. Come in."

Fredo stepped into the cabin and stood at the end of the bed as Lia closed and locked the door. He felt awkward and unsure of how to begin. When she turned toward him, he leaned forward and tried to kiss her on her lips. She turned her face aside so he kissed her cheek instead. Lia stood in front of him and whispered for him to be still.

She slowly undressed him. She never took her eyes off his face as she undid each button of his shirt and ran her soft hands over his chest. He felt very self-conscious when he was finally standing naked and fully aroused in front of her but when Lia stepped back and dropped her bathrobe to the floor, her beauty took his breath away.

She knelt in front of him and looked up to see if he was watching her. When her soft hands touched him he groaned with pleasure and ran his fingers through her hair.

He stayed with her for over two hours until Franco knocked on the cabin door to tell him they'd be entering port soon.

Washington, D.C.
12:20 PM

The President was still angry. Even alone in his office, he wouldn't admit to himself that Oliver was a problem of his own doing. He'd nominated him for the CIA Director's position as a political reward without properly vetting him. If he had, he'd have known how utterly incompetent the man was as an executive. He buzzed his chief of staff and asked him to join him in the Oval Office.

"Did you read Oliver's report?"

"Yes sir. It appears that his call accomplished nothing more than to alert the Israelis of the existence of the android."

"I agree. I certainly did not intend for the bumbling fool to reveal that sensitive fact. I'm beginning to think it was a mistake to nominate Oliver for the CIA Director's job. I'm considering asking for his resignation. What are your thoughts?"

"The timing wouldn't be good. We're busy trying to deflect multiple scandals and the Chairman of the House Oversight Committee is firing subpoenas at us like he was using a Gatling gun. The latest public opinion polls show further declines in the number of Americans who believe you are doing a good job."

"What are latest numbers?"

"Your overall approval rating is well below 40 percent in all the major polls. A bigger concern is that several newspapers that are normally friendly have recently published articles criticizing your foreign policy decisions. With all of that going on, I think asking for Oliver's resignation might look like you're trying to find a scapegoat. I recommend waiting."

"OK. You're probably right. I'll deal with Oliver later. When you get back to your office, get the Israeli Prime Minister on the phone for me. It's 6:20 PM in Tel Aviv so he might already be at home."

A few minutes later, the President picked up the phone.

"Mr. Prime Minister, thank you for taking my call. I trust that you are well?"

"Yes, I am fine, Mr. President. May I ask the purpose of your call? I was just sitting down to dinner when I was told that you wished to speak to me."

"Well, I certainly don't want to keep you from your dinner," the President said with barely masked sarcasm. "I'm sure you've been briefed about a conversation between my CIA Director and your Mossad chief."

"Yes, of course. It seemed of little consequence. Is there more to it?" the Israeli asked.

"Well, yes. Perhaps it is of little importance but I wanted to speak to you personally to confirm that Israel has not produced or deployed lifelike humanoid robots," the President said.

"Mr. President, may I speak freely?"

"Yes, please do."

"I am aware that the CIA and MI6 have just completed two days of meetings at MI6 headquarters for the purpose of evaluating a lifelike android that has come into your mutual possession. Your inquiries make it abundantly clear to me that the android was not produced by either the U.K. or the U.S. and I will tell you without equivocation that it was not produced by Israel either."

The President inhaled sharply in surprise. "Thank you for being so candid. Yes, we are in possession of a rather lifelike android robot that was recently discovered by a young couple. They foolishly kept their discovery a secret for several days before disclosing it to an MI6 and CIA agent working together on an unrelated matter. Although remarkably human in appearance, I'm told that the device is rather unsophisticated and probably of little or no military value."

Almost six thousand miles to the east, the Israeli leader wasn't surprised at the obvious deception. The American President often misrepresented facts and seemed unaware that few world leaders trusted him.

Within a few hours of taking the call from the CIA Director the previous day, the Israeli spy chief had already learned the names of every person who had attended the briefing in London. He would soon have an electronic file of the briefing slides that had been presented at the meeting but certainly had no intention of compromising the Mossad's sources by revealing that to the American President.

"I see," said the Israeli leader non-committedly. "I trust that you will let me know if this android matter turns out to be more important than you first believed."

"Yes, of course," the President responded. "Please enjoy your dinner," he said as he broke the connection without waiting for the Israeli to reply.

London, Russian Embassy
5:45 PM

Raisa Kovalenko took the call from Tengfei Chén, one of the double agents she handled. Despite his youth and inexperience, she thought he was developing well. His official duties at the Chinese Embassy in London included providing selective information to Russian SVR agents under the 1992 intelligence cooperation agreement between Russia and China. That put him in a perfect position to feed information to her that his bosses probably wouldn't want shared with their SVR Russian colleagues.

"Can you meet me for a drink at that Irish pub in Covent Garden in about thirty minutes?" Chén asked.

"Yes, I suppose so." Raisa knew there were a lot of tourists in that area so it should be a safe place to meet. Chén's official duties would provide a plausible reason for them to be together if they did see anyone they knew.

Two miles northeast of the Russian Embassy, Tengfei Chén read the intelligence report again and then logged off of his computer. He locked his office door on his way out. Twenty minutes after leaving the Chinese Embassy, he parked in a public garage and walked across the street to the pub. He took a table at the back and waited for Raisa to show up. There was a group of noisy American tourists in the pub but it was early and there were still quite a few empty tables.

Raisa came in a few minutes later and looked around until she spotted him. Chén stood to shake hands with her and waited respectfully for her to sit down.

"What would you like to drink?" a waitress asked.

"Do you have cold Bass Pale Ale in a bottle?" Raisa asked. As a matter of good trade-craft, Raisa mistrusted open glasses because it was so easy for someone to spike the drink. By varying her selections and limiting them strictly to capped bottles and pull-tab cans, she eliminated one of the most common ways an intelligence officer might use to try to kill or immobilize her.

"Yes. What can I get for you sir?" the waitress asked Tengfei.

"I'd like a Shandong Mary."

"Oh, I remember you now. You're the only one who ever orders that drink," the waitress said giving Tengfei a flirtatious glance.

"What do you have for me?" Raisa asked in a low voice after the waitress walked away.

"Have you heard about a secret meeting that took place over the past two days at MI6 HQ?"

"No, what was the subject of the meeting?"

"An extremely lifelike humanoid android they recently acquired."

Raisa knew Chén was watching to see if she reacted to his news but she'd been a spook for over twenty years and didn't give much away. "Why do you think that would interest me?" she asked in a neutral tone of voice.

"Well, my source tells me that the results of the meeting have already been briefed to the British Prime Minister and the American President. In fact, both men were briefed within a few hours after the meetings concluded. I think that suggests that the android is viewed as having national security implications. Several teams of technology experts examined the android and have concluded that it is an extremely advanced military device. They do not appear to know who made it. Some of them think the Israelis did. Some think the Chinese. Some think the Russians. What is clear is that neither the Brits nor the Americans know where the android originated," Tengfei told his handler.

"Yes, that is interesting. How was the android discovered?" Raisa asked.

"Two recent Cambridge doctoral graduates, an American man and a Maltese woman, found the android buried in the sand in about 70 feet of water a few miles east of Malta. They initially kept their discovery a secret but eventually disclosed it to an MI6 agent who was working with a CIA agent apparently in connection with the assassination of the ECB president," Tengfei told her.

"Again, this is all very interesting but of what use is it?" Raisa said feigning disinterest to encourage the young agent to tell her everything he knew.

"The android and the man and woman are being kept under protective guard in three rooms on the top floor at the back of an old

apartment building in Vauxhall that's used as an MI6 safe house. Only one MI6 agent is on duty at the front entrance after 10:00 PM. The MI6 and CIA agents who brought them to London are staying at the safe house too but have separate rooms on the same floor at the front of the building."

"It has occurred to me that a small special operations team could probably abduct the android and the man and woman without too much difficulty. However, if you are going to do it, it should probably be tonight. MI6 has a habit of moving people they are keeping in protective custody around every few days. The subjects have been in this Safe house for three days already."

Raisa took a sip of her ale but didn't speak for several long moments as she considered what the young Chinese agent had told her. She'd already decided that she would arrange the abduction as soon as she could disengage from Tengfei.

"You seem well-informed on what is almost certainly a top-secret matter for MI6 and the CIA. How confident are you of the accuracy of what you have told me?" Raisa asked.

"I am totally confident," Tengfei replied. "You can take this to the bank, as the Americans like to say."

"How can you be that sure?"

"The information came from China's Comment Crew based in Shanghai. They are officially known as the People's Liberation Army Unit 61398. They have stolen enormous amounts of top secret military robotics information from the Americans and the Brits. They are one of the best computer hacking teams in the world and they have multiple back doors into American and British computer systems at defense contractor facilities and even at the CIA and MI6. This is absolutely reliable information."

"OK, I'll be in touch. Do you mind taking care of the bar tab?" Raisa asked as she stood and walked away without saying anything more.

Sitia, Crete
21:20 PM

The yacht was tied up for the night at the marina in Sitia, Crete. The Rinaldi brothers and the two fireflies had gone ashore to explore the old city. It was not a major tourist destination according to the travel guides but the photos and descriptions seemed to suggest that it had its own charm. Abramo and his wife had finished their dinner and were sitting in the main cabin reading.

“You know they are having sex don’t you?” Donatella asked.

Abramo sighed, wishing he didn’t have to have this conversation. He had been dreading it ever since the young people had started doing what he and his wife had feared. Donatella was a devout Catholic who believed that all sex outside of marriage was a sin. Abramo knew that she was very upset.

“Yes. It would be impossible to hide in such tight quarters.”

“Have they no shame? The walls are so thin that I can hear everything. It makes me feel dirty to have two whores having sex with those young men only a few feet from our cabin. I am very uncomfortable about this, Abramo. I never thought we would be in this situation when we agreed to take the yacht to your client.”

“I am sorry my dear. I had hoped it might not happen but I did not feel I could refuse my client’s request. This unpleasantness will be over soon. We will arrive in Alexandria tomorrow evening and have a nice holiday together before we fly back to Italy. Please try to ignore them for one more day.”

The Rinaldi brothers and the fireflies returned to the yacht at 9:20 PM. They’d walked all through the old town and then had a nice dinner at a small café near the waterfront. After only a few minutes of polite conversation, they said goodnight and went below. Fredo and Lia went to her cabin. Franco and Teresa went to the owner’s cabin. It wasn’t long before the sounds of their lovemaking could be heard even in the main cabin. Donatella began to cry. Abramo understood how unhappy she was and tried to comfort her but she pushed him away. They didn’t go to their own cabin until after midnight when the sounds from below finally stopped.

Sunday, June 1

Vauxhall, London
1:00 AM

The MI6 Safe house was a drab four-story brick apartment building located less than a half-mile from MI6 headquarters. Raisa Kovalenko and Boris Rogozin were waiting in a utility van parked in the alley behind the building. Raisa was tense. As a veteran of many missions, she knew that a lot could go wrong on this kind of operation.

At precisely 1:00 AM, a shaped-charge attached to an electrical transformer across the street from the front of the apartment house exploded putting the immediate neighborhood in darkness.

Inside the building, the MI6 officer on duty went immediately to the ground floor front window and saw the burning remnants of the transformer just as he heard Phil Shaw's voice in his headset.

"What happened?"

"It looks like the transformer across the street blew."

"Is the building still secure?"

"Yes sir. The battery backup on the security system kicked in when the power went out. The panel is all green but we won't get the cameras and the recorder back until regular power is restored.

A coded knock at Phil's door signaled that Al Flores was checking in. Phil opened the door and Flores stepped into the room.

"Everything OK?"

"Yes, it looks like it. A transformer exploded across the street. It's not uncommon in these old, run-down neighborhoods."

At 1:02 AM, another transformer exploded a block down the street, again drawing the attention of the duty officer on the ground floor and the MI6 and CIA agents on the top floor. None of them heard the sound of breaking glass at the back of the building, carefully timed to coincide with the sound of the second explosion.

At the same instant that the second transformer blew, the window to Tiera's room exploded in a cascade of shattered glass. A second later, a very dangerous-looking woman dressed in black and

wearing a mask stepped into the bedroom. Brandishing an assault pistol with a tactical flashlight on the accessory rail, the special ops agent pointed the gun at Tiera and motioned for her to keep quiet. She put a gag in Tiera's mouth and taped it in place with utility tape. She then blindfolded Tiera with a black sleeping mask. Working quickly, she bound Tiera's wrists with a nylon zip-tie and pushed her down onto the bed while she bound her ankles and then injected her with a drug that rendered her unconscious within seconds. Tiera was in her underwear and barefooted when her assailant put her over her shoulder and carried her out the door and down the back stairs.

Next door, the scene was much the same in David Logan's room. He was tucking his shirt in and buckling his trousers when his window shattered. The deadly Sig Sauer P556 SWAT assault pistol in his assailant's right hand was an unmistakable warning that resistance would get him killed. He too was gagged, blindfolded, bound with nylon ties and drugged. The special ops agent was a large, powerful man who easily lifted David onto his shoulder and then carried him down the back stairs.

Two other agents entered the third room where they expected to find the android. The room was empty.

Nahbi's keen hearing had detected their approach when they leaped onto the roof and ran across it to the back of the building. He had just barely been able to hear them whispering to each other and had realized that they represented an attacking force of some kind. He'd immediately slipped out of his room and gone to the stairs leading to the roof, thinking that he might intercept them. When he'd reached the roof access door, he had seen the service access switch for the door alarm and deactivated it. He had stepped onto the roof and begun to look around when he heard the door click shut behind him and had belatedly realized that the door had a hydraulic closer. The door could not be opened from the roof without a key.

A moment later, Nahbi heard the sound of the first explosion and ran across the roof to the front of the building to see what it was. As he looked around, he realized that the attackers had jumped down onto the roof from the slightly higher roof of the adjacent building. If they had approached that way, he could at least get off of the roof

and possibly get back into the MI6 safe house building where Tiera and David were. He knew that they were probably in danger so he wanted to get to them as quickly as he could.

With his powerful legs, Nahbi was able to jump high enough to get his hands on the parapet wall of the adjacent building. He pulled himself up and headed for the roof access door. Unfortunately, it too was locked. As he was considering his options, the second explosion occurred a block down the street. He ran across the roof to the front of the building and saw a second transformer in flames. Under normal conditions, his hearing could have detected the sound of the breaking glass even with the much louder sound of the second explosion. But, standing on the roof, only about 100 meters away from the transformer and at nearly the same height, he was just too close to the explosion.

The Russian agents had waited on the window ledge outside of the three rooms until the second explosion provided acoustic cover for them to smash the window glass and enter the rooms. As the sounds of emergency vehicle sirens drew closer, the last two special ops agents made a hasty exit down the stairs and out the back door into the alley. Boris Rogozin pulled the van up to the back door of the old apartment building while Raisa opened the sliding door on the van's side. A few seconds later, the van was speeding down the alley before slowing to make a left turn onto a secondary road that would lead them away from the MI6 safe house.

"Where's the android?" Raisa shouted at the Russian Spetsnaz Alpha Group team leader.

"He wasn't there and we didn't have time to search the building for him. You wanted this operation to be sanitary with no killing and no clues about who carried it out. If we'd searched the building, we would have ended up in a gun battle with the MI6 and CIA agents. It would have gotten very ugly very fast. We did the right thing," the team leader shouted back at her.

Raisa realized that he was right and just nodded silently. She was already thinking about her next move.

Gwadar Port, Pakistan
6:05 AM

At 6:05 AM, the container ship Empress IV prepared to get underway from Gwadar port in western Pakistan. Her captain had graciously invited his only passenger to watch the ship get underway from the bridge. Yousef stayed out of the way but observed and listened as the ship's captain issued a continuous string of orders.

"Single up the stern lines. Cast off the bow lines. Rudder hard to port. Main engines all back slow. Bow thruster hard to port. Half thrust."

As the huge ship's bow moved slowly away from the pier, the captain continued giving orders. "Cast off the stern lines. Hoist the ensign. Rudder amidships. Main engines all stop. Bow thruster all stop. Bow thruster amidships. Rudder right ten degrees. Main engines all ahead slow."

Gradually turning to starboard and gaining speed, the Empress IV moved seaward from the unusual hammerhead formation that made Gwadar a natural port. Yousef heard the ship's navigator take control of the ship at the outer buoy.

"This is the navigator. I have the conn. Helmsman, come to new course 205 degrees. Make turns for twenty-five knots."

The navigator asked Yousef if he'd like to see the ship's route to Suez. A large-scale navigation chart was taped to the navigation table on the starboard side of the bridge. The navigator had plotted the entire route in red grease pencil on an acetate overlay. Each course change was marked with GPS coordinates and annotated with the approximate time.

On its first day out of Gwadar, the ship would remain on course 205 degrees true for 325 nautical miles until about 7:30 PM when it would be just east of Masirah, a desert island off the coast of Oman.

The ship's captain had directed the navigator to plan the voyage so the ship would transit the narrow Straits of Hormuz to enter the Red Sea in late afternoon on the third day out of Gwadar. Although the Empress IV was equipped with the latest satellite and radar navigation devices, supplemented by sonar, it was safer to make the trip through the narrow and often congested passage in daylight.

It was 2,522 nautical miles from Gwadar to Suez. The navigator told Yousef that the trip would take the Empress IV about four and a half days.

Yousef thanked the navigator and walked aft to watch Pakistan's coastline receding in the distance. He had seen the container with the Ambassador's limousine loaded late the previous afternoon. As he'd been instructed by Ahmed Malik, he'd placed a satellite tracking device on the container when he locked it. He knew the exact position of the container on the top layer near the port side of the ship. Other nearly identical containers were stacked around it but he could still pick it out. He was satisfied that his cargo was secure in the trunk of the car inside the container and absolutely safe for now. For the first time in four days, he could relax. He was tired. When the coastline of his native land was no longer visible, he went to his cabin to sleep. There was little for him to do for the next few days anyway.

Vauxhall, London
1:57 AM

It was almost 2:00 AM when Phil Shaw placed a call to the duty officer at MI6 headquarters.

"This is Phil Shaw, ID number 76515. I need to speak to Sir Lionel immediately. It is a matter of national security. He knows who I am. Please have him call me on this number as soon as possible. I'll be waiting for his call."

Five minutes later, Phil's phone rang with the caller ID and incoming phone number suppressed.

"Hello, this is Phil Shaw."

"Mr. Shaw, this is Sir Lionel Smythe. I understand you want to speak to me."

"Yes sir. I'm afraid I have some bad news. The MI6 safe house was attacked by some kind of special operations team a few minutes after 1:00 AM. Nahbi believes they were Russians. They have abducted Mr. Logan and Miss Aquilina. We believe they intended to capture the android too but by a freak bit of luck, they didn't get him. The agents present in the house were distracted by two

exploding transformers that were used as diversions. An MI6 forensics team is here now but so far we don't know for sure who the attackers were."

"I see," said Sir Lionel. "Have you or agent Flores notified the Americans yet?"

"No sir, we've been pretty busy. You're the first person I called after calling for backups and a forensic team."

"I'll take care of them. I'll call Roger Benson and Mrs. Moore and let them decide who else to notify on their side. I'll call the Prime Minister's chief of staff and let him decide whether to wake the PM or not. Are you sure that you have sufficient manpower to protect the android?" Sir Lionel asked.

"Yes sir. We have 20 armed personnel in and around the building. We've moved the android to an interior room on the first floor. There are two armed agents inside the room with him and two more in the hallway outside. Others are posted throughout the building and outside. We have four unmarked cars in the neighborhood with two armed men in each car. Short of a full military assault, which I don't expect, I'm sure we can protect the android. I plan to move him to the MI6 building later this morning after the forensics team is done here."

"This is very unfortunate and deeply troubling. Please contact me through the duty officer at any time if you need to," Sir Lionel said. "If there's nothing else, I have some calls to make."

"No sir. Again, I'm sorry for waking you," Phil Shaw said as he heard Sir Lionel hang up. He wasn't sure the Director heard him.

Alexandria, Egypt
7:05 PM

Abramo Sartori slowed the big Ferretti yacht to 5 knots as he steered it past the breakwater entrance to the Eastern Harbor of Alexandria, Egypt. He steered toward the yacht club's pier a few hundred meters south of the impressive Citadel of Qaitbay. Hundreds of boats were anchored in the harbor so he was tense as he threaded his way among them. He couldn't help thinking how horrible it would be to have brought the beautiful yacht safely such a

long distance only to collide with another boat in sight of the final destination.

Ibrahim Al-Jabiri and two other men were standing on the pier waiting for them. Abramo cut the throttles to an idle and expertly swung the yacht alongside the pier letting it drift gently sideways until it touched the rubber fenders. The two uniformed Ghanem Company employees took the lines tossed to them by the Rinaldi brothers and made them fast. Abramo cut the engines and went aft to meet Mr. Al-Jabiri.

"Salam alekum," Ibrahim Al-Jabiri said as he shook hands with Abramo. "Welcome to Alexandria. I trust that the voyage went well?" he asked in perfect English.

"Buongiorno," Abramo replied. "Yes, we had a good voyage, thank you."

Al-Jabiri welcomed Hakeem Ghanem's nephews back to Egypt and told them their mother was anxious to see them.

"This is my wife, Signora Donatella Sartori," Abramo said to Al-Jabiri as he formally introduced her. "And this is Signora Lia Pedrazzini and Signorina Teresa Giachetti." Abramo noticed the appraising look in Al-Jabiri's eyes as he saw Teresa for the first time. Al-Jabiri then gave Lia a closer look and Abramo could almost read the man's mind marveling that such an attractive married woman was a prostitute.

"My men will load your luggage into the company truck and will deliver it later to the hotel and to Mr. Ghanem's home after they have secured the yacht at the company's pier," Al-Jabiri told them. "I've hired a stretch limousine to take you to Mr. Ghanem's home a few kilometers west of the city. I've also made reservations for Signora Pedrazzini and Signorina Giachetti at the Golf Porto Marina hotel. It is considered by many to be the finest hotel in Alexandria. It has a lovely swimming pool and a lounge that accommodates the tastes of international travelers. I'm sure they will be very comfortable there. We can leave as soon as you are ready," Al-Jabiri told them. "The drive along the waterfront is pleasant and takes about 30 minutes."

The reunion of the Rinaldi brothers with their mother an hour later was emotional for them all. She hadn't seen them in several years and could not get over their transformation into handsome young men. Mr. Ghanem was a gracious host. His home was spacious and light with a marvelous view of the Mediterranean from a wide covered porch that stretched from one end of the house to the other. Dinner that first night was a memorable feast. Abramo and Donatella were tired and said goodnight early.

Monday, June 2

Amersham, England
7:15 AM

David opened his eyes slowly and realized that his arms and legs were tied to a chair. He was very cold. Tiera was tied to another chair about ten feet in front of him. They were facing each other and they were both naked. She was already awake and was obviously relieved to see that he was apparently OK.

David's head was pounding and his vision was still blurred. He'd been barely conscious when his attacker had hoisted him over his shoulder with a curse and a grunt as he strained under David's weight. David had heard him mutter *odin tyazhelyy syn suka* which he knew meant *one heavy son of a bitch* in Russian. Their abductors were definitely Russians.

"Well, good morning Mr. Logan. I hope you've had a nice nap," said a woman's voice from across the room. "Your girlfriend has been awake for some time and she has been very worried about you."

"Who are you?"

"All you need to know is that your lives are in my hands. Cooperate and answer my questions and you will be released unharmed. But, if you make me angry, I assure you that you will regret it."

David saw a slight motion in the dimly-lit corner of the room. It was a stocky, powerfully-built man who had just shifted his weight from one leg to the other as he leaned against the wall.

"What do you want to know?"

"Where is the android?"

"I don't know. He went to his room about the same time that Tiera and I did. I haven't seen him since several hours before you broke into our rooms."

The woman nodded to the man in the corner. The man bent to pick up a large plastic bucket. He walked toward David with a menacing grin visible on his face as he came into the part of the room that was lighted by a single bare bulb hanging from the ceiling. He walked around behind David.

Without any warning, the man poured a 20-liter bucket of ice-cold water and crushed ice over David's naked body. The shock was breathtaking.

"Are you sure that you don't know?" the woman asked again.

"No," David said as he began to shiver from the cold. "I don't know. It's just like I told you."

The woman nodded to the man again. This time, he poured a bucket of ice-water and crushed ice over Tiera. She gasped with the shock but wasn't caught by surprise the way David had been.

"What about you, Miss Aquilina? Where is the android?"

Tiera's teeth were chattering as she stammered that she didn't know either.

"Oh, that's too bad. I'm very sorry that you have both decided not to cooperate," the woman said in a threatening voice. She nodded again to the man who walked around behind the chair that David was tied to. David tried to turn his head to see what the man was going to do just as he felt two sharp points pressed against right shoulder and several million volts from a high-powered Taser surged through his body. The first sensation was of intense pain. Like most Taser victims, he screamed. Then the convulsions and muscle spasms began.

Tiera began screaming uncontrollably in terror as David's body convulsed. A moment later, violent muscle spasms wracked his body and he lost control of his bladder. The convulsions were horrible to watch. Tiera began to cry and begged the woman to stop hurting him.

"Tell me where the android is," the woman asked again.

Tiera was so distraught after watching what the man had done to David, that she could not answer the woman. She could only shake her head.

"Let's give Mr. Logan a few minutes to recover. I'm sure he wouldn't want to miss Act III," the woman said ominously.

It took almost ten minutes for the muscle spasms to stop so David could focus on his tormentor.

"Look, we've told you we don't know where the android is. You can torture us as long as you like but our answer won't change. Don't you get it? We don't know where he is."

"I think you do and I think you will tell me," the woman said menacingly." At first I thought I might let you watch your girlfriend find out what a Taser feels like. But, I think I have a better idea. You see, naked young women excite Boris and I can tell that he is very attracted to Miss Aquilina. I think he would enjoy touching her, wouldn't you Boris?" the woman said while watching David's eyes to gage his reaction.

"Touch her again and I'll kill you."

"Oh, I think not Mr. Logan," the woman taunted him as she nodded to the man she'd just called Boris.

Boris walked around behind Tiera and looked straight at David as he leaned over her shoulder and placed his two big hands over her breasts. He pinched her nipples and tugged upward on her breasts with obvious pleasure. He leered at David as he continued to fondle Tiera's breasts. Tiera was sobbing softly in fear and embarrassment and then, mercifully, she fainted.

David was lunging against his restraints and managed to move the chair a few inches. The woman tipped the chair over on its side and pulled it around so that David could watch Boris.

"Mr. Logan, I'm sure you can figure out what part of your girlfriend's lovely body Boris really wants to touch. I haven't decided how far I'll let Boris go. It's really up to you," the woman told him.

David almost never used vulgar or profane language but the string of epithets that poured from his mouth would have embarrassed a Navy Bosun's mate. "You Russian whore, I promise you I will kill you both if that monster touches her again," David said through clenched teeth.

"Ah, there you go again, Mr. Logan, making idle threats." The woman nodded again to Boris.

Boris moved to Tiera's right side and put his big hand on the inside of her leg a few inches above her knee. He stroked the inside of her leg while grinning at David. His hand began to creep upward. David was violently angry now. His face was drained of all color as he thought about this ogre violating Tiera.

"Stop! Call off your perverted dog," David shouted. "I don't know where the android is but I know who does. Maybe I can persuade him to swap the android for Tiera. The man's name is Phil Shaw. He's an MI6 agent. His unlisted phone number is in the call history of the cell phone in my pants pocket."

The woman motioned for Boris to get the phone. She touched the on/off switch and watched the screen as the phone loaded its operating system to connect to the wireless network. The signal strength was good. Brief messages flashed across the screen as some built-in applications started up.

Suddenly, the woman cursed loudly and kicked David's chest viciously. "Boris, we've got to get out of here right now! The phone has a location beacon in it. MI6 has almost certainly been waiting for this phone to be turned on so they could pinpoint its location. Get their clothes. Keep them covered while they get dressed. Handcuff them with nylon ties and gag them but don't tie up their feet. They need to be able to walk. Then bring the car around to the side of the warehouse. Hurry!" Raisa Kovalenko shouted.

8:20 AM

A white JetStar Cable TV service van was parked 100 yards from the old warehouse. Nathan Lavi was behind the wheel and Gavriella Adler was beside him in the passenger's seat. Avi Ben-Shimon and Daniyel Shaltiel were in a blue Florist's van backed up to a loading dock at the other end of the block. The warehouse they were watching was located in an industrial park near the small town of Amersham in the northwestern outskirts of London near the M25 ring.

Levi Reznik had assigned Gabe to lead the super-secret Kidon unit. He had sent them to England to abduct Raisa Kovalenko and bring her to Tel Aviv to face Israeli justice. Like most Kidon units the team was small. Gabe knew that Raisa had tortured and sadistically mutilated one of the Mossad's best agents before killing him and tossing his body in a ditch outside of Adana, Turkey.

Gabe had studied the Mossad's file on Kovalenko so she knew that Raisa was one of the top field agents of the Russian Foreign Intelligence Service known by the acronym SVR. Levi had told her that the SVR was the successor to the old KGB First Chief Directorate from the Cold War era. The file on Raisa indicated that she was one of Russia's most ruthless interrogators. She was known to prefer chemical and psychological methods but Gabe knew from several reports in the file that she did not hesitate to use torture and mutilation to achieve her objectives. Gabe had also noted that Raisa typically killed her captives when she had extracted the information she wanted.

It had taken Gabe's team several days to locate Raisa in London and another day to plan how to take her down and get her out of England without creating an international incident. They had kept her under constant surveillance and were ready to take her down when the Mossad Director had learned about the android and given them a new assignment.

Unfortunately, the Mossad's intelligence unit didn't know where the android was. Gabe had suspected that Raisa might know after they'd observed her meeting with Tengfei Chén, a Chinese intelligence officer known by the Mossad to be a Russian double agent. With no other leads, they had continued to keep Raisa under

surveillance. It was risky because Raisa was an experienced agent. She might spot them or shake them off her trail at any moment. But Gabe thought Raisa was the best chance they had so they'd stuck with her.

Hoping for a lucky break, they had tailed Raisa and the man with her to the MI6 safe house neighborhood the night before when the Russians had abducted David Logan and Tiera Aquilina. Dressed all in black for night ops, Gabe had snuck into the alley on foot and watched the Russian special ops team enter the building next to the MI6 safe house. Faced with a heavily-armed Russian team, and fully aware that any gun battle would have disastrous consequences, she had decided to back off and wait for another opportunity. After the attack, her team had tailed the Russians to the warehouse on the outskirts of London.

Although Gabe had seen three men and one woman leave the warehouse almost immediately, she didn't know how many other agents might be inside. She had decided to wait and watch. She'd used the time to identify Raisa's associate and to download his file. The man was Boris Rogozin, also an SVR agent. He was a veteran of the Second Chechen war and was often teamed with Raisa. The file on him indicated that he was a powerful bull of a man who acted as Raisa's bodyguard and provided the brawn to complement Raisa's brains.

Gabe's team had pointed sensitive directional microphones at the windows at the front of the warehouse and had heard the screams of David Logan and Tiera Aquilina although they hadn't been able to pick up normal conversation. When they heard Raisa shouting at Boris it was obvious that the Russians would be leaving with their captives. Gabe told both drivers to maneuver to bracket the vehicle Raisa and her captives were in at a safe distance but to be prepared at an instant's notice to storm the Russian vehicle to rescue the captives. If they could take Raisa alive, so much the better. Boris was expendable.

Three minutes later, Raisa and Boris loaded David and Tiera into a black Audi sedan and headed south on the A355 secondary road toward the M20. Gabe was studying a satellite image of the area and

saw that there was a forested area about a mile south of the A404 intersection.

Avi had passed the Audi on a straight stretch of road to put the florist van in the lead position. Gabe radioed him to get ready to slow suddenly and turn the van sideways to block the road when he entered the section of road lined with trees. Her plan was for the Cable TV van to come up behind the Audi and do a similar maneuver to trap the Audi between them. Gabe told her team to be ready to rush the Audi. Gabe hoped Raisa would surrender without gunplay but there was no way to be sure. This was probably the best opportunity they would have.

Forty seconds later Gabe saw the Audi's taillights come on and saw the car come to a stop, blocked by the Florist's van now turned broadside on the narrow country lane. Before the Cable TV van came to a complete stop, Gabe leaped from the vehicle and ran toward the Audi with her 9mm Uzi Pro machine pistol held high and ready to fire. The rest of her team was at the doors of the Audi within seconds motioning to Raisa and Boris to get out of the vehicle.

Caught by surprise in the sudden trap, neither of the Russians had their weapons out and ready. It turned out to be easier than Gabe had dared hope.

Raisa glared at them with silent rage but did as she was told when Gabe leveled her machine pistol at her chest and told her to get undressed. Nathan handed Raisa's clothes to Tiera. Daniyel put nylon ties on Raisa's wrists and ankles and pulled a hood over her head before dumping her on the floor in the back of the Florist's van. Avi bound Boris with nylon ties and put a hood over his head before shoving him roughly into the trunk of the Audi.

Nathan helped David and Tiera into the Cable TV van to ride with Gabe and him. Daniyel got behind the wheel of the Audi. Gabe hadn't decided what to do with Boris yet. She would not murder him in cold blood but he did present a logistical problem for her. It would be hard enough to get Raisa out of England.

The three vehicles used different routes to the Mossad safe house north of Farnham Royal and parked inside the old dairy barn out of

sight of aircraft or satellite surveillance. The old stone farmhouse sat in the middle of a 40-acre farm owned by a Jewish couple who were part of the Mossad's global system of *sayanim* or volunteer Jewish helpers.

The farm was located in a rural area 10 miles northwest of Heathrow airport, and about half-way between the M40 and the M4. It offered multiple access and escape routes. As soon as she was satisfied that Raisa and Boris were securely tied up in what had been the milk cooling room of the old barn, Gabe walked up to the house. She needed to contact Levi for further instructions.

Farnham Royal, England
10:38 AM

"Levi, we have them," Gavriella Adler told her boss over the secure satellite phone link to the Mossad headquarters in Tel Aviv.

"All of them?"

"Not the android. We have David Logan and Tiera Aquilina here in the house. They're sleeping now. They've had a rough time. Miss Aquilina is still traumatized by her experience but they will both be fine after some rest. Raisa was torturing them trying to find out where the android is so the Russians don't know either."

"And you were able to take Raisa alive?"

"Yes, without firing a shot. I have Raisa and Boris Rogozin tied up in the old milk cooler room in the barn. What do you want me to do with them?" Gabe asked.

The phone was silent for several moments as the Mossad Katsa weighed several options. Finally he asked, "Did Raisa and Boris have passports with them?"

"Yes. Both of them had fake U.K. passports. "

"OK, good. The technical support team at our London embassy can make an Italian passport for Raisa using the picture from her fake U.K. passport. A courier will pick up her fake U.K. passport and return the Italian one to you sometime tonight."

"I had our operations section develop several scenarios for getting Raisa out of London and back to Israel in case you were successful. I think one of those scenarios will meet our needs."

"There is a company in Milan, Italy that specializes in transporting critically and terminally ill patients using a business jet that has been converted into an airborne ambulance. The company is owned by a retired Israeli Defense Force pilot who has done some work for us from time to time. He and his wife are both licensed pilots for twin engine business jets. Their owner-operator business is small but they make a decent living from it. I'll have our transportation section charter their plane for a flight to London to pick up a terminally ill patient and return her to Milan. They will file a flight plan showing that routing. However, on the way back, they will take a small detour to Tel Aviv."

"There is a medical supply company in London that is owned by another one of our sayanim helpers. Later today, I'll have the company deliver a medical transport gurney, some uniforms, and some other medical equipment to the farm."

"The transportation section will also schedule an ambulance and driver for tomorrow morning to transport a patient from the farm to the business jet terminal at Heathrow. The ambulance company will be told that the patient's critical-care medical technicians will accompany her so that only the driver will be needed."

"Tomorrow morning, Daniyel and Avi will dress as Emergency Medical Technicians. They will have Raisa put on a hospital gown. They will then strap her to the gurney. They will attach an oxygen bottle and a hook for an intravenous feeding bottle. About one hour before the ambulance arrives they will give Raisa an injection of Thiopental to put her to sleep. They will insert the port for intravenous drip and attach the tube from a saline bag on the gurney's hook but leave the valve closed. They will place a surgical cap on her head and an oxygen mask over her face. Covered by a blanket with the cap and mask, she will not be identifiable should the driver ever be questioned."

"Daniyel and Avi will watch for the ambulance to turn off the road into the lane leading to the farmhouse. With a show of medical urgency, they will be in the process of bringing Raisa out of the house just as the ambulance pulls up to the house."

"At the business jet terminal at Heathrow, the ambulance will enter through a security gate and proceed directly to the aircraft

parked on the flight line. If your men are questioned, they will show Raisa's Italian passport and their own fake U.K. passports. They can tell the security guard that their patient is terminally ill and being transported home so her children can see her before she dies. Since the flight originated in a European Union country and all of the crew and passengers have EU nation passports there should be no difficulty unless they are unlucky and encounter an unusually suspicious guard. If their cover story doesn't work, they'll have to improvise. Do you have any questions?"

"What about Boris?"

"Boris is just a thug. He's been the muscle to support Raisa's brains on more than one assignment. But, we don't execute people just because they're big and stupid. Let me think about Boris. I'll call you back in an hour."

"What do you want me to do with David Logan and Tiera Aquilina?"

"I'm sure that MI6 and the CIA are trying to find them. They may even still have the android we're looking for. But, the Prime Minister has just ordered Mossad to use all available manpower and resources to find some stolen weapons," Levi told her. What I'm about to tell you is for your ears only. Understood?"

"Yes."

"Five tactical nuclear weapons have been stolen from Pakistan. The Prime Minister believes they may be used to destroy Tel Aviv and the surrounding area, potentially killing up to half of our people. He has notified the U.K. Prime Minister and the U.S. President to ask for their help in finding the weapons before it's too late."

"Gabe, I'm told that the android has capabilities that far transcend those of any human and that its analytical and computational ability rivals that of some supercomputers. I think it has just become more urgent than ever that we find the android to see if we can persuade it to help us locate the nuclear devices. We need some help and we have no way of knowing how much time we have."

Gabe heard something in his voice she'd never thought she would hear from the Mossad's legendary *rock*. Levi Reznik was afraid. That made Gabe afraid too.

11:44 AM

Gabe answered her SATCOM encrypted phone with the customary Jewish greeting, "Shalom, Levi."

"Shalom," Reznik replied. "We've decided what to do with Boris. We've learned that the Director of the SVR in Moscow is very unhappy with Boris for letting Raisa be captured. The SVR already knows it was the Mossad who took Raisa down and they assume, correctly I hope, that we will give her a swift but private trial and then execute her. So, the Director wants you to hand Boris over to the SVR and let them deal with him. We don't think he knows anything that can hurt us."

"How do you want it done?"

"Tie him securely, gag him, and blindfold him," Levi told her. "Sometime after midnight tonight, have two of your men put him in a dumpster behind a fast food or convenience store somewhere near Uxbridge. Tell your men to call from a pay phone to tell the SVR where they can find him. You should be seeing the number for them to call on the screen of your phone. Did it come through?"

"Yes, I have it." Gabe grinned at the thought of putting the SVR thug in a dumpster. It was an insulting thing to do to him and it might be a long time before he lived it down. She wondered how to say dumpster diver in Russian.

"That's the easy part," Levi said. "The Director has been talking to Sir Lionel Smythe and Roger Benson. Both of them know about the stolen weapons and have been directed by the U.K. Prime Minister and the American President to do everything they can to help. The Director wants you to take Mr. Logan and Miss Aquilina to MI6 headquarters tomorrow morning. Mossad will work closely with MI6 and the CIA to find the weapons. You will be our representative on the team."

"Understood. Since Daniyel and Avi will return to Israel with Raisa, what should I do with Nathan?"

"Send him to the Israeli Embassy. Have him report to the senior intelligence officer. We'll keep him in London in case we need him. Meanwhile, he can add some manpower to a small staff that I know will be glad to have some help."

"Levi, do we have any leads on the nuclear weapons yet?"

"No. Nothing yet. We've got feelers out everywhere. Something should turn up soon. Stay in touch."

Tuesday, June 3

Farnham Royal, England
1:20 AM

At 11:10 PM, Daniyel and Avi walked from the farmhouse to the barn where Raisa Kovalenko and Boris Rogozin were tied up. Daniyel kept a silenced 9mm Sig Sauer P226 pistol pointed at Boris' head while Avi cut the nylon zip tie around his ankles and helped him to his feet without speaking. Boris was stoic. Raisa assumed that the Israelis were taking him somewhere to kill him. If Boris was afraid to die, he did not show it. Raisa could not help but admire his courage. As the Israelis led him away, he nodded to her without speaking as if to say goodbye.

After they were gone, Raisa was left alone lying on her side on the cold and damp concrete floor with her hands tied behind her. Another nylon zip tie was secured snugly around her ankles. Wearing only her underwear after the Israelis had given her clothes to Tiera Aquilina, Raisa was shivering. She wasn't gagged or blindfolded anymore, probably because no one would hear her scream and the Israelis didn't intend to let her see anything important anyway.

She and Boris had both been trying to wear away at the tough, nylon wrist restraints by rubbing them on the concrete floor whenever they were not being watched. The effort would eventually wear through the zip tie but it had been slow going because the floor wasn't very rough. She could not tell how much progress she'd made so far. But, she had every reason to believe the Israelis would come

for her once they'd taken care of Boris. She did not intend to let them kill her too.

With fierce determination, she used all of her strength to press her wrists against the floor and rubbed the nylon tie as hard as she could. She felt the burning sensation from her raw and probably bleeding skin but she kept doggedly on with her effort to free herself. She had to rest every few minutes. Two hours later, her wrists were finally free. She wasted no time trying to free her ankles. Someone might come at any moment to check on her. She had to move fast. She might get only one chance.

Raisa pushed her panties down over her hips and reached between her legs for the small nylon string that was designed to look like a Tampon cord but was attached to something very different. It took only a few seconds to retrieve the small compressed gas cartridge made of polished stainless steel that she always carried inside herself as a weapon of last resort. It was about the size of the CO_2 cartridges used in air guns and slightly larger in diameter than a super-max tampon. It had a short nozzle and a button on one end. There was a rounded plastic protective cap over the button and nozzle. She removed the cap and threw it in the corner where it would not be noticed. Raisa held the cartridge very carefully while she pulled her panties back up. She positioned the cartridge carefully in her right hand and then lay on her side with her hands behind her as though they were still restrained. She waited patiently for her chance.

That chance came only a few minutes later when the third Israeli man came to check on her. He stepped into the old milk cooling room and let the door close behind him. As he leaned over her to check her restraints, she took a deep breath and held it. She closed her eyes tightly as she sprayed him in the face with a mixture designed to instantly immobilize him and to render him unconscious within seconds.

Raisa had helped develop the weapon and knew its history and its capabilities. The gas inside the cartridge was a potentially lethal blend of pepper spray and a fast-acting nerve gas. The pepper spray had been developed by the Indian Army as a military weapon. It was derived from the Bhut Jolokia pepper, by far the hottest pepper in

the world with a Scoville rating of more than one million. The capsaicin in a Bhut Jolokia was more than 125 times hotter than the hottest jalapeno pepper and more than three times hotter than a habanero, the world's second-hottest pepper.

Raisa knew that the nerve gas fentanyl had been used by the Russians in 2002 against Chechen rebels holding 700 hostages in Moscow. A powerful gas 100 times more potent than morphine, it incapacitated its victims at low dosage. It was lethal at higher dosages as they had learned when 117 people were killed by the gas during the hostage rescue attempt. She knew that Mossad agents had also used fentanyl in their unsuccessful 1997 attempt to kill Hamas leader Khalid Mishal.

The Israeli agent went down instantly when the gas hit him in the face. He landed on his back thrashing violently in excruciating pain. Within a few seconds, he was unconscious.

Raisa moved quickly. Lifting the Israeli agent's right pant leg, she withdrew the slender fiberglass Mako knife she knew was carried by most of Israel's covert forces. Using its serrated blade, she quickly cut the nylon zip tie around her ankles and checked the Israeli to ensure that he was still unconscious. She felt in his pants pocket and found the keys to the Audi sedan. She also found two fully-loaded 15-round magazines in a cargo pocket on his trousers. He was quite a bit bigger than she was but she needed something to wear. His shirt was several sizes too big but would have to do. His trousers were OK for length but she had to cinch the belt up to the last hole to keep them from falling off. His shoes were useless to her. They were far too big.

Wasting no time, she went into the main part of the barn holding the pistol at the ready position. Luck was on her side. The Audi sedan had been parked in front of the Florist's van and behind the Cable TV van but the Florist's van was gone. Apparently the two agents had used it when they took Boris away. Raisa looked through the gap between the two barn doors and saw an old farm house about 75 meters away. If she was careful, she might be able to get away without being seen.

She got into the Audi and held the driver's door ajar enough that the interior light stayed on. She turned the ignition key to the on

position but did not start the engine yet. She found the headlight switch and rotated it to the off position so the lights would not come on when she started the engine. She then started the engine and left it idling while she got back out of the car and opened the barn doors slowly being careful to make as little noise as possible. When the barn doors were open, she backed the Audi out and drove slowly up the long driveway toward the road while watching the rear view mirrors for any sign of pursuit. There was none.

She drove south along a narrow country road without lights for a half-mile. The lights of London were reflected off the low-hanging clouds giving her enough light to see the road. The Audi's GPS display showed that she was about 10 miles northwest of Heathrow airport and about 25 miles from Central London. Five miles after leaving the farm where she'd been held captive, she turned east on the M4 and headed for the Russian Embassy near the west end of Hyde Park.

Uxbridge, England
1:30 AM

At 1:30 AM, Daniyel knew they'd finally found what they'd been looking for behind a gas and convenience store on Harefield Road near Uxbridge. They had driven around for a half-hour looking for a really disgusting place to dump him. They had chosen well. A large Norway rat had scurried away at their approach and would probably return as soon as they left. Cockroaches were all over the dumpster. Daniyel and Avi grinned at each other as they hoisted him over the rim into the filthy, evil-smelling dumpster. His SVR colleagues would not enjoy getting him out.

Tel Aviv, Israel
5:20 AM

"Shalom," Levi Resnik said as he answered the secure phone on his desk at the Mossad headquarters building in Tel Aviv. He noted that it was 5:20 AM in London. "Did your men find a nice place for Boris to take a nap?" he asked with heavy sarcasm.

"Levi, Raisa has escaped," Gabe told him at once. "When Nathan went to check on her, she almost killed him with some kind of

aerosol spray. The Embassy's doctor is here with him now. It looks like he'll be OK but he can't see yet. Apparently Raisa had a small gas cartridge hidden inside her body because we gave her clothes to Tiera Aquilina and we didn't find anything hidden in her underwear. She was able to escape in the Audi sedan that she and Boris were in when we captured them. Nathan had the keys in his pocket. She took his pistol and two magazines."

"When did this happen?" Levi asked.

"Shortly after 1:00 AM. Daniyel and Avi were away from the farm to get rid of Boris. Nathan went to check on Raisa. When he didn't come back and didn't answer my call, I knew something was wrong. I was alone in the house with David and Tiera so I moved them into the bathroom where I might be able to protect them if we were attacked."

"I called Daniyel and Avi and asked them to come as quickly as they could. They'd just finished dropping Boris into a dumpster and were already on their way. They got back to the farm a little after 2:00 AM and saw the barn doors open and the Audi missing. When they checked, Raisa was gone and Nathan was unconscious but breathing. A gas cartridge was on the floor beside him. They brought him into the house and I called the Embassy to ask them to send a doctor and two intelligence officers to provide some backup for us."

"That is most unfortunate," Levi said thoughtfully. "Are Mr. Logan and Miss Aquilina unharmed?"

"Yes."

"All right. Take them to MI6 headquarters later this morning once you have everything under control there. I'll notify Sir Lionel that it will probably be late morning before you arrive. I'll have the transportation section cancel the ambulance and aircraft."

"Levi, I'm sorry. I really bungled this."

"I won't sugar-coat it, Gabe. The Director will be furious when I tell him. Not only do we not have the android we don't even have Raisa as a consolation prize. I've consistently told him that you were one of our best agents. I'm afraid that your credibility and mine will both suffer with our new boss. We can't change that now. Everyone is focused on finding the nuclear weapons so if he's going to skin us

both, it will have to wait. Just do your job. We'll worry about the fallout from Raisa's escape later."

Vauxhall, London
10:30 AM

Phil Shaw was waiting for them in the underground parking garage at MI6 headquarters. As David and Tiera got out of the back of the van, he stepped forward to shake hands with them and to apologize profusely for not doing a better job of protecting them. He had expected their abductors to kill them and was relieved to see them alive and apparently unharmed.

"Miss Adler, welcome to MI6," Phil Shaw said as he extended his hand to Gabe. Let's go up. Sir Lionel and several others are waiting for us in the 7th floor executive conference room."

11:00 AM

Sir Lionel welcomed Gabe to MI6 and introduced her to Roger Benson. At Sir Lionel's suggestion, each of the other people in the big conference room introduced themselves to her. David watched her closely and sensed that she was memorizing everything she saw and heard.

Sir Lionel asked everyone to be seated and then opened the meeting.

"A few days ago, we were confronted with something that we feared might pose a serious threat to the national security of the United Kingdom and the United States. The android called Nahbi was examined by some of the top scientists in the fields of robotics, materials, engineering, medicine, electronics, and computational systems. However, they were unable to determine the android's origin."

"Initially, a consensus emerged that the most likely origin was Israel. However, the Israeli Prime Minister assured the American President that the android had not been produced in Israel. The U.K. Prime Minister has since spoken to the Israeli Prime Minister and is convinced that the android was not designed and produced in Israel. That left only China and Russia as remotely possible origins."

“However, we now know that the Russians and Chinese are as puzzled as we are about the android’s origin. A Chinese double-agent named Tengfei Chén alerted the Russians to the android’s existence. That led to the abduction and torture of Mr. Logan and Miss Aquilina. As these events have played out, we are now quite certain that the android was not designed or produced in China or Russia either. So, after days of intense examination and discussion, we appear no closer than we were to solving the mystery of the android’s origin.”

“Now, however, an even greater threat has emerged. Five tactical nuclear weapons have been stolen from Pakistan’s nuclear weapons assembly cantonment near Wah about twenty miles west-northwest of Islamabad. There is a grave risk that these weapons are now in the hands of radical Islamic terrorists.”

“The Israelis believe the weapons could be used to destroy Tel Aviv with a potential loss of life that might run to half of the Israeli population.”

“Each of the weapons is believed to have a yield of between 5 and 10 kilotons. For comparison, the bomb that destroyed the city of Hiroshima more than 65 years ago had a yield of about 12 kilotons. Thus, if detonated together, the combined yield of these five tactical nuclear weapons could be up to four times greater.”

“These are not the crude, dirty bombs experts have long assured us were the best the terrorists could manage. Instead, these are modern nuclear devices that are small enough to fit inside an artillery shell only 203mm in diameter and slightly less than one meter long. They are too heavy to be classified as suitcase nuclear devices but they are certainly small enough. They will be easy to transport and conceal and therefore very hard for us to find.”

“At present, we simply do not know where these weapons may be. The intelligence agencies in all three of our countries have cast a very wide net in hopes of finding clues that can lead us to the weapons before it is too late.”

”It has been suggested that we ask the android Nahbi to help. For that, we are going to need Mr. Logan’s and Miss Aquilina’s help. Nahbi has declined to help unless Mr. Logan and Miss Aquilina are

allowed to work with him. They found him and reactivated him. Curiously, he views them as his friends."

"While some of our experts doubt that the android could harbor human-like feelings of what the Greeks called phileo love for David and Tiera, others say that it appears to be quite genuine."

"We also know that Nahbi was extremely concerned when David and Tiera were abducted. He apparently blamed himself for not protecting them."

"In working with Nahbi these past few days, we have learned another quite astounding fact. This advanced electro-mechanical device, a machine in lay terms, seems to bear a sense of guilt for having previously served a man that he viewed as evil. He has expressed to David and Tiera, and to others who have interviewed him, a strong desire to behave in a responsible, decent way. He has actually said that he would destroy himself before he would become a servant to another evil, manipulative master."

"Experts in artificial intelligence and advanced robotics have emphasized that they can hardly conceive of an android displaying what can only be described as a free-will choice between right and wrong. Yet, Nahbi himself claims to be making precisely that choice. In a surprising way, Nahbi seems to have defected from the dark side, so to speak."

"So, we need help not only from the android Nahbi but also from David Logan and Tiera Aquilina," Sir Lionel concluded. "

"Miss Aquilina and Mr. Logan, would you both be so kind as to join Mr. Benson and me for a few minutes of private conversation?"

When everyone else had left the room, Tiera turned to Sir Lionel. "I need to call my parents to let them know I'm OK. They must be worried sick."

"Yes of course. Mr. Logan, I assume that you need to notify your family as well."

"Yes sir. I'd like to call my sister."

"I'll see that you are allowed to do that when we are finished here. Now, I must apologize to you. I have to remind you both that you remain bound by the official-secrets non-disclosure agreements you

previously signed. You must be very careful what you say when you speak to your families or anyone else."

"We understand."

"To my deepest personal regret, the two of you have been subjected to some very unpleasant business. I would not blame you if you felt you'd had enough. But, you heard what I said in the conference room. Nahbi will not help us unless the two of you are involved. Will you help us?"

Roger Benson leaned forward and looked directly at Tiera. "Look, I know it's not fair to either of you that you've been drawn into this. I understand that. Yet, millions of people may die if we cannot find these weapons before they can be used. We know from our experience with Al Qaeda and other Islamic extremists that the only thing that limits how many innocent people they kill is the power of the weapons at their disposal. On September 11, 2001 they killed over 3,000 people. If they'd had the capability, they would gladly have killed three million."

"If the Israeli Prime Minister's fears turn out to be warranted, as many as four million innocent Israeli citizens could die. The Israelis are paranoid with good reason but Tel Aviv might not be the target. What if it's London, where over eight million people live? If our experts are correct, and the yield of each of these devices could be as much as 10 kilotons, terrorists could disperse the weapons around the city and potentially kill nearly everyone in London. The same kind of terrible scenario will exist if the target is Paris, or Frankfurt, or Rome, or Washington, or Los Angeles. We would not ask you if the stakes weren't so high."

"Could we meet with Nahbi alone for a few minutes?" David asked. "You said he was waiting nearby."

"Yes. Most certainly. Please wait here and I'll ask him to join you," Sir Lionel replied as he and Roger Benson rose and left the room.

A few moments later, Nahbi entered the conference room and stood just inside the door waiting for them to speak first.

"Nahbi, Sir Lionel has told us that you would not help them find the nuclear weapons unless we were somehow involved. Is that accurate?" David asked him.

"Yes," Nahbi responded without embellishment.

"Sir Lionel also told us that you considered us your friends. Is that true? Tiera asked.

"Yes, that is true," Nahbi said but then continued, "I have no one else to call friend or master. The two of you found me and reactivated me. I sense that you are both people with integrity. I now have a freedom of choice that I did not have before. If I am to continue to interact with humans, I prefer to continue a close association with the two of you because I think you will try to do what is right."

"Sir Lionel told us that you blamed yourself for not being able to protect us. Is that true?" Tiera asked.

"Yes. I made a critical mistake the night you were abducted. I heard the Russians walking on the roof and whispering. I recognized that it was some kind of attack. I went immediately to the stairs that led to the door onto the roof in an effort to intercept them and thwart their attack. I successfully disarmed the roof door alarm so I could open it without triggering the alarm. But then I let the door close and lock behind me. Even with all of my knowledge and computational power, a simple thing like a hydraulic door closer defeated me because I had no practical experience with such things."

"When the first explosion occurred, I ran across the roof to the front of the building. I then realized that the Russians had gotten onto the MI6 building's roof from the higher roof of the building next door. Expecting to be able to get off the roof by that route, I climbed onto it about the time that the second explosion occurred. The roof access door on that building was also closed and locked. I was stuck on the roof for about two minutes while the Russian team took you both captive and carried you down the stairs to the door leading to the alley. I heard the vehicle's engine and some excited exchanges between the Russians as they loaded you into the van. I ran to the back of the building just in time to see the van turning left out of the alley."

"I am quite willing to help find the nuclear devices but I want the two of you to work with me. Your abilities and practical knowledge of today's world can help me avoid making other mistakes. I also want to keep you close to me so I can protect you. The MI6 and CIA agents are good and well-intentioned men, but they were not able to protect you. That is unacceptable to me. I know nothing of Gavriella Adler," Nahbi said.

David and Tiera just looked at each other for several moments. Finally, David turned to Nahbi and said, "We will help."

London, England
3:00 PM

Raisa Kovalenko was surprised to see Boris alive. Boris had been brought to the Russian embassy three hours before sunrise by the two SVR agents who had found him in the dumpster exactly where the Mossad had told them he would be. He'd showered and gotten a few hours of sleep before he was awakened and told that Raisa was in the building.

The SVR's senior intelligence officer at the Russian Embassy told them that the Director of the SVR in Moscow had been notified of their escape from the Mossad but, instead of being pleased, he was furious that they had lost their captives and allowed the Mossad to capture and humiliate them. He had ordered them to participate in a conference call at 4:00 PM London time. Raisa knew it would not be pleasant.

The Director of Russia's Foreign Intelligence Service had hardly taken a breath as he ranted for over thirty minutes about their incompetence. When he finally seemed to run out of disparaging things to say, he'd given them a new assignment and warned them that Siberia still had room for useless SVR agents who couldn't do their jobs. That threat didn't intimidate either Raisa or Boris but they both knew that another failure would mean the end of their careers and loss of the income and privileges they both enjoyed.

Wednesday, June 4

Yanbu, Saudi Arabia
5:30 AM

The Bella Maria finished loading at the Yanbu Al Sinaiyah oil terminal in western Saudi Arabia at 3:45 AM. She was scheduled to leave port shortly after sunrise and the ship's crewmen were busily getting the ship ready for sea.

Zakaria Nasser was the Belle Maria's chief engineer. He was an Egyptian with a degree in marine engineering from Cairo University and had been a ship's engineer for ten years. He was also a member of the Muslim Brotherhood. From his vantage point on the port wing of the aft superstructure, he watched the crew making preparations to get underway. He looked at his watch and realized that it was time for him to go below.

A few days earlier, he had been surprised to receive a call from Yousef Abu Shakra, the driver and bodyguard of the Egyptian Ambassador to Pakistan. He had been told to place an urgent order with a certain firm in Suez to have a special industrial oxygen cylinder delivered to him personally while the Belle Maria was waiting to enter the Suez Canal. He was told to guard the cylinder with his life and to deliver it to a certain man in Port Arthur, Texas once the ship moored at the oil-terminal on Texaco Island.

Abu Shakra had told him that the cylinder would be brought to the Belle Maria by a harbor delivery boat as soon as they dropped anchor in the holding area. It would be strapped securely to a wheeled cart similar to those used for large oxy-acetylene tanks, only smaller. The cylinder could be easily rolled around despite the fact that it weighed almost 100 kilograms. He was told to arrange for the cylinder to be hoisted aboard under his close supervision and then taken to his office in the engineering room where he should keep it locked up when he was not in the office. He had been curious but hadn't asked any questions. He would do as he'd been instructed.

Zakaria had made the trip from Yanbu to the refinery in Texas several times. The Belle Maria was a Suezmax tanker, the largest

ship allowed through the Suez Canal. He knew they would arrive in the holding area at the port of Suez roughly 32 hours after leaving Yanbu. There was usually a wait of several hours before the ship could join a north-bound convoy and enter the canal. It would take 12 to 16 hours to transit the canal to its northern end at Port Said.

Once in the Mediterranean Sea, the ship would head west to the Straits of Gibraltar. From Gibraltar, the ship would follow a great circle route to the Florida Keys and then travel westerly in the Gulf of Mexico to the oil terminal on Texaco Island in Port Arthur, Texas. The total distance from Yanbu to Port Arthur was about 7,200 nautical miles. Zakaria knew that it would take the Belle Maria 18 days to make the trip.

MI6 Headquarters, London
8:05 AM

David and Tiera had breakfast together in the level B1 cafeteria in the basement of the MI6 headquarters building and then took the elevator to the B2 level at 7:30 AM. David knew that a lot of people had worked through the night to set up the work area they would be using.

The previous evening, Sir Lionel had called them together to tell them that he had decided to put Nahbi in charge of the task force and to explain why. He had told them that there was no question that Nahbi's intellect, logical ability, and memory capacity far surpassed those of any human. Recognizing a few doubtful expressions as he looked around the room, Sir Lionel had freely admitted that Nahbi was not an experienced intelligence officer and that he had never even been a member of an MI6 task force, let alone been in charge of one. Gordon McFarland had solved that problem by suggesting that Nahbi study and memorize all of the after-action reports of every major MI6 task force over the previous twenty years along with everything in the MI6 files about several important CIA and Mossad cases. By the time Nahbi had finished the assignment, he was more highly-qualified to lead the team than anyone else.

Nahbi requested, and Sir Lionel approved, having David serve as his chief of staff. David was a proven leader and his experience in

Afghanistan had included covert operations with Pakistan's Army in the remote mountain regions along the border between the two countries. He could also speak Urdu and Pashto, two of Pakistan's most important languages.

Sir Lionel had assigned Gordon McFarland to be the team's Executive Sponsor. His primary responsibility would be to coordinate the combined resources of the several intelligence agencies to provide whatever support the team needed.

Sir Lionel had suggested that the team be named Task Force 3 as a subtle reminder that the search for the nuclear weapons was a three-nation joint effort. Task Force 3 would consist of Nahbi, David Logan, Phil Shaw, Pete Nocona, Al Flores, Gavriella Adler, and Tiera Aquilina. They would live and work in the basement of the MI6 building until they located the nuclear weapons.

Each of them had been assigned individual quarters on the B1 basement level that were similar to a small hotel suite except there were no windows. The cafeteria was at the end of the hall. Room service was available twenty-four hours a day.

David knew that Nahbi and Gordon had worked most of the night to identify the equipment and communication links the team would need. In less than eight hours, the MI6 technical support personnel had converted one of several 4,000 square foot controlled-access rooms on the B2 basement level of the MI6 building into a well-equipped command center.

The rest of the TF3 team was already in the room when David and Tiera arrived. An MI6 technical support supervisor gave them all a short briefing about how the space was configured.

He told them that each team member would have a dedicated work station equipped with three flat screen monitors connected to a dedicated Hewlett Packard Z920 computer. The modified HP Z920 computers were among the fastest work station computers available. Each of the HP computers was itself part of a networked computer grid within MI6 that used a form of opportunistic supercomputing that allowed multiple computers to participate as elements of a virtual super computer. The result was that each work station had flexible access to whatever computer processing power

was needed for a specific task. The entire system was connected to high-speed fiber-optic communication links to several Internet hub computers giving the TF3 team the fastest and most reliable Internet connections possible.

The tech support supervisor told them that three of the twelve workstations would normally be unmanned but that they had been programmed to automatically receive and re-route decoded data streams from spy satellites operated by GCHQ in the United Kingdom, by the CIA and NSA in the United States, and by the Mossad in Israel. Task Force 3 would not have direct control over the orbital positioning of the spy satellites but any orbital adjustment request they made would be accommodated as soon as possible. Sir Lionel had already told them that the TF3 mission had the highest national security priority in all three of the cooperating countries.

Two of the work stations were unassigned but available for the use of any visitors who might need them or for possible additions to the TF3 team.

Two administrative support work stations were located on opposite sides of the only access door and were manned on alternating shifts by seasoned veterans of many previous MI6 special task force operations.

A large open area at the other end of the room was outfitted as a conference area complete with multiple flat-panel screens and a conference table that could seat twenty people. When desired, each of the projection screens could display a commercial television channel that experience had shown was sometimes useful during national or international crises.

Nahbi called the kick-off meeting to order at 8:05 AM. Only the permanent members of Task Force 3 were present.

"Good morning," Nahbi greeted them. "As you know, our job is to find the nuclear weapons as quickly as possible. Each of you will have a specific primary role but we will collaborate and help each other so the functional boundaries are not hard and fast. We'll adapt as circumstances change and new information becomes available."

"Tiera, you will spend most of your time doing on-line research to acquire specific information I ask you to find for me."

"David, I want you to work closely with GCHQ, NSA, and the Mossad communications analysis section to set up appropriate key-word filters to intercept potentially useful communications and to analyze them. Your broad knowledge of Semitic languages should enable you to screen questionable communications efficiently. I want you to bring to me anything that you think is important enough to merit my attention."

"Pete, since you are the most experienced and senior member of the team so I'd like for you to coordinate our efforts with those of the CIA and Mossad. We need to be sure they get any information we have and that they share what they have with us.

"Phil, I want you to act as the team leader for terrorist threat identification. I'd like for you, Al, and Gavriella to review whatever is known about individuals and organizations that might plausibly be involved in the acquisition and potential use of the nuclear weapons. I'd like to see a short description of each one you identify along with their current location if possible."

Nahbi then explained his own role. "My job will be to assimilate everything the rest of you come up with. I will use my ability to correlate large amounts of information very quickly in order to make probability estimates for various scenarios. I have already concluded that it is a virtual certainty that the weapons could only be transported out of Pakistan by ship. The devices are too heavy to be handled as commercial air cargo without raising suspicion. With Afghanistan to the west, China to the north, and India to the east, there are no viable land routes for transporting the weapons out of Pakistan by car or truck," Nahbi told them. "It's been five or possibly six days since the weapons were stolen from the Wah cantonment. Allowing two days to move them to a port facility at either Karachi or Gwadar, that means the weapons might have left Pakistan four or five days ago."

"Tiera, your first assignment is to research all ship movements into and out of Pakistan. Pay particular attention to container and general cargo ship movements and especially to those bound for ports in Muslim countries."

"We will get together again at 1:00 PM today for updates and any necessary adjustments in our approach." Demonstrating his mastery of modern English idioms and good leadership technique, Nahbi made them all laugh when he concluded by saying, "*Let's Rock and Roll.*"

1:00 PM

David had expected that Nahbi might call on him first in tacit recognition of his status as his deputy so he was ready.

"David, have you been able to get key-word filters installed on the various streams of monitored communications?" Nahbi asked.

"Yes, the folks at NSA were very helpful. They already screen for most of the key-words and phrases we'd be interested in. Unfortunately, the volume is staggering. NSA is literally watching message traffic from all over the world. Their supercomputer is already one of the fastest on Earth but even it is barely able to handle the data volume NSA monitors. It will take me several more hours to devise some way to filter what they're feeding me to a level we can cope with. The teams at GCHQ and Mossad were also very helpful. I'm cross-checking their key words with those of NSA to see if they've thought of some filter strings that NSA hasn't."

"Pete, do you know who your go-to contacts are in each of the agencies?"

"Yes. At the CIA it'll be my boss, Roger Benson. Here at MI6, we'll go through Sir Lionel for anything Phil and I can't handle alone. Gabe's boss, Levi Reznik, will be our senior level contact in the Mossad. I'm pretty confident that the three agencies will work together effectively to find the weapons."

"Tiera, what do we know about ship movements so far?" Nahbi asked.

"Not very much, I'm afraid. During the time period we're focusing on, there have been 23 arrivals at the Port of Karachi. Of those, ten were container ships and one was a general cargo ship. The rest were tankers. I'm still trying to find out departure dates and destinations for all of them. The port's web site isn't updated very often and seems to have a lot of erroneous information."

"I've drawn a blank on the Port of Gwadar in Western Pakistan so far. Gwadar was turned over to the Chinese last year for further development and port management. I haven't yet found a website showing arrivals and departures from Gwadar. I'm still working on it."

Nahbi made a suggestion. "Ask if any of the agencies have high-resolution satellite photos of Pakistan's ports. You might be able to determine ship's movements that way if on-line research isn't working. Also, contact Lloyd's of London, Seven Seas and other shipping insurance companies to see if they can furnish Pakistan arrival and departure information for ships they insure."

"Phil, what can you tell us so far about the bad guys?"

"We're just getting started. In Pakistan, the obvious choices are Lieutenant General Parvez Jhalawan, Ahmed Malik, and Dr. Bashir Ghilzai. We did learn something interesting that may be pertinent. Two days after the theft of the weapons, the bodies of the two Pakistan soldiers who were involved in the theft were found by some children playing in a grove of trees. They'd both been shot in the head at close range."

"We know that Ahmed Malik met with the Sicilian Mafia boss, Enrico Favaloro, probably in connection with the assassination of the ECB President. However, we can't be sure that was the purpose of the meeting. Malik was almost certainly aware of, if not actively involved in, the theft of the weapons. That suggests that we need to put Enrico Favaloro on our list."

"A former Egyptian Army officer named Akil El-Sayed was the apparent successor to Osama bin Laden as the leader of Al Qaeda. He was near the top of the American's list of most-wanted terrorists until he was killed by an American Navy drone in Libya on 9 May. He had met earlier in the day with the Egyptian Ambassador to Pakistan, Hassan Al-Zeid, so we will add Al-Zeid to our list of possible bad guys.

"We've already come up with a fairly long list of individuals and militant organizations from Afghanistan, Iran, Iraq, Egypt, Libya, Turkey, Yemen, and even the United Kingdom, the United States, and several western European countries that have large expatriate

Muslim populations. We've hardly begun to think about Indonesia with its large Muslim population."

"Radical Islamic terrorists are not the only suspects although for now they're at the top of our list. North Korea is another possibility given its recent regime change and the heightened tension with South Korea. We know they've bought nuclear technology from Pakistan in the past just as both Libya and Iran have. However, North Korea already has nuclear weapons so it's hard to see why they would be involved. We've even considered the Irish Republican Army. Nuclear weapons would give the IRA a powerful bargaining position in their desire for Ireland to become independent of the United Kingdom."

"We're trying to devise some way to filter the list of possibilities so we can concentrate on determining the movements and ancillary connections for the highest probability candidates. I think we're going to need to put what we do know on a single computer and then ask you to download it directly so you can do your magic correlation and probability analysis. Otherwise, it would be a miracle if we could narrow the list down to a high probability subset of likely candidates," Phil concluded.

"Send me links to all of your files. I'll review what you have so far to see if I can devise some short-cuts for you."

Nahbi then gave the team his own assessment of the current situation. "Pending more information, the working theories and assumptions with the highest statistical probabilities are these:"

"One or more high-ranking civilian or military leaders of Pakistan's government were involved. Let's focus on those high-ranking officers and civilians known to be sympathetic to militant Islamic organizations. Give your highest priority to those with suspected involvement in previous transfers of nuclear technology and secrets to Iran and North Korea."

"The enlisted personnel were executed because they knew too much. They were merely the means of getting the weapons out of the nuclear cantonment area and delivering them to someone. Try to find links between those two unfortunate men and anyone high up in the military or civilian government."

"The weapons were almost certainly transported to either Karachi or Gwadar by car or truck to be loaded onto a ship. They were most likely transported together for security reasons. The combined weight of all five weapons would be close to 1,000 pounds so only a truck or a large SUV or sedan with heavy duty suspension could have been used. Focus on connections between military and government officials who possess such vehicles or who have access to them. Bear in mind that the number of people involved has to be kept small in order to maintain the requisite secrecy."

"It is highly probable that the weapons have already left Pakistan. Cargo and tanker ships cruise at between 15 and 25 knots. That suggests that the ship carrying the weapons could already be 1,500 to 3,000 miles from Pakistan depending on the departure date from one of the ports. If we can narrow the list of candidate ships somewhat, we may be able to contact ship owners for the signal codes for the ship's global tracking systems."

"The high-probability targets for the weapons are Israel and large cities in Western Europe and the United States. Whoever has the weapons now possesses a very large hammer. They will not use it to crush gnats. It is possible that there could be up to five separate targets or some smaller number with more than one device used against a single target. When we're finished here in a few minutes, I'd like to brainstorm what criteria a terrorist organization might use to select the target or targets."

"I do not think the weapons are being routed to the southeast around the southern tip of India. There are no apparent high-value targets in that direction for thousands of miles. Instead, I think it likely that the weapons are being routed through the Suez Canal into the Mediterranean or possibly around the southern tip of Africa."

"If Israel is the target, then the logistics of getting the weapons into position will be quite challenging for the terrorists. The Israelis are on high alert so the weapons would almost certainly be intercepted if the terrorists tried to land them along Israel's Mediterranean coast. The most feasible way to get one or more weapons into Israel would be to offload them at Port Said at the north end of the Suez Canal and then drive them overland through the Sinai to Khirbat al-Adas at the southern end of the Gaza Strip.

The Muslim Brotherhood controls the northern Sinai and Hamas controls the Gaza Strip so the terrorists would be on friendly territory until they reached the Israeli border."

"Although the Gaza Strip is one of the most densely-populated areas on Earth, the area to the east of the Armistice Agreement Line in Israel is mostly irrigated farmland with relatively few people. The Erez border crossing at the north end of the Gaza Strip is heavily guarded and anyone crossing is subjected to intense scrutiny. Rather than risk Erez, I think the terrorists might use a tunnel from somewhere in Gaza into the farming areas as they've done many times before. A very large tunnel was recently discovered by the IDF running over a mile from near Abasan al-Sa'ir in Gaza to a field three kilometers west of Ein HaShlosha. There are lots of potato farms in that area and trucks are everywhere that could be used to transport the devices once they were inside Israel."

"If the target or targets are in Western Europe, then the routing would almost certainly be via the Suez Canal. Given the civil unrest in Greece and Turkey, it is unlikely that either of those countries would be on the infiltration route. That suggests Northern Italy, Southern France, or Southeastern Spain as the most likely ports of access to the continent. Let's do some research to identify the weakest security of the several potential ports in that area."

"If the target or targets is in the United States, then the routing would almost certainly be via the Suez Canal and then into the Atlantic Ocean via the Straits of Gibraltar. From there, any of the East Coast ports would be potential destinations. However, Gulf Coast ports cannot be ruled out."

"Based on what we know and can reasonably assume, it is probable that the weapons left Pakistan four or five days ago aboard a ship bound for the Suez Canal. Depending on the type of ship and its cruising speed, the weapons may have already reached the Suez Canal although I doubt that they have yet had time to enter the Mediterranean."

"It is highly probable that the nuclear devices have been removed from the artillery shell cases and concealed in some innocuous-appearing container. I have evaluated the most likely alternate containers and believe that a steel cylinder designed to hold

industrial gas, such as acetylene or oxygen, is the most likely probability. Such cylinders are large enough to enclose the nuclear devices and heavy enough to pass a casual inspection. However, any metal container that is at least 203 mm in diameter and approximately one meter in length could be employed to conceal the devices."

"Finally, the probability analysis thus far has been focused on ocean-going ships that cruise at between 15 and 25 knots. It is possible that the weapons could have been placed aboard a cruise ship or large yacht instead. However, the cruising speed would still be in the same range."

"It is also possible that the weapons have already been separated. I hope not because that would make our task infinitely more difficult."

"I will work around the clock until we find the weapons," Nahbi told them. "Fortunately, I do not get tired although I realize that each of you must get some rest in order to remain effective. I propose that you all work two seven-hour shifts with the first shift starting at 6:00 AM followed by a one-hour lunch break at 1:00 PM. The second shift will run from 2:00 PM until 9:00 PM. That will give you nine hours for sleep and getting some exercise. The schedule is not hard and fast but I think it best if there is a long period each day when we are all available. If you want to work longer hours than I've suggested that's entirely up to you."

Thursday, June 5

Suez, Egypt
4:35 PM

It was warm and humid at the southern entrance to the Suez Canal. Two hours earlier, the Empress IV had moved from the holding area anchorage to a pier with four cranes and was ready to off-load several containers. Yousef Abu Shakra was already waiting on the pier with his one small bag. He could see the blue container

with the Ambassador's car in it on the top layer of the huge stack of steel shipping containers.

Yousef watched as a big hammerhead crane lowered the container with the Ambassador's car in it onto the back of a transport truck on the pier. The Egyptian driver tightened the hold-down fasteners and was about to climb back into the cab when Yousef walked over to him. He offered the driver a nice tip to let him ride in the truck to the nearby container storage yard where the car would be removed from its container and turned over to him.

An hour later, Yousef turned left out of the container storage yard's fenced enclosure and drove northeasterly along the water toward the center of the town of Suez, Egypt. He had made arrangements to spend the night at a villa six miles north of town that was owned by a member of the Muslim Brotherhood. Sometime after dark, with help from the villa's owner, he would remove the green tank from the trunk of the Ambassador's car and strap it to a sturdy two-wheeled cart in the back of a delivery van parked in the garage below the villa's elevated residence.

In the morning, he would drive the delivery van to a service pier where he would supervise the tank being loaded onto a port delivery boat. He would stay with the tank until he saw the Chief Engineer of the Belle Maria leaning over the rail to personally supervise having the cart hoisted aboard. When the Chief Engineer signaled that he had the tank safely on board, the second phase of Yousef's assignment would be complete.

MI6 Headquarters, London
9:08 PM

"Want to come to my room for a little while?" Tiera asked as she and David walked toward the elevator.

"Sure, if you promise there'll be no monkey business." David wondered if she recognized the phrase she'd used that night at the old stone cottage on her father's estate.

Tiera leaned forward to look into the retina scanner at the door to her room and waited for the click that signaled the door was

unlocked. She and David stepped into the room and let the door close.

Tiera immediately put her arms around his neck and gave him a long and passionate kiss that caught him a bit by surprise. As he returned her kiss he became aroused and knew that Tiera could feel the pulsing against her leg. She put one of her legs between his and pressed it against him so she could feel his erection. It took all of his will power to turn aside and pull away from her. He ran his fingers through her hair and gave her a gentle kiss on her forehead.

"Hey," he whispered softly. "I thought there wasn't going to be any monkey business."

"That's what you said," Tiera said with a pouting look on her face. "I didn't agree to those terms and conditions. You can't blame a girl for trying. Hey, want to take a shower with me?" she asked with an impish grin.

David laughed and shook his head slowly, "You're incorrigible. I wonder what you'd do if I said yes."

"Say yes and you'll find out quickly enough."

"You know I can't do that no matter how badly I'd like to."

"Why, David? Why? I know you love me and I can tell that you want me. Why do we have to torture ourselves so?" Tiera asked sadly.

"You know why. If we made love and then never married we'd both be sleeping with a ghost for the rest of our lives. No matter how much we loved the person we married, there would always be memories of the pleasures we'd shared with each other. What if you married another man and he couldn't satisfy you in bed. Would you spend the rest of your life comparing him to me? That would be a terrible tragedy for you both. Surely you know how hard it is for me to be firm about this. I want you with every fiber of my being but I believe with all my heart and soul that it would be wrong if we haven't made a lifelong commitment to each other in marriage."

David looked into Tiera's eyes and then said, "Think about it this way. Your father is rightfully proud of that fine red wine he produces on the estate when all around are unremarkable wines that satisfy less-discriminating palates. My dear, sweet Tiera, wait for the fine

wine to mature. Don't settle for anything less than the very best and rarest of the finest wine you can drink from this cup of life. Be patient. We have something very important to do right now. Let's get through this and then take some time to make the decisions we both know we'll have to make. Hold on to the sure and certain owledge that I love you so very much."

Tiera nodded and gave him a wan smile. "OK. If there's not going to be any monkey business, then this tired girl needs her beauty rest. Get out of here so I can take a shower and get to bed. I love you too you big brute. Good night."

Like everyone on the TF3 team except Nahbi, David knew that Tiera was exhausted. The work was both tedious and intense. After more than fourteen hours, the human members of the TF3 team were mentally wrung out and painfully aware of just how big the haystack was and how small the needle. Still, David thought it had been a highly productive day in terms of getting data channels established and beginning to sift the enormous amount of information they hoped would finally give them the clues they needed to find the nuclear weapons.

9:30 PM

Sir Lionel locked his office door and was on his way out of the building. As he was walking toward the elevator, he saw that Gordon McFarland's light was still on and walked down the hall to ask him a few questions.

"Am I interrupting?"

"Oh, good evening sir. No. Not at all. I'm about ready to call it a day."

"Gordon, do you think it was a good idea to put the android in charge of the task force?"

"Yes. Absolutely! Clearly, he is uniquely qualified but to succeed every supervisor must gain the respect of his subordinates. Nahbi has done that. The rest of the TF3 team members have all told me that he's brilliant and untiring but of course we expected that."

"Phil Shaw told me that Nahbi can analyze in seconds data that has taken them hours to collect and that even with the rest of them

feeding him data, it seems like Nahbi is always waiting on them. Tiera told me that Nahbi uses those times when he's waiting for input to conduct thousands of data searches from his own work station."

"When I asked if he had any concerns, David Logan told me that Nahbi had set a grueling pace they were all struggling to keep up with. Yet, David also pointed out that Nahbi is a highly effective supervisor. They all seem to like having him lead the team because he multiplies their effectiveness."

"Gavriella said that Nahbi is totally attuned to what they're working on and often provides helpful suggestions that save them time and help avoid wasted effort. Al Flores told me that he's never worked for a boss who was always good-natured and tactful the way Nahbi is. Al said that when one of them goes to him for help, Nahbi always smiles and seems genuinely pleased that they've come to him."

"David told me two other things that reinforce my conviction that your decision to put Nahbi in charge of the team was the right one. As you know, David was an Army officer who led men in combat in Afghanistan. In that capacity, he had a moral responsibility to do everything he could to protect the lives of his men. It is easy to see that he carries both physical and mental wounds from that time in his life. But that experience has made him a good judge of leadership ability. David told me that it's almost like Nahbi read every book that has ever been written on the art and science of effective leadership and has assimilated the best ideas and incorporated them into his personal leadership style. I pointed out to David that was precisely what Nahbi had done."

"But, the other thing David told me was the clincher. He said they all had a powerful sense that they are part of an exceptional team under the direction of a remarkable leader. He said the team believes in each other and feel that if anyone can find the weapons before it is too late, it's them."

Friday, June 6

Suez, Egypt
2:03 PM

Yousef Abu Shakra had been waiting patiently for almost an hour on the patio of a waterfront café. Although it wasn't unusually hot, a large umbrella provided welcome shade from bright sunlight. A pair of binoculars was lying on the table. He had a clear view of the holding area anchorage just south of the entrance to the Suez Canal.

A few minutes after two o'clock, he saw the Belle Maria enter the holding area and drop anchor. A pilot boat went alongside almost immediately.

Forty minutes later, Yousef was standing in the bow of a small, flat-bottomed utility boat when it went alongside the giant Suezmax tanker. He scanned the rail above for the face in the photograph. He finally saw the Chief Engineer leaning over the rail near a small boom crane the ship used to hoist minor cargo aboard. The Chief Engineer had seen him too and they nodded at each other in recognition. The delivery boat had several pallets of lettuce, citrus fruits, dates, canned goods, and spare parts that the ship's supply officer had ordered. Yousef asked that the oxygen cylinder be transferred first. A few minutes later, the Chief Engineer gave him a thumbs-up signal and moved out of sight.

An hour after the modified oxygen tank and its secret contents had been loaded aboard the Belle Maria, Yousef parked the delivery van at the villa. He immediately got into the Ambassador's limousine and headed for Alexandria.

Twenty-three kilometers north of Suez City, Yousef slowed down as he queued up behind several container trucks and a bus. When he reached the checkpoint, he showed the customs and immigration officer his passport and diplomatic papers. He was waved through without the limousine being inspected. It was 108 kilometers from the checkpoint on the dusty Suez-Cairo road to where he crossed the Nile River north of downtown Cairo near the town of Shubra Al Khaymah. After he crossed the river, it was 207 kilometers to the Ambassador's home west of Alexandria.

Six and a half hours after leaving Suez, Yousef hit the button for the garage door opener at the Ambassador's villa overlooking the Mediterranean Sea. He'd gotten stuck in a massive traffic jam on the east bank of the Nile River for over an hour but had otherwise made good time.

He was tired but quietly satisfied by his success in bringing his cargo safely to the Ambassador's residence as he'd been ordered to do. He checked his cargo and then relocked the limousine's trunk. He then went straight to his quarters at the back of the compound to call Ambassador Al-Zeid to tell him he'd arrived in Alexandria and that everything had gone as planned. He knew that the Ambassador would notify General Jhalawan.

Alexandria, Egypt
3:15 PM

Franco stroked Teresa's bare back as she lay beside him in her room at the Golf Porto Marina Hotel. Her skin was soft and warm. It was very pleasant in the room with the sliding door open to the balcony overlooking the beach and the blue waters of the Mediterranean Sea.

Franco was relaxed and happy. He had stayed away from Teresa for three long days. When he'd called her, he had been afraid that she wouldn't want him to come. Her obligations under her agreement with his uncle had technically ended when they arrived in Alexandria. She would have been entirely within her rights to tell him no. But, to his great joy, she had laughed with delight at the sound of his voice and told him to hurry.

Their pent-up desires had been released in a passionate explosion that left them both panting and sweating. They'd showered together and then made love two more times. They'd showered again and then sat naked and cross-legged in the middle of the bed eating little sandwiches and fruit that Teresa had ordered from room service. Teresa was fondling him again and he was beginning to respond when his phone rang.

It was his uncle asking where he was. Franco told him he'd gone for a drive. His uncle asked him to come to the house because he

wanted to talk to him. Franco told him he'd be there in a half hour. Teresa made a face when she heard him say that.

"I have to go. I'm sorry. I would love to stay with you but I just can't. I'll call you when I can."

5:25 PM

Ten minutes after Franco left, Teresa's phone rang.

"Hello?"

"Signorina Giachetti?" a man's voice asked.

"Yes, who is this?"

"This is Ibrahim Al-Jabiri. Mr. Ghanem asked me to speak to you to see if you would like to make some more money."

"What does he have in mind?" Teresa asked cautiously. In her experience, when a man used the phrase *make some more money*, he usually wanted her to do something perverted or painful.

"I'm in the hotel now. Could you meet me on the patio beside the swimming pool in a few minutes?"

"OK. I'll be down in five minutes."

Ibrahim Al-Jabiri was seated at a table beneath a big umbrella. To her surprise, he stood as a courtesy when she approached and shook hands with her in a friendly way.

"Thank you for meeting with me. I think you will like what I have to say," he said. "Please sit down. Can I order something for you?"

"No, thank you. I'd like to hear what Mr. Ghanem has in mind."

"Mr. Ghanem is very pleased with the new yacht but there are some modifications he'd like for the Ferretti factory to make to the flying bridge. He's asked Signor Sartori to take the yacht back to Italy and has offered to pay him a very nice bonus. Signor Sartori has graciously agreed to do as Mr. Ghanem has requested."

"In the original agreement, Mr. Ghanem offered to pay you and Signora Pedrazzini 10,000 euros each for a five-day cruise followed by a five-day, all expenses paid holiday in Alexandria and first-class airfare back to Italy. He did not require you to provide your customary services to his nephews but only to be pleasant companions for them. I understand that perhaps the young men

behaved as young men often do and that you and Signora Pedrazzini have been very good companions for them both. Mr. Ghanem is pleased and is happy to pay the bonus that was mentioned. I have envelopes here for you and Signora Pedrazzini. Each envelope contains 7,000 euros to complete Mr. Ghanem's agreement with you both."

"Please thank Mr. Ghanem for us," Teresa said. "May I hear what Mr. Ghanem now proposes?"

"As you may have already guessed, Mr. Ghanem would like for you and Signora Pedrazzini to return to Italy on the yacht. His nephews will help Signor Sartori handle the yacht on the return trip. Signor Sartori is a licensed marine instructor and will continue to teach them about the technical aspects of the yacht and navigation so they can obtain master yacht certificates once they return to Italy. Mr. Ghanem desires that his nephews be able to bring the yacht back to Alexandria by themselves when his requested modifications are complete."

"Mr. Ghanem has authorized me to offer another 10,000 euros to both of you with the possibility of another 2,000 euro bonus for you both if your services are satisfactory. He would like for you and Signora Pedrazzini to remain with the yacht until it reaches Venice. He will then provide first-class airfare for you back to Bari. If you agree, it will represent a total compensation of 24,000 euros each for about 16 days of your service. May I inform Mr. Ghanem that you will accept his generous offer?"

Teresa looked at him thoughtfully before replying. "I cannot speak for Lia although I believe she will agree. In any event, I would be happy to accept Mr. Ghanem's offer. I will talk to Lia and call you this evening."

"Thank you. I will await your call," he said.

6:30 PM

"Will the fireflies return with the yacht?" Hakeem Ghanem asked his General Manager. The two men were sitting in Ghanem's study at his villa west of Alexandria. Ghanem would not relax until this last detail was taken care of and the yacht was safely on its way.

"I believe they will," Al-Jabiri told his employer. "Signorina Giachetti has essentially already said yes. She will speak to Signora Pedrazzini and call me with their decision this evening."

"I've asked Franco to come see me when you and I are finished. How much do you think I should tell him?"

"We must know if he can be relied upon to do what must be done once the yacht arrives back in Venice. If you wait, you'll have to explain it to him over the phone and there would be some risk that he might not be willing. I think you must explain the courier role he and Fredo will play while he is here," Ibrahim suggested. "Then you can gauge his reactions and decide if you are willing to trust your nephew with a critical role in the most important blow that any of us will ever strike against the infidels. If you are not completely satisfied that he will do as you ask, we will have to make other plans."

Hakeem Ghanem was silent for a moment before saying, "I think Franco will agree to transport the devices but I also think he would balk at what must be done before he and Fredo leave Venice."

"Fredo is clearly infatuated with Signora Pedrazzini. The man I had watching the hotel this afternoon told me that Franco had been in the hotel for several hours and left only minutes before you arrived. I'm sure he was with Signorina Giachetti. We must assume that my nephews now have emotional involvement with these two young women."

"But I have given much thought to this. My nephews' predictable reticence is not a significant problem. I will arrange for a limousine to pick up the fireflies at Signor Sartori's home to drive them to the airport. The driver will handle the part that I don't think I could trust my nephews to do."

"It is absolutely critical that the fireflies agree to return with the yacht. If the yacht is boarded for inspection, I want the officials to see a harmless, middle-aged Italian couple and four attractive young people. The purpose of the voyage to Alexandria is perfectly believable since Abramo is a licensed yacht broker with many wealthy Arab clients. He can show the blueprints you made to explain that his customer wants factory modifications made to the

yacht. Everything that he and his wife know is entirely routine and legal. If they are questioned closely, the fact that the two young women are prostitutes hired as companions for my nephews will only strengthen what is otherwise an entirely plausible cover story," Ghanem concluded.

Al-Jabiri's cell phone rang. "Mr. Al-Jabiri, this is Teresa Giachetti. I've spoken to Lia and she is willing to do as Mr. Ghanem has requested. When will we leave?"

Al-Jabiri told her the yacht would leave Alexandria Sunday morning. He thanked her and hung up. "They will do it."

A few minutes later, Franco knocked on the door to his uncle's study. When he left an hour later, Hakeem Ghanem was satisfied that his nephews would carry out their part of the plan.

MI6 Headquarters, London
8:02 PM

Nahbi looked around the room and recognized the team's fatigue. "You've all done some great work. Here's where we stand as of this evening."

"We're almost certain that the nuclear weapons were stolen at the direction of Lieutenant General Parvez Jhalawan with help from Ahmed Malik and Dr. Bashir Ghilzai. We're reviewing what we know about their movements and meetings over the previous month to see if we can identify other persons who may be involved."

"We're still not sure how the weapons were transported from Wah to either Karachi or Gwadar but Tiera has identified eight container ships and one general cargo ship that left Pakistan between the 28th of May and the 2nd of June. Of those nine ships, seven were bound for the Suez Canal. We will focus our attention on those seven ships."

"Tiera also identified fourteen large yachts with sufficient speed and range that left Pakistan in that time period. However, for various reasons, we have eliminated all of them as potential transport vessels for the weapons. It is still possible that the weapons might be transferred from a large ship to a private yacht

either while underway or at some port of call so we'll have to be alert to that possibility."

"The most likely target cities in Western Europe are Paris, Frankfurt, and London. Potential second-tier targets include Madrid, Brussels, Amsterdam, and Berlin. In the United States, the most obvious target is Washington, DC. New York is a second-tier possibility. I want to concentrate on message chatter between the various bad guys that mentions any of those cites."

"If the terrorists plan to attack Israel, it will almost certainly be Tel Aviv. However, my analyses increasingly indicate that Israel is not the target. Although Israel is hated by the Islamic extremists, they would accomplish much more by attacking the United States or one or more of the major Western European cities while killing fewer of their own people and without sowing radioactive contamination in a region they want to occupy."

"When all factors are considered, the European ports of Barcelona, Marseille, Toulon, Monaco, Genoa, and Venice appear to have the most porous security for cruise ships and luxury yachts. Any of the container ports could provide a point of entry with only moderate risk of detection." None of the major U.S. ports can be considered to have porous security. I think it is likely that the infiltration point in the United States would be a secondary port such as one of the Gulf Coast ports in Louisiana or Texas."

"Tomorrow, I want to concentrate on the seven ships headed for the Suez Canal," Nahbi told the team. "I want to know who owns them and the nationalities of the ship masters and senior officers. I want to know where they are as of noon tomorrow."

"I still want to know how the weapons were transported from Wah to one of the Pakistan ports. I also want a full cross-reference to anyone suspicious who met with General Jhalawan, Ahmed Malik, or Bashir Ghilzai recently."

"I'll need a biographical summary of the senior members of Al Qaeda, the Taliban, and the Muslim Brotherhood, particularly in Pakistan, Afghanistan, and Egypt." I also want a similar bio for the senior leaders of those organizations in each of the high-probability target cities."

"I think it's time we found out what reconnaissance assets can be brought to bear once we identify the most probable transport vehicles. Phil, I'd like for your team to contact the appropriate military and civilian agencies to see what we'll have to work with."

"Get a good night's sleep. I think tomorrow is critical. It is probable that the weapons have either already reached the Suez Canal or soon will."

Saturday, June 7

Alexandria, Egypt
7:32 AM

Shortly after sunrise Saturday morning, Ibrahim Al-Jabiri parked the Ghanem Company's cargo van beside the garage at the home of Egypt's Ambassador to Pakistan. Yousef Abu-Shakra was waiting for him.

The two men transferred what appeared to be four unusually heavy scuba tanks from the trunk of the Ambassador's limousine to a cradle in the back of the cargo van. When they'd finished loading the tanks, both men got into the van and drove east toward Alexandria.

The Ghanem Equipment Company facilities were located in a crowded industrial area in the Al Qabbari district on the west end of Alexandria's main harbor. The two-story office building was modern and attractive. The executive offices on the top floor had an excellent view of the harbor. The machine shops and warehouses behind it were rusted metal buildings surrounded by bins and dumpsters full of scrap metal and industrial waste.

A ten-foot high chain-link fence topped with razor wire enclosed a large lay-down yard where several flatbed trailers loaded with oil field equipment awaiting repairs or overhaul were parked. Along the west side of the enclosure was a row of boat cradles for large yachts temporarily in the yard for engine overhauls. Several tall aluminum poles capped with flood lights provided bright illumination to support night work and provide security lighting. The company had

two parallel 40 meter long finger piers with tracks on each side for a huge straddle crane used to lift large yachts and transport them to the storage cradles. A sloped concrete ramp at the shore end of the piers allowed smaller boats to be launched or recovered from boat trailers.

Twenty five minutes after leaving the Ambassador's villa, Al-Jabiri parked the van on the company piers near where the Ferretti 690 yacht was moored.

Thirty minutes later, all four tanks were strapped into a vertical rack inside the new scuba tank storage cabinet on the aft main deck of the yacht. Al-Jabiri locked the cabinet. He set the yacht's alarm system before he and Abu-Shakra stepped back onto the pier. One of the company's armed security guards saluted Al-Jabiri as he drove the van off the pier.

The nuclear devices hidden inside the fake scuba tanks had already come almost three thousand miles by land and sea. Their next destination was over twelve hundred nautical miles away and that would still not be the end of their journey.

Yousef thought his part in General Jhalawan's plan was finished. He was wrong.

MI6 HQ, London
5:00 PM

Nahbi was reviewing the biographies of known terrorists that Phil and his team had assembled. There were a lot of them. He was thinking of the best way to narrow the list when Tiera poked her head into his cubicle. David was with her.

"Can we talk to you for a few minutes? David and I think one of the weapons may be on an oil tanker named the Belle Maria. We also think we know how the weapons were taken out of Pakistan."

Nahbi nodded and waited for Tiera to continue.

"The Egyptian Ambassador to Pakistan is a man named Hassan Al-Zeid. He is a senior member of the Muslim Brotherhood. Al Flores found out from his CIA contacts that Al-Zeid had a secret meeting with General Jhalawan at the General's villa in Janawai on 15 May. David found out that the previous day the NSA intercepted

and decoded a message from the Egyptian President ordering Al-Zeid back to Egypt. The message directed the Ambassador to have his limousine shipped back to Egypt as well. His driver and bodyguard, a man named Yousef Abu-Shakra, is also a member of the Muslim Brotherhood. He drove the car from Islamabad to the Gwadar port and supervised having it put into a vehicle container. It was loaded onto the container ship Empress IV that left Gwadar Port at 6:00 AM on Sunday, the first of June."

"Why do you think the weapons were in the Ambassador's car?"

"It took us a while to fit the pieces of the puzzle together. It began with the Egyptian President recalling Ambassador Al-Zeid on 14 May and directing him to ship his limousine back to Egypt. The Ambassador had lunch with General Jhalawan the next day. The weapons were stolen two weeks later in the late evening of 28 May."

"The Chinese now run the Gwadar Port under a management agreement with the Pakistan government and they are sticklers for bureaucratic process. However, David pointed out that the Ambassador's diplomatic status would allow the vehicle to be loaded with little or no inspection. The container ship transmitted bills of lading to the insurance company for each container loaded at Gwadar Port. The bill of lading for the container holding the Ambassador's car was roughly one-thousand pounds heavier than it should have been. The nuclear devices weigh just less than 200 pounds each so that could account for the unusual weight. Abu Shakra was listed as a passenger on the Empress IV."

"If the weapons left Pakistan inside the Ambassador's vehicle on a container ship, what makes you think one of the weapons is now on the tanker?" Nahbi asked her.

"The NSA intercepted a call from Abu Shakra to the Chief Engineer of the Belle Maria directing him to place an order with a certain company for an oxygen bottle. The Chief Engineer is an Egyptian member of the Muslim Brotherhood named Zakaria Nassar. NSA also intercepted his call to the industrial gases company in the Port of Suez."

"The Empress IV moved to the container pier at the Port of Suez late in the afternoon of Thursday, 5 June. The Ambassador's car was

off-loaded immediately. The Belle Maria reached the Port of Suez the next day on Friday, 6 June. Shortly afterward, a harbor service boat delivered a medium-size, green industrial oxygen bottle to the Belle Maria's Chief Engineer. A man fitting Yousef Abu Shakra's description was on the service boat. You told us that the nuclear devices could be hidden in something like an industrial gas bottle. We think one of the weapons has been concealed in an oxygen bottle and delivered to the Belle Maria. The ship is bound for the Texaco Oil Terminal in Port Arthur, Texas via the Strait of Gibraltar," Tiera concluded.

"Where is the Belle Maria now?" Nahbi asked.

David answered. "According to the insurance company's satellite tracking system, she is part of a convoy of ships that is approaching the northern end of the Suez Canal at Port Said. She will enter the Mediterranean about an hour from now."

"Where are the other weapons?"

"We don't know," Tiera said. "Abu Shakra may still have them or he may have already transferred them to one or more other ships."

"We need to find Abu Shakra. He can tell us where the other weapons are," Nahbi said.

"He's in Alexandria," David told him. "Just before midnight last night, the NSA intercepted a cell phone call he made to Ambassador Al-Zeid saying that he had arrived in Alexandria and that everything had gone as planned."

"Where is Ambassador Al-Zeid?"

"He's in Cairo staying with friends. He and his wife arrived there yesterday afternoon from Doha, Qatar. He has a meeting with the Egyptian President Monday morning at 10:00 AM," Tiera told him.

"How do we know that?" Nahbi asked.

"The Chief of Staff to the Egyptian President keeps us well-informed. He passes information to a member of the staff of one of the Egyptian Shura Council who is a senior member of the Muslim Brotherhood. The staff contact is actually an Egyptian double agent working for the CIA."

Nahbi pressed the intercom button on his desk to ask Phil Shaw, Pete Nocona, Al Flores, and Gavriella Adler to join them.

When they were all together in Nahbi's cubicle, he told them, "I need to know if any of your agencies have an experienced intelligence agent on the ground in Alexandria, Egypt. We need to interrogate an individual who is unlikely to cooperate with us willingly and it must happen tonight. Check with your operations folks and get back to me immediately. This is top priority," Nahbi emphasized.

"Pete, see what the CIA can do about mobilizing some reconnaissance assets. Phil and Gabe, I'd like for you to contact your agencies with the same objective. Ideally, I'd like to have a submarine shadow the Bella Maria. At some point, we may want a U.S. Navy P-3 Orion out of Sigonella to do some fly-bys. We're going to have to board the ship but before we can we're going to need high-level government approvals. While we're waiting on approval and commitment of the necessary assets to accomplish the boarding and inspections, we need to be sure the weapon is not transferred to another vessel."

"It's almost two thousand nautical miles from Port Said to the Strait of Gibraltar so the Belle Maria will be in the Mediterranean for four or five days. During that time, the weapon could be transferred to a smaller boat, such as a private yacht. The military and political folks will have to decide which naval vessel will intercept and board the tanker. The sooner that can take place, the better. Every hour that passes is another opportunity for the weapon to be transferred again."

Twenty minutes later, Pete, Phil, Al, and Gabe were back in Nahbi's cubicle. Phil went first. "One of MI6's best field agents is in Alexandria but Pete thinks there might be a better option."

Pete took that as his cue. "The nuclear-powered aircraft carrier USS George H.W. Bush is operating in the eastern Mediterranean. She's been conducting Sixth Fleet training exercises but, more to the point, she has two platoons from SEAL Team Eight aboard as part of a Deployment for Training, what the Navy refers to as a DFT."

"We've been discussing this among ourselves," Phil said. "We think simply directing a field agent to try to penetrate the compound security at the Ambassador's villa and then trying to get something useful out of Abu Shakra does not have a high probability of success."

"We think having SEAL Team Eight extract Abu Shakra for questioning is more likely to succeed," Pete said. "Initial questioning could begin on board the carrier but he could be flown directly to London if necessary. Alternatively, we could fly an interrogation team to the carrier while the extraction was in progress. In any event, if we simply tried to interrogate him in situ, but did not neutralize him, he would warn the terrorist leaders that we were hot on their trail. We certainly don't need for them to become even more cautious until we know where the weapons are. If he just disappears, they will wonder what happened but won't know anything for sure."

Nahbi nodded and was silent for a few moments as he considered multiple options and calculated probabilities. He then asked a question. "Is it possible to deploy a SEAL Team that quickly? Could we actually assault the Ambassador's compound and kidnap Abu Shakra on such short notice?"

Pete answered. "Yes. SEAL Team Eight continuously trains for this kind of mission. All of the equipment they would need is already on board the carrier. SEAL Team Eight is one of the Navy's most experienced units and they'll have good intel. The CIA agent in Alexandria has confirmed that Abu Shakra is the only person at the compound right now. The Ambassador and his wife are in Cairo and none of the other staff have quarters on site. The CIA can orbit a UAV over the compound to provide real-time imagery and the carrier can provide air support if it turns out to be needed. The Iwo Jima, one of the Navy's Wasp class amphibious assault ships, is in the area conducting joint training with the carrier group. There's a Marine Corps Expeditionary Unit on board in case backup by a quick reaction force is needed. Normally, this kind of snatch and go mission requires extensive planning and training with mockup buildings and multiple scenarios but I am absolutely confident that SEAL Team Eight can execute this mission successfully on short notice.

The Ambassador's villa is 28 miles west of Alexandria in a community of luxury villas known as Kazablanka. It sits on a low rocky knoll overlooking a sandy beach. There is a short staircase from the beach to the sea-side gate into the compound. Abu Shakra's quarters are inside the fenced compound but are separate from the main house. It is very accessible from the sea."

Pete continued to explain why he thought the SEALs were the right approach. "A SEAL Team platoon normally consists of 16 SEALs but they are often divided into either two squads or four elements. I've operated with SEAL Teams before. They are very good at what they do. If there was more time to plan and prepare, the SEALs might go in with a full platoon or more. I'm not a SEAL ops planner but I'm guessing that they'd drop an inflatable boat and four of their best men from a MH-53E Sea Dragon or a V-22 Osprey several miles off-shore and then go ashore in the middle of the night to take Abu Shakra alive. Once they had him, they'd return to a pickup point offshore. Typically, they would sink the inflatable at the pickup point to simplify the recovery."

"Do you think the President of the United States would approve such a mission?" Nahbi asked.

"That's a good question," Pete agreed. "I think we'd have to hope that the NSA Director, who is an Army Lieutenant General, could persuade him. I doubt that the current CIA Director could be counted on for support but no President would hesitate to act when there are nuclear weapons in the hands of terrorists. So, yes, I think the President will approve the mission."

"OK, we'll ask for SEAL Team Eight support. Good work," Nahbi told them.

Nahbi immediately called Gordon McFarland to brief him on the situation and to solicit all possible support from Sir Lionel and the Prime Minister.

Alexandria, Egypt
8:00 PM

Abramo had insisted that they all sleep aboard the yacht so they could get an early start Sunday morning. He'd felt guilty when

Franco and Fredo's mother cried and held onto her sons until the last possible moment.

The rented limousine's driver stopped to pick up Lia and Teresa at the hotel. By 6:00 PM everyone had stowed their luggage and gone ashore to enjoy their last night in Egypt. Abramo and Donatella walked to a nearby waterfront restaurant to have a quiet dinner together. The Rinaldi brothers and the two fireflies had dinner in a small Greek restaurant a few blocks from the marina. By nine o'clock, everyone was back on board and in their cabins. Donatella put ear plugs in her ears so she wouldn't have to listen to the sounds the young people were making.

Port Said, Egypt
8:15 PM

An hour after dark, the Belle Maria cleared the breakwater at the northern end of the Suez Canal and entered the Mediterranean Sea. An hour later, her master ordered a course change onto the second leg of the route the ship would follow toward the Straits of Gibraltar. In the engineering spaces below, Zakaria Nassar took one last look at the mysterious oxygen tank before he locked the door to his office and headed up to his cabin. He thought the tank probably contained poison gas and was very nervous having it in his office.

Mediterranean Sea
9:00 PM

Israeli Defense Force Lieutenant Colonel Abner Myerson was the commanding officer of the Israeli submarine Tekumah. He maneuvered the submarine to take station off the starboard quarter of the contact designated Tango 6 where he would be able to read the ship's name on her stern. When the submarine was in position, he brought it to periscope depth just long enough to confirm that the contact designated Tango 6 was indeed the Belle Maria. He'd been ordered to shadow the tanker while it remained in the Tekumah's top secret op area. The sonar operator on watch had been tracking the tanker since shortly after it entered the Mediterranean Sea from the northern terminus of the Suez Canal. He had enough plot points to determine that Tango 6 was steaming at 16 knots on a course of

330 degrees. At 1015, Tango 6 changed course to 282 degrees and increased speed to 18 knots. The sonar operator recognized that the ship was following a common sea lane for tankers bound for the Strait of Gibraltar and reported the course change to the officer of the deck.

Sunday, June 8

Alexandria, Egypt
2:30 AM

From a quarter-mile offshore, Navy Lieutenant Mark Hays studied the line of oceanfront villas through a pair of night vision binoculars. He had already identified the Ambassador's villa and was watching to be sure there were no people on the beach at this hour. The Chief was monitoring the video feed from the CIA's RQ-170 Sentinel UAV orbiting silently overhead. The four-man element of SEAL Team Eight would not go ashore until the Lieutenant gave the word.

The moon had set more than an hour earlier at 1:19 AM. However, a few of the nearby villas had perimeter lighting so the assault team would not have the benefit of total darkness. Fortunately, the low bluff above the beach would provide some cover until they were ready to enter the compound.

The Zodiac F470 Combat Rubber Raiding Craft, known by its acronym CRRC, rocked gently as the team waited for the signal to land. The boat was 4.75 meters long and was powered by a compact and lightweight 55 HP outboard motor with pump jet propulsion and a shrouded impeller. It could carry a maximum of eight people at 15 to 18 knots.

The CRRC had been dropped four miles offshore by an MH-53E Sea Dragon helicopter from the aircraft carrier George H.W. Bush steaming slowly 60 miles offshore. The SEALs had jumped into the water from a height of about twenty feet. The trip from the drop zone to the beach had taken 30 minutes at 10 knots to minimize noise from the outboard motor.

Each of the four SEALs was armed with a 9mm sound-suppressed Heckler & Koch MP5SD submachine gun with four 30-round magazines. In addition, each carried a Sig Sauer P226 MK25 9mm semi-automatic pistol with three 15-round magazines and a DeGroat suppressor. Because their mission was to capture Abu Shakra alive if possible, the SEALs were using full metal jacket NATO ammunition instead of the more lethal jacketed hollow points. All of the men had Emerson CQC close quarter combat knives strapped to their legs. The blades were made from steel salvaged from the ruins of the World Trade Center.

The SEALs wore black wet suits with hoods, black rubber diving boots, and thin black gloves. They were wearing black Kevlar vests and helmets that would provide protection for their vital organs and some protection against a head shot from the back or side. Each man had a set of night-vision goggles, and their faces were blackened with waterproof grease. Swim fins, diving masks, and snorkels were lashed to the gunnels of the CRRC but would not be used except in an emergency.

All of the SEALs wore amphibious-assault, bone-conduction headsets with microphones certified for depths of up to 20 meters. One advantage of the headsets was that they did not use ear pieces that would block ambient sounds. Another advantage was that the operator heard the transmissions via bone-conduction through the face instead of through a speaker or earpiece that might be overheard by an adversary. The Lieutenant and the Chief Petty Officer also had encrypted satellite communication radios with highly accurate one-meter GPS capability built in.

Lieutenant Hays gave the hand signal to proceed. A few minutes later, the CRRC slid quietly onto the sandy beach. The Chief remained with the CRRC to defend their means of retreat. The Lieutenant and the other two men advanced up the slope single file to the gate into the compound. One of the SEALs inspected the gate carefully for any sign of wiring that might be part of a perimeter security system. There was none. The gate had a simple latch on the inside but was not locked. Within a few seconds, they were inside the compound. There were two non-rotating security cameras

mounted on both sides of the main residence but the area around the staff quarters was not within the field of view of either camera.

Lieutenant Hays studied the staff quarters for a few moments to verify the intel that it was a small apartment for a single occupant. There was a double sliding screen door on the right that opened onto a small covered patio. The apartment's living room was visible through the double doors with the help of the night-vision goggles. A large window on the left was undoubtedly the bedroom. He moved quietly to the side of the bedroom window and cautiously peeked inside. He could see a man lying on the bed and could hear him softly snoring through the screen. Either the apartment was not air conditioned or the occupant preferred fresh air. He made a hand signal to the others that there was one man inside.

The screen door was latched on the inside but it took only a few seconds to cut the plastic screen material and reach inside to open the door. The Lieutenant gave the signal to move in.

Inside the apartment, two of the SEALs moved quietly down the narrow hallway to the bedroom. The first SEAL was in a low crouch position so the second man could fire over him if necessary.

Yousef Abu Shakra had heard the slight sound of the sliding screen door opening and was waiting for them with his 9mm Beretta pistol. As soon as he saw two men in special operations gear, he shot the first one in the forehead. His aim was good and the SEAL fell dead instantly. The second SEAL fired a quick double-tap to Abu Shakra's chest and he went down immediately without firing another shot. Lieutenant Hays moved into a backup position behind his team mate but instantly recognized that the gun play was over. He knelt beside the downed SEAL to check for any pulse. There was none. The man was dead.

The other SEAL was checking Abu Shakra and signaled that he was still alive.

Both bullets had entered Abu Shakra's muscular chest but had apparently missed his heart and not exited from his back. He was unconscious but his external bleeding was manageable. Lieutenant Hays quickly tore some bed sheeting to make a compress bandage and plugged both bullet holes with wads of the cotton sheet. By the

time he'd done that, the other SEAL had torn several long strips from the sheet. They bandaged him as well as they could. The Lieutenant picked up the dead SEAL and shifted his body into a fireman's carry position. The other SEAL did the same with the unconscious Abu Shakra. They retreated to the beach as quickly as they could with their loads.

Before they could leave, however, they needed to search the compound to see if the weapons were there. They would have to hurry. One of the neighbors might have heard the muffled sound of the three gunshots. Lieutenant Hays and the other SEAL went back to the compound and straight to the garage. They forced the side door and immediately saw the Ambassador's black limousine parked inside along with a Land Rover SUV. They pried open the trunk of the limousine but it was empty. The SUV was unlocked but it too was empty. They quickly searched the rest of the garage but there was no evidence that the weapons had ever been there. The Lieutenant realized they were running out of time and he doubted that the weapons would have been stored in the main residence anyway. As far as he could tell, the weapons weren't on the compound. He signaled that it was time to go.

As soon as the CRRC was a few hundred feet offshore, Lieutenant Hays called the carrier to ask for an assisted pickup only two miles offshore in accordance with the mission's contingency plan. A pickup that close to shore risked an angry protest from the Egyptian government but it couldn't be helped. They had to get Abu Shakra to a doctor as quickly as possible. The Lieutenant advised the duty officer that the team had one fatality and a badly-wounded captive. The Chief and the other SEAL were stoic but Mark knew they were grieving just as he was. They had lost a good friend. If their captive died, it would all have been in vain.

7:17 AM

Abramo Sartori steered the yacht past Alexandria's East Harbor breakwater and increased speed to 15 knots on a northerly course. He and Donatella had enjoyed being tourists but they were both ready to go home. If the good weather held, the return trip would take only four days. With the Rinaldi brothers to help drive, and the

extra fuel capacity Hakeem Ghanem had specified, the yacht's maximum range was in excess of 500 nautical miles between refueling stops. It was 328 nautical miles from Alexandria to Sitia, Crete. Abramo expected to tie up to the fuel pier in Sitia marina before dark.

USS George H.W. Bush
8:09 AM

Lieutenant Hays hadn't felt like trying to sleep after they'd returned to the ship. All SEALs know that their profession is one of the most dangerous in the world but this was the first time he'd ever lost one of his men. He would have to write a letter to the SEAL's widow but he just wasn't up to it yet. He showered and went forward to check on their captive.

Yousef Abu Shakra was under armed guard in the intensive care unit of sick bay. Two Marines in combat utility uniforms were posted nearby. Both had M4 carbines, the compact variant of the M16 Assault Rifle. The Navy hospital corpsman on duty told Mark that Abu Shakra would live thanks to their prompt first aid and the skill of the Navy doctor who operated on him. The doctor had removed two 9mm full metal jacket bullets. One of them had done considerable internal damage after glancing off of one of Abu Shakra's ribs. Mark already knew that an interrogation team would land on the carrier within the hour but it was obvious that it would be some time before Abu Shakra could answer questions and there was no guarantee that he would give them the information they needed.

MI6 HQ, London
9:05 AM

Gabe stuck her head into Nahbi's cubicle. "You asked us to identify the available tracking and boarding assets. Here's a quick run-down."

"The Israeli submarine Tekumah made positive ID and tracked the Belle Maria for a couple of hours last night until she moved out of the sub's assigned patrol area. Belle Maria's last reported course was 282 degrees at 18 knots so she should be about 60 nautical

miles north of Mersa Matruh, Egypt by now. Tiera is checking the satellite locator to confirm."

"Al Flores spoke to the duty operations officer at Sixth Fleet headquarters in Naples about an hour ago. The USS Virginia, a nuclear attack submarine, is currently attached to the Sixth Fleet and may be able to take over shadowing the tanker if ordered to do so. The Navy never releases location information on their nuclear submarines without a direct order from the SECDEF or the President so we don't know if Virginia is in position to help. Al also talked to the Commanding Officer of NAS Sigonella in Sicily who told him that the Trident Maritime Patrol Squadron, VP-26, is currently attached to NAS Sigonella."

"VP-26 has four of the older Lockheed P-3C Orions available. They can remain airborne for about 12 hours using their ability to shut down one or two engines to conserve fuel. Normal cruising speed is 300 knots, giving them a surveillance radius of about 1,800 miles from Sigonella. That means that two P-3Cs can cover the entire Mediterranean with some reserve fuel capacity when operating out of Sicily."

"Phil Shaw spoke to the Admiralty's Fleet Battle Staff in Portsmouth. One of the U.K.'s frigates, the HMS Sutherland, is operating in the western Mediterranean and might conceivably be used to board the Belle Maria. HMS Sutherland is currently in port at Gibraltar so the ship is technically under the authority of Sir Theodore Macfarland, the current Governor and Commander in Chief of Gibraltar," Gabe concluded.

Nahbi thanked her and was about to turn back to his computer when Al Flores appeared.

"Bad news, I'm afraid. One member of SEAL Team Eight was killed by Abu Shakra during the extraction. Abu Shakra was seriously wounded and is in critical condition aboard the carrier. The interrogation team may be on board by now but it will be some time before Abu Shakra can be questioned."

"Yes, that is unfortunate," Nahbi responded. "But at least Abu Shakra is alive so we may still get the information we need."

Monday, June 9

Sitia, Crete
6:00 AM

Franco was at the helm when his uncle's yacht cleared the breakwater at Sitia and headed for Lixouri on the Greek island of Kefallinia. It was 347 nautical miles away so they'd gotten an early start. At the yacht's rated cruising speed of 27 knots, they should reach the quay in Lixouri around 7:00 PM. He was tired but happy after spending the night with Teresa in the owner's cabin. They had made love until they were both exhausted and then had fallen asleep in each other's arms. Teresa had still been asleep when he'd left the cabin.

Mediterranean Sea
8:43 AM

Chief Warrant Officer Russell Clark was the pilot and aircraft commander of a U.S. Navy P-3C Orion on a special reconnaissance mission over the central Mediterranean. Just before nine in the morning, he and his copilot made positive visual identification of the Belle Maria roughly 300 miles southeast of NAS Sigonella steaming on a westerly course. They reported the sighting and the information was passed to MI6 headquarters in London.

Cairo, Egypt
10:00 AM

"As-salamu aleikum," said the Egyptian President as he shook hands with his former Ambassador to Pakistan.

"Aleikum as-salam."

"Be seated. We have much to discuss," the President said. "I'm sure you are aware by now that your villa was attacked early Sunday morning by a special operations team and that Yousef Abu Shakra is missing. I understand there was a great deal of blood on the floor of his bedroom. It is being analyzed now to see if it was his."

"Yes, I was informed this morning by our mutual friend, Hakeem Ghanem. Do we know who carried out the attack?"

"Not for certain," the President replied. "The Americans seem the most likely. They have a nuclear-powered aircraft carrier conducting training not far outside of our territorial waters. It is a poorly-kept secret that most American Carriers have SEAL Team detachments on board. However, given the tensions we are experiencing here in Egypt, I do not want to publicly accuse them unless I am certain they carried out the mission. There is no physical evidence but that seems the most likely scenario. Do you know why your villa would be attacked and why Abu Shakra would be abducted?"

Hassan Al-Zeid had expected the question but had no good way to reply without violating the instructions he'd been given by General Jhalawan. He decided to probe to see what the President might know.

"Is it possible that I was the target and that Abu Shakra was trying to defend the villa against the assailants?" the Ambassador suggested.

"Yes, that is possible. However, I cannot help but wonder if this had something to do with whatever is going on between you and General Parvez Jhalawan. You should know that I am not pleased that you are apparently taking orders from General Jhalawan and that I am being kept in the dark regarding the reason," the Egyptian President said bluntly. Unless you are prepared for me to declare you a traitor, I strongly advise you to tell me what is going on. I will not tolerate you serving another master," the President told Al-Zeid hotly. If you think I am bluffing, consider how easily I could declare you a traitor and have you shot. You have friends in the Muslim Brotherhood but you also have enemies."

Hassan Al-Zeid was suddenly very afraid. He knew that the President was not bluffing. He had a choice to make. Either he answered the President's questions or his lovely young wife was going to be a widow before the day was out. He was afraid of both men but the General was far away. In the end, it was not a difficult choice to make.

"I understand. I will tell you all I know."

Over the next two hours, Hassan Al-Zeid described his meeting with Akil El-Sayed and his lunch meeting with General Jhalawan.

He told the President that the reason General Jhalawan had insisted that he be recalled was so his limousine, with its diplomatic privilege, could be used to transport stolen nuclear weapons out of Pakistan. He described the role played by Hakeem Ghanem and his General Manager, Ibrahim Al-Jabiri. He explained Abu Shakra's role and concluded by surmising that the western powers had identified his part in the theft and transport of the weapons. He truthfully told the President that he did not know the targets or timing of the intended use of the weapons although it seemed clear to him that General Jhalawan had both targets and a timetable in mind. He also told the President that he believed Jhalawan was ambitious and extremely dangerous.

When Al-Zeid had told him everything he knew, the President tapped a button on his intercom and two armed soldiers came into the Presidential office.

The President stood and looked directly at his former Ambassador. "Hassan Al-Zeid, you have been found guilty of treason against the Arab Republic of Egypt. As the elected President sworn to protect our nation, I hereby condemn you to death by firing squad. You will be executed within the hour. I advise you to make your peace with Allah if you can."

MI6 HQ, London
2:00 PM

Pete Nocona asked everyone to join him in the conference area. What he told them was stunning.

"I have just received a call from Langley. The CIA's contact in the office of the Egyptian President's Chief of Staff has confirmed that Ambassador Al-Zeid did meet with the President this morning in Cairo. They were together for almost three hours. Shortly after their meeting ended, Ambassador Al-Zeid was summarily executed by a firing squad. An hour later, his 29-year-old wife was beheaded by Islamic zealots who accused her of being a Lebanese whore and then dragged her headless body through the streets."

Nahbi had half expected something like this. Al-Zeid's secret meeting with General Jhalawan made it clear that the Ambassador was taking orders from both the Egyptian President and the head of

Pakistan's Inter-Services Intelligence Agency. The Egyptian President's hold on power was already very shaky. He could ill afford to have one of his senior administration officials showing signs of questionable loyalty.

"This was predictable," Nahbi told the team. "If Ambassador Al-Zeid had ever read the Christian Bible, he might have remembered the verse that says *No man can serve two masters: for either he will hate the one, and love the other; or else he will hold to the one, and despise the other.*" The Egyptian President could hardly afford to have one of his senior people taking orders from a Pakistani General."

Gavriella asked if the Ambassador's execution provided any useful clues in their search for the nuclear weapons.

"No. I don't think so," Nahbi answered. "We already knew that Al-Zeid was involved and that his driver had been the means of getting the weapons out of Pakistan. In all probability, the Egyptian President was not a confidant of General Jhalawan. I think the Ambassador's execution was merely an exercise of unrestrained power by an angry thug masquerading as a political leader. Al-Zeid embarrassed the Egyptian President by not confiding in him and thereby gave the President ample reason to doubt his loyalty. Among Islamic zealots and terrorists, questionable loyalty is the same as a signed death warrant."

USS George H.W. Bush
1:15 PM

Lieutenant Hays was talking to the Navy doctor when the cardiac monitor beside Yousef Abu Shakra's bed suddenly began to emit the steady tone that indicated his heart had stopped. Within seconds, the doctor and three hospital corpsman were at his bedside trying to save his life.

The doctor pulled the defibrillator paddles from the crash cart and prepared to administer a potentially life-saving electrical shock to Abu Shakra's heart. When he saw that the hospital corpsmen were clear, he triggered the device and watched the monitor for signs that the heart had begun beating again. When he saw that it hadn't, he triggered the device again. The second jolt did the job.

Abu Shakra's heart resumed its normal rhythm. They had saved his life but he was still in critical condition.

Mark Hays knew the interrogation team would just have to wait.

Tuesday, June 10

Adriatic Sea
3:00 PM

The yacht left Lixouri harbor on the Greek island of Kefalonia at 6:00 AM headed for Vieste, Italy 323 nautical miles away. At 27 knots, they would arrive about 6:00 PM local time. They entered the Adriatic Sea two hours after lunch. The seas were calm and it was a warm, sunny afternoon. Fredo was driving the yacht from the flying bridge when Franco and Teresa came up the ladder.

"Fredo, would you mind steering from the main cabin for the next couple of hours?"

"Why?"

"Teresa and I want to sunbathe together."

Teresa was wearing a pair of white shorts and a white bikini top. Franco noticed that his brother couldn't seem to take his eyes off her breasts. The soft, stretchy material of her bikini top barely contained her ample breasts and her large nipples protruded noticeably through the thin fabric. Franco remembered Fredo saying he wanted to make love to Teresa too. It was obvious that his brother was still having fantasies about her.

"OK, sure." Fredo said. Franco took the helm for a few minutes while Fredo went down to the main cabin.

One of the nice features of the Ferretti 690 yacht was the large enclosed deck area just forward of the flying bridge's steering console. There was a tinted acrylic windshield all around the area and there were custom-fitted cushions that completely covered the deck like several jig-saw puzzle pieces. With the pads and windscreen, it was a very pleasant place to sunbath.

When Fredo signaled that he had the helm, Franco and Teresa got undressed. They lay on their backs beside each other for a little while enjoying the warmth of the afternoon sun and the gentle breezes on their bare skin. After a few minutes, Teresa rolled onto her side and ran her fingers through the hair on Franco's chest. They did get some sun but it was incidental.

London, England
11:10 AM

Sir Lionel Smythe had been expecting the call from the duty officer at the Admiralty.

"Sir Lionel, I was asked to let you know that a few minutes after 11:00 AM the Prime Minister signed the order authorizing the HMS Sutherland to intercept, board, and inspect the Belle Maria at the earliest possible opportunity."

"Thank you for letting me know."

Sir Lionel knew that the decision to use one of the Admiralty's ships had been discussed and agreed to by both the United States and Israel. It was generally believed that such an overt act by either the United States or Israel would be unnecessarily inflammatory among the Arab nations of North Africa. The call confirmed that the Prime Minister had directed Sir Theodore Macfarlane, the Governor and Commander in Chief of Gibraltar, to sign orders effecting that decision.

Sir Lionel knew that such unusual orders would be given to the Commanding Officer of HMS Sutherland in person if possible. He knew Commander Reginald Burton well and considered him a fine officer. They were fortunate that a suitable ship and able commander was in the right place at the right time.

Sir Lionel passed the information to Gordon McFarland who in turn called Nahbi to let him know. In Gibraltar, HMS Sutherland prepared for sea.

USS George H.W. Bush
1:15 PM

Lieutenant Hays was with the lead interrogator when he asked the Navy doctor when they could begin to question Abu Shakra. The doctor said possibly the following day if he continued to improve.

Yousef Abu Shakrah had regained consciousness. He was still hooked up to the cardiac monitor and had an oxygen mask over his nose and mouth. The doctor had reclassified his condition as stable.

The senior member of the MI6 interrogation team called Nahbi to tell him the bad news. Nahbi simply asked to be kept informed.

Marina di Vieste, Italy
9:45 PM

Lia knocked softly on the door to the owner's cabin. Teresa and Franco had just finished taking a shower together but hadn't bothered to dress.

"Yes, who is it?" Franco asked.

"It's Lia. Can I come in?"

Franco wrapped his towel around his waist and glanced at Teresa lying on the bed. She covered herself before nodding to Franco that it was OK to open the door.

"What is it, Lia?" Teresa asked her friend.

"Fredo wants to do a four-way. He was a virgin before this trip and he wants to make love to you too, Teresa. He knows that we have been paid very well and he seems to think we won't say no."

"What did you tell him?"

"I said I would talk to you and Franco. I told him if the two of you want to do it, I'll go along. You know I'd prefer not to but I don't see how I can really refuse. What do you both think?"

Franco glanced at Teresa and then looked back at Lia. "The answer is no. Stay here, I will tell him."

"Wait, Franco," Teresa said. "What reason will you give him? From his perspective, Lia and I are professionals who have been paid to provide our customary services."

"Do you want me to answer in front of Lia?" Franco asked softly.

"Lia already knows how you feel. I've told her a little but she would have known anyway. Lia is a very sensitive person with remarkable empathy for other people's feelings."

Lia turned to Franco and asked him, "Franco, do you really intend to tell your brother that you've fallen in love with a firefly and that he can't enjoy her because you're claiming her for yourself? Are you that sure of your feelings?"

"There are practical issues as well. Teresa can't afford to retire from being a firefly. She doesn't make nearly enough from her nude modeling to pay even her most essential bills, let alone to finance her college studies. How will you feel when she returns to Bari and what she does for a living? You don't want to share her with your brother. What about with many men?"

"I am deeply sorry for you. This is a very difficult thing but I advise you not to proclaim your love for Teresa until the two of you have discussed what happens after we reach Venice. For now, I think you should tell Fredo only that you think Teresa might just conceivably be the woman who could make you happy. Don't say you're in love with her. Only say that you don't want to complicate matters by doing a four-way. He'll be disappointed of course. We can all see the hunger in his eyes when he looks at Teresa. But you are his big brother. He admires you. I'm confident that he will accept your answer."

Franco looked at Teresa for a long moment before he said, "OK. I'll tell him what you've suggested."

Wednesday, June 11

Adriatic Sea
8:40 AM

The yacht was 50 miles east of Pescara, Italy. Franco and Teresa were sitting on the aft main deck. Franco knew they couldn't defer the discussion any longer. The yacht had left Vieste at 6:15 AM and would enter the Venice Lagoon in less than eight hours.

"Teresa, I've been thinking a lot about what will happen to us after we reach Venice." He hesitated a moment before continuing. "Would you consider coming to Rome to live with me? I make a good income and if we were living together, I think I make enough that you could still go to school without having to work as a firefly. If you wanted to continue your nude modeling, I wouldn't really mind. That would give us time to get to know each other better. I really think you are the right woman for me but I understand and respect your caution."

"Doesn't Fredo live with you? I don't think it would work for all three of us to share an apartment."

"Yes, but I think he'd like to get a place of his own, especially now that he's discovered that sex is even better than he thought it would be. He told me there are several girls at work that like him. I think he's already scheming how to get them into his bed. He's not going to want to live with me after this trip. I've got some money saved. I'll offer to put up the deposit and first month's rent for him so he could move out almost immediately."

Teresa said nothing for several minutes as she considered what Franco had proposed. Franco wisely gave her time to think.

"I won't say yes or no just yet. The University of Bari is on its summer schedule. I didn't enroll in any courses for the first half of the summer term but had planned to take a psychology course during the second half. I've made enough money on this trip that I don't have to work for a while. So, here's my counter-proposal."

"I will come to Rome for two weeks and stay with you in your apartment. While you're at work, I'll visit the nearest campuses of the Sapienza University of Rome and talk to some of the professors and students. I'll find out how Sapienza tuition costs compare to UoB. I'll use the Rome Metro to see how easy it is to get from your apartment to the campuses. Sapienza requires entrance interviews before I could be accepted. I'll find out if my grades and test scores are good enough to get in. I think they are but I must be sure."

Teresa looked straight into Franco's eyes. "I'd like to meet your friends and go to dinner at some of your favorite places. I'd like to go to some music concerts with you and visit some of the Roman ruins

and parks around the city. I will do our laundry and keep the apartment clean and neat while I'm staying with you but you need to know that I will never be the proverbial *barefoot and pregnan*t housewife. I will eventually want children but I also plan to have a professional career."

"I need to know more about you. It may surprise you to learn that I attend church regularly. I know that what I do for a living is wrong in the eyes of the Catholic Church. I have to live with that. I came from a very large and very poor family but I didn't want to marry just to get financial security. So, I do what I have to do to break the chains of poverty that have shackled my family for generations. Being a firefly pays for my education and gives me a chance. I need to be sure that you won't obsess about what I've done to make a living. It would ruin any chance we might otherwise have of being happy together."

"Fredo told me that he converted to Islam only because he thought that was what you and your mother wanted. I hope you're not offended but neither of you seem very devout. Perhaps that's not a bad thing."

"It may be true that many Muslims are peaceful. Yet, it is equally true that many are not. To me, it is beyond barbaric for Islamic terrorists to bomb school buses in Israel and then strap bombs around their own children in the name of Jihad. I'm sorry, but I do not consider people who murder children to be human. In my eyes, they are rabid animals that should be exterminated. You need to understand how strongly I feel about that. So, before I make a long-term commitment to live with you or maybe even marry you, I want to know more about what you really believe and what sort of moral compass guides your life."

It was Franco's turn to be silent as he considered what Teresa had said. Finally, he spoke.

"I was afraid you might just say no. I'm elated that you will come for two weeks. I know you don't want me to say it, but I do love you. I can hardly bear to think of life without you. Your plan is a good one. I must trust that these next two weeks will be only the first steps toward a life together."

"Franco, do not think for an instant that I do not love you too. I do. But that is really not the question. We must both find out if our newly-discovered feelings toward each other could grow and mature into the kind of love that would sustain and nourish a marriage through a lifetime of both good times and bad." Teresa leaned over to give him a tender kiss. It was the first time she'd given him a serious kiss that was not an expression of passion.

USS George H.W. Bush
11:25 AM

Lieutenant Mark Hays and the leader of the MI6 interrogation team were having lunch together in Wardroom #3. Mark was vaguely aware that the President was giving a speech on one of the flat panel displays but the sound was turned down and no one was paying attention because it had already aired several times. The major cable news shows were notoriously repetitive.

"Mark, we're not getting anywhere. Abu Shakra has refused to provide any useful information. We were with him for over three hours today and he told us nothing of any value. The Navy doctor finally told us we'd have to let him rest. I've sent a message to London asking for further instructions. We'll try again in the morning but I think we're wasting our time with this guy."

Mediterranean Sea
5:55 PM

HMS Sutherland intercepted the Belle Maria 216 nautical miles east of Gibraltar an hour before sunset. The tanker had immediately stopped her engines when ordered to prepare to be boarded. Even so, it took the massive ship nearly twenty minutes to come to a complete stop.

Eighteen enlisted personnel and two officers from the Sutherland went aboard to begin the search. With the information provided by TF3, the fake oxygen tank was discovered almost immediately in the Chief Engineer's office. A Royal Navy Bomb Disposal Chief Petty Officer supervised the transfer of the suspected nuclear weapon to HSM Sutherland.

Four hours later, the officer in charge of the boarding party radioed to Commander Burton that they had found no other suspicious devices. Until the oil could be off-loaded, it wasn't possible to search the tanks.

The Belle Maria was ordered to follow the Sutherland into port at Gibraltar for further inspection but it did not appear that the other nuclear devices were on board the ship.

Commander Burton provided a situation report to the Admiralty in Portsmouth at 2315 local time. That report was forwarded immediately to TF3 in the basement of the MI6 headquarters building. Nahbi was the only member of the TF3 team who wasn't in his room for the night.

The Sutherland and the Belle Maria entered the harbor at Gibraltar a little before noon the next day. Zakaria Nasser and the nuclear device were immediately placed aboard a Royal Air Force Boeing C-17 Globemaster III cargo plane and flown directly to RAF Brize Norton 65 miles west north-west of London.

Phil Shaw and Al Flores were waiting at Brize Norton when the plane landed to take Zakaria Nassar to MI6 headquarters for questioning. The Bomb Disposal Chief Petty Officer told them that he and the suspected nuclear device were headed for the Atomic Weapons Establishment facility near Burghfield.

Port Alberoni, Venice Lagoon
6:15 PM

Franco slowed the yacht as they approached the no-wake zone in the channel between Lido and Pellestrina islands. Abramo was standing nearby in case he needed help but Franco was confident that he could bring the yacht safely into port without help. Abramo called the port office to let them know he was returning but the office was closed for the day. A recorded message asked him to leave the name of the boat and its mooring location so a Customs officer could visit the yacht in the morning to process the necessary paperwork.

By 7:10 PM, they had moored the yacht in Alberoni Marina's large-yacht moorage facing the Venetian Lagoon.

Abramo and Donatella said good night and walked to their home a hundred meters north of the yacht basin. The Rinaldi brothers and the two fireflies slept on board.

In the owner's cabin, Franco lay on his side watching Teresa sleeping beside him. She had a smile on her face and had even laughed softly in her sleep once, perhaps dreaming about the pleasures they'd shared earlier. Franco was wide awake, thinking about what his uncle had asked him to do. He hadn't told Teresa yet.

"Teresa, wake up. I need to talk to you."

"Hmm, what is it?"

"My uncle has asked Fredo and me to deliver some equipment to a company in Geneva. We should be back in Rome in five or six days."

"So, what am I supposed to do in the meantime?"

"I'm very sorry. When I asked you to come live with me, I assumed you would want to go home to Bari for a week or two to pack additional clothes and take care of personal business. I thought Fredo and I would have plenty of time to take care of my uncle's business before you came to Rome. When you said you'd come immediately, it caught me by surprise. I was so happy that you would come to Rome with me, that I just couldn't tell you right then. I was afraid you would change your mind."

"When will you leave?"

"We need to catch the 6:15 AM Lido di Venezia ferry in the morning. At that time of day, Abramo told me to allow 30 minutes for the drive and 30 minutes to get in line to be sure we'll be boarded for the 6:15 sailing. That means we need to leave here no later than 5:15 AM," Franco told her. "We have to load some minor equipment items in my SUV so I'll have to be up and showered no later than 4:00 AM."

"Just how will Lia and I get to the airport?"

"Abramo said he would be glad to take you but my uncle has arranged for a limousine to take you and Lia to the airport. It will take almost two hours to get to the airport with the ferry and traffic so the driver will pick you up at Abramo's house at 3:30 PM. Your flight is scheduled to leave Marco Polo International at 6:35 PM

tomorrow afternoon. It makes one stop and you will arrive in Bari at 10:40 PM. My uncle will have another driver waiting for you in the baggage claim area at the Bari airport. He'll have a sign with your name on it. You should be home before 11:00 PM tomorrow evening."

Teresa shook her head slowly in disappointment. "You should have told me sooner. I was looking forward to going to Rome with you. Now, I'm not so sure it's a good idea. Call me when you get back to Rome and I'll let you know then if I'm still willing to come."

"Please don't change your mind. This is something I just have to do. My uncle was very kind to my mother after my useless father divorced her. My father won an ugly custody battle for Fredo and me and then threw my mother out of the house with very little money. I don't know what might have become of her if my uncle had not taken her into his own home. I could not say no to my uncle. I hope you can understand and forgive me for not having the courage to tell you sooner."

Teresa's angry look softened. "OK, go take care of your uncle's business. I'll probably get over my irritation. I was just caught by surprise. I'm sorry if I was grouchy." She gave him her best seductive look. "We still have almost five hours before you have to shower and leave. You may have to let Fredo drive because you're not going to get much sleep."

Thursday, June 12

Port Alberoni, Venice Lagoon
3:55 AM

Teresa was awake but sleepy and tired after hours of passionate love-making. She heard Franco open the bathroom door and watched through nearly closed eyes as he dressed. She enjoyed looking at his muscular, tanned body. Sex with Franco was the best she'd ever had with any man. Considering what she did for a living that was saying quite a lot.

Franco came over to the bed and leaned over to kiss her goodbye. She opened her eyes and gave him a tender, loving kiss. "Be careful on the road and call me every day. I'll see you in Rome in about a week."

"I love you," Franco said softly. "I've got to go."

Teresa watched as he closed the cabin door behind him and then she drifted off to sleep.

Fifteen minutes after saying goodbye to Teresa, Franco parked his dark-green Iveco Massif on the pier beside the yacht. He and Fredo loaded the four modified scuba tanks into the back of the SUV and then piled swim fins, masks, and wet suits on top. They put their duffel bags on the back seat along with a folder containing diving literature for dive sites in the Portland and Weymouth areas of South England. At 5:10 AM, they headed north on the Via Sandro Gallo toward the Venezia di Lido ferry terminal. Fredo drove.

Innsbruck, Austria
12:25 PM

Franco stopped for petrol and fast food at a service plaza a few kilometers west of the Innsbruck airport on the A12 Autobahn. The route he'd planned would take them through Ulm and Stuttgart. West of Stuttgart, they would turn northward. They still had almost 400 miles to go. He expected to reach their destination sometime after 10:00 PM. They would stop somewhere along the way to buy enough groceries for three days.

Port Alberoni, Venice Lagoon
3:30 PM

Teresa was sitting at the Sartori's kitchen table reading a magazine when the doorbell rang.

Donatella went to the door to greet the limousine driver. Two men were standing on the porch. One was wearing a chauffeur's uniform. The other was dressed in slacks and a sport coat. Both men had on dark sunglasses.

"Buongiorno, Signora Sartori," said the driver. "Are the ladies ready?"

"Yes, their luggage is here by the door. Signora Pedrazzini is in la toilette. They'll be with you in a moment."

"May I speak to them before we load their luggage?" the driver asked. "I am required by my company's rules to verify their identity from their passports. I've also been directed to have your husband sign the voucher for the limousine service to the airport."

"Yes, of course," Signora Sartori replied.

When they were all together in the living room, the driver and the other man suddenly drew semi-automatic pistols. Both guns had silencers fitted to their barrels.

"I'm afraid there's been a change of plans," the driver told them. "We won't be leaving for a while. It is important that you do exactly what we tell you. Any attempt to attract attention or to escape will end badly for you. To ensure that you do as I say, my friend is going to tie your hands and put tape over your mouths. You will then be taken into the bedroom to lie on the floor until it is time for us to leave. Your feet will also be tied. I must warn you that you are now in a very dangerous situation. You will not even be allowed to go to the bathroom. If you cannot wait, I'm afraid you will just have to relieve yourselves where you lie."

Donatella and Lia both began crying. Abramo was terrified but bravely tried to comfort his wife. Teresa watched the men closely. She had already concluded that the men intended to kill them all, probably after dark. In a flash of intuition, she realized that there was some connection between the equipment delivery Franco had described and the situation they now faced. Bitterly, she wondered if Franco had known that they would be killed when he had kissed her goodbye.

The driver covered them with his pistol while the other man handcuffed them with nylon zip ties and put duct tape over their mouths. One by one, he led them into the bedroom and pushed them down to the floor before putting another zip tie around their ankles. When all four were lying on the bedroom floor, the second man took the women's luggage and purses out to Abramo's Alfa Romeo Giulietta hatchback. He then returned to the house and assumed guard duty over the captives.

A few minutes later, the driver left in the limousine. He parked it in a public parking space along the Via Malamocco about two miles north of the Sartori home. Before leaving the limousine, he removed the chauffeur's cap and jacket and replaced them with a windbreaker and a ball cap from a small duffle bag. He locked the duffle bag in the trunk of the limousine and walked to a dark-blue Fiat that the other man had parked there earlier in the day. He drove to the nearby Alberoni Marina and parked along the street on the Strada della Marina a block north of the Strada della Droma intersection. While it was still daylight, it was important that the Sartori neighbors not see a strange vehicle parked outside the home for several hours.

He got out of the car and walked to a shaded park bench overlooking the marina within view of the car. He took a candy bar out of his pocket and then touched the icon on his smart phone to open the E-book he was currently reading. He was less than a half-mile from the Sartori home but he would not return there until late evening.

MI6 HQ, London
3:20 PM

The Chief Engineer from the Belle Maria had arrived at MI6 headquarters less than an hour after the C-17 touched down at the RAF base at Brize Norton. He had been taken to an interrogation room on the second floor. Nahbi had decided that he would conduct the interrogation personally with Pete Nocona, Phil Shaw, and Gavriella Adler in the room with him. David, Tiera, and Al would observe through the one-way glass.

It was not certain that Zakaria Nassar even knew the contents of the fake oxygen bottle he had taken custody of in the Port of Suez. Nahbi had decided to focus on how he had been directed to receive the oxygen bottle.

"Good afternoon Mr. Nassar," Nahbi began. "As you undoubtedly know, you are being questioned in connection with the green oxygen bottle you had in your office aboard the Belle Maria. I would like to know how it came to be in your possession."

Nassar gave a predictably evasive answer. “It was delivered to the ship while we were at anchor in Suez waiting to join a north-bound convoy the next morning. I don’t understand why an oxygen bottle would be of interest to you. We use quite a lot of oxygen aboard the ship for various purposes.”

“So the bottle contained only oxygen? Is that what you want me to believe?” Nahbi challenged him.

“Yes. What else would it have contained?” Nassar replied with a genuinely blank look on his face.

“Ah, well that is the question, is it not?” Nahbi said blandly. “Did you order the bottle to be delivered to the ship?”

“Yes. I sent an order for the oxygen to Suez while we were en route from Yanbu Oil Terminal in Saudi Arabia. There is nothing unusual about that. I often place orders for spare parts and other materials while we are underway so they will be ready to take aboard when we reach our next port.”

“So, this was a routine order you placed?” Nahbi asked.

“Yes, of course,” Nassar answered.

“Isn’t it true that you received a phone call from Yousef Abu Shakra on the 4th of June instructing you to place the order?” Nahbi asked. “I should warn you that your conversation with Abu Shakra was recorded. If you like, I can have it played back for you. Will that be necessary?”

Zakaria Nassar remained defiant, “If you have the recording, then why ask me?”

“Because if you cooperate, you may not find yourself being shipped to Guantanamo Bay to enjoy the company of other Islamic terrorists until you die of old age. I understand that you have a wife and two sons. If you ever hope to see them again, I strongly advise you to cooperate by answering my questions truthfully,” Nahbi told him sternly.

The threat worked. Over the next two hours, Zakaria Nassar admitted that he had received instructions from Yousef Abu Shakra that included ordering the oxygen bottle, securing it, and then delivering it to a man at the Texaco Island Oil Terminal in Port Arthur, Texas when the Belle Maria made port.

When the interrogation was completed, the TF3 team members were unanimous in their belief that the man knew nothing else that would be useful.

4:10 PM

After confirming with the Navy doctors that the prisoner could safely make the trip, Nahbi ordered Abu Shakra flown to London under close guard with a medical support team. Nahbi specifically requested that SEAL Team Eight personnel be used to guard him. He was fully aware that SEALs were seldom used to guard prisoners unless the subject was of exceptional importance, as Abu Shakra certainly was.

Shortly after 6:00 PM, a Grumman C-2A Greyhound was launched from the USS George H.W. Bush. Abu Shakra was strapped to a medical gurney and was closely guarded by Navy Lieutenant Mark Hays and the SEAL Team Eight enlisted man who had shot him.

With a refueling stop at the U.S. Navy base in Naples, the trip to RAF Brize Norton would take more than nine hours at the propeller aircraft's fuel-efficient cruising speed of 250 knots. It would be sometime after 4:00 AM London time before Nahbi could begin to interrogate him.

Friday, June 13

Port Alberoni, Venice Lagoon
1:00 AM

The Mafia assassin who had posed as the limousine chauffeur parked the Fiat in front of the Sartori residence and got a heavy, hard-sided roll-aboard suitcase out of the trunk. He knocked lightly on the front door and it was opened almost immediately.

"Any problems?"

"No, but the bedroom smells like a sewer. Ten hours is a long time to expect anyone to hold their bladders and bowels. I'll be glad to get this over with."

"Did you find the keys to the boat?"

"Yes, they were hanging on a hook by the back door. I waited until after dark to be sure the boat would start. It started on the first try. The fuel tank is almost full. There are stairs leading down to the dock beneath the house. I don't think they can be seen from the nearby houses," the accomplice told him.

"OK, let's get them down to the boat. Unfortunately, there's a full moon tonight and it doesn't set until just before dawn."

"Are we going to let them walk to the boat?"

"No, we'll have to carry them. I'm not going to take a chance that one of them might decide to make a break. By now, they've probably figured out they'd have nothing to lose by trying to escape so we're not going to give them a chance."

"The lagoon is three miles wide at this point. We'll take them out to the middle and drop them overboard. The suitcase I brought has four lead weights in it and some more nylon zip ties. I don't want to take a chance that gunshots might be heard. Sound really carries across the water. We need to have plenty of time to get away before anyone starts wondering what has happened to these people."

"You mean we're not going to kill them first?"

"No, they'll be dead soon enough anyway."

It took the two men twenty minutes to carry all four of their victims to the boat. The second man tied a 30-pound lead weight to their ankles using the nylon zip ties. All of them were in shock as they realized what was going to happen to them.

It took only a few minutes to reach the center of the lagoon. The Mafia assassin put the boat in neutral and let it drift. One by one, the two men dropped the terrified victims over the side of the boat to a horrible death. Teresa was last.

The two men moored the Colombo 32S Aliante in the slip beneath the Sartori residence. They checked for anything that might help police track them and then went up the stairs to the house to check it too. The foul smell of the human waste in the bedroom was the only clue they could not eliminate.

At 4:30 AM, they locked the front door and went down the front stairs to the cars. The assassin drove the Fiat and the other man drove Abramo's Alfa. The Lido di Venezia ferry would leave the Lido side of Venice Lagoon at 5:25 AM so there was plenty of time to get to the ferry's staging area.

The crossing took 35 minutes. The ferry docked at the Venice Tronchetto terminal at 6:00 AM. The second man drove Abramo's car to the giant parking garage and then to the top floor in the long-term parking area. He locked the keys in the car and took the elevator to the ground floor. He walked across the street and got into the passenger-side front seat of the Fiat. The assassin handed him an envelope containing 10,000 euros. The two men shook hands and the second man got out of the car. The assassin drove away.

ISI HQ; Islamabad, Pakistan
6:20 AM

Thirty-five hundred miles to the east of Venice, and five time zones later, Ahmed Malik went in person to General Jhalawan's official quarters as soon as he received the news.

"What is so important that you wake me at this hour?" General Jhalawan demanded to know.

Ahmed Malik answered in his customarily direct manner. "The Belle Maria has been boarded by the HMS Sutherland about two hundred miles east of Gibraltar. The Royal Navy has removed the weapon from the ship and has arrested the ship's Chief Engineer on suspicion of possession and potential use of a weapon of mass destruction."

Lieutenant General Parvez Jhalawan was instantly furious. His face was flushed and his fists were clenched. "How in the name of Allah did this happen?" he almost shouted at Malik. "How did MI6 find out about the device on board the tanker? Your security precautions were apparently not very good. This is very bad. It means that our blow will not cripple the Americans as we planned."

Malik was not in the least afraid of the General but he was wise enough to be deferential and to provide a calm response.

"One of my deep-cover agents inside MI6 has kept me fully informed about the very talented group of people that has been assembled to work with the android named Nahbi. Their team has been given the code name TF3. They were selected by Sir Lionel Smythe personally and ordered to find the weapons. As you know, Sir Lionel is one of the most respected old-school spooks in the world. He is a very effective administrator but he has probably forgotten more about the art and science of intelligence work than most will ever know."

"The TF3 team has been working in the basement of the MI6 headquarters in London since shortly after the weapons left Pakistan. In addition to the android, who is functioning as the supervisor of the group, there are field agents from MI6, the CIA, and the Mossad. There is also a disabled veteran American Army officer who holds a doctoral degree in Semitic languages. The last member of the group is a young woman who is a citizen of Malta. She has a doctorate in computer science. They are being supported by Gordon McFarland, one of the best applied technology experts anywhere in the world. It is an impressive team," Malik told the General.

"Do you think Ambassador Al-Zeid told the Egyptian President anything substantive before he was executed?" Jhalawan wanted to know.

"I feel sure that he told the Egyptian president everything he knew in an effort to save his life. However, he did not know about the Belle Maria," Malik responded. "I think the TF3 team was probably able to identify the Belle Maria through good trade-craft. After all, they have the combined resources of MI6, GCHQ, CIA, NSA, and Mossad. That is no feeble collection of intelligence-gathering capabilities. With the android to assimilate and correlate the various information streams, it was probably inevitable that they would deduce at least part of your plan." Malik said.

"What about Bashir Ghilzai? Do you think he might have sold out to a higher bidder after you told him that you would be sending him to Germany to prepare the weapons?"

"No sir, I don't. I think he is far too fearful for his life to risk your wrath. However, there was a member of his immediate office staff

that may have been supplying some information to parties unknown. He has been eliminated just in case. In any event, he would not have known much. He may have overhead Dr. Ghilzai talking on the phone a few times but it is difficult to imagine that he could have provided information of any significant value."

"I still don't understand how the TF3 team identified the Belle Maria. I understand that Abu Shakra has been abducted, probably by the Americans. Could he have told them?" General Jhalawan wanted to know.

"No sir, I don't think so. Abu Shakra is probably dead. Our contact in the Egyptian President's Chief of Staff's office has told me that there was some blood on the floor in Abu Shakra's quarters and that most of it was his. I must assume that the NSA intercepted phone calls and other messages between Yousef Abu Shakra, the Ambassador, and probably the Chief Engineer aboard the tanker. Few people realize the extent of the NSA's ability to covertly intercept and analyze email, phone calls, fax transmissions, and even encrypted diplomatic communications. The NSA has what is almost certainly the fastest supercomputer on Earth at Fort George Meade in Maryland. They are building an even more advanced facility in Utah. I'm sure you've seen the media frenzy over recent disclosures about the NSA's global surveillance. Yet, even the media does not begin to appreciate the full extent of NSA's capability," Malik explained.

"Where are the other devices now?"

"Hakeem Ghanem's two nephews arrived in Aarbergen, Germany late last night. The older nephew called his uncle just before midnight to let him know they had arrived. They are staying in a garage apartment above an automotive repair shop owned by a long-time member of the Muslim Brotherhood in Germany, also known as the Islamische Gemeinschaft in Deutschland or simply the IGD."

"Have the Italians been eliminated?"

"Yes. Enrico Favaloro provided a two-man hit team at my request. The yacht broker and his wife and the two young prostitutes now lie at the bottom of Venice Lagoon," Ahmed Malik said.

"The more I think about it, the more I think that perhaps Signor Favaloro knows too much. Please make sure that he cannot point any intelligence or law enforcement agencies toward us," General Jhalawan told Malik. "We cannot afford to take the blame for what is going to happen. That would ruin everything we've worked for."

"Yes sir. I'll take care of it," Malik said.

"Another thing, Ahmed," said the General. "I think that Dr. Ghilzai and his young engineer protégé should rest in peace once their work is completed. Similarly, I think perhaps Hakeem Ghanem, his General Manager, and his nephews should also awake in paradise once the devices have been turned over to those assigned to place the weapons."

"The nephews will pose no great problem. However, I wonder if it is wise to risk open warfare with the Muslim Brotherhood in Egypt if we assassinate two of their senior officers. Are you sure you want to do this?"

"It is necessary. We cannot eliminate the nephews without alienating Ghanem anyway. The key will be to accomplish the task without leaving a trail that can be traced to us," the General told him.

"Ahmed, there is one more thing I want you to do. Either capture or destroy the android. He poses a grave threat to our plans."

"I understand. Yet, it will not be easy to do. At present, he is inside an impregnable fortress and will not come out until the weapons have either been found or used. Let me think about it. Perhaps I can devise a way to do as you wish."

Although there was no point in revealing why it was so, Malik knew that it would be far more difficult than the General could possibly imagine. He also knew that it would be unwise to eliminate the young engineer assisting Dr. Ghilzai too soon.

Venice Lagoon
2:30 AM

Unbelievably, Teresa was alive. The assassins had not realized that most of the Venice Lagoon was very shallow with an average depth of less than two meters. The only deep areas were in the

dredged channels. Abramo's boat had been in the deeper ship channel between Alberoni and the industrial port on the other side of the lagoon when the others had been dropped into the water. By the time the men had pushed Teresa over the side, the idling boat had drifted south over shallower water.

The lead weight attached by a zip tie had hung several inches below her feet. As soon as she was tossed overboard, the weight had plunged to the bottom dragging her with it. Bound hand and foot, she was helpless. With her lungs filled with a precious last breath of air, the upper part of her body was quite buoyant so she had floated vertically above the weight for almost a minute after the lead weight settled into the mud.

Teresa had held her breath as long as she could and had heard the sound of the boat moving away. She'd almost given up. The fiery pain in her lungs was unbearable. Involuntarily, a burst of air from her burning lungs had escaped through her nostrils. That had reduced her body's buoyancy to neutral. She had been about to give up and draw water into her lungs when her feet had touched the bottom. She'd instantly realized that the water was very shallow. She'd lunged upward and managed to get a quick breath of air before being pulled back beneath the surface. The 30 pound lead weight dragged her back underwater immediately but she was in excellent condition and could overcome the handicap of the weight until she became too tired to continue.

By repeating the lunging motions, she'd managed to breathe. With each quick trip to the surface, she'd caught glimpses of the area around where she'd been dropped overboard. There had been wood pilings nearby that marked the edge of the channel used by oil tankers bound for the industrial port across the lagoon. She had begun lunging at an angle instead of straight up and had soon reached the pilings.

The pilings were lashed together with rusted wire rope and were encrusted with razor sharp mussel shells. By looping the nylon tie on her wrists over one of the bolts that held the wire rope, she had been able to rest and catch her breath. She had rubbed the nylon tie against sharp edges of the mussel shells. They were almost as good as a knife. Within a few minutes, she had freed her hands. She had

pulled the tape from her mouth and had finally been able to take a really good breath. She had rested for several minutes and looked around to see if there were any boats nearby. There hadn't been. She had not been able to get to the tie around her ankles to free them or remove the lead weight. She was safe enough but would have to wait for help.

Shortly after dawn, one of the clam fishing boats known as a vongolara passed near her. She had shouted and caught their attention. An old man and his son had helped her on board and cut the nylon zip tie from her ankles. She asked if they had a marine radio or cell phone but they did not. She asked them to take her to the Alberoni Marina, which they were glad to do.

Once on shore, Teresa found a phone and called the police. Five minutes after her call, a police car with two policemen in it had arrived. She'd told them what had happened and urged them to call for boats to search the area to see if any of the others had somehow survived.

She had been taken to the Polizia di Stato substation in Malamocco where she had been questioned by the Commissario Capo and a female detective. She had told them everything she knew including her suspicion that there was some connection to the delivery that Franco's uncle had asked him to make in Geneva.

A little after noon, the female detective had told her that the bodies of Abramo, Donatella, and Lia had been recovered. Tragic emotions that she'd been holding back could no longer be kept in check. She had wailed pitifully in despair at the terrible news. She had felt deeply saddened at the death of Abramo and Donatella. They had both been decent people. But it was the knowledge that kind, gentle Lia would never return to her husband and little girl that forced racking sobs of unbearable grief from her.

Teresa had no clothes, no passport, no money, and no place to stay. A police officer made arrangements for her to stay at the Casa Madonna Venicia near Alberoni for a few nights. She was assigned to a semi-private room and given a clean change of clothing.

The Casa Madonna Venicia was a church-sponsored residential community for people with disabilities and psychiatric disorders.

Teresa didn't care. She was emotionally and physically exhausted and deeply grateful for a place to sleep.

MI6 HQ, London
4:25 AM

Abu Shakra was still tied to the medical transport gurney by restraining belts. The gurney had been placed on a table in the middle of the interrogation room and propped up at one end so he could see his interrogator. He was fully alert and obviously still defiant. A doctor was on call nearby but would not be permitted to observe the interrogation.

Just as when the Belle Maria's Chief Engineer had been interrogated, Pete Nocona, Phil Shaw, and Gavriella Adler were present in the room with Nahbi.

David, Tiera, and Al were again observing through a one-way mirror. Despite the early hour, Gordon McFarland had joined them. Lieutenant Mark Hays was also with them. Nahbi had told Mark that there was no way to know how Abu Shakra would respond. If he continued to refuse to answer questions, Nahbi wanted the young officer to understand that he was determined to find out what Abu Shakra knew by whatever means were necessary. Far too many innocent lives were at stake to be squeamish about the interrogation methods. Nahbi told Mark that he would rather be guilty of treating one man inhumanely than to have the deaths of millions of innocent people on his conscience. Nahbi emphasized that there might later be accusations that the interrogation had violated the Geneva Convention rules even though, technically, they did not apply to Abu Shakra. He did not want to put the young officer in the awkward position of having appeared to condone whatever methods Nahbi was forced to employ. Mark Hays was a career Naval officer but Abu Shakra was the enemy and had killed one of his men. He opted to observe the interrogation.

Nahbi wasted no time.

"Yousef Abu Shakra, you have been taken prisoner and brought to this place because of your role in the theft and transport of nuclear weapons. Do not deceive yourself. You are utterly without hope of rescue because none of your associates know where you are

or even if you are still alive. Whether you live or die is entirely up to me. I will ask you some questions and you must give me truthful answers. I warn you that I will not hesitate to use my considerable knowledge of the art and science of torture if you try to avoid giving me the information I want. You will answer me or I will take you through a hell you cannot imagine."

David and Tiera, especially, were shocked to hear Nahbi speak that way.

"He knows what he's doing," Gordon McFarland told them. "Abu Shakra is a very tough man and he does not fear death. But, like any human, he fears intense pain, disfigurement, and unknown horrors. He will try to conceal his fear but Nahbi is intent on terrifying him to persuade him to give us the information we need. That is probably the only hope we have of extracting the information from this man."

"Couldn't we just inject him with sodium pentothal, the truth serum, to get the information?" Tiera asked.

Gordon shook his head and then answered her question. "Barbiturates such as Sodium pentothal don't really work as truth serums the way you've seen in the movies. It is true that they do weaken resolve and make people more compliant to pressure. Barbiturates decrease higher cortical brain functioning. Because lying is more complex than telling the truth, suppression of the higher cortical functions *may* lead to uncovering truth because such drugs make the candidate loquacious and cooperative. However, they talk so much that discovery of the desired information is often lost in a fog of excessive and typically irrelevant talk. Moreover, unless the interrogator knows exactly what he or she is seeking, the probability of extracting the desired information is quite low."

David then asked, "Would Nahbi really torture this man? He told us that he would not harm any human."

"No, that's not exactly what he said," Tiera clarified. "What he actually said was that he would not knowingly harm any *innocent* person. This man is not innocent by any stretch of the imagination. Nahbi is trying to save thousands or even millions of innocent lives. I think he will do whatever he has to do to accomplish that purpose."

"Tiera is right," Gordon told David. "We must hope that Nahbi succeeds."

The observers were astounded at Nahbi's ability to verbally terrify Abu Shakra without resorting to physical means. All of them were quietly thankful that Nahbi was not their enemy.

But Abu Shakra was tougher than anyone expected. Before he told Nahbi what he knew, Nahbi was forced to use physical torture as well. Even the professional intelligence agents were shocked at how Nahbi proceeded once it became clear that Abu Shakra would not yield to mental pressure alone.

Tiera had been unable to watch after Nahbi had begun drilling into Abu Shakra's front teeth with a diamond bit in a cordless drill. He had applied a steady, light pressure and gone slowly to allow the drill bit to become red hot as it penetrated the nerve tissue at the center of each tooth. When Nahbi sprayed compressed refrigerant onto the raw nerve endings, Abu Shakra's screams were horrible. By the time Nahbi drilled into the third tooth Abu Shakra was crying pitifully for something to take away the pain. Nahbi promised to give him an anesthetic if he answered his questions.

Four hours after he'd begun the interrogation Nahbi was satisfied that Abu Shakra had told him everything he knew. More than half of what he told them they already knew. The rest was already out of date and of little or no value.

Aarbergen, Germany
8:30 AM

Franco tried to call Teresa's cell phone for the fifth time. He could not understand why she didn't answer or call him back. Perhaps her phone had been lost or damaged. He knew of no other way to contact her. He did not know where she lived in Bari. He had tried to get an address from the phone company but had not been surprised that her land-line, if she had one, was unlisted. He was afraid that she might have decided not to come to Rome after all.

MI6 HQ, London
9:05 AM

"David, can I speak to you in private?" Nahbi asked.

"Yes, of course. Where?"

"My room in ten minutes."

David knocked on the door and Nahbi opened it immediately.

"Please take a seat on the sofa. I want to show you something.

Nahbi had connected a laptop computer to the plasma TV screen in his room to project an image of Ahmed Malik that David recognized at once.

"When Phil Shaw briefed us about Malik, did you notice that he did not give a date and place of birth as he did for all of the other suspected terrorists and conspirators?"

"Yes, but I didn't think anything of it. Why?"

"I've done an exhaustive search and there is no record anywhere of Malik's birth. I thought I recognized him when Phil projected his photo in the conference room. At first, I thought it had to be merely a surprising similarity to someone else."

"I examined dozens of photographs of Malik that were taken over a period of more than 30 years. Let me show you," he said as he cycled through several images showing dates in the lower right-hand corner. "As you can see, he is not showing any signs of aging. He looks exactly today as he did more than three decades ago. I now know who he is and where I've seen him before."

"Where?" David asked, somehow sensing the answer.

"He was in Jerusalem in 58 AD. He was a bondservant to a wealthy member of the Sanhedrin named Ananias ben Nebedeus. He was the vocal leader of the mob that tried to kill Paul before the Roman commander intervened. He was also one of the 40 men Joazar persuaded to take a sworn oath to kill Paul. His name wasn't Malik then. It was Ammiel. Like me, he had no surname."

"Are you sure of this?"

"Yes. Ahmed Malik is also an android."

"Why are you telling me this in private? Why not tell the whole team?"

"You are the only one who hasn't ruled out the possibility that I was present in Jerusalem almost two thousand years ago. Even you have doubts but you are the only member of the team who firmly believes in the existence of intelligent beings who are able to move in and out of time at will."

"Unlike the others, you have kept an open mind about my origin. Everyone else, including Tiera, believes I am a contemporary military creation. If I told them that Malik is also an android, and that he was in Jerusalem at the same time I was, they would roll their eyes in disbelief and I would lose all credibility with them. They might even begin to suspect that I had ulterior motives or at least some kind of conflict of interest. We can't afford that right now. Until we find the other nuclear weapons, I must say or do nothing to undermine the team's confidence in me."

"But there's another reason. If anything should happen to me, it is essential that at least one member of the TF3 team knows that Malik is not human."

David nodded thoughtfully before saying, "That might explain how a second-tier nation like Pakistan could have an Intelligence service that is rated the best in the world. I've often wondered how Pakistan's intelligence service could be ranked above the Mossad, MI6, and the CIA. But, if Malik is an android with powers similar to yours, and he's the head of the S-Wing, that could certainly explain it."

"Yes, I'm sure you are right," Nahbi said. "Malik's involvement means that the nuclear weapons are being controlled by an adversary even more formidable than we first thought. We've been going on the assumption that General Parvez Jhalawan was the mastermind. It now appears probable that Malik is exploiting Jhalawan's lust for power as part of a larger objective. I'm sure that Jhalawan is unaware that Malik is not human. More importantly, Malik is also a tool being used and manipulated by someone."

Saturday, June 14

Malamocco, Italy
9:00 AM

The phone in her room rang a few minutes after Teresa returned from breakfast. She had been asked to come to the reception area. The same female detective from the previous day had asked if she could come to the Police station to identify some personal articles. She'd told Teresa that Abramo's car had been found at the Tronchetto and that what appeared to be her luggage and purse were inside the car.

Her luggage and purse seemed untouched. Her passport was still in her purse and the photo verified that the items were indeed hers. Her name tag on her luggage was all the evidence the police needed to release her things to her. They asked about the large sum of money they'd found in her purse but seemed to accept her explanation since it was consistent with everything else she'd told them.

Teresa also identified the other items as having belonged to Lia Pedrazzini. There were two envelopes in Lia's purse containing a total of almost 24,000 Euros. Teresa told the police that Lia's husband was out of work. She asked if he would be able to get the money without delay. She was told that would depend on decisions made by the local magistrate.

The Commissario Capo told Teresa that her life might still be in danger but that he was not in a position to offer her police protection. He recommended that she not publicize her movements or plans until the killers were apprehended.

With the return of her money and her clothes, Teresa thanked the staff at the Casa Madonna and took a taxi to a hotel in Malamocco. The police had asked her not to leave Venice without letting them know. Teresa didn't yet know what her next move would be so she decided to stay in Venice for a few days.

She rented an Audi A3 for one week and went to a bank to use some of her cash to purchase a certified check in the amount of 2,500 euros made out to Lia's husband. She sent the check via DHL

Express. It would be delivered the following day. She hoped it would be enough to help pay the bills until Lia's earnings from the trip that had cost her life could be released to her husband. She couldn't bring herself to write a note. She wouldn't have known what to say to a man she'd never met.

Her cell phone battery had run down. After she recharged it, she saw that Franco had tried to call her several times. If he had known what would happen after he left, why would he have tried to call her? She wasn't ready to speak to him. She needed more time to collect her thoughts.

MI6 HQ, London
10:00 AM

Dr. Angus Dunbar, Chief Nuclear Scientist at the United Kingdom's Atomic Weapons Establishment facility near Burghfield, was cleared by security at the main entrance and escorted to the TF3 command center. Nahbi asked the rest of the TF3 team to join them in the conference area. Dr. Dunbar had already told him the essence of his findings over the phone but Nahbi wanted the team to hear it directly from the scientist.

"Thank you for meeting with me on such short notice," the scientist told them. "I have the results of our analysis of the weapon. I'm afraid the news is very bad."

"As I think you already know, this device is conceptually a descendent of the American W33 tactical nuclear artillery shell designed to be fired from the M110A2 self-propelled howitzers. Those devices could be adjusted in the field to produce yields of either 5 or 10 kilotons," the scientist told them.

"The Americans also had one variation that produced a yield of 40 kilotons. It was what is known as a boosted fission weapon. What that means in layman's terms is that a small amount of fusion fuel was used to increase the number of neutrons released. The rate of fission was increased so much that more of the fissile material was able to undergo fission before the core explosively disassembled."

"We expected that the weapon found on the tanker might be a boosted fission weapon with potential yield of up to 40 kilotons.

What we found was utterly surprising and far more dangerous. The device recovered from the Belle Maria is not just a nuclear weapon, it is a neutron bomb."

"Let me provide some historical context to help you understand what this means," Dr. Dunbar said.

"By design, a neutron bomb normally produces slightly less blast and heat damage than a fission or fusion weapon. However, it releases an enormous pulse of high-energy neutron particles that are lethal to humans. Most people exposed to the barrage of neutron particles near the blast center will die immediately. Most people within a radius of up to five miles will die a day or two later from massive tissue destruction. These high-energy particles can penetrate thick, protective materials such as reinforced concrete buildings and even tank armor."

"The neutron bomb was conceived by Samuel Cohen at the Lawrence Livermore National Laboratory in 1958. The United States successfully tested a neutron device in 1962. During the 1970s, the Carter administration proposed modernizing the U.S. nuclear arsenal by installing neutron warheads on Lance missiles and 8-inch artillery shells to protect Western Europe against a potential attack by numerically superior Soviet forces. In the face of European resistance, President Carter deferred deployment. France then tested a neutron device in 1980. In 1981, President Reagan re-authorized the production of neutron warheads for the Lance missiles and 8-inch artillery shells. The artillery shell variant was designated the W79. Starting in 1996, the Americans began to retire all of their neutron warheads. The last W79 artillery shell was dismantled at the Nuclear Security Administration's Pantex facility outside Amarillo, Texas in 2003."

"Pakistan's nuclear scientists have leveraged their knowledge of American designs to produce both strategic and tactical nuclear weapons to repel a numerically superior Indian Army force. The device recovered from the Belle Maria is an innovative hybrid design that is capable of causing complete destruction of most buildings in the blast zone and near total mortality of all humans within a radius of five miles," Dr. Dunbar concluded.

Nahbi was watching the faces of the TF3 team members during Dr. Dunbar's presentation. He was not surprised to see that they were stunned. With four weapons still unaccounted for, and each assumed to have the same destructive force as the weapon recovered from the Belle Maria, the potential loss of life was hard to imagine. Just one of the missing weapons could wipe out the entire central city and surrounding area of any of the great cities of northern Europe and kill every person in a thirty square mile area.

Depending on which cities were selected as the targets, the four remaining weapons could kill ten to twelve million innocent people, including six to eight million children. Twelve million deaths would be four thousand times the number of people killed by Al Qaeda in the September 11, 2001 attacks against the United States.

If the weapons were detonated simultaneously, the terrorists could kill more innocent people in a single day than Adolf Hitler's Nazis killed in all of World War II.

Malamocco, Venice
2:20 PM

Teresa had not seen the limousine and could describe the murderers only generally. The Police had very little to go on in their efforts to track down the killers. Forensic technicians had uncovered absolutely nothing helpful from the Sartori residence or the boat. It was clear that the killers were professionals.

Late in the afternoon, the limousine was discovered parked in Malamocco and the chauffeur's hat and jacket were found in the trunk. There were no prints or other clues. Hair strands were recovered from the hat as possible DNA evidence. The police were not surprised to learn that the limousine had been stolen the day before it had been used in the murders.

The Italian Polizia di Stato checked the video cameras at the border crossings from Italy into France and Switzerland to see if they could identify the time and place where Franco Rinaldi's SUV had left Italy.

The most direct route from Venice to Geneva would have been the A5/E25 crossing into France that connected with the N205 into

Geneva. There was no record of his vehicle having made that crossing.

They also checked the video camera recordings where the E27 crossed the border into Switzerland. Again, there was no record of his vehicle. They found no record that his vehicle had crossed into Switzerland north of Milan where the A9 connected to the A2 in Switzerland.

It had finally occurred to them that Franco might have lied to Teresa about Geneva being his destination. Sure enough, when they checked the video camera recordings where the A22 connected to the Austrian A13 south of Innsbruck, they finally knew he had headed north instead of west.

Franco's SUV had crossed into Austria at 11:17 AM on 11 June. More than three days later, he could be anywhere in northern Europe. Lacking any other clues, they contacted INTERPOL in Lyon, France and asked for a bulletin to be issued to law enforcement agencies throughout northern Europe in the hope that someone would see the vehicle and report it.

The female detective called to tell Teresa that Franco and Fredo Rinaldi were being treated as criminal suspects because of their possible connection to the murders and attempted murder. Teresa didn't know what to think.

MI6 HQ, London
6:45 PM

Nahbi looked up from his workstation to see Phil Shaw, Tiera, and David standing at the entrance to his cubicle.

"Nahbi, we may have a thin lead on the four missing weapons," Phil said. "I just received a call from Greg Deveaux at INTERPOL headquarters in Lyon. Greg has been asked by the Italian Polizia di Stata to issue an alert to all law enforcement agencies in France, Germany, Belgium, the Netherlands, and England to watch for a dark-green SUV belonging to Franco Rinaldi."

"Abu Shakra said the weapons were on the yacht when it left Alexandria last Sunday morning. He told you that the Rinaldi brothers were Hakeem Ghanem's nephews and that both of them

were low-level members of the Muslim Brotherhood. Although he didn't know their assignments, it seems reasonable to assume that their role is to deliver the weapons somewhere in Europe. Unfortunately, he didn't tell us what he knew until almost forty hours after the yacht reached Venice so the proverbial horse was already out of the barn."

David chimed in. "The reason INTERPOL has become involved is that the yacht broker, his wife, and one of the two Italian prostitutes on the yacht were murdered by drowning in Venice Lagoon the day after the yacht returned to Venice. They were killed a little after 1:00 AM early Friday morning. The Italian State Police believe it was a professional hit. They want to question the Rinaldi brothers since they were on the yacht when it returned from Egypt."

"The other prostitute who was on the yacht miraculously survived. That's how we know when the others were murdered. She told police that one of the killers posed as a limousine driver. She also said the Rinaldi brothers had been asked by their uncle Ghanem to deliver some equipment to Geneva. At first, the police could not pick up their trail. It turned out that Geneva wasn't the destination. The brothers crossed the Italian border into Austria and were clearly northbound. The SUV was refueled at a service plaza outside of Innsbruck. Even though the fuel was purchased with cash, the service station has cameras on the pumps that are positioned to read license plates in case someone doesn't pay. After Innsbruck, the trail went cold. Apparently, they are not using a traceable cell phone and are paying cash for anything they buy so there's no credit card trail."

"What's the name of the prostitute who survived and where is she?" Nahbi asked.

"Her name is Teresa Giachetti and she's in a hotel in Malamocco on Lido Island," Tiera answered.

"Tiera, get in touch with her," Nahbi directed. "See if she is willing to come to London. We need to talk to her. There may be something useful she can tell us. The police questioning would have been focused on the murders. They might have missed something we could use. If she agrees to come, we'll probably need to clear it with the local police."

"We know there are four devices still unaccounted for and that they were concealed in scuba tanks aboard the yacht. Abu Shakra did not know where they were to be taken after they arrived in Venice."

"Still, we learned quite a lot from him. He told us that he received his initial orders from Ambassador Al-Zeid and subsequent orders from Ibrahim Al-Jabiri. The Ambassador told him that General Jhalawan had ordered the theft of the weapons as part of a grand plan to cripple the western powers and usher in a new world order governed by Islamic law."

"Abu Shakra also told us how the weapons left Pakistan and how one device was transferred to the Belle Maria. He told us that Al-Jabiri helped him load four devices onto the yacht. We may safely assume that Hakeem Ghanem has a senior role as well given that he is Al-Jabiri's boss, is also a senior member of the Muslim Brotherhood, and directed his nephews to deliver what almost certainly are the other devices to a destination still unknown."

"We still do not know the time-table or the targets. It is probable that only General Jhalawan and perhaps Ahmed Malik know those details. All of our work will be tragically in vain if we do not find the answers to those two critical questions soon."

Frankfurt, Germany
8:42 PM

Franco parked his SUV in the enormous parking garage at the Frankfurt Airport. It was a long walk from the car to the baggage claim exit in Terminal 1. He had not realized it would take so long to get from the car to the baggage claim area so he and Fredo were late.

Dr. Bashir Ghilzai and a younger man were impatiently waiting for them as they approached the area where they were to meet. As they had been instructed, Fredo held up a sign with the hand-printed word *Diamar* on it to identify them to Dr. Ghilzai.

Dr. Ghilzai was clearly in a foul mood. He tersely introduced his associate only as one of the engineers who worked for him. Fredo took Dr. Ghilzai's luggage. The two men had changed planes in Istanbul to Lufthansa flight LH1301 and were tired from their long

flight. Franco suggested that he go get the car and meet them at the curb to save them the long walk.

Franco had not realized that he would have to exit from the parking garage, go through the toll booths, and then follow a circuitous route through heavy traffic and several traffic lights to return to Terminal 1. It took him thirty-five minutes. When Dr. Ghilzai got into the car, it was obvious that he was very angry.

"I have reserved two rooms at a small hotel two blocks from the garage," Franco told Dr. Ghilzai. It is not fancy but is clean and they serve a continental breakfast each morning. It is 34 miles to Aarbergen from the airport, mostly on the A3 Autobahn. It will take about forty-five minutes."

Sunday, June 15

MI6 HQ, London
10:45 AM

Tiera buzzed Nahbi's line. "Teresa Giachetti will arrive at London City Airport about five o'clock this afternoon. Phil Shaw and I will pick her up at the terminal and bring her here. You should be able to speak to her by six o'clock."

"Fortunately, there is a small airport with a grass runway at the northern end of Lido Island so we didn't have the delay of getting her to the Marco Polo International airport on the mainland."

"The transportation section upstairs has chartered a Cessna Caravan to fly her directly from the Aeroporto Nicelli Venezia Lido to London City Airport. It's about 800 miles and the Caravan can cruise at about 160 knots with more than adequate range for a non-stop flight. The Italian police had no objection to her leaving Venice when I told them that she would return after her meeting with us."

"Good work." Nahbi said. "Let us all know when she arrives."

Aarbergen Germany
1:30 PM

Dr. Ghilzai had already confirmed that the auto repair shop had all of the necessary tools and two heavy steel tables normally used for transmission repairs. He was anxious to complete his work and leave.

He and Tariq Zardari carefully removed three of the nuclear devices from the scuba tanks and placed them in polished stainless steel carbon dioxide tanks normally used by bars and restaurants for carbonated beverage dispensers. Following instructions they'd received from Ahmed Malik after the device on the Belle Maria had been intercepted, they left one of the devices in the modified scuba tank.

Zardari fitted each of the four devices with a modified GSM cell phone connected to the detonator. An electrically small antenna, commonly known as an ESA, was glued to the top of each tank for the best possible reception. At the appropriate time, an encrypted text message would be routed to the devices simultaneously through the Eutelsat 10A communications satellite positioned in a geosynchronous orbit at 10 degrees east longitude. From that position, the satellite's coverage included all of Europe, Africa, and the Middle East. Prior to the interception of the device on board the Belle Maria, the plan had been to use the Iridium satellite network to trigger the device in the United States. That capability still existed if needed since all of the modified GSM cell phones were quad band units able to receive signals all over the world.

6:00 PM

All that remained was to transport the devices to the target cities and place them in their designated locations. Dr. Ghilzai briefed the Rinaldi brothers on what their roles would be after they left Aarbergen.

Fredo accepted his assignment without complaint but Franco was unhappy with the revised plan because it would mean he would be gone much longer than he'd originally thought. He was afraid that Teresa might be so angry that she wouldn't come to Rome after all.

Franco's uncle had not told him what the scuba tanks actually contained. After he'd seen that the contents of three of them had been transferred to CO_2 tanks he had begun to suspect that he and Fredo might have been transporting some kind of poisonous gas or biological warfare chemical. Although they had joined the Muslim Brotherhood at their uncle's urging, neither of the Rinaldi brothers wanted any part in killing innocent people. Franco decided to call his uncle.

Hakeem Ghanem's mobile phone did not display a caller ID so he answered very cautiously. "As-salamu Alaykum," he said without mentioning his name.

"Uncle Ghanem, this is Franco. Do you have a few minutes?"

"Yes, of course," Ghanem responded as he belatedly realized that the number he'd seen on his phone's screen was from the pre-paid GSM phone that Franco had been using.

"Uncle Ghanem, can you tell me a little more about what you've asked us to do? It's not difficult to see that it involves something more than simply making equipment deliveries."

Ghanem had been expecting Franco to call. The young man was intelligent and thoughtful so it was not surprising that he had questions. Ghanem had been provided with a prepared story for just this situation.

"Yes. Certainly," Ghanem said. "You are correct that the scuba tanks are not what they seem. I'm sure you've noticed that they are heavier than a normal scuba tank. They are actually very sophisticated electronic surveillance devices with small nuclear power supplies in their bases that will last for years. That is why they are so heavy."

Ghanem continued with the cover story. "As I'm sure you know, the western nations employ a large number of incredibly expensive surveillance satellites that none of the Islamic nations can yet match. To partially neutralize that advantage, scientists aligned with the Muslim Brotherhood here in Egypt have developed devices that can receive certain kinds of radio and telephone signals. Those signals are then encrypted before they are transmitted via one of the

commercial satellites to the Egyptian General Intelligence Service in Hadaeq Al Qubah, near Cairo."

"The surveillance devices need to be placed close to the top of tall buildings to receive and transmit effectively," Ghanem told his nephew. "From an intelligence perspective, the United States, the United Kingdom, France, and Germany are the most valuable sources of information."

"I'm sure you can understand the need for secrecy. It would be very easy for the western nations to remove our hidden listening posts if they knew of their existence. The devices are predominately passive. That means they spend most of their time simply receiving messages and cannot be tracked because they are not transmitting. Sometime after midnight each day, the devices compress the information they've gathered that day and send a short burst transmission to the GIS here in Egypt via one of the communications satellites. The actual time when the devices are transmitting is so short that it is impossible to triangulate their location."

"The scuba tanks and the CO2 tanks are merely convenient containers that will not arouse suspicion. Dr. Ghilzai and his associate are involved to ensure that the devices are properly handled and placed. Do you have other questions?" Ghanem asked.

Franco paused for a moment before answering. "Thank you for explaining that to me. I am relieved to know that the equipment we are delivering will be used for peaceful purposes. I do have one question."

"When you asked us to deliver the equipment to Germany, I understood it would take only a few days. Now, with the revised plan that Dr. Ghilzai explained, I will be gone for two more weeks. Would it be possible for someone else to take the scuba tank to the United States? I would really like to go home as soon as possible."

Ghanem decided to nip that thought in the bud. "I am ashamed of you, Franco," he said in an angry tone of voice. "You have been given a very important job to do. I have placed my trust in you and have told other senior members of the Muslim Brotherhood that you are trustworthy. Is this what I can expect from you in the future?

Will you only accept convenient assignments that do not interfere with your personal life? Is this how you repay my kindness to your mother and show loyalty to our cause?"

Franco cringed under the verbal attack from his uncle. "I am sorry, Uncle Ghanem. I do not wish to seem ungrateful for all you have done for my mother and for Fredo and me. We will do as you've asked."

"Good," Ghanem said curtly. "Now, there is something else I need to tell you. There is reason to believe that police in northern Europe are watching for your vehicle. It is possible that they have discovered that I am sympathetic to the Muslim Brotherhood. Because you are my nephew and recently visited me here in Alexandria, the police are apparently trying to monitor your movements."

"As a precaution, I want you to hide your SUV in an old barn ten miles south of Aarbergen near Bärstadt. The garage owner will show you where to park it. Use other vehicles from now on. The garage has two compact sedans available as loaners. Until this assignment is complete, I want you and Fredo to use those vehicles. Do you understand?"

"Yes," Franco responded. I will move my vehicle this evening. Is there anything else?"

"No. I will call you if anything changes. Goodbye," Ghanem told his nephew.

MI6 HQ, London
6:00 PM

"Thank you for coming Signorina Giachetti. I do not think our talks will take very long but I assure you they are extremely important," Nahbi told her.

"I understand that Franco Rinaldi told you that he had been asked to deliver some equipment for his uncle. Did he tell you what kind of equipment?" Nahbi asked.

"No. He told me only that he'd been asked to deliver some minor equipment items to Geneva and that he could not say no to his uncle

because he'd been kind to Franco's mother. He said it would take only a few days."

"I'm sure you are aware by now that Geneva was not the destination. We believe the so-called equipment items have been taken to one of the northern Europe countries. Do you know any reason why Franco might have lied to you about the destination?"

Teresa's eyes filled with tears and she could not answer immediately. When she had regained control of her emotions, she said, "No. I have wondered about that a thousand times. He said he loved me. Yet, he lied to me and then some men killed three innocent people and tried to kill me too. It is hard not to believe that he knew something that he did not tell me. However, he did try to call me several times after the killers took us out to drown us. I do not understand why he would try to call me if he'd known that I was supposed to be killed."

"It seems possible that Franco and his brother do not know what they are involved in," Nahbi told her. "They may be only couriers who have not been told the full story," Nahbi suggested. "Given the relationships that developed on the cruise, it is hard to imagine that they would have been so heartless and cruel as to knowingly be complicit in plans to murder you."

"Do you have a phone number for Franco?"

"Yes, his phone number is in the call history list on my phone."

"OK. I want you to return his call right now. If he answers, tell him your phone's battery died and it took you a few days to find a replacement. Tell him you've missed him and ask where he is tonight. Don't say anything about your ordeal. We'll be listening and will record the conversation for further analysis. Try to keep him talking as long as you can. We might be able to get a cellular triangulation on his location but that is doubtful on such short notice," Nahbi instructed her.

Franco answered the phone on the second ring.

"Oh, Teresa, praise be to Allah it's you. I've been so worried about you. I've tried to call several times but the calls always went to your voice mail. Didn't you get my messages?"

"Not until just now. The battery on my phone went bad and I just got the replacement recharged enough to call you. I've missed you. Where are you?"

"We're still in Geneva. My uncle wants us to take some spare parts back to Rome so we can ship them to him."

"Franco, I don't quite know how to tell you this but I've decided that it's probably not a good idea for me to come live with you. We don't really know each other that well and I'm afraid it would not work out the way you'd like."

"Please don't say that. I love you and I miss you so very much. Please give us a chance," Franco begged her. Teresa heard two beeps just before Franco said, "I'm sorry but I have a very important call coming in from my uncle Ghanem. I have to take it. I'll call you in the morning. I love you," Franco said as he abruptly broke the connection.

"We weren't able to get a location but it's a virtual certainty that he lied about being in Geneva," Nahbi said. "We'll brainstorm a script for you to use in the morning. Tiera will take you to get something to eat and then to a comfortable room where you can spend the night. Once again, thank you for coming."

Palermo, Sicily
8:00 PM

Carlos Vento had just been paid the largest fee for his services that he had ever received. In his line of work, emotional detachment was essential. Still, that would be difficult this time because the assignment was not a routine contract.

Enrico Favaloro arrived at the restaurant a few minutes late. Carlos was waiting for him near the door. "How are you my friend?" Favaloro asked as the two men shook hands.

"Very well thank you. Would you like a drink before we go to our table?" Carlos asked.

"Yes, I think I would."

The two men sat at the bar for a half-hour reminiscing over memories of their long association. When the waiter tactfully reminded them their table was ready, they took their drinks with

them. Over the next two hours, they enjoyed a fine meal and talked of many things. When they were finished, Carlos suggested that they go to a new gentlemen's club for some entertainment and a night cap. Enrico readily agreed. Carlos said he'd been wanting to ride in Favaloro's new Lamborghini Aventador LP700 roadster and asked if they could ride together.

A few blocks from the restaurant, Favaloro stopped at a red light. He barely felt the prick when a short needle on a specially-designed ring on Carlos' left hand touched him lightly on the back of his neck. Surprised, he turned to look at Carlos just as the batrachotoxin R began to take effect.

The poison that Carlos had chosen was from the Phyllobates terribilis, also known as the Golden Poison Frog. Ten times more potent and faster acting than the tetrodotoxin produced by the blue-ringed octopus, batrachotoxin R was the most potent neurotoxin known. It killed by permanently and irreversibly blocking nerve signal transmissions to the muscles.

Within seconds, Favaloro's heart went into cardiac arrest. He was dead before the light changed. Carlos got out of the car and walked several blocks back to where he had parked. Once inside his car, he called an unlisted number in Islamabad, Pakistan to advise his client that the assignment had been completed.

The autopsy the next day listed the cause of death as heart failure. The tiny puncture mark in the hairline at the base of Favaloro's neck was never found.

Aarbergen, Germany
10:00 PM

A little after 10:00 PM, a white delivery van pulled into the small parking lot beside the automotive repair garage in Aarbergen, Germany. The signs on the van indicated that it was owned by Steinbach Beverage GmbH located in Steinbach am Taunus five miles from downtown Frankfurt. The company employee driving the van was a member of the IGD, a front organization for the Muslim Brotherhood. Franco had been told to expect him and raised the roll-up garage door so the driver could park the van inside out of sight. He closed the door as the driver got out of the van.

"Guten Abend," Franco said.

"Hallo," the driver replied without offering to shake hands. "I am here to pick up a canister you have pressure tested for us. I was told that you have tested it at one-hundred and seventy-six percent of its designed pressure rating. Is it ready?"

Franco nodded as he heard the secret code that identified the man. The unusual pressure test number was the key. "Yes. Come with me," he said.

The driver spent over an hour with Dr. Ghilzai and the young engineer in the garage's office. They gave him a detailed briefing about what he was to do with the CO2 tank without telling him what it contained. They told him that it was heavier than a standard CO2 tank but that it could be easily moved around using a typical delivery dolly.

Zardari gave the driver a sealed envelope containing the address and a floor plan diagram marked with the exact location where the tank was to be placed. He told the driver that he would receive a text message on his phone with a date and the authentication phrase *Light and Knowledge*. He was instructed to place the CO2 tank in the designated location within two days after the date he was given. When the tank was in place, he was to send a one-word reply to the text message. The word was *Jasmine*.

While the driver was being briefed, Franco and Fredo transferred one of the modified CO2 tanks to the back of the delivery van.

Dr. Ghilzai wanted to be sure the driver understood his instructions. He walked with him from the office back to the repair bay where the van was parked. "You are sure that you understand what you are to do?" Dr. Ghilzai asked the driver one last time.

"Ja, sicher," the driver answered.

A few minutes before midnight, Franco raised the roll-up door and watched as the driver backed the van out of the garage. Franco waited to close the door until the van was out of sight.

Monday, June 16

London, MI6 HQ
7:00 AM

Unaware that Teresa was in London and that her time was one hour earlier than his, Franco waited to call her mobile phone until eight o'clock in Germany. Nahbi knew that Franco would think Teresa was in Italy and had anticipated that his call might be early. At Nahbi's direction, Tiera had taken Teresa to breakfast at 5:30 AM so they were ready when Franco called. Sitting in the TF3 conference area, Teresa waited until the third ring as she'd been instructed. Nahbi and the other TF3 members were all listening in on the call and it was being recorded.

"Buongiorno," Franco said as she answered his call. "I hope I haven't called too early."

"No, I've been up for some time. Are you still in Geneva?" she asked as she'd been told to.

"Yes," he lied to her again. "We'll be here for at least another eight or ten days. The parts and equipment items my uncle wants us to take back to Rome aren't ready yet. Apparently, some of the components haven't arrived here in Geneva yet. He wants us to wait until all of the parts are ready so we can ship a single crate with everything in it. I feel really bad but I won't be home for maybe two more weeks. I hope you aren't too angry with me. I really feel like I have to do this," Franco said with a worried tone in his voice.

"Look, Franco, I can't just sit around waiting for you. I need to make a living and I need to register for the second summer session at the university. You didn't even do me the courtesy of telling me about this until just a few hours before you left Venice. Last night, you hung up on me abruptly when the call came in from your uncle. Now, you tell me you won't be home for another two weeks. I'm sorry, but that's just not acceptable. It is totally unfair and unreasonable. So, go take care of your little project. If you want to see me again, you'll have to come to Bari. I'm not going to arrange my life totally around yours. I told you that I want to have a career of

my own and that I'm not going to be anyone's barefoot and pregnant little wife waiting patiently at home," Teresa told him angrily.

"Teresa, please don't be angry with me. I understand how you feel and I don't blame you. I wish I could simply say no to my uncle but I just can't."

"Well, that's your choice and it has consequences," Teresa said harshly. "You said you loved me but you have now twice placed loyalty to your uncle above your feelings for me. If I am not the most important person in your life, then I will not be in your life at all."

Nahbi silently signaled that they had triangulated Franco's location.

"Will you continue to work as a firefly?" Franco asked softly.

"Yes. I have little choice. And Franco, when you are tormented by thoughts of me making love to other men, just remember that I was willing to give that up for you. Your devotion to your uncle has cost you very dearly. I hope it was worth it. Goodbye," she said as she disconnected the call.

Tears were rolling down Teresa's cheeks. Tiera put her arms around her and just held her until her crying stopped.

"Let me walk you back to your room," Tiera said. "I think you need some time alone after that."

"No, I'm OK. I know he lied to me again. I want to know where he really is," Teresa said.

Nahbi answered her question. "He's in a small town near Frankfurt, Germany. Unfortunately, it is typical of most small towns in Germany. The houses are very densely grouped so the police will have to go door to door in a radius of about a quarter mile. It will take several hours to search the area."

"Do you think he knows about the murders?" Teresa asked.

"There is no way to be absolutely sure at this point. If he knows about them, he would also know that you alone survived. The tone of his conversation with you suggests that he does not know what happened. It is hard to imagine that he would be brave enough or callous enough to call you if he had any knowledge that someone tried to murder you only hours after he left you," Nahbi said.

"Now what?" Teresa wanted to know. "I can tell there's more to this than a murder investigation. Can't you tell me what's going on?"

All of the TF3 team members glanced at Nahbi. It was his call.

"What I'm about to tell you is absolutely top secret information. I will not ask you to sign an official secrets document but I must have your solemn promise not to discuss what I am about to tell you with anyone."

Teresa's face paled but she nodded her agreement.

"Five nuclear weapons were stolen from Pakistan two weeks ago. They were carried by container ship to the Suez Canal. One weapon was placed aboard an oil tanker that was intercepted in the Mediterranean five days ago. The other four weapons were transported by car from Suez to Alexandria where they were placed aboard Hakeem Ghanem's yacht for transport to Venice."

"Ghanem is a senior member of the Muslim Brotherhood. Either he or someone higher up in the terrorist organization ordered you and the others murdered to cover the trail. Franco and Fredo are couriers being used to transport the weapons to where the terrorists intend to detonate them. We don't think they know what they are carrying and I doubt that they knew about the plans to murder the rest of you who were with them on the yacht. We hope they still have the weapons. We have very little time. So, please excuse me," Nahbi said. "I would like for you to remain here in case we need for you to talk to Franco again."

"Yes, of course," Teresa told him.

Aarbergen, Germany
8:15 AM

Tariq Zardari and Fredo left the garage first. They drove south through the western outskirts of Wiesbaden and crossed the Rhine River near Mainz. From there, they drove south on the A63 to its junction with the A6 near Kaiserslautern. They crossed the border into France just west of Saarbrüken and then followed the A4 to Montévrain, a town twenty miles east of the center of Paris.

They arrived at the Fleur-de-lis motor hotel just before five o'clock. Their room had been reserved and pre-paid by a travel

agency claiming to represent the International Association of Industrial Engineers. Tariq showed the reception clerk a phony ID with the association's logo on it and was given the room key.

At 10:30 PM, right on schedule, Fredo met their contact in the lobby and escorted him to their room. For the next hour, the engineer gave the man a thorough briefing including how he would know when to place the device and what the authentication phrase and confirmation word would be. When Zardari was finished, Fredo went with the man to let his vehicle into the underground garage.

After the device had been successfully transferred to the man's vehicle and he had left, Fredo and Tariq slept for a few hours. They left the key in the room and drove out of the parking garage at 4:00 AM on their way back to Frankfurt.

Five miles after they crossed the Marne River, Tariq told Fredo he needed to relieve himself. Fredo pulled off at the next exit and then turned south for a couple of miles to a wooded area. When Fredo pulled over and stopped, Tariq pointed a silenced pistol at him and told him to get out of the car. Fredo instinctively realized that the engineer intended to kill him. As soon as he was out of the car, Fredo ran for his life toward the trees. Zardari put two quick shots into his back and then walked over to him and shot him once more in the head.

Zardari dragged Fredo's body a few meters into the woods before going back to the car. He got behind the wheel and took a few moments to wipe the gun clean before heading for Frankfurt. When there were no cars visible behind him on the A4, he slowed down and moved over to the shoulder before tossing the gun out the window.

Oxfordshire, UK
8:30 AM

Sulaiman el-Masri was reading the business section of the London Times as he sipped his second cup of coffee. He was one of the fifty richest men in the world and the second wealthiest Arab expatriate in the United Kingdom. He and his Algerian wife lived on a beautiful country estate near London.

Two years before, Sulaiman had quietly acquired five million shares of Bombardier preferred stock on the grey market at a cost of more than 100 million dollars. Over the months that followed, he had acquired an additional ten million shares of the Canadian aerospace company's publically-traded common stock. With those purchases, he had become the largest single stockholder in the company. He had used his votes to elect his 26-year-old son to the Board of Directors.

Like the sons of many wealthy Arabs, Jamel el-Masri had been educated in Canada and England. So far, he had shown little interest in business. His father hoped that serving on the board of the aerospace company might encourage his only son to prepare to take over the family's multi-billion dollar global interests before it was too late.

Sulaiman el-Masri had been diagnosed with amyotrophic lateral sclerosis in January. Although he was taking the drug Riluzole, he knew that his life-expectancy was very uncertain. Still, he hoped for the best. After all, an internationally acclaimed physicist had been diagnosed with the disease fifty years ago and was still alive. So, perhaps there would be time for Jamel to mature and prepare to take over the family's business affairs.

Jamel's only true passions were scuba diving and flying. He had persuaded his father to purchase one of Bombardier's new Global 8000 executive jets. He had obtained his multi-engine pilot's license in record time and had then qualified to pilot the Global 8000. Jamel was an enthusiastic advocate for the new aircraft that had the greatest range and highest operational ceiling of any business jet in the world. Sulaiman hoped that his son's love for the extraordinary aircraft might eventually engender an interest in the business affairs of the company that produced it.

As a conservative businessman Sulaiman would have been astounded and deeply embarrassed to learn that his wife had supported and encouraged the rise of the Muslim Brotherhood in the UK without his knowledge. The growing number of Algerian Islamists who used London as an operational base for global terrorism had led French security forces to derisively refer to the city as Londonistan.

The oldest brother of el-Masri's wife was the leader of the radical faction of the Muslim Brotherhood in London known as the Armed Islamic Group or AIG for short. Jamel admired his charismatic uncle and had secretly joined the Muslim Brotherhood while in graduate school at the Imperial College of London. Jamel wisely concealed his militant Islamist ardor from his moderate, pro-western father, but his mother was fiercely proud that her only son would one day fight against the western infidels.

Aarbergen, Germany
9:45 AM

Franco and Dr. Ghilzai left the garage ninety minutes after Fredo and the engineer. Franco had a small gift-wrapped package in the bottom of his carry-on bag. Tariq Zardari had given it to him just before he and Fredo had left for Paris and had told him to give it to the owner of the charter diving boat when he arrived in Key Largo.

It was 550 kilometers from Aarbergen to where they would put the car on the Eurotunnel Shuttle train at Calais for the trip under the English Channel. Dr. Ghilzai was carrying a false Italian passport. As Italian citizens and nationals of a country in the European Economic Area he and Franco did not need visas to enter the United Kingdom.

Franco followed the A3 in a northwesterly direction to Cologne where he turned west onto the A4. He was relieved that the traffic was light. The A4 became the A76 at the border between Germany and the Netherlands and then changed again to the A2 at the Belgian border. From Brussels, he followed the A10 to its intersection with the A18 near Ostend. The highway number changed again to the A16 at the French border. Passing just south of Dunkerque, they arrived at the Eurotunnel terminal in Calais a little after three in the afternoon.

Franco drove the loaner car onto one of the Eurotunnel Shuttle train's vehicle transport cars. He and Dr. Ghilzai stayed in their car for the 35 minute crossing. At Folkstone, they followed the M20 to their hotel near the town of Maidstone. At 10:00 PM, they met with the first of their two U.K. contacts. Dr. Ghilzai briefed the man before Franco helped load the third CO2 tank into his cargo van.

London-Oxford Airport
10:00 AM

Jamel el-Masri paid and tipped the taxi driver and walked into the terminal building at the London-Oxford Airport dragging his roll-aboard luggage and a briefcase behind him. He was excited and eager to get airborne on the first short leg of the trip.

The sleek Bombardier Global 8000 executive jet was parked in front of the hanger where it was kept. The maintenance crew had already completed the pre-flight inspections and topped off the fuel tanks. The Global 8000 tanks held 7,200 gallons of jet fuel giving the aircraft a maximum range of 7,900 nautical miles.

Thirty minutes later, Jamel turned left onto the main runway and brought the aircraft to a stop. He made his final instrument checks and then increased engine thrust to full power before releasing the brakes. The aircraft accelerated quickly and lifted off smoothly 26 seconds later. The flight to Southampton would take less than thirty minutes even with the air-traffic control re-routing around the RAF Brize Norton airspace.

Tuesday, June 17

London, MI6 HQ
9:08 AM

"Hello," Nahbi said as he took the call.

"Guten Morgan, Herr Nahbi. This is Detective Franz Mueller. I am with the Kriminalpolizei Department of the Landespolizei in Hesse. I was the officer in charge of the search conducted in Aarbergen yesterday at your request. I'm afraid we did not find the green SUV registered to Herr Franco Rinaldi or any proof that it had ever been there."

"We used twenty-five two-officer teams of Schutpolizei to conduct door-to-door inquiries. They showed photographs of the Rinaldi brothers and the SUV to everyone they contacted. Many of these police officers work in that district and are thoroughly familiar with the town and surrounding area. We have no credible reports

that a green SUV with Italian license plates was seen in the community and no one recalled seeing either of the brothers. I'm sorry we couldn't be of more help."

"You said you had no credible reports," Nahbi responded. "Does that mean one or more people claimed to have seen such a vehicle?"

"Well, yes," Detective Mueller admitted. "An elderly woman said she saw a dark-green vehicle leave an automotive repair garage in Aarbergen late Sunday night. Her eyesight is apparently not very good and she did not see the license plate. However, our officers questioned the garage owner and he said the lady must be mistaken. He was very sure that no green SUV had been in his shop recently."

"Were there any other reports?"

"Yes, there was one other but the officers doubted its reliability," Mueller answered. "At 10:27 PM Sunday night, an officer on routine patrol detained and questioned a fifteen-year-old boy and a thirteen-year-old girl after he discovered them having sex in the woods near the intersection of Scheidertalstrasse and the B54 arterial. He did not charge them with any crime but did drive them home in view of the late hour and their youth."

"As part of our search, one of our officers reviewed the patrol reports for the past several days. Two of our officers followed up with the teenagers late yesterday afternoon. Questioned separately, the teenagers told differing stories about having seen an SUV when they were crossing the B54 on their way to the woods. The boy was emphatic that the vehicle was an Italian Iveco Massif 4X4 with two men in it. The girl said it wasn't an SUV and there was only one man in the vehicle. She also thought it was dark blue. However, they both agreed that it had turned south onto the B54 toward Michelbach."

"Are there any traffic cameras in the area that might have recorded the SUV?" Nahbi asked.

"Unfortunately, no," Detective Mueller replied.

"Why did your officers doubt the teenaged boy's account? Isn't it curious that he came up with the exact make and model of Franco Rinaldi's SUV," Nahbi asked rather sharply.

"I understand your point," Detective Mueller responded. "However, the officers who questioned him had already shown him

a photograph of that make and model and asked if he'd seen a vehicle like it. The senior officer felt that the boy simply told them what he thought they wanted to hear."

"I see," said Nahbi. "Is there anything else?"

"No, but I'll call if we find anything new," Mueller told him.

After the call ended, Nahbi sat quietly for several minutes as he considered what the German policeman had told him. He then asked the other members of TF3 and Gordon McFarland to join him in the conference area.

"I've just been given some disappointing news," Nahbi told them without preamble. "The German police did not find the green SUV or the Rinaldi brothers. However, there were two witnesses who claim to have seen the SUV in Aarbergen late Sunday evening. The police do not consider either witness to be reliable but after hearing the details, I disagree. I feel sure the Rinaldi brothers were in Aarbergen. I think the vehicle was moved to keep us from finding it. More importantly, it is likely that the weapons are no longer in that area and may even have already been taken to the target cities. I don't have to tell you that we need a bit of luck now."

Al Flores asked the questions they were all thinking.

"How can we possibly find the weapons now? We don't know the target cities or where in those cities the weapons will be deployed. We don't even know the time frame for their use. Do you think there is any realistic possibility that we can still find the weapons in time?"

Nahbi smiled that gentle, enigmatic smile they'd all come to recognize as what Tiera called his *adult-explains-to-children look.*

"Try not to be discouraged. If anyone can find the weapons in time, it is this team. I want each of you to go back over every clue from the time the weapons were stolen until they apparently arrived in Aarbergen. Try to think like a brilliant terrorist mastermind might. In a sense, I'm asking you to make educated guesses based on what we know and what we suspect. I can calculate probabilities and we can proceed on those outcomes until we have something better but I am not human. You are. To me, that means one of you might

be able to think enough like the terrorist mastermind to deduce at least the broad outlines of the attack plan."

Nahbi continued. "I believe General Jhalawan, or someone close to him, is the mastermind of this attack. We know that Ambassador Al-Zeid met with Akil El-Sayed in Egypt and then with General Jhalawan in Pakistan. Sayed wrote extensively on the subject of strategies that Al Qaeda could use to attack the western nations. I feel certain that Jhalawan saw something in El-Sayed's writing that he felt he could use. I believe the Ambassador met with El-Sayed to explore and develop those concepts. We can use that clue," Nahbi told them.

"David, I want you to read every strategy paper you can find that El-Sayed wrote. Look for common themes. I want to know just how El-Sayed thought Al Qaeda could inflict great harm on the United States and the other western nations."

"Gabe, the Mossad and the Israel Defense Force know more about Islamic terrorism than anyone. I want you to plug into the collective wisdom of the most experienced Mossad and IDF officers. In every terrorist attack that succeeded, there were lessons learned just as there were in the attacks that failed or that fell short of the objective. The terrorists have never had nuclear weapons before so they will have to modify their approach. We need to know what your colleagues think. Their experience in dealing with Muslim terrorists cannot be duplicated and might just provide a critical piece of the puzzle."

"Phil, I'd like for you and Al to contact the best psychological warfare experts in the U.S., the U.K., France, and Germany. Look for techniques a brilliant terrorist mastermind might use to inflict the maximum psychological damage on the civilian populations of the western nations."

"Tiera, I want you to contact the anti-terrorism units at the federal level of the same four countries. Ask them for their lists of high-value targets and what anti-terrorism countermeasures are either already in place or available to be activated on short notice. Also, ask them for any dates that might have special significance to terrorists mounting an attack on their countries. This year, Ramadan begins on Saturday, June 28. That's only eleven days from

now. Given that the weapons are already in northern Europe, and any delay risks their discovery, it seems likely that the attack will come before the onset of Ramadan. With all of that in mind, I think we have only a few days to find the weapons."

"Gordon, I'd like for you to contact the most brilliant technologists you know. Ask them two questions: What technology exists that we might be able to use to find the weapons and what technology exists that a well-funded and well-organized terrorist group could employ. For example, do any of the military satellites have the ability to locate nuclear devices from space that we haven't been told about? I think it likely that cellular phone systems will be used to trigger the devices. Do the communications experts have any ideas about how such signals could be identified in real time and potentially blocked? I realize that's a long shot but I think we must look under every one of the proverbial stones," Nahbi told the Wizard of MI6.

"Gordon, I need for you to do something else too," Nahbi said. "Teresa Giachetti is still in the building. I'm going to have her call Franco to apologize for being so angry with him. I'll coach her about techniques for keeping him on the phone as long as possible. I'd like for you to coordinate a massive effort to triangulate on his phone signal. He could be anywhere in northern Europe by now but I think the high probability areas are the central districts of Frankfurt, Paris, and London. Let's cast a wide net in the hope that we'll get lucky in locating him."

London, Canary Wharf
10:00 AM

"Good morning and welcome back, Mr. Aquilina," the executive assistant to the Chairman of the HSBC bank said in greeting. Mr. McGregor will be with you in a moment. He's wrapping up a conference call with our Hong Kong office. He knows you're here. Can I get something for you?"

"No, thank you. I'm fine," Matthias told her.

Matthias and Maria Aquilina had arrived at the Four Seasons Hotel at Canary Wharf the previous afternoon on a trip that would include both business and pleasure.

Matthias had asked for the meeting at the nearby world headquarters of the HSBC bank to discuss the global economic situation in the aftermath of the assassination of the ECB President three weeks earlier. A successor for Volker Schuhmacher had not yet been named and the critically important vacancy was hampering efforts to stabilize the financial systems of both Greece and Spain. Matthias had some ideas about who the successor should be and he wanted to compare notes with the President of HSBC.

"Matthias, it is so good to see you," Reginald McGregor said in his customary booming and exuberant voice. "Come in, come in. I trust that your family is well?" McGregor inquired with a raised eyebrow.

"Yes, we are all fine. Maria is still grieving over Volker's death but she is coping. I think coming with me to London to spend some of my money on clothes and accessories will be therapeutic for her," Matthias said with a forced smile.

"Yes, yes. Of course," McGregor agreed. Whenever my wife is depressed, her shopping sprees always cost me at least a thousand euros. If she's really depressed, the bill can be much higher," he said with a laugh. "What's on your mind? I'm sure you didn't come all this way to discuss how our wives spend our money."

"Have you given much thought to who you'll support to replace Volker?"

"Yes, and I suspect you and I have the same person in mind. How do you see the votes lining up among the board of governors?" McGregor asked.

The two men talked for over an hour and then had lunch in the HSBC staff restaurant. It was a pleasant, sunny day so Matthias decided to walk back to the hotel. A block south of the HSBC building, he turned west along South Colonnade Street. He did not see the man following him.

London, MI6 HQ
1:00 PM

"Are you ready Teresa?" Nahbi asked.

"Yes, I think so."

"Remember to do whatever you can to keep him on the line. Our chances of determining his location are poor but if you can keep him on the phone for at least five minutes, we've got a chance. Go ahead. Call him now."

Franco answered her call on the second ring. Telephone company technicians in five countries began trying to pinpoint his location by triangulating on his cell phone's signal. MI6 technicians in London began making a digital recording of the conversation.

"Franco, it's Teresa. I've called to apologize for being so angry yesterday. I do love you and I didn't sleep much last night thinking about how mean I'd been to you. I'm really sorry. Will you forgive me?"

"You had a right to be angry. I truly understand. I love you too. I think yesterday was maybe the worst day of my life thinking I'd never see you again. Do you really believe there might still be hope for us?"

"Oh, yes. Definitely. I know you feel obligated to repay your uncle's kindness to your mother. I thought about that for a long time last night and realized that if I was in the same position, I'd probably feel just as you do. Actually, I admire you for your sense of loyalty to your family."

"You don't know how happy your call has made me."

Teresa took a deep breath and began to repeat exactly what Nahbi had coached her to say.

"Franco, there is still something we need to clear up between us. This is a little awkward but it's important to me so I've got to say what's on my mind. You've told me twice now that you were in Geneva. I know you use a pre-paid SIM card in your phone that does not transmit a caller ID. But, you may not have realized that it does show the country code once a connection is made. I didn't think anything of it the first time you told me you were in Geneva."

"I'm not a technical whiz so it didn't dawn on me until later that the country code was wrong. I know the country code for Switzerland is 41 because I've gone on holiday there several times. The country code that was displayed on my phone both times when we talked was 49, the code for Germany. Look, I can understand

that your uncle may be secretive about his business affairs but I don't like thinking that you lied to me. Please tell me the truth."

Teresa knew that it was critical that Franco believe the lie Nahbi had coached her to tell him. Franco's cell phone and its pre-paid SIM card did *not* transmit the country code. Nahbi had explained to her that he was gambling that Franco wouldn't know that. They would soon know if his bluff had worked.

"I'm sorry that I lied to you," Franco said. "My uncle Ghanem insisted that no one should know where we were. I suspect that he does not pay the import duty on equipment and parts he buys from international sources."

"So, you've been in Germany all this time?" Teresa asked. "Is Fredo still with you?"

Franco hesitated a moment before he answered. "Yes, we've been in Germany for the past five days. And, yes, Fredo is still with me," he lied.

"Just where in Germany are you?"

"I guess you'll figure it out from the country code anyway so I may as well tell you. I'm in England but my uncle will be furious if he finds out I've told anyone where we are."

Teresa didn't have to fake her surprise. "What are you doing in England? Are you really picking up repair parts or was that another one of your uncle's lies?"

"We've brought some minor equipment items to a man my uncle does business with here. I don't know the details but it's all very secretive. It may be some sort of black market deal. I wish we'd never told my uncle we'd do it."

Nahbi silently signaled that they had succeeded in triangulating Franco's location. His admission that he was in England had made the task much easier. The bluff had worked.

Teresa nodded to Nahbi to show she understood.

"Franco, I do love you but I'm really confused by all of this. I don't know whether I can trust you or not. Let me think about what you've told me. I'll call you in a day or two. OK?"

Franco desperately wanted to find some way out of the tangled web of lies and deceptions he'd woven but he already knew that he'd be in the United States in less than 24 hours. The next time she called, she'd see the 01 country code that everyone knew was assigned to the United States. He couldn't think fast enough to find a solution so he simply agreed to wait for her call.

Seventy miles away, in the basement of the MI6 building in London, Nahbi was barking orders rapid-fire to mobilize all available police to converge on the Southampton area as quickly as possible. He wanted an all-out effort to apprehend Franco before he slipped away again.

They didn't know what kind of car Franco was driving or where in the city he might be but they at least knew his general area. Every police officer would have photos of Franco and Fredo. They might get lucky.

Southampton, UK
1:30 PM

Jamel had told Franco to take the copilot's seat before he taxied to the end of the runway and did his pre-flight checks. When he was satisfied, he released the brakes and the Global 8000 was airborne less than 30 seconds later.

Jamel checked his instruments again before putting the jet into a slow, banking turn westward toward the United States. Twenty-four minutes after takeoff, he leveled off at 48,000 feet and throttled back to 480 knots. It was three thousand miles to Linden, New Jersey. With the four hour time zone difference, he expected to land around 4:00 PM local time.

Their suitcases were stowed in the luggage compartment aft along with their scuba diving equipment. One of the scuba tanks was two inches longer than the others and much heavier. A gift-wrapped box in Franco's luggage held what appeared to be a box of Almond Roca candy.

London, West Ferry Circus Park
2:45 PM

Matthias stopped one block south of his hotel in a small park in the middle of West Ferry Circus. He sat down on one of the park benches to enjoy the sunshine. A moment later, a powerfully-built man sat down on the bench beside him. Matthias was surprised to hear the man speak to him.

"Mr. Aquilina, listen carefully," Boris Rogozin told him in a low voice. "If you want to see your wife alive again, you must do exactly as I tell you."

"Who are you?"

Boris ignored the question. "I will take you to your wife."

"Why should I believe you?"

"Call your wife's cell phone."

Matthias called Maria's mobile phone number. She answered at once but she was hysterical and he had difficulty understanding her.

"Maria, calm down. Where are you?"

"I don't know she cried. There is a woman pointing a gun at me and she said she will kill me if you do not do as they tell you. Matthias, I'm scared. I think she means what she says."

Matthias thought quickly and decided he had little choice but to do as the man told him. It seemed likely that a big ransom demand would be made. It was no secret that he was a wealthy man. If it was only a matter of money, he could deal with that.

"Stay calm, I'll be there soon."

Chichester, U.K.
3:30 PM

Dr. Ghilzai had left the Southampton Airport a few minutes after Jamel and Franco had taken off. He'd decided to drive along the southern coast of England on his way back to Frankfurt and had stopped several times along the way to enjoy the scenery. He was surprised when his phone rang. It was Tariq Zardari.

"Dr. Ghilzai, I have just received new instructions. Ahmed Malik told me that he tried to reach you but you didn't answer your phone. Where are you now?"

"I'm a few miles east of Portsmouth heading toward Folkstone on the A27 highway. I just passed Chichester. Why?"

"I'm just about to load the car on the Eurotunnel train at Calais. I'll meet you at a motor hotel in Ashford this evening. I'll call you with the address when I find a place to stay and brief you when we meet," the engineer said as he hung up.

Dr. Bashir Ghilzai sensed something suspicious about the call. Tariq should be somewhere near Frankfurt by now. Instead, he was in Calais preparing to cross the Channel into England. He'd alluded to a new assignment but had given no clues. It was possible that there was some problem with the device that he and Franco had transferred in Maidstone. But, the more he thought about it, the less plausible that possibility seemed. If the device needed to be modified or turned over to someone else for placement, he was imminently well-qualified to do that alone. There was no obvious reason why the young engineer needed to be diverted to meet him.

Bashir Ghilzai was one of the world's foremost nuclear scientists. He had a verified I.Q. of 162 and his brain was fairly screaming a subliminal warning to him. Something was very wrong. The more he thought about it, the more he suspected that General Jhalawan had ordered the young engineer to kill him now that his role was completed. He remembered the cold fear that had gripped him when General Jhalawan had threatened his life in Islamabad.

Having long since realized that his transfer of nuclear technology to Iran and North Korea might eventually force him to leave Pakistan, Dr. Ghilzai had moved much of his wealth to Switzerland and New Zealand. Perhaps it was time to retire. He could not risk meeting with his former protégé and it appeared that he could not return to Pakistan either. He pulled off the road into a service plaza and sat in the car to think. After twenty minutes, he headed north toward London.

London, MI6 HQ
4:00 PM

Tiera's mobile phone vibrated in the pocket of her slacks.

"Hello," she answered non-committedly, half expecting it to be a wrong number. It wasn't.

"Miss Aquilina, I'm sure you recognize my voice. Do not say anything. Just listen. You will never see your parents alive again unless you do exactly what I say. Your parents are unharmed and quite safe for the moment. They have nothing I want so there was no need to torture them in case you wondered. They will either be released unharmed or I will kill them. That depends entirely on you and the android. Listen carefully. When I hang up, I want you to tell the android that you need to speak to him in private. I will call your cell phone again in fifteen minutes. When you answer, use the speaker so you can both hear what I have to say. If you tell anyone or try anything, your parents will die." Tiera heard the dial tone as Raisa hung up.

Tiera was terrified. From what Gavriella had told her, she knew that Raisa Kovalenko would not hesitate to kill her parents. She went immediately to Nahbi's cubicle.

"Nahbi, can I speak to you in private? It is very important. Could you come to my room for a few minutes?"

Nahbi looked surprised but nodded. Tiera said nothing until they were inside her room. She told him about the call she'd received. Nahbi listened carefully but asked no questions. At exactly 4:15 PM, Tiera's phone rang again. She pressed the speaker button to answer the call. Raisa wasted no time.

"Nahbi, you hold the keys to how this little drama will end. Tiera's parents will be released unharmed when you surrender yourself to me. If you do not, I will kill them."

"Your talents are of great interest to my country. As you undoubtedly recognized, the assault on the MI6 safe house was intended to capture you. Miss Aquilina and Mr. Logan were of collateral value only because at that time they knew more about you than anyone," Raisa said.

"How do you propose to make the hostage exchange so I will know that Tiera's parents will not be killed once you have me?"

"Within five minutes after I hang up, you and Miss Aquilina must leave the building by the south exit and walk to Vauxhall Station. Someone will be watching to verify that you have done as I've instructed."

"Take the train toward Stanmore. I will call you on Tiera's phone with your next instructions." The line went dead.

"Don't worry, Tiera," Nahbi said gently. "Raisa will not harm your parents if we do as she's told us. Do you have a spare battery for your phone?"

"Yes, it's on a charger by the bed. I'll get it."

Four minutes later, Nahbi and Tiera exited from the MI6 building and walked one block to the Vauxhall Tube Station. They bought tickets and stood on the platform to wait for the train. Nine minutes later, they were headed north.

4:54 PM

David walked over to Nahbi's cubicle. He'd finished reading everything that Akil El-Sayed had written about Al Qaeda strategies. He thought he understood the terrorist leader's mindset and wanted to discuss his conclusions with Nahbi.

Nahbi wasn't there so David walked over to Tiera's cubicle expecting that Nahbi might be there. Tiera wasn't in her work area either. Puzzled, David called Tiera's room but there was no answer. He tried Nahbi's room too and again got no answer. Although it was unusual, David assumed they were probably somewhere in the building and would return soon.

London, Buckhurst Hill
5:08 PM

Following Raisa's phoned instructions, Nahbi and Tiera got off at Victoria Station and changed to the Dockyards Light Railway train headed toward Upney.

After they'd been on the DLR train for ten minutes, Tiera's phone rang again. She handed it to Nahbi so he could memorize everything Raisa said.

"Get off the train at Bow Church Station," he heard Raisa say. "Cross over the platform to the Mile End Station. Take the Central Line train toward Epping."

Nahbi and Tiera did as Raisa had instructed. After they'd been on the Central Line train for a few minutes, Raisa called again and told them to get off the train at the Buckhurst Hill Station and wait for further instructions. While they were standing on the platform, Tiera's phone rang again. Once again, Nahbi took the call.

"Walk north a short distance to the B170. The street signs will say Roding Lane. Walk east about one-quarter mile to the Rous Road intersection. Follow a pathway south through the trees for about 250 feet. You will come to a clearing with a junior-size soccer field," Raisa told them.

"Tiera's parents will be sitting on the ground in front of the eastern goal. Tiera can walk to mid-field but must not approach her parents closer than that until I tell her she can. Her parents are both wearing explosive belts with radio-controlled detonators. I will be watching you from the trees. If you make any suspicious moves, Tiera's parents will die a gruesome death right before her eyes."

"You will see a wheelchair in front of the western goal. You will walk to it and sit down. Boris will step out of the trees and come to where you are sitting. He will place steel manacles on your wrists and ankles. He will then place a blanket over your arms and legs to conceal the manacles. When he signals that you are securely restrained, I will join Tiera at the center of the field and show her how to disarm the controller once I give it to her."

"Boris will take you to a van parked nearby. When he signals that you are safely in the van, I will hand the controller and the keys to the explosive belts to Tiera and leave."

It took less than ten minutes to reach the soccer field. Tiera began to cry when they came out of the woods and she saw her parents sitting blindfolded back to back on the ground in front of the goal. The explosive belts were plainly visible. Her parents were

utterly helpless and Tiera was terrified knowing that their lives were in the hands of a ruthless woman who would not hesitate to kill them.

"It will be over soon," Nahbi whispered as he gently touched her shoulder and motioned for her to walk to the center of the field.

Nahbi walked to the wheelchair and sat down. Boris came immediately from the trees and placed specially-hardened, high-strength steel manacles on his wrists and ankles just as Raisa had described. Boris covered Nahbi's arms and legs with a blanket and started pushing the wheelchair toward a small parking lot near the east end of the field. A van with a hydraulic lift for a wheelchair was parked there.

Boris loaded Nahbi into the van and then put foam plugs in his ears and a heavy black hood over his head. He gave a two-tone whistle as the signal to Raisa. She joined him a few moments later and they drove away. It was only 20 miles to the Russian Embassy near the west end of Hyde Park but they would take a meandering route to ensure they were not followed.

After Tiera removed the explosive belts from her parents and disarmed the controller, she called David. She told him briefly what had happened and asked that he arrange for them to be picked up at the Buckhurst Hill Station. David kept her on the line while he called Gordon McFarland. Twelve minutes later, the Superintendent of the police station in Buckhurst Hill and another officer arrived to take them to the MI6 headquarters.

London, MI6 HQ
6:30 PM

Sir Lionel Smythe and Gordon McFarland sat quietly in the conference area as Tiera told them what had happened. Neither man spoke until she was finished.

"Tiera, I can understand that you could not allow Raisa to murder your parents. Still, losing Nahbi at this critical time is very troublesome," Sir Lionel said with classic British understatement. "After discussing it with Roger Benson and Levi Reznik, I've decided to put David in charge of the task force in Nahbi's absence."

Gordon could tell that Nahbi's abduction was a devastating blow to the TF3 team's morale. They had lost a brilliant leader and a remarkable personality they all considered their friend. He knew that each of them understood why Sir Lionel had decided to put David in charge. David's leadership qualities were obvious to them all but he was not Nahbi.

"Do we have any idea where the Russians have taken him tonight or how they will get him out of the country?" Sir Lionel asked as he looked around the table.

"He's in the Russian Embassy," Gordon told them.

"How do you know that so soon?" Sir Lionel asked.

"Several days ago, Nahbi came to me concerned that multiple foreign governments would undoubtedly continue to try to abduct him. He had designed an advanced tracking device that would be almost impossible to detect. I had my best electronic technician build it. It looks just like a small version of the other modules in the cavity at the back of his skull. It is color-coded just like they are and has the same multi-conductor ribbon cables although they are dummies. Unlike his other systems, however, this one does not use power from his internal power module. Nahbi felt that any competent engineer or scientist would quickly identify the power module in his lower back and disconnect it to immobilize him. So, this tracking device has its own internal lithium-ion battery that can power the unit for up to a year."

"The beauty of Nahbi's design is that it is completely passive unless it receives a certain high-frequency interrogating signal. When it does, it transmits a reply that lasts only a tiny fraction of one second. However, that brief signal can be detected by the intelligence reconnaissance satellites operated by the CIA and GCHQ. Triangulating on that short burst signal, Nahbi's location can be determined within a 3-meter radius."

"As soon as I heard what had happened, I began sending query signals every few minutes. There is no question about it. Nahbi is in the Russian Embassy in Kensington Palace Gardens on the west side of Hyde Park."

"Gordon, you never cease to amaze me," Sir Lionel said.

"Can't we have our foreign office contact the Russian Ambassador and demand Nahbi's release?" Phil Shaw asked.

Sir Lionel frowned as he considered Phil's question. "No, I don't think so. If Nahbi was a U.K. citizen, we might be able to do as you suggest although it would take days or even weeks. However, as an android of uncertain origin, and therefore not a citizen, the Russians would be on solid ground to simply refuse our request. They would probably deny Nahbi is even in the Embassy. Knowing how the Russians operate, I wouldn't be surprised if they suggested that we've made the whole thing up and that he doesn't even exist. There really wouldn't be anything we could do about it. Diplomatic Immunity is a rather strong protection for them in this case. Moreover, Nahbi's existence is known only to the intelligence communities and political leadership of a few countries. We could not, for example, press a claim at the United Nations where our friends are pitifully few. Military tacticians know that a full frontal assault is not usually the best line of attack. I think in this case, we're going to have to find some way to outsmart the Russians."

London, Ritz Hotel
7:00 PM

Mikhail Prokoviev's Dassault Falcon 7X was parked at Biggin Hill Airport 15 miles southeast of his hotel. The former RAF fighter base had become a preferred London airport for executive jets from all over the world.

The Russian oligarch was in London on business. He and his latest trophy girlfriend were staying at the Ritz hotel in a suite that cost over four thousand pounds per night, the equivalent of almost seven thousand dollars.

A little after 7:00 PM, he got a call from the Director of the Russian Foreign Intelligence Service in Moscow. He knew instantly that it was something important. Sergei would not be calling him at 11:00 PM Moscow time otherwise.

"Mikhail, I'm sorry to have to do this to you but I've been ordered by the President to borrow your aircraft for urgent SVR business," Sergei Kosygin told him.

Prokoviev understood very well that there were certain overhead costs associated with the preferential treatment and lucrative advantages he received from the corrupt Russian government. Perhaps this wouldn't be much of an inconvenience.

"When will you need the aircraft and for how long?"

"Almost immediately for about three days. I cannot tell you more than that. It is a matter of utmost secrecy. Your pilots will fly the plane to Moscow tomorrow morning and bring it back on Friday."

Prokoviev was relieved. He had planned to remain in London at least through Sunday afternoon so he could afford to be agreeable.

"Sergei, my old friend, no apology is necessary between us. I will place a few calls immediately. My crew always keeps the aircraft ready to go at a moment's notice."

London, MI6 HQ
8:00 PM

David remembered a sergeant major once telling him that officers should never run because it spooked the troops. He took a deep breath and made a conscious effort to appear calm.

"For now," David told the members of TF3, "we'll keep doing what Nahbi told us to do with one exception. We're going to have to work through the night on this new problem. I'm sure this won't be the first all-nighter for any of us."

"Phil, I'd like for you to have a covert police surveillance cordon set up around the Russian Embassy immediately. We need to know if the Russians try to move Nahbi. I think they'll try to get him out of the country tonight or early tomorrow morning."

"The Russians will probably try to use an executive jet. They can't afford to risk being intercepted by the security checks at Heathrow or Gatwick. My best guess is that they'll bring in an executive jet or use one that's already here. We need to be ready to prevent them from getting off the ground if possible."

"Tiera, talk to the operations folks upstairs," David said. "Find out if they can get the police to put a hostage rescue SWAT team on standby immediately. It is possible that we'll have to storm an aircraft or otherwise resort to force. I don't think they'll try to use a

military jet because it would draw too much attention. However, the Farnborough Air Show is coming up in a couple of weeks. It's possible that the Russians might already have a suitable military aircraft parked there. See if you can find out."

"Gabe, you know more about Raisa than any of us. Try to guess how she'll play this. Look at all of her options and get back to me as soon as you have a short list of plausible scenarios."

"While we try to prevent the Russians from getting Nahbi out of the country, or destroying him if they can't, we still need to find the nuclear weapons. Except for Al, the rest of you should spend the night trying to do what Sir Lionel suggested. We need to outsmart the Russians."

"Al, I want you to call Roger Benson immediately. Tell him what's happened and that we still don't know where the weapons are. Ask if the CIA has assets in Pakistan that could be used to abduct General Jhalawan. The clock is ticking and he may be our best chance to find the weapons in time. His private residence is in a small village some distance from Islamabad. It seems possible that an elite team might be able to penetrate his security just as SEAL Team Six did when they took out bin Laden."

"And Al, ask if the CIA or the Air Force could use an armed drone to eliminate General Jhalawan if we run out of time and options. I fully realize the potential political ramifications but the alternative would be far worse."

"I'd also like for the CIA to update General Jhalawan's and Ahmed Malik's locations as frequently as they can. I feel sure that one of those two men will give the signal to detonate the weapons. If it comes to it, I'd like to have the option of taking them out. It would have to be a pre-emptive strike. We can't afford to wait for them to dramatically reveal their intentions."

"I'll ask Sir Lionel to notify the political and intelligence service leaders."

Linden, New Jersey
4:12 PM

After a seven-hour flight and brief air traffic delay, Jamel landed the Global 8000 at the Linden, New Jersey Airport and taxied to their assigned parking spot. He was tired but felt strangely elated.

A courtesy van pulled up to the aircraft a few minutes later and the driver helped them unload their luggage and scuba gear. Franco had to help him with the special tank. Jamal noticed the driver's questioning look and explained that it was an old tank that couldn't be pressure certified anymore so it had been partially filled with lead as an anchor for their inflatable diving platform. That seemed to satisfy his curiosity. They cleared immigration and customs without incident and were met at the terminal by the limousine driver Jamel had arranged.

Twenty miles north of the airport, they crossed into lower Manhattan via the Holland Tunnel. With the rush-hour traffic, it took another twenty-five minutes to cover the last three miles to the Marriott Marquis hotel.

Before leaving England, Jamel had reserved one of the hotel's Times Square View rooms for seven days. He had spoken directly with the hotel manager and requested that they be given a room on the 45th floor if possible. The hotel manager did a little research and discovered that Jamel's father was one of the wealthiest men in the world. He'd called Jamel back almost immediately and had assured him that his request would be honored.

Jamel had made dinner reservations for 9:00 PM at the View Restaurant located on the 48th floor of their hotel. It was the only restaurant in the city that revolved and the food was famously good.

The nighttime view of Manhattan was spectacular. As the restaurant revolved, they could see the JP Morgan Chase and Citigroup buildings less than a mile away. The Federal Reserve Bank and the New York Stock Exchange were three miles to the south.

London, MI6 HQ
9:05 PM

"David, I want to make a suggestion," Gavriella said as she appeared at the opening to his cubicle. She had given a lot of thought to what she was about to say.

"Fire away."

"I agree that Raisa will try to get Nahbi out of the U.K. as soon as possible, maybe even tonight or early in the morning," Gabe told him. "If MI6 or British police do the take-down, the Russians will say the British have violated the sanctity of diplomatic immunity."

"Yes, I'd already thought about that. I suspect that Sir Lionel has too."

"Some of what I'm about to tell you is top-secret information within the Mossad. I could be stripped of my rank and even imprisoned for telling you. You know that I was the leader of the Mossad team that freed you and Tiera and took Raisa and Boris into our custody. I don't know if you knew that my team was watching as the Russians abducted you and Tiera. We didn't intervene because it would have led to a gun fight. We don't work that way. We always try to finesse situations and, whenever possible, we try to accomplish our purposes without even revealing that we were there. So, I chose to follow the Russians and keep them under surveillance while hoping for a better opportunity."

"We didn't storm the old warehouse because we didn't know how many Russians were in there. I was pretty sure that you and Tiera had been taken by a Spetsnaz Alpha Group team and I didn't want to tangle with them if it could be avoided. Though the Russian Alpha Group teams are less well known than the American SEAL Teams, they are arguably just as good. They also have more latitude than their American counterparts when a mission involves ethical issues."

"After our interdiction operation was successful, my boss decided to keep the rest of my team here in London just in case they were needed again. What I'm telling you is that Israel has the ability to reactivate my Kidon team with less than an hour's notice. I'll have to get approval from my boss but I feel sure he'll agree. If an Israeli team does the take-down, the Brits will have what the CIA calls

plausible deniability. The Prime Minister's cabinet members will be able to say it was apparently the work of a foreign special operations team and thereby rob the Russians of their charge that diplomatic immunity was breached. What do you think?"

David looked intently at her for several moments as he considered her proposal and then said, "I like it. Let's do this in two phases. See if your boss will give his approval. If he does, then you and I will call Sir Lionel."

Gavriella called Levi at home since it was almost midnight in Tel Aviv. "Levi, I'm sorry to call so late but I need your approval for something."

Less than five minutes later she was given authorization to do as she'd proposed. She and David then called Sir Lionel directly. He called them back a few minutes later after conferring with the Prime Minister. Gabe's proposal was given a green light.

"David, I'm leaving the building to join my team. You can reach me on my secure phone at this number," Gabe told him.

Wednesday, June 18

London, Russian Embassy
12:43 AM

David was exhausted but he knew everyone else was too. He was studying some London maps when his intercom buzzed. It was Phil Shaw. "I just got a call from the police inspector supervising the surveillance of the Russian embassy. A black embassy sedan with diplomatic license plates just left the compound with two men in it. Using their night vision goggles they were able to determine that neither man matched any of the photos we gave them but both men are wearing some kind of uniform. The inspector told me he'd ordered the car followed and wanted to let us know."

"Good. Tell him to maintain the cordon surveillance and report anything that might be even remotely relevant. Ask him to let us know where the black sedan goes."

London, Israeli Embassy
1:30 AM

"Sorry to get you out of bed at this hour but I don't think you'll mind losing a little sleep tonight when you hear about our mission," Gabe said with a fierce grin on her face. "It's payback time."

"We have two objectives tonight. Our top priority is to prevent the Russians from getting the android out of the country. It's possible that the Russians will try to destroy the android rather than give him up. We need to prevent that if at all possible. Our second priority is to regain custody of Raisa Kovalenko and Boris Rogozin. This will unfold fast so we'll have to improvise as we go."

"I've asked for two vehicles. An official U.K. Civil Aviation Authority sedan is on its way to us as I speak. It should be here within ten minutes. It's unmarked but has a windshield barcode sticker for the Operations and Safety division that will automatically open any of the flight line security gates at any civilian airport in the country. That's one of the vehicles we'll use to tail the Russians. The other vehicle is an unmarked utility van that's already parked outside."

"Daniyel, I want you and Avi to load your gear into the utility van and be ready to leave twenty minutes from now. Suit up and get into your war paint for night ops. Nathan, you can put our gear in the CAA sedan when it arrives. You'll drive and I'll ride with you," Gabe told them. "We'll try to avoid gun play but we'll do what we have to do. The Russians must not get the android out of the country."

"The London police have the Russian Embassy under continuous covert surveillance. We'll be using the same encrypted radios they use so we'll hear all of their reports in real time. I want to move our vehicles to the north and south ends of Kensington Palace Gardens so we are positioned to start tailing the Russians as soon as they leave their Embassy. We'll use the two-car rotating-tail technique so whichever vehicle picks up the Russian vehicle will have to guide the other vehicle into position to take over the tail."

"I've also asked for MI6 to coordinate with MI5 to get several miniature surveillance drones airborne as soon as the Russians leave the embassy. I want to be sure they don't elude us. The drones

will transmit real-time images back to MI5 where operators will be ready to redirect us in case we lose the Russian vehicles. I've also asked for two military helicopters to be on standby just in case."

"I'm guessing the Russians will use an executive jet that's already on the ground at one of the nearby business jet airports. The four most likely airports are London City, Biggin Hill, Farnborough, and Blackbushe. We're trying to find out if there are any Russian-owned business jets on the ground at any of them right now but it will probably be sometime tomorrow before we know."

"London City Airport is closest to the Russian Embassy but Biggin Hill has become a popular airfield for business jets and is only a little farther away. Farnborough and Blackbushe are roughly 30 miles from the Russian Embassy. Farnborough hosts the International Air Show but we've confirmed that there are no Russian military aircraft on the ground there yet."

There was a knock at the door. The Israeli Embassy's Military Attaché entered the room and told Gabe that the CAA sedan had arrived.

Gabe looked around the room with that same fierce grin her team had seen before. "I hereby declare that bear season is now open. Let's go hunting, shall we?"

London, Biggin Hill Airport
1:39 AM

Less than 10 minutes after Gabe finished briefing her team, the London Police tail reported that the Russian Embassy's vehicle had entered the flight line gate at Biggin Hill Airport.

Gabe wasn't surprised. She'd already guessed that Biggin Hill would be the Russian's escape route. She checked with Gordon McFarland who confirmed that the signal from the GPS unit in Nahbi's head was still coming from the Russian Embassy. Gabe told her team to sit tight.

Seventeen minutes after the Russian vehicle arrived at Biggin Hill, the police on site reported that the two men were wearing pilot's uniforms and had boarded an executive jet parked in a row of other jets on the east side of the airport. The police provided the jet's

tail number and described the aircraft as white with blue and gold trim but no other visible markings. The Israelis waited.

London, MI6 HQ
2:07 AM

Tiera came into David's cubicle a few minutes after receiving the report from the police surveillance team at Biggin Hill airport.

"David, I've got Gabe on the radio. I'm putting it on the speaker so you and she can both hear what I have to say."

"I've got the information on the aircraft. It's registered to the Siberian Energy Corporation. It's one of the largest of the Russian Oil and Gas conglomerates with significant holdings in the Priobskoye field in western Siberia. The biggest shareholder is a Russian oligarch named Mikhail Prokoviev. He's one of the wealthiest men in Russia and is a close friend of the Director of the Russian Foreign Intelligence Service."

"The aircraft is a Dassault Falcon 7X. It's a large-cabin, ultra-long-range business jet with three engines. It has a maximum range of 6,000 nautical miles. It's only 1,600 miles from London to Moscow so it would be a non-stop trip of just over three hours. Prokoviev's pilots are both former Russian fighter pilots so don't take them lightly. They are probably armed."

"Gabe, the entrance to the Biggin Hill terminal building will be a left turn from the southbound A233. About 70 meters east of the A233 your team will need to make a right turn to approach the security gate that leads to the flight line. Normally, departures are made from the boarding area in front of the terminal building beneath the control tower. However, the SEC corporate jet is parked near the eastern boundary of the airport. To reach it, your team will go through the security gate and then turn south along the taxiway. You'll cross the southern end of the main runway and then drive easterly paralleling the secondary runway until they run out of pavement. You should be able to see the SEC jet from there."

"I've asked for a London Metropolitan Police Service helicopter based at Lippits Hill to do a low-level pass along the eastern side of the Biggin Hill Airport. The LMPS uses the EC-145T2 rotary wing

aircraft with a maximum speed of 150 MPH so they can get there quickly. Fortunately one of their helicopters was already in the air on the east side of the city when I called. It will reach the Biggin Hill Airport a few minutes from now. All of their helicopters have both visible light and infrared photography capability. They will transmit digital photos of the Falcon and the surrounding area directly to your tablet computer. "

"Gabe, do you have all of that? OK, good luck," Tiera said as she broke the connection.

David thought to himself that things were about to get interesting. As a combat veteran, he knew that people might die before the night was over.

When Tiera left, David called the Superintendent of the London Metropolitan Police Department to make an unusual request for support at the airport.

London, Russian Embassy
2:10 AM

"A Jaguar Daimler funeral hearse has just entered the compound at the Russian Embassy," the police inspector told Gabe and her team over the secure radio. She clicked her transmit button three times to signal that she'd received the message.

In the basement of the Russian embassy, Nahbi was seated on a stool in the middle of a large room. He was still wearing the steel shackles and hood. Boris Rogozin carefully fitted an unusually bulky motorcycle helmet over Nahbi's head and buckled the chin strap. It was a standard fiberglass helmet with several layers of Kevlar ballistic fabric molded over it as a blast shield. Two pounds of a shaped PE4 plastic explosive charge was fitted inside the back of the helmet with an embedded detonator wired to a cell phone receiver. Raisa had a small GSM cell phone with one of the speed dial buttons assigned to the phone number for the receiver inside the helmet. She would use it to vaporize Nahbi's computer brain if he or anyone else tried anything. Her orders were to bring the android to Moscow or destroy it.

The funeral home personnel brought a metal casket on a dolly to the service entrance as they'd been instructed to do. Boris and one of the embassy's SVR agents brought the casket inside and put Nahbi in it before closing and locking it. They wheeled it outside and watched as the funeral home personnel loaded it into the hearse. Boris got into the passenger's seat of the hearse to ride with the driver. Raisa and the other funeral home employee got into a black embassy sedan. Raisa told him to drive so she could keep her hands free. The hearse exited from the embassy and turned south toward Kensington Road. The sedan followed so Raisa could keep the hearse in view.

Gabe's secure phone rang.

"Gabe, this is Gordon. The tracking signal from Nahbi has gone dead. Since they're using a hearse, I'm guessing they've hidden Nahbi inside a metal casket that blocks the signal."

Gabe and Nathan saw the hearse and sedan turn east on Kensington Road and waited until it was several hundred feet ahead before following. Daniyel and Avi raced east on Bayswater Road and then turned south on Park Lane. They took over shadowing the hearse near Buckingham Palace Gardens. Gabe and Nathan turned west on Kings Road and then south on Eccleston Street to follow a parallel route. Based on Tiera's research, Gabe knew where the Russians were going but she wanted one of her team's two vehicles to keep them in sight at all times. She and Nathan took over the tail again just before the A202 crossed the Vauxhall Bridge.

London, Biggin Hill Airport
3:05 AM

The air-traffic control supervisor on duty in the Biggin Hill tower saw the hearse stop in front of the flight line gate. He'd been expecting it and hit the button to open the gate. He watched as the hearse and a black sedan drove through the gate and then turned right toward where the Falcon executive jet was parked 600 meters south of the tower.

The Russian Embassy had notified him an hour earlier that the body of a Russian diplomat was being transported back to Moscow for an official funeral. An embassy employee had faxed copies of the

deceased person's diplomatic passport, diplomatic credentials, and death certificate to the control tower thirty minutes earlier. The pilots had already filed their flight plan.

The phone in the control tower rang a moment later. It was the Superintendent of the London Metropolitan Police. The control supervisor listened carefully to the instructions he was given. He looked out the south window of the control tower in time to see several vehicles pass through the gate onto the flight line. One of them was an armored bomb squad vehicle. Using binoculars, he could see that people were already boarding the Falcon. The hearse and sedan pulled away as the door to the executive jet was closed. A moment later, he heard the pilot tell the duty air traffic controller that they were ready to taxi.

Israel, Mossad Headquarters
5:12 AM

Gabe's secure phone rang. "Gabe, this is Levi. Where are you right now?"

"We've just passed through the flight line gate at Biggin Hill airport. The bomb squad is ready to play their role. Why?"

"There's been a change of plans and you're not going to like it. The Foreign Affairs and Defense Committee of the Knesset has been meeting in emergency session for several hours. The Director and I have just received a phone call from the Prime Minister ordering us to bring the android to Israel."

"Levi, I can't believe what I'm hearing. We're trying to find nuclear weapons and the android is our best hope. If we take him to Israel now, millions of innocent people could die. Tell me this is a bad joke," Gavriella said stiffly.

"I'm sorry but we have our orders. Once the Russians exit the aircraft, you are to take control of it and fly it to Tel Aviv. Bring Raisa and Boris with you. Daniyel was General Avigur's pilot when he was in the Israeli Defense Force and he's qualified to fly the Falcon. Nathan was a fighter pilot before joining the Mossad in case Daniyel needs any help."

"Levi, I can't believe you're asking me to do this. Without Nahbi and now without me too, the Task Force 3 team will be decimated at the most critical time. Do you really expect me to do this?"

"I expect you to obey your orders. The FADC and the Prime Minister feel that the threats we face from Iran and other militant Islamists have escalated so sharply that the survival of Israel is at stake. The consensus view is that Israel has no choice but to take control of the android and to use him to defend our country against bitter, hate-filled enemies who would like to see Israel destroyed," Levi explained. "If it's any small consolation, the Prime Minister has assured me that you and Nahbi can continue to provide support to the Task Force from Mossad headquarters."

Gabe thought for a moment before saying, "Levi, I understand my orders. I want you to modify them slightly."

"I don't have much latitude, Gabe. What do you propose?"

"I will send the android to Israel as ordered but I'd like to remain in England to do what I can here," Gabe told him. "I can't abandon the rest of the team. Their morale has already been dealt a serious blow. Once they find out that we've double-crossed them, their anger is predictable but I'm even more worried that David may not be able to keep them motivated in the aftermath of such discouraging news. With Nahbi and me both gone, there will be only five members of Task Force 3 remaining. Do you have enough latitude to let me stay here until we find the nuclear devices?"

Levi was silent for several moments before he said, "OK, Gabe. Unless I'm overruled, you can stay in the UK for now."

Before he hung up, Levi gave Gavriella additional information that took some of the sting out of her orders.

London, Biggin Hill Airport
3:20 AM

"Falcon seven-xray, this is Biggin Hill Tower. Be advised that there is a bomb on your aircraft. Please shut down your engines at once and exit the aircraft. A London Metropolitan Police Bomb Squad unit is already on its way to your location."

"Biggin Hill Tower, this is Falcon seven-xray. Can you repeat your last please?"

"Roger, Falcon seven-xray. The London Metropolitan Police Force has received credible information that one of the service personnel employed by the refueling contractor has placed a bomb on your aircraft."

Onboard the Falcon, Raisa was furious. She shouted at the pilot that it was a trick. She insisted that he begin to taxi at once. He refused so she pressed a compact 9mm Makarov pistol against the side of his head and told him to do as she'd directed. She was surprised to immediately feel the muzzle of another pistol pressed against her right temple. The copilot told her to hand her weapon to the pilot or he would splatter her brains all over the cockpit. She hesitated only a moment before doing as he ordered.

Both pilots had served in the Russian Air Force and had been extensively trained as body guards for Mikhail Prokoviev. Raisa could not intimidate them. She argued with them and threatened them but to no avail.

The pilot disarmed Raisa while the copilot kept her covered. He searched her for other weapons and had her empty her pockets. After a quick examination, he let her put everything back in her pockets, including her cell phone. He then covered her with her own pistol as he followed her into the passenger cabin keeping her between himself and Boris. He ordered Boris to put his weapons on the seat beside him to move toward the exit door without making any sudden movements. Boris could see the gun pointed at Raisa's head so he did as he was told.

As the bomb squad's armored vehicle pulled up beside the plane with its red lights flashing, everyone on board deplaned except for Nahbi. A uniformed policeman escorted the Russians to a waiting passenger van. Two explosive ordnance specialists in full protective gear stood beside the plane waiting until the bus was far enough away to be out of the danger zone.

When they reached the terminal, two London policemen escorted them to a room normally used by airport security personnel and asked them to be seated. Raisa was extremely suspicious and kept

her hand in the right pocket of her slacks with her thumb on the speed dial key of the GSM cell phone.

A few moments later, Gabe and her team entered the room. As soon as Raisa saw the Israelis, she pressed the send button and began to laugh.

"Nathan, see what she's got in her pocket," Gabe ordered.

"It's a small cell phone," Nathan told her a moment later.

Without looking at it, Gabe instinctively knew why Raisa had laughed. She'd used the phone to trigger an explosive device attached to Nahbi. Something primitive and dangerous exploded inside Gavriella's mind. She knocked Raisa to the floor with a viscous blow to the side of her head. "What have you done?"

Raisa touched her head where Gabe's pistol had struck her. "You can tell Levi Reznik that he loses again," she sneered. "The android's head has just been vaporized by two pounds of PE4."

"Nathan, do a body cavity search on Raisa and then get them into the passenger van," Gabe told him. "I need to see for myself if what Raisa has just said is true. Regardless, the rest of you need to get airborne as quickly as possible."

The bomb squad was still at the aircraft when they pulled up. Nathan and Avi made sure that Raisa and Boris were secured while Daniyel began to prepare for takeoff. The police bomb squad unloaded the coffin and cut the locks. Gabe dreaded what they would find.

When the hinged lid of the coffin was raised, there was no sign of an explosion. Nahbi was restrained by steel manacles and was wearing a bulky helmet of some kind but did not appear to have been harmed. One of the bomb squad specialists carefully removed the helmet and carried it a safe distance away to the middle of the grassy area beside the runway. The other bomb squad specialist removed the hood from Nahbi's head. Gabe stepped to the side of the coffin and looked inside. Nahbi was smiling up at her. "Well, Gabe, I am glad to see you," he said calmly.

4:03 AM

They helped Nahbi out of the casket and the bomb squad cut the steel manacles from his wrists and ankles. Gavriella pulled him aside to speak to him in private.

"When Raisa told me what she'd done, I thought I'd never hear your voice again. Why didn't the explosives detonate?" Gabe asked.

"Strangely enough, the fact that she failed in her attempt to detonate the shaped charge in the helmet was due to her religious heritage," Nahbi explained. "Although Tiera's research indicated that Raisa is an atheist, we know that her parents were devout members of the Russian Orthodox Church. Orthodox caskets are always made entirely of wood. Raisa didn't realize that in the UK, as in the United States, most caskets are made of galvanized 16 gage steel painted in a variety of colors. The radio signal from the cell phone tower could not penetrate the heavy gage steel. If the casket had been made of wood, she would have succeeded."

"Amazing. Look, I've got a lot to tell you and not much time. This rescue, just like the one that wrested David and Tiera from Raisa's grasp before, was done by a Mossad Kidon team under my command. I suggested to David that having the Mossad take down Raisa would make it easier for the UK Government to disavow all knowledge to avoid diplomatic problems. My proposal was approved by the Prime Ministers of the United Kingdom and Israel."

"Our team had a lot of help from the London Metropolitan Police Service, including the bomb squad. Two of my men are qualified pilots. They will fly the Falcon jet to Tel Aviv to deliver Raisa and Boris to our judicial system where they will be tried for murdering an Israeli citizen. But, there's more."

"I've been ordered to send you to Israel on the plane. The Israeli Knesset and the Prime Minster feel that Israel's survival is at a critical point. They believe that your unique skills might make the difference. I'm sorry to have to say this, but as the commander of the team, I am under orders to ensure that you are on board when this plane takes off even if I have to use force."

"I see," said Nahbi. "What else?"

"They initially wanted me to return to Israel too. I've negotiated modifications to my orders that will allow me to remain here in the UK as part of TF3. You will be allowed to continue to support TF3 from the Mossad headquarters in Tel Aviv. My boss and the Prime Minister understand fully that we don't yet know how to stop the use of the nuclear devices. Our leaders are not monsters but their sworn duty is to defend Israel and they are doing what they feel they must do. I don't like their decision but, after thinking about it, I'm forced to admit that they are doing what we expect our leaders do. They are putting the interests of their people first."

Nahbi looked at her intently as he considered hundreds of possible scenarios and their most probable outcomes. Finally, he responded to what Gabe had told him.

"I will do as your government has ordered. I do not want to put you in the position of having to use force against me and I certainly do not want to have to use my abilities against you. I am pleased that you will remain here. Using video conferencing, I do not think having me work from Israel will be a serious handicap. So yes, I will go to Israel," Nahbi told her.

"Nahbi, there is something else. I was told not to tell you this until I found out whether you'd agree to go to Israel without being forced. The Knesset has authorized the Prime Minister to grant you full Israeli citizenship in exchange for your service to our country."

That was not a scenario that Nahbi had considered. It would provide him with both citizenship and civil rights. It also meant that after nearly two thousand years he would be going home.

London, MI6 HQ
5:45 AM

"Welcome back and congratulations," David said as Gabe came through the door into the TF3 secure area. "Where's Nahbi?"

"Please, will all of you take a seat in the conference area? I've got a lot to tell you," Gabe said with obvious strain in her voice.

When they were seated and waiting expectantly, Gabe told them the bad news. "Nahbi won't be coming back. My government ordered me to send him to Israel and directed me to use force if

necessary. Fortunately, I didn't have to. Once Nahbi heard the details, he agreed to go."

The first reaction that registered on everyone's face was utter disbelief. That was quickly replaced by dark anger. Tiera spoke first.

"You must be either crazy or incredibly brave to come back to us with that news. Surely you must recognize that this is the worst possible thing that you could have told us. We were all afraid that Raisa might destroy Nahbi. That would have been horrible and we all prayed that it wouldn't happen. Instead we find that he's unharmed but that a country and a person we thought were our friends are not. How could you come back knowing that you'd betrayed us?" Tiera asked hotly.

David held out his hand as a signal to Tiera to be quiet.

"Tell us the whole story," he said to Gabe in a remarkably calm voice.

None of them interrupted as she told them everything. When she was finished, Al Flores stood up and began pacing back and forth.

"Let me get this straight," Al said in a bitter and angry tone of voice. "Israel's Knesset and Prime Minister have abducted Nahbi when we are only days away from the possible detonation of four nuclear devices with a combined explosive potential of up to ten times that of the atomic bomb dropped on Hiroshima. Are you telling us that they are willing to risk millions of innocent lives in order to gain control of Nahbi for Israel?"

Before Gabe could respond, Phil Shaw piled on.

"Nahbi realized almost from the beginning that Israel was not threatened by the devices stolen from Pakistan. But what you're telling us means that once Israel's leaders knew the devices weren't targeted on Tel Aviv, they focused solely on Israel's self-interest and in doing so essentially threw several large cities in Western Europe and possibly the United States under the nuclear bus. I tell you flatly that Israel's name will join that of Adolf Hitler and Nazi Germany in eternal infamy if millions of people die as a result of your government's decision."

David could see that Gabe's emotions were barely under control. She took a deep breath before she responded.

"You have not said anything that I didn't say to my boss or that he hadn't already said to our Prime Minister. I don't expect you to agree with their decision but I think you owe it to me to at least let me tell you something you don't know."

"Israeli intelligence has absolutely reliable information that Iran already has several nuclear devices of sufficient yield to destroy Tel Aviv. The American President said repeatedly that he would never allow Iran to obtain a nuclear weapon. Well, it's too late. He talked tough while he postured and preened in front of the cameras but did nothing constructive to help Israel face this threat."

"You all know that as soon as the new Iranian President was sworn in, he issued a public statement saying that *Israel is a wound on the body of the world of Islam that must be destroyed*. When those words were uttered by the leader of a nation that already has nuclear weapons, it became clear that Israel faces imminent mortal danger. The indecision and inaction of the American President, and his open hostility toward our Prime Minister, make it abundantly clear that Israel can expect no help from the west. Our leaders have done what they felt they must to give Israel a chance to survive. I am not happy with their decision but, as I told Nahbi, they have done what leaders should do. They have put the security of their country first."

"I have returned here this morning in the hope that once you've all had time to think this through you'll understand and will forgive me for following my orders. I promise each of you that I will continue to do my very best to help find the nuclear devices before it is too late."

It was absolutely quiet in the conference area for several long moments. Finally, David spoke as only a wise leader could.

"Gabe, I want to thank you and your team for what you accomplished tonight. When you left here a few hours ago, I wasn't sure I'd ever see you alive again. I fully expected Raisa and Boris to put up a fight. I am amazed that you were able to capture them and rescue Nahbi without bloodshed."

"I know you are just as disappointed as the rest of us that Nahbi won't be rejoining us here but I take your leaders at their word that

he will continue to work with us using video teleconferencing. I think, on balance, that tonight's operation was a remarkable success. Things might have turned out tragically otherwise."

David looked around the table and then said, "All of us need to remember that Israel is a small country of fewer than eight million people surrounded by 300 million Muslims who do not recognize Israel's right to exist. Her leaders can't afford to make mistakes. Ask yourself what you'd have done if you'd just learned that your worst enemy had nuclear weapons and was openly telling the world that your country must be destroyed"

"It's been a long night and we're all tired. Let's get a few hours' sleep."

Tel Aviv, Israel
9:45 AM

The Dassault Falcon landed at Tel Aviv's Ben Gurion Airport after a five-hour, 2,200 mile flight from London. Levi Reznik was waiting on the flight line in an unmarked car to take Nahbi to Mossad headquarters to meet the Director.

After lunch with the Director, Nathan took Nahbi to a nearby apartment complex where the Mossad leased several furnished apartments for short-term use by field intelligence officers when they were in-country. Clothing and food had been put in the apartment in anticipation of Nahbi's arrival.

Nahbi knew that Nathan was exhausted and eager to go to his own apartment for some much-needed sleep. Nathan took a few minutes to explain the apartment's secure computer system and told Nahbi they would be picked up in front of the apartment complex the following morning.

After Nathan left, Nahbi sent a message to David that he was safely in Israel. He spent most of his first night in Israel analyzing potential locations for placement of the nuclear devices.

Croydon; South London
8:30 AM Time

Once he'd made his decision, Dr. Ghilzai used his tablet computer to find out how to apply for political asylum in the United Kingdom. It was sixty miles from Chichester to the Border Agency Offices in Croydon on the south side of London. The offices were closed by the time he got there late Tuesday afternoon so he'd checked into a motor hotel for the night. He ignored the calls from Tariq Zardari and was waiting at the Border Agency Office when they opened Wednesday morning.

He knew that he would have to find an attorney to represent him since he could be convicted for having used a false passport to enter the country. If convicted, it would jeopardize his request for asylum. However, the information he possessed was of such value that he had little doubt that his request for asylum would eventually be granted.

He told the receptionist that he was there to request political asylum. She told him to take a seat and that someone would be with him shortly. A few minutes later, a woman called his name and escorted him to a small interview room. She told him that she would be his case owner and would deal with every aspect of his request for asylum.

The woman was pleasant but thoroughly bureaucratic and painfully slow. After a few minutes, Dr. Ghilzai interrupted her and told her that he had information of vital national security interest that should be communicated to the Director of MI6 immediately. That got her attention and she left the room to speak to her supervisor. Her supervisor called the duty officer at MI6 headquarters and mentioned Dr. Ghilzai's name. The MI6 duty officer checked with his supervisor and then transferred the call to David's room.

"Mr. Logan, this is the supervisor of the Border Agency Offices in Croydon. We have a man here who says his name is Dr. Bashir Ghilzai. He said you would recognize his name."

David listened for several moments and then told the Border Agency officer that an MI6 officer named Phil Shaw would be there within thirty minutes. He called Phil's room as soon as he hung up.

"Phil, this is David. I'm sorry to wake you so soon but I need for you and Al to pick up Dr. Bashir Ghilzai at the Border Agency Asylum office in Croydon as soon as you can get there. This may be the lucky break we've needed. I'll order a car and driver for you and tell Al to meet you at the main entrance in ten minutes. Bring Dr. Ghilzai to the conference room when you get back."

London, MI6 HQ
10:15 AM

David knew that Dr. Ghilzai was a security risk so he did not want the nuclear scientist to even see the area where the TF3 team worked. He told Phil and Al to take him to an interrogation room on the second floor of the MI6 building. Tiera, Pete, and Gavriella joined them but Nahbi was not yet available.

"Good morning Dr. Ghilzai. My name is David Logan. I will conduct this initial interview with you. I understand that you have requested political asylum in the United Kingdom. May I ask why?"

"Before I answer any questions, I want a written guarantee that I will be granted asylum. I am in possession of information that is of vital importance to the security of the United Kingdom and several other countries. I am willing to divulge that information in exchange for political asylum and personal protection."

David gave Dr. Ghilzai a penetrating look. "I'm sure you realize that no such guarantees can be provided until we know more about the basis of your request for asylum and can evaluate the information you have. However, I anticipated your request for some type of assurances and have invited two Parliamentary Under Secretaries of State to hear what you have to say."

"The Honorable Justin Crandall is the Parliamentary Under Secretary of State for International Security Strategy in the Ministry of Defense," David said. "If he is convinced that the information you have is of compelling importance to the security of the United

Kingdom, he can recommend that you be granted asylum on the basis of national security."

"Dr. Elizabeth Simmons is the Parliamentary Under Secretary of State for Borders and Immigration. Based on Mr. Crandall's recommendation, if she is satisfied that your circumstances satisfy the criterion for asylum, she has the authority to waive the normal process to approve your application."

David wanted to keep Dr. Ghilzai off balance. "I must warn you that you are in a very precarious position. You have entered the United Kingdom using a false passport. You could be convicted and imprisoned for up to ten years for that offense alone. Alternatively, you could be immediately deported back to Pakistan."

"Please do not threaten me," Ghilzai said forcefully. "I am here today because I have been threatened by someone I fear far more than any of you. Lieutenant General Parvez Jhalawan is the new Director of Pakistan's Inter-Services Intelligence Agency. He has a reputation for eliminating anyone who displeases him. A few weeks ago, he told me that he would torture me and kill me if I ever told anyone what I am now prepared to tell you in exchange for asylum and protection. General Jhalawan has a global reach. As long as he is alive, I will never be safe from his wrath without some form of deep witness protection by a sovereign nation."

"Since I was brought to MI6 headquarters as soon as my name was known, I assume that you either suspect or know that I was involved in the theft of the nuclear devices from the Wah cantonment and their subsequent movement and placement."

David nodded but said nothing.

"Your assumption is correct. I have been involved at nearly every point. General Jhalawan made it very clear that if I did not do as he asked, he would have me killed."

"I led the team that designed those weapons and know better than anyone the devastation they can cause. I know where they are and what General Jhalawan intends to do with them. I will tell you everything I know in exchange for asylum and personal protection. Do we have an agreement?" Dr. Ghilzai asked looking first at David and then at the two ministers.

David played his role perfectly. “Dr. Ghilzai, I do not wish to offend you but surely you must know that we already knew most of that. From our perspective, you are a member of a terrorist conspiracy intent on murdering thousands of innocent people. Why should we believe you would now cooperate to help avoid the horror that you yourself helped create? What evidence can you provide to convince us that you actually know something of value to us?”

“If you knew where the devices were, we would not be having this discussion,” Ghilzai said somewhat sharply. “I am fully aware that you intercepted the device aboard the Belle Maria. Clearly, if you knew where the other weapons were, you would not need me. But, you do not know where they are, do you? You are running out of time. I think that without my help, you will not find the devices before General Jhalawan detonates them.”

David glanced at the two government ministers before saying, “Dr. Ghilzai, please excuse us for a few minutes.”

Phil Shaw and Al Flores took Dr. Ghilzai to a small room across the hallway to wait.

David looked around the room. “I’d like to hear everyone’s thoughts, please.”

Mr. Crandall spoke first. “It all hinges on whether he really knows where the weapons are. There are two risks I see. He may think he knows but his information may be out of date or he may have been intentionally misled for security reasons. Also, he may only know the approximate locations.”

Dr. Simmons then said, “Based on what MI6 and TF3 have told me about the deteriorating conditions and new leadership in Pakistan, I am satisfied that Dr. Ghilzai’s situation meets our government’s criteria for granting asylum. Unless there is objection, I am prepared to authorize asylum for him immediately.

“I think Mr. Crandall has put his finger on the critical issue here,” Gavriella said. “We do not know how current Dr. Ghilzai’s information is nor do we know how detailed it is. David, my advice is for you to continue to play hardball with him. Try to force him to give us more detail before we grant the assurances he wants and take the pressure off him.”

Tiera nodded and then said, “I agree with Gabe. I think Dr. Ghilzai is terrified of General Jhalawan. You can exploit that fear to extract more information from him. From what we know of Ahmed Malik, I suspect that Dr. Ghilzai may fear him even more than he does General Jhalawan.”

David looked around the room and saw that there was consensus before asking Tiera to have Phil and Al bring him back.

When Dr. Ghilzai was seated, David stood on the opposite side of the conference table and looked directly at him.

“Dr. Ghilzai, I have conferred with my colleagues. We are not convinced that you possess sufficiently detailed information regarding the location of the devices, how they will be detonated, and when. The unanimous view is that we should send you back to Pakistan to face General Jhalawan and Ahmed Malik. Your reputation has not engendered admiration for you. To us, you personify the barbaric, inhuman face of radical Islamic evil. I am going to ask you three specific questions. Your fate will depend on your answers and whether or not we believe you.”

“First, do you know the specific location where each device has been placed?”

Dr. Ghilzai’s face was ashen as he admitted that he did not. “I know what cities they have been taken to. I do not know the specific locations. However, I think I know how to find out.”

“How?”

“There is a young nuclear engineer who has been my protégé for several years. I have reason to believe that he is currently in England and that there may be a way to take him into custody for interrogation. I was supposed to meet him last night but I was afraid that he had been ordered to kill me so I went to the Border Agency office instead.”

“I see. Do you know the technical details of how the devices will be detonated?”

“Yes,” Dr. Ghilzai replied.

“Do you know when they will be detonated?”

"No, only that it will probably be before the beginning of Ramadan. You must move quickly to find and disable the devices before Jhalawan can detonate them. I would also advise you to treat my presence here with utmost secrecy. If General Jhalawan learns I've been questioned by MI6, he will detonate the devices immediately. Although none of the devices have yet been put into final position, they are already in the target cities. From General Jhalawan's perspective, it would be better to detonate them in a sub-optimum location than risk having them found and deactivated."

A few minutes later, Dr. Simmons returned to the conference room after taking a phone call from the Foreign Secretary. She told Dr. Ghilzai that his request for asylum and personal protection had been granted. With that news, Dr. Ghilzai relaxed visibly and immediately began to tell the TF3 team what he knew.

"The targeted cities are Frankfurt, Paris, London and New York. Unfortunately, I do not know the precise locations. To ensure that no one person knew the entire plan, each of us was given only the information we needed to perform our role. Just before we left Islamabad, Ahmed Malik gave Tariq Zardari, the young nuclear engineer who assisted me, four sealed envelopes containing the addresses and detailed floor plans showing where each device was to be placed. Zardari gave one to each of the men assigned to place the devices in Frankfurt and Paris. He gave the other two envelopes to me for the teams that would deliver the devices to London and New York. I did not open them."

David frowned. "The device on the Belle Maria was headed for the United States. Are you saying that two devices were targeted on U.S. cities?"

"No. General Jhalawan's plan originally had only one device targeted on the United States," Dr. Ghilzai replied. "The other four were intended for European cities but when you intercepted the Belle Maria, he had to revise his targeting."

David nodded and then said, "From what you've told us, it appears that the precise locations may only be known to General Jhalawan and Ahmed Malik. Earlier, you told us that your protégé might know the specific locations. However, what you just said

suggests that Tariq Zardari probably doesn't know either. What makes you think he does?"

"I believe Zardari probably opened the envelopes and then resealed them. It's the kind of thing he would do."

"The weapons will be moved to their final destinations by trusted members of the Muslim Brotherhood within forty-eight hours after they receive the text message *Light and Knowledge* on their cell phones. When the devices are in place, each man will reply to the first message by texting the word *Jasmine* back to the same address."

"Each of the devices has a GSM quad-band international cell phone installed that will be used to remotely activate a four-hour timer attached to the detonator. However, if a slightly different text string is transmitted, the timer will be bypassed to detonate the devices immediately."

"Do you know the phone numbers of the GSM cell phones?" Tiera asked.

"No, I don't. One of the things Tariq did as part of our activation sequence was to test the GSM phones and then install new SIM cards. I do know that the SIM cards were pre-paid cards sold by Telenor Pakistan. Such SIM cards are essentially untraceable. They are sold by the tens of thousands in airports, drug stores, and cell phone stores all over the world. Trying to trace Telenor cards would be especially difficult since Telenor is one of the largest mobile operators in the world with over 140 million subscribers."

"Do you know if General Jhalawan and Ahmed Malik's mobile phones are also subscribed to Telenor Pakistan's system?" Tiera asked.

"That seems likely, although I do not know for sure. The mobile phones the government provided for my staff were on the Telenor network. In any event, Ahmed Malik is a very technologically-advanced person and he can command any technical resources he might need. I strongly suspect that he will use a pre-paid GSM SIM card in an unlocked phone that has been acquired specifically for this project. He certainly would not use his own personal mobile

phone or place the activation calls from a traceable government phone."

"General Jhalawan has enormous ambition." Ghilzai told them. "He would not want to be blamed for the carnage that will occur if his plan succeeds. I feel sure that he envisions himself filling a power vacuum that he thinks will arise following the detonation of the devices. His ego is extraordinary. I believe his goal is to become the head of a new Islamic world order once he has dealt a crippling blow to the western democracies."

David asked, "What can you tell us about the devices themselves?"

"They are two-stage plutonium-based linear-implosion neutron bombs with design yields of 40 kilotons. They are modernized versions of the American W79 artillery shells first tested in 1962. In the decades since the American neutron device was developed, nuclear technology has advanced significantly. However, it was my pioneering research at Wah that found a way to reshape the nuclear material to create a more efficient super-critical mass. That breakthrough allowed weapons as compact as these to achieve previously unattainable yield efficiencies. The massive release of high-energy neutron particles will kill virtually every living thing within a five-mile radius of their point of detonation. Beyond that, out to a distance of eight to ten miles from the blast center, there will be delayed health issues that will eventually kill many more people. Although the explosive blast and shock wave of a neutron bomb is lower than that of a typical fission device, most buildings in a three-mile radius will be completely destroyed."

"The devices for Frankfurt, Paris, and London have been concealed in polished, stainless steel carbon dioxide tanks. The apparent purpose was to allow them to be placed inconspicuously in a restaurant or bar that uses CO2 for soft drinks and draft beer taps. To maximize the destructive result, the devices should be detonated 300 to 1,500 meters above ground. That means they will almost certainly be placed near the top of tall buildings. Each device weighs approximately 200 pounds."

"The device for New York City is concealed in a modified scuba tank identical to the one you found on the Belle Maria. It was flown

to the United States from Southampton by Jamal el-Masri, a member of the Armed Islamic Group, the most militant of the Muslim Brotherhood factions in the United Kingdom. He is the son of one of the wealthiest Arabs in the U.K. and the nephew of the leader of AIG. Franco Rinaldi, Hakeem Ghanem's nephew, is with him. I do not know which airport in the New York City area was their destination but the aircraft is a Bombardier Global 8000."

"You told us that there might be a way to capture Tariq Zardari so we could question him. What did you have in mind?" David asked.

"By now, he has almost certainly reported to Ahmed Malik that I did not join him Tuesday night as I was supposed to. Malik may already suspect that I've defected and requested asylum. But, if you act quickly, I think you might still lure Zardari into a trap."

David listened as Dr. Ghilzai outlined what he had in mind.

"I will call him and tell him that I was involved in a serious automobile accident on my way to Ashford and that I was unconscious and bleeding badly when the emergency medical team arrived at the site. I'll tell him that I have been in the intensive care unit all night and have just been allowed to place a phone call."

"Tariq Zardari is a very smart young man so you will need to cover all bases. Ideally, there would have been a serious traffic accident along my logical route to Ashford that he can verify with a call to local police. Then, you would need to coordinate with a local hospital to create a cover story that included me being admitted. I assure you that Tariq will check. It would be helpful if you could route the call through the hospital's switchboard so he would see the hospital's caller ID when he answered my call. Although I could use my cell phone, routing the call through the hospital would add credence to what I tell him. You would also need to coordinate a cover story with the local police and the EMT ambulance company. Again, I cannot over-emphasize that Tariq will check my story every way he can think of. Malik will do his own independent checking. If you are to succeed in luring Tariq into the trap, you must make sure they can confirm the truth of what I tell him."

"I will tell him that the doctors have told me that I cannot leave the hospital for several days but that friends and family members can visit me once I'm moved to a private room this afternoon. If Tariq has been told to kill me, as I suspect, he will come to the hospital to make sure I never leave it alive. There is no way to know what method he will try to use but as I've told you, he is a very smart young man. You must not underestimate him."

David was silent for a few moments as he considered what the scientist had proposed.

"I don't think a hospital would allow us to set a trap inside the hospital that might endanger other people. Instead, I think it would be better if you tell Zardari that you will be released from the hospital at 3:00 PM and ask him to pick you up. We'll have several unmarked vehicles ready to surround and block his car once you identify him to us. He might still try to shoot you so we'll have you wear a bullet-proof vest under your clothing. With a little luck, we should be able to take him without gunplay."

"The car Zardari will be driving is a dark-blue four-door Volkswagen Jetta sedan," Dr. Ghilzai told David.

David looked at the other members of TF3 with a raised eyebrow. "What do you think? Any suggestions?"

"I think it just might work," Al Flores said at once. The rest of the team nodded their concurrence.

"OK, that's the plan. Phil, I'd like for you to work with the local police and medical facilities to get this set up just as quickly as possible. We don't have much time. If Tariq thinks Dr. Ghilzai has defected, he'll probably try to get out of the country as quickly as he can. Al and Gabe can work with you."

"Tiera, please have a room assigned to Dr. Ghilzai on the B1 level near our rooms and arrange for an armed officer to be with him at all times. Also, ask Gordon McFarland if he can arrange cell tower triangulation on the phone call in case Zardari doesn't take the bait."

"I'll ask the NSA, GCHQ, and the Mossad to add the key words *Light and Knowledge* and *Jasmine* to their message screening and to route any hits to our terminals immediately," David said. "OK

everyone, let's get moving. I'd like for Dr. Ghilzai to place the call within the next two hours."

Eastbourne, U.K.
3:00 PM

Phil Shaw knew he was walking into extreme danger as he pushed Dr. Ghilzai's wheel chair through the front door of the hospital a few minutes after three o'clock. He couldn't help wondering if he would ever see his little girl again. He was disguised as a male nurse dressed in pale blue hospital scrubs. Dr. Ghilzai's head was bandaged and he had his left arm in a sling. Beneath their clothing, both men were wearing Kevlar bullet-proof vests. Phil had a Sig Sauer P226 semi-automatic pistol inside his waistband in front where he could reach it quickly. He had a Sig Sauer P938 subcompact semi-auto in an ankle holster on his right leg. Both weapons were loaded with 147 grain 9mm jacketed hollow points.

Al Flores and Gavriella Adler were in two unmarked cars parked nearby in positions that would allow them to quickly block Zardari's escape. Two London Police Force special operations officers were in taxicabs posing as drivers waiting for a customer. Four other officers were either sitting or standing nearby. All of them were wearing bullet-proof vests under their clothing and each of them was armed but had been ordered not to kill Zardari unless there was no choice.

At five minutes past three, a blue Volkswagen pulled into the driveway and stopped in front of the main entrance a few feet from where the wheel chair was sitting. Before anyone could react, Zardari shot Dr. Ghilzai twice. The first bullet sliced through the scientist's neck and severed the carotid artery. The second bullet punched a neat hole in the middle of the Pakistani scientist's forehead. Ghilzai was killed instantly.

Zardari floored the accelerator pedal and the blue sedan leaped forward only to crash into the side of the car Al Flores used to block his escape. Air bags deployed in both cars. Before the air bag in the Volkswagon deflated, Phil Shaw was already beside the car pointing his pistol at the side of the young engineer's head. Less than 60 seconds after Zardari had stopped his car at the entrance, he was in MI6 custody. One of the special operations officers advised him of

his Right to Silence, the British equivalent of the American Miranda Rights.

London, MI6 HQ
5:20 PM

Tariq Zardari was taken to an interrogation room on the second floor of the MI6 building and handcuffed to a strong metal chair. David conducted the interrogation with Pete, Phil, and Gabe in the room. Tiera, Al, and Gordon McFarland observed through the one-way glass. David knew that time was running out.

"Mr. Zardari," David began, "You are fortunate that you have committed your crimes in the United Kingdom where capital punishment is still prohibited. Even so, you are likely to spend the rest of your life in a maximum-security prison. British prisons are not nearly as hospitable as those in the United States. A life sentence with no possibility of parole means that the rest of your life will be a personal hell for you as an educated young man. You will live twenty hours each day in a 10 foot by 12-foot cell that you share with another inmate. Because you are young and handsome, it is likely that you will be raped repeatedly and have things done to you by other inmates that you cannot imagine. You will live in continuous fear of other, more powerful inmates."

Tariq Zardari blinked but said nothing.

"The British are not as reluctant to use force as many Europeans but, even so, they do not allow the use of torture. However, I should warn you that I am not a citizen of the United Kingdom. The nature of your crimes is so heinous that British officials will look away if I decide to use torture to extract the information I want from you. I consider myself a civilized man. Yet, to save millions of innocent lives, I will not hesitate to subject you to both physical and mental pain of the most horrendous sort. Do you understand?"

Zardari remained silent though his body language indicated that David's threats were affecting him.

"David is trying to handle Zardari the way he thinks Nahbi would, isn't he?" Tiera asked.

"Yes, and I'd say he's off to a ripping good start," Gordon McFarland replied. "Did you see the look on Zardari's face when David mentioned that he would probably be raped? I'd say that David has already succeeded in terrifying him though the young man is doing a creditable job of hiding his fear."

"This can't be easy for David," Tiera said. "I know that he is adamantly opposed to torture. Although he is a combat veteran, he is essentially a peaceful man. I've heard him say that we must not use the same barbaric methods our enemies do. I don't think his deep religious faith would let him actually torture anyone. For him to even threaten torture, he must think there is no other way to get this man to talk."

"I'm sure you're right on all counts," Gordon told her. "Yet, there is a real danger that Zardari will not yield to verbal threats alone. Remember that even after Nahbi's brilliant interrogation of Abu Shakra, he finally had to use physical torture to get the man to talk. If David makes the threat, he must be willing to follow through. Otherwise, Zardari will recognize that David has been bluffing. If it comes to that, I doubt that we'll ever get Zardari to tell us what he knows. Keep your fingers crossed."

"I want to know where the devices will be placed," David told Zardari.

Zardari remained silent.

"I think you will eventually tell me what I want to know anyway so there is really little point in forcing me to torture you," David said. "You can never go home. Even if we sent you back on the next flight, General Jhalawan or Ahmed Malik would first torture you to extract information and then kill you. If you do not tell me what I want to know, then I will torture you."

"Horrible as it can be, torture is a delicate matter because it is very easy to go too far. Each person's tolerance for pain differs. Some people have died of shock and heart failure after only one of their fingers was cut off while others have stubbornly resisted even as they lost all of their fingers and toes and then their hands and feet. Some have given in only after being castrated. Still others have finally yielded after having one of their eyes brutally gouged out.

Some are admirably brave but, in the end, no one can resist escalating torture indefinitely. The Americans learned that in Vietnam. Some of their finest officers eventually yielded to torture even though they had been extensively trained to resist it."

"I'll ask you again. Where will the devices be placed?"

Still, Zardari said nothing.

"OK, my friend, you have brought down hell fire and brimstone on yourself," David told him softly. "Phil, bring my tools."

Phil brought David a black leather bag and sat it on the table in front of Zardari.

"Let me explain what each of these tools is used for," David said as he took the first item from the bag. "These beautiful, chrome-plated cutters are used to snip off fingers and toes, one joint at a time. This garrote with a thin stainless steel wire can be used to shorten your penis or to remove your testicles in one swift and intensely painful motion. This is a dentist's drill. I can use it to drill into the nerves of your teeth without anesthetic. As you can see, I have some very interesting tools at my disposal."

For the next several minutes, David described what each tool in the bag did as he arranged them neatly on a towel where Zardari could see them. Those watching saw the terror mount in Tariq Zardari's eyes but still he remained silent.

"Mr. Zardari, I have no sympathy for the radical Islam that you and your associates advocate and practice. If I have to mutilate you to save innocent lives, then I will do it."

"Phil, cut his clothes off," David directed.

When Zardari was completely nude, David sat down in a chair a few feet in front of him.

"Where are the devices going to be placed?"

Zardari shook his head slowly. David bowed his head for several moments and then picked up the chrome-plated cutters. He looked directly at Zardari as he slowly opened and closed the cutters. "I had hoped that I would not have to do this to you," David told Zardari. "It is so unnecessary."

Tiera had tears in her eyes as she turned to Gordon McFarland. "When David bowed his head, I know he was praying that he would not have to do this. But, I think he has decided that he has no choice. I wish there was some other way. I can't bear to think of the pain this is causing him."

Then, as if in answer to David's silent prayers, Zardari finally spoke.

"I do not know," he said in a strained whisper. "Only General Jhalawan and Ahmed Malik know. I had a sealed envelope for each of the weapons that gave the address and a detailed floor plan showing precisely where the weapons were to be placed. Dr. Ghilzai and I were not given that information as part of the security compartmentalization. Even though I participated in briefing the men who will place the weapons, I do not know the contents of the envelopes that Dr. Ghilzai and I gave to them."

"I don't believe you," David said. "Dr. Ghilzai told me that he felt sure that you'd opened the envelopes and then resealed them. He said that was precisely the kind of thing you would do."

"Dr. Ghilzai was wrong. I did not open the envelopes. I admit that I considered it but I was too afraid so I didn't. I cannot answer your question," Zardari insisted.

David leaned forward in his chair as he looked directly into Tariq Zardari's eyes. "Mr. Zardari, you will eventually tell me the truth. Why subject yourself to unbearable pain and permanent disfigurement unnecessarily?"

"You do not understand these men," Zardari whispered. "There is no decency or mercy in either of them. I would never have killed Fredo Rinaldi or Dr. Ghilzai except that Ahmed Malik threatened my family. He told me that if I did not kill them, my family would be sold to a man in Thailand who traffics in women and children as sex slaves and that I would never see them again."

Tears ran down Tariq Zardari's cheeks. "Please understand, my wife was only sixteen when we married and still a virgin. She is a sweet and gentle person. She is so shy that she will not even make love to me with the lights on. I love her so much that the thought of her being forced to have sex with many strange men almost drove

me crazy. I decided I would do whatever I had to so she would never experience the horrors Malik described. My little girls are only nine and eleven years old. Malik told me they would bring a very high price as sex slaves because Thai men prefer young girls. I have done what Malik ordered me to do to protect my family. My life is worth nothing to me compared to the love I have for my wife and my two little girls. I would gladly burn forever in hell's fires to save my family. If Malik thinks, even for a moment, that I have told you anything, he will carry out his threat."

David leaned back in his chair and looked around the room at the three intelligence officers. He could tell by the looks on their faces that they all knew that Zardari had not faked what he'd just said. It was clear that the man was terrified. Instead of the monster they'd thought they were dealing with, they all realized that the young engineer was a pawn in something so evil that he had been powerless to resist it.

David sat quietly thinking for several moments and then faced the one-way glass window. "Tiera, have some clothes brought for Mr. Zardari."

"Phil, please remove his restraints but keep him under close guard.

"Mr. Zardari, you have persuaded me that you do not know the buildings and precise locations where the weapons will be placed," David told him. "I need to confer with my colleagues. We may be able to help each other," David told the emotionally-drained young engineer. "I'll be back in a few minutes. Pete, would you and Gabe come with me please?"

The three of them joined the rest of the team in the adjacent observation room for a quick discussion.

David spoke first. "I believe he's telling the truth. I don't think he knows the contents of the envelopes and I think he has killed at least two people in what will probably prove to have been a futile attempt to save his family. Do you all agree?"

Tiera nodded and said, "Until he told us what Malik had threatened to do to his family, I thought he was some kind of monster who was simply refusing to answer your questions. I

watched him closely as he told you about his love for his family and his fears about what Malik would do to them. I don't think he could have faked that."

Pete and Al both nodded. Gabe said, "I agree with Tiera. I don't think he was faking."

"What do you think, Gordon?" David asked.

"I agree that he wasn't faking his emotional narrative. I think there is no doubt that he believes Malik will carry out his threat if he does not do as he's been ordered. I'm not entirely convinced that he doesn't know more than he's told us, though. He may not know the precise locations but my instincts are that he knows things that might help us find the weapons."

"I agree," David said. "I think we might persuade him to cooperate by offering him a miracle."

"What do you have in mind?" Gabe asked.

"I'm not even sure we could make all of this happen but what if we could persuade the U.K. government to grant him a conditional pardon for killing Dr. Ghilzai? What if we could obtain authorization to have a black ops team kidnap his family and get them out of Pakistan safely? What if he was offered witness protection for himself and his family in exchange for cooperating fully to help us find the weapons?"

Gordon McFarland responded to David's hypothetical scenarios. "A conditional pardon and witness protection for Zardari might be possible. I'm not sure about a black ops extraction though. I'm pretty sure the U.K. government would not do it. To my knowledge, the Israeli's don't have either presence or access to carry out such a mission inside Pakistan. Only the CIA or the U.S. Navy SEAL Teams are probably capable of successfully executing such a mission. I can't help but wonder if the American President could be persuaded to authorize it."

"Gordon's right that Israel does not have boots on the ground or sufficient means of access inside Pakistan to carry out an extraction mission," Gabe told them. "Even if we did, I'm not sure our Prime Minister would authorize it."

"OK," David said. "Let's see if I can get him to cooperate on the hope that we might be able to move his family to safety and make it possible for them to eventually be reunited."

A few minutes later, David sat down across a small conference table facing Zardari.

"We've decided that you are probably telling us the truth," David began. "We know a great deal about Ahmed Malik so your description of the threats he made ring very true to our ears." David paused for a moment and then said, "I have a proposal to make to you that may be mutually beneficial."

"I want you to cooperate with us fully in every way possible," David told Zardari. "We understand that you do not know the precise locations where the weapons will be placed but we all agree that you probably know some things we don't. Our hope is that by working together, we may be able to fill in enough pieces of the puzzle to deduce the locations in time to prevent the detonation of the devices. I do not have the authority to provide any guarantees to you but I have conceived a strategy that might work."

"The first element of the strategy will be to create a bogus news story about the deaths of two men outside a hospital in Eastbourne. Subject to some refinement, the story will be that a patient that had just been released was killed in an execution-style drive-by shooting this afternoon. The assassin was then killed when his vehicle crashed into another car while fleeing the scene. Investigators have determined that both men entered the United Kingdom using counterfeit passports. Police are still trying to find the true identity of the men."

"We'll have a makeup artist work on your face so we can take a photograph that appears to be a morgue photo of an unidentified dead man. We'll get a similar photo of Dr. Ghilzai with a bullet hole in his forehead."

"I'm sure that one or two of the scandal rags will be more than happy to run our story about two mysterious dead men along with gruesome photos of them and the wrecked car with blood all over the windshield. It's just the kind of sensational news item many of the grocery store checkout aisles have on prominent display. The

article will include a police request for any information about the identity of the two men."

"With a bit of luck, the story will find its way to General Jhalawan and Ahmed Malik. They should conclude that the automobile accident simply saved them the trouble of eliminating you."

"The threats to your wife and children reminded us of the monstrous evil we face from radical Islam. If you help us, we will try to help you," David told Zardari.

"In exchange for your unqualified help and cooperation, I will propose that you be granted a limited U.K. pardon for the murder of Dr. Ghilzai under extenuating circumstances related to national security. I will also propose that a special operations team abduct your family and get them safely out of Pakistan. If the operation succeeds, your family would be brought to the United Kingdom. You and your family would then be inducted into a deep-cover witness protection plan."

"I give you my solemn word that I will do my very best to gain approval for these proposals. However, you must understand that I cannot guarantee that I will succeed. Still, it seems to me that what I have proposed may be the only hope you have that your family will ever be together again," David said.

The amazed look on Tariq Zardari's face spoke volumes. "Only a truly good man would show such compassion toward my wife and little girls. And only a wise man would see a possible way to save them. I will do whatever I can to help. I pray that your proposals will be approved and that your plan will succeed. But, even if it does not, the fact that you were willing to try has created a debt that I can never repay."

Forty minutes later, Pete Nocona and Al Flores were with David when he dialed into a secure conference call with the Director of the National Intelligence Service in Washington, DC. The Directors of the CIA and NSA were also on the call. David summarized the results of the interrogation of Tariq Zardari and then made a formal request to the DNI for a CIA or SEAL Team to extract Zardari's family from Pakistan. Although the Director of National Intelligence position required Senate confirmation, the DNI was appointed by

the President and reported directly to him on all matters relating to national security. As a political appointee, he would do nothing contrary to the President's policies.

After listening to David's presentation, the DNI muted his phone and discussed the request with the CIA and NSA Directors. After less than two minutes, the DNI came back on the line to tell David that his request could not be approved. The only explanation given was that the benefit to the United States was very modest when weighed against the risk of an adverse reaction from the governments of Pakistan and other Muslim nations.

David thanked the DNI for his time and broke the connection. Al Flores cursed bitterly under his breath. David knew that Al was a devout Catholic and had never heard him use profanity or vulgar language before.

"Don't those guys get it?" Al exploded. "Where's the unqualified support we were promised?"

"I suspect that the Directors of the CIA and NSA both advised against an extraction that might be traced to the United States and there's some merit in that cautious view," David said. "I'm disappointed, of course, but I'm not really surprised. We've had more support from the Brits than we have from our own government. For now, let's not mention that my request was disapproved."

Janawai, Pakistan
10:30 PM

General Jhalawan was sitting at his desk sipping a cup of strong coffee and reading some papers when his housekeeper showed Ahmed Malik into his study. He was surprised to see Malik, especially at such a late hour.

"You must have news."

"Yes, and I wanted to tell you in person," Malik said. "Tariq Zardari carried out my orders. He shot and killed Dr. Ghilzai as he was leaving the hospital. The young fool then killed himself by crashing into another car as he was trying to escape. Several British tabloids have published sensational photographs of both men's

bodies and the wrecked car. I have confirmed that the wreck Ghilzai was involved in and the incidents at the hospital actually occurred. It appears that those loose ends have now been eliminated."

"Very convenient," General Jhalawan mused. "Are you quite sure that this was not an MI6 hoax?"

"Yes. I have checked all the pertinent facts," Malik answered. "Both men are dead. The police are still trying to determine their true identity. The Brits have reviewed the security camera files at the Immigration booth at the Eurotunnel. They know that Ghilzai and Zardari entered the country using fake Italian passports. The police have traced Zardari's car to the repair garage in Aarbergen but the owner of the garage died two nights ago of carbon monoxide poisoning. It seems that he was working late and did not provide for adequate ventilation while he was running an engine in the shop."

General Jhalawan smiled. "Well, Ahmed, once again you seem to have taken care of the details."

"Sir, there is something else I'd like to discuss with you," Malik said. "You asked me to have Hakeem Ghanem and his General Manager eliminated. At the time, you may recall that I wondered aloud if that was wise. I feel that I must ask you again if you are certain that is what you want me to do."

"You must have some good reason for questioning my decision twice now. What is it?" Jhalawan asked sharply.

"Sir, you know better than I that Al Qaeda grew out of the Muslim Brotherhood. We have been very successful in using trusted members of both groups to execute your plans. However, with the situation in Egypt growing more precarious by the day, I think Ghanem and Al-Jabiri may be more valuable to us alive than dead. I believe both men are trustworthy. With the death of Ambassador Al-Zeid, we do not have another fully-vetted and trusted high-level contact within the Egyptian Muslim Brotherhood."

Jhalawan stared at Malik for a long moment before replying. "Those two men are the strongest remaining links to me through you. When we eliminate the men who place the devices, we will have swept the trail clean. I can see that you have given this a great deal of thought and I know that you would not normally question my

orders at all let alone twice. For that reason, I will consider what you have said and let you know my final decision. But Ahmed I must warn you that if I decide to affirm what I have previously ordered you to do, I will not tolerate any further questioning of my orders. Is that clear?"

"Yes sir. I fully understand."

Jhalawan saw that Malik had something else on his mind. "What else?" he asked.

"You also told me to capture or destroy the android. Unfortunately, the Russian SVR found a way to lure him out of the MI6 building before I did. Two of their most experienced field agents kidnapped the parents of the young Maltese woman and then did a hostage exchange for the android. The android apparently willingly gave himself in exchange for the lives of Mr. and Mrs. Aquilina."

"So, the android is now in Russia?" Jhalawan asked irritably.

"No sir. The Israelis have him," Malik admitted.

"How in the name of Allah did that happen?" Jhalawan exploded.

"An Israeli Kidon team used a bomb hoax to get the Russians off their plane to gain custody of the android. Apparently, the Israelis double-crossed their British and American colleagues and used the Russian executive aircraft to fly the android to Tel Aviv. I do not know the android's current location but an educated guess is that he is inside the Mossad headquarters in Herzliya."

"Why would the Israelis bite the two hands that feed them?" General Jhalawan asked.

"They are concerned that the Iranians either already have or soon will have nuclear weapons. The new Iranian President has affirmed Iran's intent to destroy Israel. I think the Israelis hope the android can help them find a way to disrupt or destroy Iran's nuclear program. The Israelis justifiably have no confidence in the American President. Certainly, he does not appear to be as committed to Israel's defense as previous American administrations. For the Israelis, old friendships have a lower priority than their survival."

"Yes, yes. That is all old news," Jhalawan said irritably. "What I'm wondering is whether the Israelis have hard intelligence that the

Iranians already have one or more nuclear devices. If they do, that adds a new and potentially troublesome complication to our plans."

"Yes sir. I understand. Do you still want me to devote some resources to either destroy the android or find a way to get him out of Israel?"

"No. His removal from the team working at MI6 probably eliminates any chance they have of finding the devices before we detonate them. In that sense, I'd say the Israelis may have done us a favor. For now, let's just let that dog lie."

London, MI6 HQ
6:00 PM

"Sir Lionel, I need some advice," David said as he entered the old spymaster's office.

"About what?"

"I know that Gordon told you that the Director of the National Intelligence Service has disapproved my request for either a CIA team or a SEAL Team to extract Tariq Zardari's family from Pakistan. I was hoping that you might see something I've missed. Is there any way we could possibly get them out of Pakistan before Ahmed Malik carries out his threat against them?"

"Do you still feel they are at risk now that you've faked Tariq's death?" Sir Lionel asked.

"Yes sir, I do. Both Jhalawan and Malik probably consider Tariq's family a loose end that needs to be tied up."

Sir Lionel leaned back in his leather chair and put his finger tips together with his index fingers tapping lightly on his chin as he considered what David had asked. He didn't like the thought of granting a pardon to a murderer but realized that the deal David had struck with Zardari was probably necessary under the circumstances. Looking at David, he reflected that the young man was a rarity. He was an absolutely ethical natural leader. Yet, he was also a courageous, battle-tested warrior who had received the Secretary of the Army Award for Valor. He deserved better support than the American President and his political appointees were providing.

"Yes. There may be a way. Kidnapping has been part of Pakistan's history for centuries. Many wealthy British colonials were kidnapped for ransom in the 19th century. Since the 1980s, slum gangs have made a lot of money preying on business families in Karachi and Islamabad. More recently, criminal gangs operating along Pakistan's border with Afghanistan have been kidnapping the children of high-profile, wealthy families and holding them for ransom."

"Many of the hostages have been taken to the Waziristan region along the Afghan border. Unfortunately, that is a Taliban stronghold and the frequent target of CIA drone attacks. The hostages are often subjected to great hardships as they are forced to walk many miles through some of the most rugged and inhospitable terrain on Earth."

"I have broad discretion in providing resources to your task force. I will authorize funding for one of the tribal warlords to kidnap Zardari's family and to take them through a mountain pass into Afghanistan. Once across the border, they will be delivered to an undercover MI6 agent who will see them safely aboard a military aircraft bound for England. It will be a difficult and possibly terrifying experience but it's the best way I can see to get them out of Pakistan. Your ruse to persuade Malik and Jhalawan that Zardari was dead should keep them from suspecting MI6 involvement. It will appear to be just another instance of the family of an educated professional being kidnapped for ransom."

Thursday, June 19

Janawai, Pakistan
7:30 AM

Malik's cell phone vibrated softly in his pocket. As he flipped it open, he saw that it was General Jhalawan. "Good morning sir."

"Ahmed, I've decided that there is no way to keep Hakeem Ghanem from finding out that I ordered the deaths of his nephews. It is simply too obvious. Once he realizes that the order came from

me, his continued loyalty would always be in doubt. Al-Jabiri is loyal to Ghanem so both men must awake in paradise and the sooner the better."

"Yes sir. I will take care of it."

"There's something else I've been thinking about all night. We are very close to achieving our objectives. I don't want to take any unnecessary chances that the devices will be found and disarmed. Osama bin Laden failed to strike the mortal blow and it ultimately cost him his life despite our government's best efforts to covertly shield and protect him. I do not want to make the same mistake he made."

"What do you have in mind, sir?"

"I feel sure that the task force is working around the clock now trying to find the other four devices. The Russians may have helped us a bit by removing the android. However, I think it likely that he is still supporting the task force. The Israelis need to show that they remain loyal to their British and American friends so it seems logical to me that they would allow the android to help in any way he can."

"I agree."

"You previously referred to the MI6 building as an impregnable fortress. Early this morning, it occurred to me that there is a way to disrupt the work of the task force in a devastating way from outside of that fortress. To use the western vernacular, we can pull the rug out from under them at the most critical time. Here's what I want you to do."

Malik listened carefully and then said, "Yes sir. I will make the arrangements immediately."

Tel Aviv, Israel
8:30 AM

Nathan and Nahbi were waiting at the curb when a black Toyota Land Cruiser pulled up in front of the apartment complex. Levi Reznik was driving and the Mossad Director was in the front passenger seat. Nathan and Nahbi got in back.

"Shalom. We have something special for you this morning," the Director said over his shoulder. "We're going to take a little boat ride."

After a short two-mile drive, Levi parked the Land Cruiser in a reserved parking space at the north end of the Marina Hertslya. They walked a hundred meters to the end of the northernmost of the Marina's piers where a Morena-class rigid-hulled inflatable boat was tied up. Members of the Israeli Defense Force's elite naval commando unit known as Shayetet 13 saluted the Director as he approached. Levi, Nahbi, and Nathan followed him aboard. A few minutes later, the RHIB was outside the breakwater heading north at twenty knots through moderate seas. Salt spray exploded at the bow each time the boat slammed into a wave. It was a beautiful day to be out on the water.

Ninety minutes after they left the marina, the boat turned toward the shore. Nahbi knew exactly where they were even though it had been almost two thousand years since he'd last seen this coastline.

The helmsman slowed the boat and steered it into a small mooring area beside the Citadel Café in the Caesarea National Park. The Director was the first ashore and he motioned for Nahbi to join him.

Over the next two hours, Nahbi walked through the ruins of what had once been a thriving seaport. The Director timed their walk to bring them back to the Citadel Café at noon. As they approached the café, Nahbi saw several armed security personnel posted strategically around the building. He soon learned why.

"Nahbi, it is my great honor to introduce you to the Prime Minister of Israel," the Director said.

The Prime Minister smiled and shook hands with Nahbi. "Welcome to Israel. Or should I say, welcome home? I understand that you sailed from this port a very long time ago so I thought perhaps this venue would be appropriately symbolic."

If the Prime Minister was skeptical of Nahbi's story, he gave no sign of it.

The entire café had been reserved. Their table overlooked the old harbor. Nahbi was surprised at how relaxed and informal the Prime

Minister was. He was a big man with strong features. He was dressed casually in slacks and an open-collared shirt. Nahbi soon learned that he possessed a keen intellect and a razor-sharp wit. The leisurely lunch was both memorable and enjoyable.

A few minutes before 2:00 PM, the Prime Minister stood up and asked Nahbi to join him on the terrace overlooking the harbor.

Standing beside Nahbi, the Prime Minister told him, “One of Israel’s leaders once said that the state of Israel is the national state of the Jewish People and is a democratic state in which all its citizens – Jewish and non-Jewish – enjoy fully equal rights.”

“I apologize for our decision to bring you to Israel either with or without your consent. It was a rude thing to do but to our minds absolutely necessary. We are fighting for our survival. We need your help to ensure that Iran can never use its nuclear weapons capability against us. In exchange for your commitment to Israel, we offer you full citizenship and rights that are identical to those of other Israeli citizens. You will be able to own property, marry or have a domestic partner if you wish, establish and run a business, enter into contracts, and pursue your own happiness as you see fit. Are you willing to join us?”

“Yes.”

“Very well then. Israel does not use a sworn oath of allegiance like the United States does. But, we do require you to make this solemn pledge.”

“Do you pledge allegiance to Israel as a Jewish and democratic state and promise to honor the laws of the state?”

“Yes, I do.”

“Then, by my authority as the Prime Minister of the State of Israel, I declare that you are a citizen of Israel from this day forward. Welcome home.”

The Prime Minister motioned to his aide who brought him a leather folder.

“Inside this folder, you will find an Israeli passport and certain other citizenship documents. You will also find a bank book for an account that has been established for you at the First International Bank Group. The account has a current balance of one million

Israeli New Shekels which is approximately equal to 275,000 dollars or about 200,000 Euros. You will receive a salary and retirement benefits for your work at the Mossad so that you can live independently just as other employees do."

"Thank you Mr. Prime Minister. This is far more than I dared hope for."

The Prime Minister shook Nahbi's hand again and looked directly into his eyes for several moments before turning aside to say, "Well, Mr. Director, I think you may have finally hired someone smarter than you. I trust that your vanity can stand it," the Prime Minister said with a broad smile.

London, MI6 HQ
1:00 PM

David waited until 9:00 AM Washington time to place the call. The Executive Assistant to the Director of the National Intelligence Service put him on hold while she checked to see if the Director was available. After being kept on hold for several minutes, David's call was put through.

"Good morning sir. Thank you for taking my call. I need your help."

"In what way?"

"I am convinced that we are only a few days away from the detonation of the four remaining nuclear devices. Before he was killed, Dr. Ghilzai told us that he felt certain that General Jhalawan would detonate the devices before the beginning of Ramadan. That's nine days from today. I'm afraid we may not find them in time. There's just too much we don't know. I think our best chance of stopping General Jhalawan is to abduct him and Ahmed Malik. For that reason, I am asking you to intercede for us with the President to obtain authorization for a top priority extraction."

"Mr. Logan, I understand your concerns but I seriously doubt that the President will authorize kidnapping a high-ranking member of the Pakistan government and the head of their Intelligence Service."

"Yes sir, I expected that would be your answer. But, I must ask that you try. We are facing the possible death of several million people unless we can find and disarm those weapons. We've already had conversations with the Brits, the French, and the Germans about possible evacuation but there's a huge problem with that concept."

"What problem? I would think that evacuation was such an obvious response that I find it hard to believe that they would oppose it."

"Actually sir they don't. It's our Task Force that recommends against evacuation."

"Why?"

"We're sure that General Jhalawan is closely monitoring the situation in each of the target cities. If he finds out that mass evacuation orders have been given, he'll detonate the weapons where they are without waiting until they've been placed in the optimum locations. Millions of lives are at stake here regardless. If they are not evacuated, and we can't find the bombs, many will die. But, on the other hand, if we order evacuation, Jhalawan will detonate the devices and the people will die anyway. It's a no-win situation. That's why I most urgently ask you to find some way to help us before it's too late."

"Mr. Logan, the President is being advised by the Secretary of State, the Secretary of Defense, and the Chairman of the Joint Chiefs on this issue. All of them are telling him that they don't think Jhalawan will actually detonate the devices. They have told the President that Jhalawan will use the threat of detonation as leverage in a high-stakes poker game. They believe that like Osama bin Laden, Jhalawan wants the United States to withdraw all of its forces from the region. Both cabinet secretaries are telling the President that Jhalawan will make his demands at the last minute and that we'll then have an opportunity to negotiate with him. The President is convinced that the devices will not be detonated. So, he's not inclined to approve anything that might be construed as a hostile act on the part of the United States."

"But, what if he's wrong?"

"It's his call. I'll present your request but I can almost guarantee that the President will not approve it. I'll call you back as soon as I've spoken to him."

2:00 PM

Right on schedule, Nahbi's familiar face filled the big screen in the TF3 conference area. Gordon McFarland sat in so he could brief Sir Lionel.

"Good afternoon and welcome back," David told Nahbi. "Congratulations on your citizenship."

"Thank you. I miss all of you, of course, but I must admit that being made a citizen with full rights is something I never expected."

OK, let's get started," David said.

"A few days ago, Nahbi asked me to read everything I could find that had been written by Akil El-Sayed regarding Al Qaeda strategies. His writings are extensive but there is an obvious common thread. The militant Islamists believe that the west is too strong to be defeated militarily so they have adopted asymmetrical warfare using terrorism."

"Like Osama bin Laden, El-Sayed was convinced that the west's Achilles Heel is its financial system. He quoted Ralph Waldo Emerson's famous line to the effect that if you strike at a king you must kill him. He made numerous statements in his writings that were highly critical of bin Laden for his failure to strike a mortal blow. He argued that all Osama bin Laden did was anger the metaphorical king leading to the death of many Al Qaeda leaders."

"Akil El-Sayed clearly believed that destruction of the west's financial systems was the best way to bring about a collapse of their military, economic, and political power. We know that Egypt's Ambassador to Pakistan met with El-Sayed and then with General Jhalawan. I think it is safe to assume that Jhalawan intends to use the nuclear devices to strike a mortal blow against the west's financial systems."

Nahbi expressed agreement. "I have come to the same conclusion but it is not yet obvious which targets he has selected. Tiera, were you able to obtain the lists of high-value targets that I asked for?"

"Yes. It's a long list of government offices, military bases, public water and power supplies, transportation hubs, refineries, and similar infrastructure. All four governments have assigned lower priorities to financial institutions in the belief that public safety should come first. The stock exchanges and major banks are in the third tier of likely targets. There is a broad consensus that the terrorists prefer the most dramatic targets, such as the U.S. Capital Building, the Pentagon, and the U.K. Parliament Building."

"The American Department of Homeland Security distinguishes between discreet targets suitable for small teams of terrorists and more dramatic targets that require careful planning and well-coordinated execution by a larger number of agents."

A lively discussion then took place regarding how to narrow down the list of possible targets.

"Dr. Ghilzai told us that the devices would likely be placed near the top of tall buildings. If we merge that criteria with the financial system objective isn't it probable that the devices will be placed in one of the tallest bank buildings in the target cities?" Al Flores asked.

"Dr. Ghilzai also told us that three of the four devices are concealed inside stainless steel CO2 tanks suggesting that the devices will be placed in either a restaurant or a bar. Do we know which of the tallest bank buildings have a restaurant or bar near the top floor?" Phil Shaw asked.

Tiera answered both men's questions. "Yes and no. In Frankfurt, that suggests either the Deutsch Bank Twin Towers or the new European Central Bank tower. Although it's a trade center rather than a bank, another possibility is the Messeturm tower just west of the Deutsche Bank towers. However, it does not appear that there are restaurants or bars on upper floors in any of those buildings. I'm still trying to find out if there are tenant dining rooms on upper floors in any of those buildings or if there might be other tall buildings that do have a restaurant on an upper floor."

"In London, it will almost certainly be one of the tall buildings at Canary Wharf. HSBC, Citigroup and numerous other banks have offices there. HSBC is the second-largest bank in the world.

Citigroup is fifteenth. Three of the tallest buildings in the United Kingdom are located at Canary Wharf. However, with the possible exception of some small executive dining rooms that may have been added by various tenants, none of the Canary Wharf skyscrapers have restaurants or bars on upper floors."

"BNP Paribus and Crédit Agricole are the two largest banks in France. Crédit Agricole is the world's fourth-largest bank and BNP Paribus is sixth. However, the Paris headquarters for both banks are low-rise buildings. A more likely location in Paris would be the Montparnasse Tower. At 690 feet tall, it is the 14th tallest building in the European Union. Le Ciel de Paris restaurant is located on the 56th floor and is listed as having the highest panoramic bar in Europe. The headquarters for Crédit Agricole is less than a half-mile away. The BNP Paribus headquarters building is a little over two miles north of the Montparnasse Tower and therefore well within the radius of maximum destruction and loss of life. I think we have to put the Montparnasse Tower near the top of our list for Paris."

"In New York City, the most likely targets appear to be either the Citigroup or JP Morgan Chase headquarters buildings in mid-Manhattan. Both buildings are about four miles north of the Stock Exchange and Federal Reserve Bank. The Empire State Building is more central but it's hard to see how the device could be gotten past the building's strong security." The new World Trade Center building is nearing completion and is already the tallest building in New York. However, it's on the south end of the city and somewhat distant from the big banking centers. I considered the possibility that General Jhalawan might select it as a target just to demonstrate that American resolve to rebuild the WTC was in vain," Tiera concluded.

"Why use CO2 tanks if they weren't going to put the devices in a restaurant or bar?" Gabe wondered aloud.

"Maybe they made a bad assumption or had some flawed information," Tiera said. "When I was doing my research, I came across several references that said the HSBC staff restaurant at Canary Wharf was the largest in Europe and that it was located on one of the top floors of the building. Actually, the staff restaurant is located on the first floor. Perhaps they made the decision to use the

CO_2 tanks before their location research was completed or maybe there are flaws in their research. In any event, a CO_2 tank is a pretty harmless-looking container. Nearly everyone has seen them and would not be surprised to see one on a delivery cart or in an elevator."

"But, that means the devices could be placed almost anywhere near the top of a tall building. It could be in a mechanical room, a janitorial closet, or in an empty office suite," Phil Shaw pointed out.

"Nahbi, have you developed your own list of likely buildings?" David asked.

"Yes. I spent most of last night analyzing the possibilities. Tiera's briefing did a good job of identifying the high-probability targets."

"In London, the focus should be on the Canary Wharf area as she indicated. The likely target buildings are the skyscrapers at One, Eight, and Twenty-Five Canada Square. Those three are among the tallest buildings in the U.K. and two of them are bank headquarters. In descending order of probability, I rank the HSBC building at Eight Canada Square as the most likely target building. The Citigroup headquarters at twenty-five Canada Square is number two and One Canada Square is number three."

"In Frankfurt, Tiera's list was almost identical to mine. I've always thought there was a strong correlation between the assassination of the ECB President and General Jhalawan's plan so I initially ranked the new ECB headquarters building as number one. By destroying the ECB headquarters, Jhalawan would create utter chaos in the European financial systems for all of the EU members. I initially ranked the Twin Towers of Deutsche Bank as number two. I never thought the Messeturm Tower was a high probability but it is taller and in roughly the right area so I didn't rule it out. In any event, these three buildings are within two miles of each other so detonation in any of them would destroy the others as well as most of the downtown area."

"However, late last night I discovered that there is another very tall building in Frankfurt that is in an even better location for Jhalawan's purpose. The Main Tower is 656 feet tall and has a revolving restaurant and bar on the 53rd floor. Just as an aside, the

tower is named after the Main River that also gives Frankfurt am Main its name. I initially overlooked it because it's not a bank headquarters and several Frankfurt skyscrapers are taller. But then I discovered that the Standard and Poor's credit rating agency is the building's main tenant. S&P is a major player in global financial markets so it does fit the financial system criteria."

"Because of its central location and height, detonation at the top of the Main Tower would destroy nearly all of the major banking buildings in Frankfurt as well as the European headquarters of the Standard and Poor's rating agency. The ECB headquarters is a mile and a half away but the Commerzbank and Deutsch Bank headquarters are within a quarter mile. I recalculated the probabilities for the various possible sites and now rank the Main Tower as number one with the ECB building as number two followed by the Deutsche Bank twin towers."

"I agree with Tiera's assessment that the Montparnasse Tower is the most likely target building in Paris. The headquarters buildings for Crédit Agricole and BNP Paribus are considerably lower probabilities according to my analysis but because they are both among the world's largest banks, we cannot rule them out. There are some newer skyscrapers in the Nanterre area northwest of downtown Paris. However, those buildings are roughly six miles from the center of the city and the other large bank headquarters so my analysis assigns lower probabilities to them."

"New York City is more difficult. Dr. Ghilzai told us that the weapon for New York was concealed in a scuba tank like the one we found aboard the Belle Maria. That suggests that the location for the New York City device is not a restaurant or bar where a scuba tank would be utterly out of place. Unfortunately, I have been unable to identify any relationship between a scuba tank and anything in Manhattan. Yet, I believe the scuba tank does fit into a cover story of some kind so I'll keep working to find some link we can use," Nahbi told them.

Tariq Zardari had listened intently to the discussions but had thus far had nothing to contribute. With Nahbi's comment about the scuba tank, he broke his self-imposed silence.

"I think I know what the link is. Jamel el-Masri loves flying and scuba diving. He piloted his father's Bombardier 8000 from Southampton to the airport in Linden, New Jersey. Franco Rinaldi is with him. Before they left Southampton, I gave a gift-wrapped cardboard container of Almond Roca candy to Franco to be delivered to the diving tour operator when they reached Key West, Florida. The package is actually a bomb that will be detonated soon after their aircraft leaves New Jersey on its way to the Kendall-Timiami Executive Airport about fifteen miles south of Miami International Airport. A Muslim Brotherhood agent will be watching the Linden airport and will trigger the bomb using a cell phone about an hour after the plane takes off. There was a lot of diving equipment on the aircraft when it left Southampton so a scuba tank containing the weapon would be inconspicuous and would be consistent with their cover story of a diving vacation. I'm sure that tank will be placed somewhere in New York City but I don't know where. I heard Jamel talking to Franco about a diving tour they had scheduled to Wreck Valley off the New Jersey coast on the day after their arrival. I don't know if that was a ruse or if they actually intended to go diving. I suspect that it was a ruse."

"Do you know where they were going to stay?" Tiera asked.

"No, but based on what I do know, I would guess that they are probably in a Manhattan hotel waiting for the signal from General Jhalawan."

"Tiera, check the arrivals logs at the Linden airport," David suggested. "See if you can pick up their trail and what names they were using when they cleared immigration and customs. They probably took a taxi from the airport into Manhattan. If we get lucky, we might be able to find which hotel they went to. Although I doubt that Jamel has filed his out-bound flight plan yet, anything is possible. Ask the airport if he gave a departure date and next destination when he parked the aircraft. Pete, see if you can arrange to have their plane put under continuous surveillance. If they show up at the airport, we might be able to take them into custody for questioning."

David swiveled in his chair to face Al. "Contact the military high commands in the four targeted countries to set up a teleconference

with their best nuclear bomb squad leaders. Tariq told me that after the weapon on the Belle Maria was intercepted, Malik had ordered him to add tamper-proof circuits that will detonate the weapons if they are not handled in precisely the right way. Tariq has prepared some diagrams and checklists showing how the devices can be disarmed. I considered having you contact the Metropolitan Police bomb squads but they are not equipped for nuclear devices. Only the military experts are trained for what we're facing."

David then posed a question to Gordon McFarland. "Gordon, does the technology exist to detect nuclear weapons from satellites or at least from some distance away?"

"Unfortunately no. In fact, even a Geiger Counter that uses the most advanced version of the Geiger-Müller counter, which is basically an ionization chamber connected to some electronic circuits, would have to be close to the device to register the Alpha and Beta particle emissions. Alpha particles are ionized, low-velocity helium atoms. They cannot travel more than four to seven inches through air and a single sheet of paper will stop them. Beta particles are electrons that travel faster and can penetrate further than Alpha particles but the limit for a Beta particle is still only about ten yards in open air or several millimeters through paper, cardboard, or living tissue."

"Gamma rays are similar to x-rays in that they are a form of electromagnetic radiation. Gamma rays can travel up to a mile in open air and can penetrate more deeply through living tissue than Alpha or Beta particles. However, the metal containers will act as a partial shield which will reduce the number of detectable gamma photons and probably eliminate the escape of any Alpha or Beta particles. When the shielding effect of the containers and the surrounding building materials is factored in, it is unlikely that we can detect the relatively low level radiation from the devices without being in close proximity. High-energy neutrons can be detected at considerable distance but the devices will not emit them in detectable numbers until detonation."

"My research indicates that a company in the United States manufactures what is arguably one of the best portable radiation survey and detection meters currently available. If we could obtain

enough of them on short notice, local law enforcement officers could be quickly trained to use them. But, unless we can narrowly focus the search radius, it's hard to see how we could use portable radiation meters to find the weapons."

"OK. That's too bad. I had hoped for a technical solution to our needle-in-the-haystack problem but I'm not really surprised," David said.

"I've just talked to the folks at the National Security Agency. So far, they haven't picked up any text messages with the phrase *Light and Knowledge* in any language they track. NSA is currently monitoring roughly three-quarters of all cell phone messages originating anywhere in the world so it's possible that the message has been sent but not picked up. However, I don't think so. I doubt that the message has gone out yet. I have wondered if there was any significance to the phrase *Light and Knowledge* and the word *Jasmine*. Does anyone know?"

"Yes," Tariq answered. "*Light and Knowledge* is a reference to the star on Pakistan's flag. *Jasmine* is the national flower of Pakistan."

David nodded and then asked, "Gordon, is there any way we could block the cell phone transmissions?"

"In practice, probably not," Gordon said. "In theory, it might be possible to devise a digital filter that would screen every in-coming call or text message and then delay or cancel the further transmission. From a technical perspective, that's not substantially different than what the television networks do when they insert a delay in their broadcasts to protect the public from horrific graphic images or other communications deemed unsuitable for distribution. However, the networks are dealing with known feed sources and time frames. We don't have that luxury. To block the signals from Jhalawan, we'd have to shut down the entire cell phone systems in the target countries for an extended period. There's just no plausible way we could do that."

"I suspected that would be your answer," David said. "I don't think the devices have yet been placed in their final locations. Dr. Ghilzai told us that the Muslim Brotherhood agents were instructed

to place the devices within forty-eight hours of receipt of the message. That indicates that the planned detonation is probably no sooner than two days from today. Dr. Ghilzai also thought the detonation would occur prior to the beginning of Ramadan on the twenty-eighth. That suggests that the window we're looking at is not more than five or six days, say from the twenty-first through the twenty-seventh."

"I wonder if there's any way to find out which CO_2 vendors make deliveries in the target areas," Tiera said thinking out loud. "In all probability, the tanks will be brought to the buildings by delivery trucks that provide regular service to the buildings. There can't be that many companies that provide carbon dioxide to the plausible target buildings."

"Check with the taxation authorities," Nahbi suggested. "It's likely that they have records of the sales or value-added-taxes collected for the various products and services. Using computerized records, it should be possible to identify the names of CO_2 and beverage vending companies that have reported sales in the most likely target buildings."

"Good! Tiera can follow up on that," David said. "Phil, I'd like for you and Gabe to contact civil defense authorities in each of the target cities to see what contingency plans they have in place that might help us find the devices. Do they have bomb-search strategies that we could use?"

Pete Nocona pointed out that most bomb-search procedures rely heavily on trained dogs to sniff out potential explosives, which wouldn't work to locate nuclear weapons.

Al Flores reminded the team that the devices might be encased inside a larger container so focusing solely on trying to find CO_2 and scuba tanks might be a mistake. Expanding that thought, he pointed out that the devices could be inside shipping crates marked for delivery to the building maintenance departments or inside a refrigerator or piece of furniture being delivered to a tenant, or any number of other possibilities.

Gabe added that the large trash cans used by janitors could hold one of the tanks and that they are already on wheels so moving the heavy devices wouldn't pose a problem.

Watching the back and forth discussions among the team members, it was obvious to David that the team was starting to doubt that they could find the devices in time. As the clock continued to tick, and they seemed little closer to finding the weapons, their morale and confidence was ebbing.

David's combat experience had taught him that maintaining their morale was essential. Soldiers in any conflict must believe that they can win or, at the very least, that their cause is so just that they are willing to sacrifice their lives if necessary to uphold what is right. The Task Force 3 team was comprised of exceptionally intelligent people so a superficial rah-rah pep talk wouldn't work. They'd see through it instantly and that might make things worse.

"Listen to me, please," David began. "I've fought these guys before. Jhalawan and Malik aren't that different from the barbaric warlords and Taliban leaders I encountered every day in Afghanistan. These monsters don't value human life and see nothing wrong with using children as mobile bomb platforms. They feel some perverted sense of evil righteousness when they see someone beheaded. They are absolutely delighted when they are able to kill or maim the soldiers who are trying to maintain some semblance of civilized law and order in the world. They are utterly evil. They see the West as weak and decadent. The sad thing is that sometimes we act weak, which only emboldens them to acts of greater evil. But, they are so arrogant that they always make mistakes. That's how we'll beat them."

"It's not surprising that we're feeling the pressure. But, we've got at least a couple of days and a lot can happen in that time. Just take care of your assignments. We're solving this puzzle, piece by piece. We intercepted the device on the Belle Maria and we'll find the other four weapons too."

"You all know that I was wounded in Afghanistan and that I lost some good friends there. For me, the words *Never Forget* are not just a 9/11 slogan. One of my cousins died in the terrorist bombing of the Khobar Towers in Saudi Arabia. I was only eleven years old at

the time but Jeff Logan was like a big brother to me. I miss him still. I was fourteen when another cousin lost both legs and one arm in the terrorist attack on the USS Cole in Yemen. I remember how sad it was watching his young wife trying to be brave when he came home. My uncle David, my father's only brother and the man I was named after, died in the September 11th attack on the Pentagon."

"I would like nothing better than to get married, have some kids, and live in peace but Islamic terrorism has already spilled a lot of my family's blood. I am determined to do whatever I can to defeat radical, militant Islam. We all know the quotation attributed to the British philosopher Edmund Burke that '*The only thing necessary for the triumph of evil is that good men do nothing*.' This battle isn't over. Don't think for even an instant that it is. Hang tough."

3:00 PM

After the teleconference ended, Gordon McFarland provided a status update to Sir Lionel.

"How is David handling the pressure?" Sir Lionel asked.

"There's no question he's feeling it but he's outwardly calm and in firm control. I wish politicians on both sides of the Atlantic had even a fraction of his leadership ability. He's an impressive young man."

"How did the team react to Nahbi's participation in the teleconference?"

"It was very positive. Nahbi jumped right back into his role of making suggestions that saved time and improved results."

"Was there any sense that his participation undermined David's leadership of the team?"

"Not at all. In fact, Nahbi himself set the tone by showing deference to David as the team leader. I'd say the leadership transfer has gone surprisingly well."

"It appears that we will have a very narrow window of opportunity to find and disarm the weapons after either NSA or GCHQ picks up the Jasmine signal. Is that the way you see it?"

"Yes," Gordon answered. "Detonation could come at any time after the weapons are in place. It could be minutes or days."

"David believes the detonation signal will be transmitted before the beginning of Ramadan on the 28th. I think he's right. Since the time of the appearance of the new moon differs by time zone, it is not clear what event or time General Jhalawan will see as the beginning of Ramadan. My own view is that Jhalawan plans to detonate the devices a day or two before the start of Ramadan to allow time for the news to reach Muslims everywhere before the onset of Ramadan. In my view, the precise moment of the beginning of Ramadan is not really the critical issue."

"We have to hope that either the NSA or GCHQ will pick up the *Light and Knowledge* signal to place the devices. We have a short list of likely buildings and David has asked for law enforcement teams to be on standby for continuous surveillance once the message goes out. If we get lucky, the surveillance teams might recognize the delivery of the weapons. Unless Jhalawan fears that we are close to finding and disarming the weapons, in which case he would detonate them immediately, I think we'll have at least 48 hours after the *Light and Knowledge* signal is transmitted. We might have more but I wouldn't count on it. If I were in Jhalawan's shoes, I'd detonate them soon after I received the *Jasmine* signals that the devices were all in place. I wouldn't risk having them vulnerable to discovery any longer than necessary. We won't have much time and there's a lot of ground to cover."

"The team unanimously believes the U.S. President has miscalculated badly," Gordon continued. "They all think that Jhalawan will detonate the weapons soon after they are in place to minimize the chances that they will be discovered and disarmed. Al Flores is bitterly angry at his President's willingness to risk millions of lives based on what Al sees as his naïve and foolish confidence that evil men will behave in a civilized way. I heard him mutter under his breath that only idiots try to negotiate with rattlesnakes."

"Gordon, do *you* think we'll find them in time?"

"I hope so sir. I truly hope so. Will the Prime Minister order the evacuation of London if it looks like we've run out of time?"

"I don't think so. He apparently agrees with the task force's opinion that Jhalawan is watching and that he would detonate the devices in place at the first sign of mass evacuation. The PM has

discussed the issue with the Queen, a few members of Parliament, and the Mayor of London. I understand that they all agree that an evacuation order would likely result in detonation. They are hoping and trusting that we'll find the weapons in time. There is a top-secret planning effort underway at MI5 for first responders and other civil defense measures just in case. The Foreign Minister told me earlier today that the other nations have decided not to order evacuations either so it's entirely on our shoulders."

"I assume that means you won't order an evacuation of MI6 either."

"I've ordered a few senior people and critical staff to be away from London for the next nine days. I can't very well order a general evacuation contrary to the PM's decision but I feel it is important to ensure that enough people would survive to provide some limited continuity of our intelligence capability. Normally, I would have asked you to be elsewhere too but I think you and I need to be here to the very end, no matter how it turns out."

"Yes sir. I understand."

Sir Lionel punched the speed-dial number for David's cubicle in the basement.

"David, this is Sir Lionel. I apologize for the short notice but the Prime Minister has asked me to come to Number 10 to brief him at five o'clock today. I'd like for you to go with me to be sure we can answer any questions he may have. My driver will pick us up at the front door at 4:30 PM. Coat and tie are appropriate."

London, Number 10 Downing Street
5:00 PM

The Prime Minister's housekeeper asked them to wait in the living room. The PM joined them two minutes later and asked them to be seated.

"Mr. Logan, I am pleased to meet you. Sir Lionel's decision to put you in charge of the task force is the best recommendation you could have with me. He is a shrewd judge of talent so his endorsement carries great weight."

"We all felt that identification of the Belle Maria was an incredible demonstration of the intelligence-gathering and analytical capabilities of your team. Frankly, I was amazed that you were able to do it. You and your team have my sincere appreciation and admiration for what you accomplished. Now, to current matters, do you know where the other four devices are?"

"No sir. Based on interrogation of several people, we know they are already somewhere in the cities of London, New York, Frankfurt, and Paris but we do not know exactly where."

"What is being done to find them?"

Over the next thirty minutes, David gave the PM a thorough briefing. When he was finished, the PM asked a few questions and then asked, "Is there anything I can do to help?"

"No sir. Not that I can think of. I still hope that we will find the weapons in time but I tried to hedge our bets. I was disappointed that the President would not approve having the CIA or a SEAL team abduct General Jhalawan and Ahmed Malik so we could interrogate them. The abduction and interrogation of Abu Shakra was very helpful and I had hoped that we might be able to repeat that success. I subsequently asked for a drone strike and that was disapproved as well. I now think it's too late for those actions so we're focused on finding and disarming the devices before they can be detonated."

"Is there anything you'd like for me to communicate to the leaders of the other three countries?

Sir Lionel had warned David to be ready for that question. "No sir. With the recent public outrage over what is being sensationalized by the media as a violation of privacy by the NSA, we've gotten some push-back from the French and Germans about NSA's efforts to intercept the signals from Jhalawan. But, I've spoken to the NSA Director and he's assured me that the French and German objections won't matter. NSA can still screen the calls using a variety of top-secret methods. Sir Lionel has given me similar assurances that the efforts by GCHQ do not depend on French and German cooperation. So, for now at least, I can't think of anything I'd like for you to communicate to the other leaders."

The Prime Minister nodded and then stood to indicate that the briefing was over. He thanked them for coming and expressed his confidence that they would be successful.

London, MI6 HQ
7:00 PM

After having dinner together in the cafeteria, Tiera and David went to her room for some time together. The long hours and pressure were taking a toll on them both.

When they were alone, David put his arms around Tiera and gave her a tender kiss. She returned his kiss but seemed distracted and soon pulled away from him.

"David, I'm scared. We might die here in this building far from our homes and families if the device here in London is not found and disarmed in time. I've been thinking of my parents and Nicholas and I realized that I may never see them again. I couldn't stop crying last night. I almost called you but I know you've got a lot on your mind so I didn't want to add my worries to yours. When I got in bed, I pretended that my pillow was you and I wrapped my arms around it and just cried and cried. I don't know what time I finally fell asleep but I was exhausted when I got up this morning. This really isn't like me. I've never been overcome by emotion this way before. Do you really think the teams will find the weapons and be able to disarm them in time? I know that you always try to appear calm for everyone else's sake. But what do you really think?"

"I wish you had called me," David said as he reached out to gently caress her cheek. "You are the most important person in the world to me and I don't like to think of you suffering alone. But, to answer your question, yes. I do think we will find all of the weapons in time. The teams of people we are working with are absolutely amazing. I've never seen such cooperation among multiple agencies in multiple countries before. Even in the midst of World War II, the allies squabbled continuously. Eisenhower had his hands full trying to keep Montgomery and Patton from killing each other instead of the enemy. It's been much easier for me because everyone has been pulling together all the way. So yes, I think we will find them in time."

"I also do not think we will die here even if the unthinkable should happen and the device here in London actually detonates. We are almost five miles from Canary Wharf and therefore on the periphery of the high-mortality zone. More importantly, we are living and working underground and would be shielded from most of the neutron radiation by the concrete and steel of the building plus several feet of earth and rock. The MI6 building is of modern design and construction. It is well outside of the primary blast zone so it would almost certainly survive the blast. We are not going to die here. You will see your family as soon as this is over."

Tiera snuggled up beside David on the couch and lifted her face to let him kiss her again. She unbuttoned his shirt and ran her fingers through the hair on his chest in a loving, non-sexual way. David could see that she was exhausted both physically and emotionally. It wasn't long before she fell asleep. He carried her to her bed a little after midnight. She gave him a groggy kiss as he put her in bed and pulled the covers over her without undressing her. She was already asleep again before he turned out the light.

Friday, June 20

London, MI6 HQ
1:00 PM

David looked at the clock. He reviewed his notes and then spent a few moments in a thankful, silent prayer. He knew that without the disarming briefing Tariq Zardari was about to give, the nuclear devices would probably detonate even if they found them in time.

A few minutes before the scheduled start time for the teleconference, the nuclear ordnance teams from the United States, France, and Germany began to log on using secure satellite communications links and the two-level passwords they'd been given. The team from the U.K. was physically present in the TF3 conference room in the basement of the MI6 building. All of the team members were active-duty military personnel that had

received specialized training in handling, arming, and disarming various nuclear weapons. All were experts in their field.

Multiple large-screen monitors in each of the teleconference centers were configured so the participants could see each other. One of Gordon McFarland's technicians was acting as the media engineer to display the diagrams and checklist that Tariq had prepared.

When all of the teams were logged on and visible to each other, David introduced himself, the members of Task Force 3, and Tariq Zardari. He then asked each team leader to introduce his team.

"I'm sure you'd all like a status update before we begin," David said. "As of now, we still do not know where the nuclear devices are or where they will be placed. Once we intercept the *Light and Knowledge* message, the high-probability buildings in each of the target cities will be under continuous surveillance by undercover law enforcement personnel who have been thoroughly briefed."

"We also have digital links routed from the security cameras at all building entrances to a room here at MI6 equipped with seventy-two monitors connected to digital recorders. We can switch between the various feeds if we need to but the basic configuration is for eighteen monitors to be semi-dedicated to each of the four countries. This allows us to watch multiple entrances to several buildings at the same time. The security camera data feeds are already being monitored around the clock."

"Our objective is to recognize when the devices are brought into the buildings so we can mobilize your teams to take possession of the devices to disarm them."

"Federal law enforcement agencies in each of the targeted countries are also working around the clock to locate the weapons. Task Force 3 has the overall lead role in gathering, analyzing, and disseminating information. We are in continuous communication with the FBI, MI5, The French Sûreté, and the German GSG 9. We also have regular contact with senior political and military leaders. In simple terms, the communication lines are open in all directions and cooperation has been excellent."

"I will now turn the briefing over to Tariq Zardari. He will familiarize you with the weapons and the tamper-proof mechanisms that must be defeated in order to disarm the weapons."

Tariq launched into his briefing without preamble. "I believe you all know that these weapons were developed in Pakistan as part of a defensive strategy for the border disputes with India. As originally configured, they were designed to be fired from the American-made M110A2 eight-inch howitzers. Pakistan owns approximately 250 of those self-propelled artillery pieces."

"The Pakistani weapons are based on the American-designed W33 and W79 nuclear artillery shells from the Cold War era but they are more powerful due to technical advances in the way the critical mass is shaped. Like the American W79 shells, these are neutron bombs. They weigh approximately 200 pounds and can fit in a cylinder that is eight inches in diameter and approximately thirty-eight inches long."

"These devices have an explosive force of approximately 40 thousand tons of TNT. To put that in perspective, each of these devices is three to four times more powerful than the bombs that destroyed Nagasaki and Hiroshima. In reality, they are more of a strategic weapon than the tactical weapons originally designed and fielded by the Americans. The underlying design premise was that Indian forces would outnumber Pakistani forces so badly that each artillery shell needed to be able to destroy entire battalions of invading forces deployed over several miles."

"The radius of near total physical destruction is approximately three miles depending on the nature of the terrain, the types of buildings, and the height at which the weapon is detonated. However, due to the enormous burst of lethal neutrons, the radius of near-total mortality for human beings is approximately five miles. Outside these ranges, there will still be extensive physical damage, particularly to older structures, and there will still be significant radiation sickness with delayed mortality and other severe, long-term health issues. To be very explicit, these are powerful weapons that will cause massive loss of life and physical destruction for several miles around the points of detonation."

“The devices intended for London, Paris, and Frankfurt are concealed in stainless steel CO2 tanks. The one for New York City is concealed in a scuba tank. Internally, they are identical. They have been configured to be detonated by an encrypted long-string cell phone text message.”

“After one of the five stolen devices was intercepted by HMS Sutherland near Gibraltar, the others were retro-fitted with more sophisticated tamper-proof circuitry. I’m sure that all of you are familiar with standard render-safe procedures. Unfortunately, despite universal efforts to protect EOD tradecraft secrets, the engineers who designed these weapons also knew most of the techniques and devised ways to defeat them. If the devices are not handled and disarmed in a very precise way, they will self-detonate.”

“No special tools are required to disarm the weapons. A standard EOD kit will be more than adequate. You will need a strong, all-metal folding table capable of supporting 250 pounds and standard, clip-on grounding straps for the table and each technician. You will not need the portable x-ray devices that are typically used to examine the internal components of a bomb prior to attempting to disarm it. In this case, I will show you exactly how the bombs are constructed and where the critical components are.”

“None of the obvious ways to defeat the tamper-proof circuits will work. I’ve been asked if a simple cell-phone jammer would at least temporarily defeat the mechanism. The answer is no. The designers anticipated that transporting a device toward its destination would involve moving in and out of cell phone coverage. A cell-phone jammer placed in close proximity to a cell phone only disrupts the signals being transmitted from the nearby cell phone towers. So, a cell phone jammer does nothing special that the modified weapon’s tamper-proof design wasn’t already capable of handling.”

“I’ve also been asked if simply cutting the battery wire to de-energize the cell phone receiver would work. Again, the answer is no. As I’ve explained, the tamper-proof circuits do not detonate the device if a cell signal is lost or otherwise not available. However, if power is interrupted to the receiver once the devices are armed, detonation will occur.”

"To save time, I'm not going to address every conceivable way that the tamper-proof circuits might theoretically be defeated. Instead, I'm going to provide detailed instructions on how to safely disarm the devices. I must warn you that any deviation from these instructions, no matter how slight, will detonate the device instantly."

Tariq nodded to the media engineer to signal that he wanted the first diagram projected.

"As you can see in this color-coded diagram, the nuclear weapon occupies most of the container except for a small volume near the top. Like all neutron devices, it is a fission-fusion thermonuclear weapon in which the burst of neutrons generated by the fusion reaction is allowed to escape rather than being absorbed by the device's other components. The weapon's X-ray mirrors and radiation case are shown here in a cut-away view. In a standard bomb the neutron reflection mirrors are made of uranium or lead. For these weapons, the mirrors are fabricated of chromium so the neutrons can escape. These devices release about ten times more high-energy neutrons than a fission bomb with a comparable quantity of fissile material. That is why they are so deadly."

"You can see that the detonator is located just above the nuclear device and is connected to a miniaturized control module that sits on top of it. The control module is connected to a custom-designed cell phone receiver that is connected to a multi-band miniature cell phone antenna outside of the metal container. If you look closely, you will notice a surprising number of wires. Some of them are dummies while others serve a real purpose. If one or more of the dummy wires is cut, nothing will happen. If even one of the others is cut before the disarming code is properly entered, the weapon will detonate."

"Surface-mounted on the left side of the control module, there are two miniature dual in-line package switches, each with eight toggle switches. Together, they comprise a sixteen-bit digital code panel. Normally, sixteen bits can produce 65,536 states, the number resulting from 2 raised to the sixteenth power. However, by introducing the requirement that the toggle switches must be moved

in a precise order the odds of getting the sequence right on the first try becomes several million to one. There are no second tries."

"In the enlarged window, you can see that one of the DIP switches is blue and the other is red. A typical code would require each of the toggle switches to be placed in either the on or off position without regard to the order in which the toggles are moved. Normally, so long as all of the toggles ended up in the right position, the code would be recognized as correct. However, this device is more complex. The toggle switches must be moved, or not moved, from their current positions in a specific order. Even if someone had the proper final code configuration but failed to make the changes in the precise order required, the device would detonate. Changing the position of the toggle switches is the critical part of disarming the weapon. Make just one mistake and the bomb will detonate."

"You must not move any of the toggle switches until you have announced what you are about to do and your teammate has confirmed that is the correct action. Once the correct order has been followed, and the proper configuration has been achieved, the weapon will be disarmed."

Tariq nodded again to the media engineer who then projected a checklist on the screens.

Tariq continued his briefing. "This checklist must be followed exactly to disarm the weapons."

"First, lay the device on its side on a metal table that has been grounded. Block the device with small plastic wedges on both sides to ensure that it can't move around."

"Carefully detach the miniature cell phone antenna. It is seated in a small spring clip that has been epoxy-glued to the top of the container. Be careful not to break the wires. They are delicate but reasonable care will suffice. Pull the antenna to one side. There is about ten inches of slack in the wires."

"Next, unscrew the top of the container by hand. It should turn fairly easily. There is a small hole in the container top through which the antenna wires passes. Make sure that the antenna wires do not bind and twist as the container top is unscrewed."

“Carefully pull the assembly consisting of the detonator, the control module, and the cell phone out of the container. Lay it on the table a few inches from the top of the container. The wires are long enough. Position it so the red and blue DIP switches are facing up and then block it so it can’t move. Orient your point of view so the numbers on the DIP switches can be read right-side up with the number one toggle to your left.”

“Then, in exactly this order, do the following.”

“On the blue DIP switch, do not change the position of toggle switch numbers three and six. You will see that switch number three is in the on position and switch number six is in the off position. Again, do not move them.”

“On the red DIP switch, do not change the positions of toggle switches one, three, five, and seven. You will see that switches one, three, and seven are in the off position. Switch number five is in the on position.”

“On the red DIP switch, move toggle switch number eight from off to on.”

“On the blue DIP switch, move toggle switch number two from off to on.”

“On the red DIP switch, move toggle switch number two from on to off.”

“On the blue DIP switch, move toggle switch number seven from on to off.”

“On the blue DIP switch, move toggle switch number four from on to off.”

“On the red DIP switch, move toggle switch number four from off to on.”

“On the blue DIP switch, move toggle switch number five from on to off.”

“On the red DIP switch, move toggle switch number six from on to off.”

“On the blue DIP switch, move toggle switch number eight from off to on.”

"On the blue DIP switch, move toggle switch number one from on to off."

"Once you have completed setting the toggle switches, locate the red wire leading from the 3-volt lithium-ion battery to the cell phone circuit board. Cut it."

"Locate the green wire leading from the control module to the cell phone circuit board. Cut it."

"Locate the black and red wires leading from the control module to the detonator. Cut them both."

"Locate the white wire leading from the control module to the detonator. Cut it."

"Cut all remaining wires between the control module and the detonator."

"Grasp the ring on the top of the nuclear core and carefully pull it out of the container."

"Further disassembly of the fissile core is not necessary. At this point, the device will be fully disarmed and can be safely transported to a secure facility for further examination and de-militarization."

Tariq answered questions for twenty minutes and then David took over again.

"We believe there will be a narrow window of time when we can disarm the weapons. Trusted members of the Muslim Brotherhood will transport the weapons to their designated target buildings and put them in place sometime in a forty-eight-hour span of time. Your teams will have to be on continuous alert and ready to move at a moment's notice. Your temporary bases of operation have been selected to be near where we expect the weapons to be placed so you can be on-site literally within minutes of notification. Each member of your team should be dressed differently and should enter the building separately."

"As the devices are disarmed, each team leader will make a voice transmission using the code words *Alpha X-Ray* for the U.S. team; *Bravo X-Ray* for the U.K. team; *Charlie X-Ray* for the French team; and *Delta X-Ray* for the German team.

"Are there any other questions?"

"Yes. I have one," the leader of the German team said. "How confident are you that the surveillance teams will recognize when the devices are delivered?"

"We cannot be sure, of course, but we know enough about these devices and their intended purpose to believe that our short-list of likely buildings includes the actual target. The National Security Agency in the U.S. has assured me that they can notify us within a few minutes of the transmission of the order to place the devices. We know from several interrogations that the agents will have 48 hours to put the devices in place once that signal is received. I think the surveillance teams will probably recognize when the devices are delivered. We have quite a few clues to help identify the delivery agent. However, there is a potential risk that we will try to mitigate."

"It is entirely possible that one or more Muslim Brotherhood agents will also be watching the buildings we are monitoring to note any evidence that the deliveries have been witnessed by those of us trying to defeat this terrorist attack. We know that the mastermind of this attack has the ability to override the control circuits to detonate the devices at any time if their interception appears likely."

"To mitigate this risk, we have placed additional law enforcement officers inside the foyers of the buildings in place of the regular front-desk building security guards. None of the outside surveillance team officers watching the several building entrances will visibly react to the suspected delivery in case they are being watched. Instead, they will key their tactical microphones two times followed by a pause and then three more clicks in quick succession to alert the rest of the team that they believe the weapons are about to enter the building. To indicate that he has the delivery agent in view, the officer inside the building will key his microphone in the old Morse code SOS international distress code of three quick clicks followed by three slow clicks followed by three more fast clicks."

"The agents making the deliveries may be armed. We cannot rule that out so gunplay is a distinct possibility. The law enforcement officers have been briefed on how to apprehend the delivery agent with minimum risk of gunfire, which would alert any Muslim Brotherhood agents outside and probably lead to detonation. Once the weapon is secured, the inside officers will make a voice

transmission over the common network summarizing the situation. That will be the signal to your EOD team to move in to disarm the weapon," David explained.

"You seem very sure that these weapons are in the hands of members of the Muslim Brotherhood. How reliable is that intelligence?" the leader of the French EOD team wanted to know.

"We have multiple confirmations that senior members of the Muslim Brotherhood have been involved in this unfolding nightmare from the beginning. We have apprehended and interrogated several of them. There is no doubt whatsoever," David told him.

"What about crowd control?" the German team leader asked.

"We cannot risk having the device detonated by any evidence that we are on-site and actively engaged in trying to thwart the plan. So, we will not take any crowd control measures. As far as a Muslim Brotherhood observer can tell, everything must appear absolutely normal. I don't want to understate the risks we face. If our intervention is witnessed, the bombs will probably be detonated without delay. We must try to gain control of the devices without alerting any bad guys who may be watching."

"Once positive possession and control of each device is achieved, the devices will be moved to a secure room on the ground floor where your EOD teams can work. One member of each team, dressed in business attire, should visit each of the short-list buildings in their city today to ensure that each team knows where the room is that you will use to disarm the device. A stainless steel table and enhanced lighting has already been set up in each of the designated rooms. The table is already grounded and wrist-grounding cuffs are attached to the table for each EOD technician."

"How much radiation will our teams be exposed to?" the American team leader asked.

Tariq responded. "The short answer is not much. You should wear your dosimeters, of course, but the amount of radiation you will be exposed to within the relatively brief time you are in close proximity to the weapons is similar to what you would get from sitting on the granite steps of a public building," Tariq told him. "I

have worked around these weapons for several years and have never even approached the maximum permitted annual total effective dose equivalent. Pakistan follows the standards set forth in the U.S. Navy's *Radiation Health Protection Manual* which are consistent with those of the Environmental Protection Agency, the Nuclear Regulatory Commission, and the Occupational Safety and Health Administration standards. European standards are similar but the unit of measure is the sievert instead of the rem."

The American team leader had another question. "You have given us the details of the sequence and final positions of the sixteen toggle switches. I'm curious how you know that. Surely you don't have that memorized."

"Actually, I do. I'm the one who devised the codes and the sequence. I can remember them because I wrote a silly poem in Urdu that provides mnemonic clues that have meaning only to me. I will never forget the poem because it is based on stories that I read over and over to my children when they were very small."

David then brought the briefing to a close. "OK. If there are no other questions, I will conclude by saying that I will be praying for your success. Thank you all."

Sunday, June 22

Woodside, California
7:10 AM

Nicholas Aquilina backed his silver Mercedes-Benz Gullwing coupe out of the garage into the bright sunlight of what looked like a lovely day for a Sunday drive. He let the engine warm up for a couple of minutes while he looked at a road map.

The Aquilina family's wealth had given him options about where to live that most students at Stanford University didn't have. Nicholas was accustomed to the comfort and privacy of his father's estate. He had decided to invest in a home in the coastal foothills several miles west of the congested areas around the campus instead of moving into an apartment. He had discussed it with his father

and they had agreed that the property would increase in value during his time at Stanford. Instead of spending more than a hundred thousand dollars to live in a luxury apartment for four or five years, he expected to pocket a handsome profit when he sold the lovely old Spanish-style home.

Just as he was about to leave, a car turned into his driveway and pulled up in front of the Mercedes. A man got out and walked up to the driver's side of the coupe. Nicholas lowered the window to see what the man wanted.

"Good morning, I wonder if you can help me. I seem to be lost."

"Where are you trying to go?"

"I'm looking for Summit Springs Road."

"Well, you're close. Go back out to Tripp Road and turn right. Summit Springs Road will be on your right in about a quarter mile."

The man leaned forward as if to shake hands. José Mendoza was in the United States illegally. He had worked as an enforcer and asesino for the Serrano brothers and their Juarez drug trafficking operation until internal fighting had almost destroyed the organization. He had been forced out when Juan Serrano had taken over. A wealthy Mexican expatriate in Modesto had hired him as a personal bodyguard and occasional contract assassin. Mendoza had been watching the target's home when he saw him back his sports car out of the garage.

The last thing the victim saw was a compact Beretta .22 caliber pistol with a silencer aimed at his head. Mendoza fired two quick shots that would not have been recognizable as gunshots even a short distance away. The man instantly slumped over dead with two small holes in his forehead. The hollow point bullets had been treated with ricin, a deadly poison, in case the victim survived the trauma of two small-caliber gunshots to his brain. There was very little blood. Mendoza bent over to pick up the two empty brass casings from the ground and then walked back to his car and drove away. There were no witnesses.

Rhome, Texas
12:30 PM

David's sister Sarah always took her grandparents to church with her. It was short drive from her home to their farm five miles west of Rhome, Texas. They were always waiting and ready when she picked them up at 9:00 AM so they could attend Sunday school before the regular church service.

Sarah's husband Jim wasn't a church-going man so he took care of their little girl and infant son while she was away at church. He didn't mind watching the kids and it was a nice break for her to be away from them for a few hours.

As she turned south off of county road 4840 onto Hall Nance road, she noticed a blue pickup truck parked at the corner near one of the natural gas wells. There was a man sitting in the truck but she didn't pay any attention to him. The truck was still there after she dropped her grandparents off but the hood was up and the man was leaning over the engine. He stood up and motioned for her to stop as she approached. In rural areas of Texas, it is worse than rude to just drive past someone with car trouble. Sarah had grown up less than a mile from where the truck was parked and had never had any reason to worry about her safety.

As she pulled up beside the truck, she rolled her window down and waited as the man approached her car.

"Do you need a lift into town?" she asked.

"You're Mrs. Clark, aren't you?" the man asked.

"Yes, I am. How did you know that?" Then she saw the gun in his hand. She floored the accelerator in a desperate attempt to get away.

As Sarah's car began to move, Sabir Abbas fired two quick shots into her head from a Ruger P94 .40 caliber pistol. She was killed instantly by the impact of two 180 grain jacketed hollow point bullets. Her car lurched to the right and came to a stop in the drainage ditch. Abbas closed the hood of his pickup and drove away. A mile north of where he'd killed the infidel, he turned east on Texas highway 114 toward Dallas. He took out his cell phone and hit a speed-dial key. "Allāhu Akbar. The job is complete," he reported tersely before hitting the end-call button.

London, MI6 HQ
9:20 PM

David had just stepped out of the shower and was toweling off when his cell phone rang. As he picked it up, he saw that it was his grandparent's number.

"David, this is your grandpa," the old man said with a catch in his voice. "I would give anything not to have to tell you the reason for my call." He paused a long moment before he said, "Your sister was murdered this afternoon right after she dropped your grandma and me off after church."

David staggered as though he'd been struck and slumped down on the edge of the bed to keep from falling. He had heard what his grandfather said but was so stunned that he could not speak for several moments.

"David, are you still there?" he heard his grandfather ask.

"Yes, I'm still here. Give me a moment," David managed to whisper.

"The Sheriff's deputies just left. The EMTs gave your grandmother a sedative and she's finally fallen asleep. I can't leave her so Jim's alone with the kids. I've asked some people from the church to check on him but I'm really worried about him. He's got to be in bad shape and there's no telling what he might do. Until I can get someone over here to stay with your grandmother, I can't leave. I called Jim's foreman and he said that he and his wife would go over immediately."

"Tell me what happened."

"Sarah dropped us off here at the house after church. I think she left about 12:30. About one o'clock, Tom Porter knocked on our door and told us that he'd just found Sarah shot dead in her car up at the corner. He'd already called 911 and told them he was coming to our house to tell us. Within ten minutes, two Sheriff's deputies came to the door and asked if we'd answer a few questions. They wanted to know if Sarah had any enemies if you can believe that. We really couldn't tell them much except that we'd seen a blue pickup truck parked at the corner on our way home. They asked if we had gotten a license number but of course we hadn't. I'm not even sure what

kind of truck it was. Maybe a Ford or maybe a Chevrolet. I just didn't pay it any attention. It's not like pickup trucks are unusual around these parts."

"How was she murdered?"

The old man began to cry. David had never known his grandfather to cry before. Even when they'd buried David's parents, the old man had hidden his own grief and been the one the rest of them had leaned on.

"David, they shot her in the head," the old man wailed pitifully. "The deputies asked if I could go to the county morgue to identify her body but Tom said he'd do it. He told me that I shouldn't let your grandmother see Sarah's body until after the funeral home fixed her up. He said it was pretty bad. David, I don't know what we're going to do. Is there any way you can come home?"

"I don't know, grandpa. I haven't told you before because I didn't want to worry you but now I have no choice. I'm the leader of a secret task force that is trying to find some nuclear weapons that terrorists intend to detonate in four different countries, including the United States, within the next few days. If we don't stop them, millions of people will die. Let me think about everything. I'll call you back early tomorrow morning your time."

"David, let's pray together before you hang up." David's grandfather's prayer was a model of grace and humility. The old deacon asked God to take care of Jim and the kids. He prayed that Jim would turn to God in his grief. He prayed that David's team would find the weapons in time and that God would give David the strength he needed. Tears were running down David's cheeks by the time his grandfather said Amen and they said goodbye.

David sat on the edge of the bed for several minutes after the call. Still wrapped in a towel after his shower, he knelt beside his bed to pray. He stayed on his knees for a long time before he stood and got dressed. He was sitting quietly on the couch in his room thirty minutes later when his cell phone rang again. He saw that it was Matthias Aquilina.

"Good evening sir."

"David, I have some very bad news and I have to ask you to do something for me. I've just received a call from a police detective in Redwood City, California. Redwood City is the small town where Nicholas bought a home. The detective told me that Nicholas was found shot to death earlier today. I can't bring myself to call Tiera unless I know you're there with her. She's a strong young woman but this will hit her harder than anything she's ever had to face. Could you go to her room so you'll be there when I call her?"

"Yes, of course. Give me fifteen minutes. Tiera may have already gone to bed. We've been working long hours and she's exhausted."

"Thank you. I hated to call you but it seemed the right thing to do. I hope you don't mind."

"No. Of course not. Thank you for allowing me to be with her when you call. Mr. Aquilina, did the police give you any details?"

"They said he was sitting in his car in the driveway and that someone shot him twice in the head. There were apparently no witnesses and there really isn't much for them to go on."

"I was afraid it would be something like that."

"Why do you say that?"

"My sister was also murdered earlier today. I just found out an hour ago. I'm sure that the man behind the nuclear terrorism attack ordered Nicholas and Sarah killed."

"Why would any human being do such a monstrous thing to innocent people?"

"I suspect that he's trying to hit Tiera and me with such a devastating emotional blow that we won't be able to do our jobs on this task force. We are only days from when he apparently intends to detonate the weapons. I'm guessing that he is doing everything he can to be sure we don't find and disarm the weapons. We know that he's a thoroughly evil man. He's already had several people killed. Ever since my grandfather called, I've been sitting here asking myself if I can find the strength to soldier on until our job is done. I've prayed about it and somehow God has calmed me and given me a clear vision of what must be done. There will be time for dealing with our grief later but not right now. Give me fifteen minutes and then you can call Tiera's room."

10:18 PM

Tiera was in her pajamas but had not yet gone to bed when David knocked on her door. He told her that he'd received a call from her father asking to speak to them both. When her phone rang, Tiera put the call on the speaker.

"Tiera, your mother and I have some very bad news. I asked David to be with you when we told you. Nicholas was found murdered earlier today."

"No!" Tiera screamed and then fainted.

"Tiera, are you there?" Her mother asked anxiously.

"Mrs. Aquilina, Tiera has fainted. Please stay on the line while I try to revive her."

David got a towel from the bathroom and wet it with cold water. He gently wiped Tiera's face and hands with the cool towel and she regained consciousness after a moment. "Is it true?" she whispered as she looked up at David with tears streaming down her face.

David could only nod.

"Tiera, can you hear me?" her mother asked.

"Yes mama, I can hear you. Papa, is it true?"

"Yes, my dear, I'm afraid it is. The police called us a couple of hours ago and I've been on the phone almost continuously answering their questions and making preliminary arrangements."

"How did it happen?"

"Someone shot him while he was sitting in his driveway apparently getting ready to go for a Sunday drive. One of the neighbors found him and called the police."

"Why would anyone want to shoot Nicholas?" Everyone loved him. Was it a robbery?"

"No. His wallet was still in his pocket with several hundred dollars in it. Whoever did it, could have taken his car but they didn't. There was no evidence that anyone tried to get into the house. The driveway is paved so there were no footprints or tire tracks and apparently no witnesses."

The look on Tiera's face was profoundly sad. David tried to put his arms around her but she pushed him away. Her voice was stronger when she spoke again.

"What arrangements have you made?"

"California law requires an autopsy in homicide cases. That will take several days and then the County Coroner will issue a formal death certificate. When that's been done, we can have his body flown home for burial. We won't try to schedule a funeral until then."

"Can you come home?" Maria Aquilina asked her daughter.

Tiera looked at David before she answered. "I have a job to do here. We still don't know where the nuclear weapons are but David is convinced that we will find them in time. I think it will be over by the time you can schedule the funeral. I'll come home then."

"We understand. Your mother and I have many friends here and Father Adami came as soon as I called him. You and David have each other and somehow I know you'll be OK. Your mother and I are so very sad that both of our families have been targeted by this evil man. I hope that you will be able to defeat him and bring him to justice. We love you both so much. Please take care of each other."

"Goodnight papa. Goodnight mama. I love you both more than I can possibly tell you. I will try to call every day."

After Tiera hung up, she gave David a questioning look. "What did papa mean when he said that both of our families have been targeted?"

David looked very uncomfortable but finally told her about Sarah.

Tiera began to cry again. "Jhalawan did this, didn't he?"

"Yes, I'm sure that's right. I think he wanted to devastate us emotionally in the hope that it would make it impossible for us to do our jobs. With Ahmed Malik supporting him, he has some of the best intelligence sources in the world. I'm sure he has a full dossier on us both and that he knows how close you were to Nicholas and how close I was to Sarah. He wouldn't hesitate to use that information against us if he could see a way to do it."

"Jhalawan is a brilliant military man. He's spent his life devising tactics to defeat his enemies, both militarily and politically. He'll do anything he can to keep us from finding and disarming those weapons. Once you and I were drawn into this battle, our families became vulnerable. I should have realized that there were no limits to what Jhalawan would do to achieve his purpose. The murder of Abramo Sartori and his wife and Lia Pedrazinni was ample evidence that Jhalawan is utterly merciless. After the Russians abducted your parents, I should have made arrangements to provide protection for the families of the entire task force."

"David, this is not your fault. Don't even think that it is. You are a good man. It is all but impossible for good men to anticipate every cruel and heartless act that an evil mind can conceive."

"I need to make arrangements to have security protection for the families of other TF3 team members immediately. I just hope it's not too late."

David picked up the phone to call Gordon McFarland.

"Gordon, this is David. I'm sorry to call you so late but it's important. I'm in Tiera's room. We've both had some very bad news and are trying to deal with it. Earlier today, Tiera's brother and my sister were both murdered. I'm sure it was Jhalawan's doing. There's no telling how far he'll go so we need to have security protection for the families of every member of the TF3 team until this is over. Can you arrange it?"

"Yes. I'll see to it at once. I'll call Sir Lionel. He's a night owl so it's not too late to call him. He'd be angry if I didn't, in fact. Where can I reach you for the next several hours?"

David looked at Tiera and she made an emphatic gesture pointing at the floor to indicate that she wanted him to stay with her.

"I'll be in Tiera's room the rest of the night."

As soon as David hung up, Tiera said, "I want you to stay with me tonight. I think we both need it. OK?"

"Sure."

"Do you want to take a shower?"

"No, I'd just stepped out of the shower when my grandfather called."

When they got into bed, they snuggled up to each other with David on his left side and Tiera's back against his chest. David's knees were drawn up behind hers. He draped his right arm over Tiera and rested his open palm softly against her pajamas over her tummy, being careful not to touch her breasts. He needn't have been so cautious. Tiera took his hand in hers and pressed it against her chest between her breasts. It was tenderly intimate but not at all sexual.

After several moments, Tiera began to speak in a soft voice. "All of the terrible things that have happened have come as quite a shock to me. I've finally begun to realize how lucky I've been and how protected from the evils of the world. Because my family was wealthy, and because Malta is a safe place to live, I've never had to face some of life's hard realities. I always had everything I needed."

"I've been thinking about the brutality that many Muslim women are subjected to. I can scarcely comprehend a religion that allows men to subjugate and brutalize women to such a degree that little girls weren't even allowed to go to school under the Taliban in Afghanistan. I always knew that putting bombs on children and blowing up school buses was barbaric and evil. But until the day when Nahbi and I stepped out of the trees and onto the soccer field at Buckhurst Hill, and I saw my parents sitting back to back with explosives strapped around them, it was not a personal confrontation with evil. It was always far away. It was never a part of my world. Now it is."

"I've always admired you for how you've dealt with the tragedies in your life. You are gentle and wise but somehow stronger than any man I've ever known. I always knew that I had never been tested the way you have been. Somewhere deep inside me, I prayed that I would be as strong as you if I ever had to be. Tonight, I am praying that I can be. I am praying for us all."

Tiera began to cry softly. "What will Jim do with an infant son and a little girl to take care of? What will Lia's husband do with a little girl, no job, and having to deal with his grief at losing his wife?

How can God allow such evil to exist in the world? How can we find the strength to deal with such tragedies?"

David just listened.

"David, I've been thinking about our time at Cambridge and our competitions on the boat crews. I've realized that I can tap into that competitive spirit and use it against Jhalawan and Malik. I will never forget Nicholas. I will miss him the rest of my life. But I will find a way to suspend my grief until this is over. Jhalawan has miscalculated. He has hurt us badly but he doesn't understand that in doing so he has given us the motivation to fight him until he is utterly defeated."

David kissed her neck. "I'm glad you understand that. I've had to make that choice and commitment several times in my life. I drew on my grandfather's stoic strength when my parents were killed. Time and again that strength and its source made it possible for me to keep doing my job when my men were killed and I had to write those sad letters to their wives and girlfriends. When I nearly lost my leg, I made a conscious decision not feel sorry for myself and to fight to regain my life. I watched other wounded men and women make the same choice. I drew on their strength and found what I needed so I could do what we called soldiering on. Tonight, on my knees, I renewed that commitment to soldier on within thirty minutes after my grandfather's call."

"I wasn't going to give you a religious speech. It just didn't seem like a good time. But, after what you just said, I'm going to quote a bible passage that summarizes the source of my grandfather's strength. He taught me this passage when I was just a scared little boy wondering why my parents had to die. He began by telling me that it was a prayer of faith written long ago by a boy about my age that was also named David. I'm sure you've heard it before but it somehow just seems like a good time to remind ourselves of its timeless truth." David then repeated the passage for the woman he loved.

"The Lord is my shepherd. I shall not want. He maketh me to lie down in green pastures. He leadeth me beside the still waters. He restoreth my soul. He leadeth me in the paths of righteousness for His name's sake. Yea, though I walk through the valley of the

shadow of death, I will fear no evil, for Thou art with me. Thy rod and Thy staff they comfort me. Thou preparest a table before me in the presence of mine enemies. Thou anointest my head with oil. My cup runneth over. Surely goodness and mercy shall follow me all the days of my life and I will dwell in the house of the Lord forever."

"You're right. I've heard that passage many times but it always seemed like some archaic old poem rather than an expression of faith in God. It never meant as much to me as it does now, hearing you repeat it. Thank you." Tiera turned to face David so she could kiss him. They didn't speak any more and soon fell asleep.

Monday, June 23

Islamabad, Pakistan
11:58 AM

Ahmed Malik was sitting in front of General Jhalawan's desk at ISI headquarters holding a cell phone in his left hand. He and General Jhalawan were both watching the clock. At precisely noon in Pakistan's capital city, Malik pressed the send button on the cell phone. The text message *Light and Knowledge* was transmitted to four cell phones thousands of miles to the west.

Clarksville, Maryland
3:06 AM

David had just returned to his cubicle when the call came in on his secure line. It was Rear Admiral Stephen Green, the Director of the National Security Agency.

"Good morning David. The *Light and Knowledge* message was transmitted from Islamabad six minutes ago at noon their time. We have the cell phone number that it was transmitted from. As we suspected, the phone used a pre-paid SIM card sold by Telenor Pakistan. Now that we have the number, we could eventually track it to a serial number on the SIM card and then maybe to the retail outlet where it was purchased. However, that doesn't seem worth

doing. I'm sure that a low-level employee made the purchase so even if we could establish a trail of custody, it wouldn't be worth much in any kind of criminal proceedings. Actually, I doubt that Jhalawan will ever be charged. We all know he's behind this but proving it in court would be extremely difficult if not impossible."

"I agree. I just realized that it's three in the morning for you. Are you at your office?"

"No, I'm at home. The duty officer at Fort Meade called me when the computer made the intercept and I immediately called you. We've been sort of expecting that it might be today so everyone was on their toes."

"Thanks for the call. Keep watching for it of course but let's hope the *Jasmine* messages never go out. If we find and disarm the weapons in time, I might use the phone number your folks just snagged to send Jhalawan a text message of my own. Well, maybe not. That's probably one of those ideas that sounds good if you say it fast. Goodnight sir."

Sir Lionel was already in his office when David called to tell him that the message ordering the weapons to be put in their final positions had been intercepted.

"So, the stopwatch is now ticking. Are all the surveillance teams in place?"

"Yes sir. Our teams know what to do. We'll find them."

"Gordon's here with me now. I authorized the protective security for the other team members a little after eleven last night right after he told me about your sister and Tiera's brother. I'm so sorry that we didn't anticipate that Jhalawan might do something like this. I've been at this game a long time and should have thought of it. Nasty business we're in. How are you both doing?"

"Better than might be expected I think. We're both determined not to let Jhalawan succeed. Tiera had some really bad moments last night but she's stronger than even I suspected. We've been together all night and we had breakfast together about an hour ago. I would say that she's very sad but not incapacitated. If anything, she may be pumping more battle adrenalin than before. She's determined to see this through. I've seen men in combat deal with the death of people

they loved like a brother and I know the signs. I think she will soldier on. I'm very proud of her."

"And you?"

"I'll be fine sir. There'll be some emotional things to deal with later but if you're wondering if I can still do my job, the answer is yes."

Frankfurt, Germany
10:22 AM

When David heard the microphone clicks from the surveillance team he went immediately down the hall to the room where all of the video feeds were coming in. The rest of the TF3 team was already in the room when he got there. Gordon and Sir Lionel came in a few moments later.

David answered an incoming call on the portable phone that connected to his work station phone over the 900 MHz wireless network in the building.

"Good morning Herr Logan. This is Ralf Kohler. I'm a field agent with the German Federal Intelligence Services. My boss asked me to call you to confirm that your MI6 monitoring team is aware that a delivery truck from a local beverage services company has just arrived in the service area at the Main Tower building."

"Yes. Thank you for calling Herr Kohler. And, yes, we are monitoring the communications and watching the video feeds. What can you tell us about the Steinbach Beverage GmbH?"

"They supply beer and wine and beverage-quality carbon dioxide to bars and restaurants throughout the area. The company is located in Steinbach am Taunus five miles from downtown Frankfurt. It has been in business for over forty years. The company is privately-owned and has a contract to provide beverage CO_2 to the restaurant and bar on the 53rd floor of the tower. The owner is a respected German-born citizen but he has a minority partner that he took in a few years ago when the company experienced financial difficulties. His partner is a wealthy Egyptian who spends a few months each year in Germany, usually in the winter skiing in the Bavarian Alps. We believe that the man making the delivery may be his son."

"OK. It looks like he's about to enter the building now. Please stay on the line."

They were all wearing their headsets and heard the SOS microphone signal clicks from the embedded officer inside the building indicating that he had the delivery man in sight. There was no security camera inside the service door so there were some anxious moments before they heard the officer announce that he had taken the delivery man into custody without incident. He told them that he'd handcuffed the man and that two other officers were now with him.

A few seconds later they heard the German EOD team leader's voice giving orders to his team. Seven minutes later, he announced that they had the device on the table and were about to begin the disarming procedure. Gordon had suggested that the team leaders wear a headband with a digital camera on it. The team leader turned his on and they could see his field of view as he started work.

It was nerve-racking to watch. The team leader was ultra-careful and methodical at every step. It seemed much longer than it really was before the control module was secured in place so the team leader could begin to move the toggle switches on the two color-coded DIP switches. Everyone was holding their breath as he announced his intent for each step and his backup technician confirmed that action was correct. Inside the MI6 monitoring room, the sound of so many people letting their breath out and then taking another deep breath would have been humorous at any other time.

Finally, the position of all of the toggle switches had been adjusted in accordance with the checklist Tariq had provided. The team leader began to cut the wires. Each audible snipping sound made everyone's heart skip a beat. When all of the wires had been cut, and the fissile core had been withdrawn from the CO2 tank, they heard the team leader exhale sharply.

"*Delta X-ray*," the team leader said. "It is done. *Einer der erfreulichen Aspekte dieses Berufs*, one of the best parts of this job."

Applause broke out instantly and there was a lot of back-slapping from normally-serious people wearing silly grins. Sir Lionel asked Phil Shaw to lend him his headset for a moment.

"This is Sir Lionel Smythe speaking. Well done all! To our German colleagues, I can only say that you have once again demonstrated the highest degree of professionalism. Thank you for your courage and for all of those many hours of training that paid off so admirably today."

"This has been a remarkable, multi-national effort. I have been amazed at the incredible cooperation and team spirit that has been evident across agencies and national boundaries. I am very encouraged for the future of civilization when I see courageous, dedicated people working together against evil forces to do what is right and good. I salute you all and pray for our continuing success throughout the remainder of today and possibly into tomorrow. God bless you all."

London, MI6 HQ
5:35 PM

David saw that the incoming call was from the Director of the NSA and picked up the phone at once.

"Hello again Admiral Green."

"David, I know you were hoping that we'd never see the *Jasmine* message but we intercepted a text message with that content about ten minutes ago. It came from a cell phone using a prepaid Vodafone UK SIM card. The call originated somewhere in New York City and was directed to the same phone number that originated the *Light and Knowledge* message earlier. I'm guessing that this call came from Jamel el-Masri. I've been monitoring the various data feeds so I already know that the surveillance teams watching the bank buildings in Manhattan haven't reported any suspicious deliveries."

"That's correct, they haven't. This means the device could be anywhere in a city of eight million people and we don't have a clue where."

"Not necessarily, it's possible that the delivery agent got the weapon into one of the bank buildings without being seen. I don't want to presume to tell you how to do your job but maybe it's time to start a search of those buildings. We don't know if General

Jhalawan intends to wait until all weapons are in place or if he will detonate them as he receives the message that each weapon is in place. We may not have much time."

"Yes, you're right. If you'll excuse me, I'll get off the phone and start trying to get search teams mobilized. Thanks for your suggestion. Goodbye Admiral."

"Good luck, David."

David buzzed Al Flores immediately and asked him to contact the NYPD to see if they could send in their best bomb squads to search the JP Morgan Chase and Citigroup buildings. He buzzed Tiera and asked her to provide a status update to everyone and to ask Nahbi to be available for a call. He then called Sir Lionel and Gordon and linked their numbers together using his phone's conferencing feature.

"See if Nahbi has any suggestions," Sir Lionel said immediately. "I don't like to even think about what Admiral Green pointed out. We've been assuming that General Jhalawan would wait until all devices were in place before sending a detonation signal. If Admiral Green is right, detonation in New York could come at any time."

"Yes sir. I've already asked Tiera to brief Nahbi and ask him to be available for my call. I'll call him as soon as we hang up."

"I hope the American President is right about Jhalawan's intentions, though I don't think he is," Sir Lionel told them. "Gordon, what's your take on this?"

"I would guess that Jamel el-Masri and Franco Rinaldi are heading for the airport already. Even though it's not rush hour, traffic is always heavy in lower Manhattan and especially through the Holland Tunnel so it could take them a while to get there. Pete Nocona arranged for police officers to watch the airplane. It's all a matter of timing now. If the surveillance team can take them into custody, we might be able to extract the information from them about where the weapon has been placed so we can get the Army EOD team there in time to disarm the device. I think we'll be cutting it pretty close."

Langley, Virginia; CIA HQ
5:45 PM

"Pete, this is Roger. David's suggestion worked. Jamel and Franco were just arrested at the Linden airport." Pete listened to the details and then thanked his boss and immediately called David.

"David, Pete. We finally got a break. I just got a call from Roger Benson. The surveillance team you asked me to have posted at the Linden airport just took Jamel el-Masri and Franco Rinaldi into custody. Jamel is still tight-lipped, but Franco is singing like a canary. He says the scuba tank is in room 4805 in the Marriott Marquis Hotel at 1535 Broadway. That's smack-dab in the middle of the Times Square area and less than a mile from the JP Morgan Chase and Citigroup headquarters buildings. It's also less than a mile from the Empire State Building."

"Thank God. I'll alert the Army EOD team immediately," David said as he hung up.

David put on his headset and touched the button on the side to connect to the Army EOD team leader in New York.

"Hello. Who's this?"

"This is David Logan in London. The bomb is in the Marriott Marquis Hotel at 1535 Broadway. I'll call the hotel manager but you shouldn't wait for them to unlock the room if I can't get through. I'll stay on the net until you've disarmed the device. Sing out if you need anything. Good luck."

"We're rolling. Be in touch."

David raised his arm and waved it in a circular motion to signal to the rest of the TF3 team that he was moving down the hall to the video monitoring room. He picked up the MI6 wireless phone and dialed Sir Lionel as he went.

They didn't have any video feeds from the Marriott hotel so they would be blind until the EOD team arrived and the team leader switched his headband camera on. David could hear the team leader giving orders. One of his men asked if they should go get one of the metal tables. The team leader said no, they had enough grounding clips and wrist bands in their kit. They could ground to the bathroom plumbing or any of the three-prong outlets in the room.

Sir Lionel and Gordon came into the room a few moments later. David was busy making calls and giving orders so Sir Lionel stood beside Tiera to watch and listen.

"I need to speak to the hotel manager at once," David said to the Marriott hotel operator.

"May I tell her who is calling?"

"Tell her that the Director of the British Foreign Intelligence Service would like to speak to her on an urgent matter," David said as he glanced in Sir Lionel's direction.

"Hello, this is Mrs. Schreiber. Can I help you?"

"Mrs. Schreiber, my name is David Logan. I am working with the CIA and other law enforcement agencies to stop a terrorist plot to detonate several bombs. I am calling you from the Secret Intelligence Service building in London. I am working for Sir Lionel Smythe, the Director of MI6. He is standing a few feet from me at this very moment."

"Please listen carefully. There is a terrorist bomb in your hotel. Within the next few minutes, an explosive ordnance disposal team from the U.S. Army will arrive in your lobby. They need immediate access to room 4805 that has been occupied for several days by Jamel el-Masri and Franco Rinaldi. Those men have left the hotel without checking out. I'm sure they left a do not disturb sign on their door."

"Please do not order an evacuation of the building. It is unnecessary and there's no time anyway. This is the second one of these bombs we've discovered today and the EOD team knows exactly how to disarm it. A mass exodus of the building could interfere with the EOD team's work. This should all be over within thirty minutes. I'd like for you to stay on the line in case we need to coordinate with you on something. I'm going to ask Al Flores of the CIA to stay on the line with you. He can answer any questions you may have."

David then called Nahbi.

"Hello my friend. We are a bit busy at the moment. The New York bomb is not in one of the bank buildings. The police surveillance team arrested Jamel el-Masri and Franco Rinaldi at the Linden

airport a little over an hour ago. Franco told them that the bomb is in the Marriott Marquis Hotel in Times Square. The EOD team and law enforcement officers are on the way to the hotel now. Are you where you can listen and watch in case I need your help?"

"Yes."

"Good. We need to talk."

As David hung up, the digital camera feed from the EOD team leader came up on the screen. The man had obviously realized that the network was blind and had switched his camera on. He was walking through the hotel lobby toward the elevator. Four minutes later, his camera showed him standing in front of the door to room 4805 and swiping a magnetic key card to unlock it.

The EOD team found the scuba tank behind the curtains on the right side of the picture window. One of the EOD specialists laid a thin aluminum sheet on the coffee table and attached a grounding wire between it and a screwdriver inserted into the grounding pin of one of the room's electrical receptacles.

Twenty-two minutes after David had taken the call from Pete Nocona, the EOD team leader began the disarming procedure. As before, the team at MI6 could only watch and pray.

Removal of the antenna and unscrewing the top of the tank went smoothly. They all watched as the EOD team leader pulled the detonator, control module, and cell phone assembly from the tank and braced it on the table so he could work on the toggle switches.

"OK, I'm ready to begin changing the toggle switches," he announced. Just as the EOD team in Frankfurt had been, the American team was methodical and careful as they followed the checklist that Tariq Zardari had provided. The first few switch changes were made safely.

"*Stop!*" the backup technician suddenly shouted. "That's wrong. Blue toggle number 7 should be moved to the *off* position, *not* toggle number 8. I say again, blue 7 should be moved to the off position."

"Roger. I am about to move blue 7 to the off position," they all heard the team leader say in a perfectly calm voice.

"That is correct. Proceed to move blue 7 to the off position."

The rest of the disarming procedure was finally completed twenty-nine minutes after the EOD team leader had removed the antenna to begin the procedure.

"*Alpha X-Ray*," he announced. "This witch is dead."

As before, applause erupted in the basement of the MI6 building. Sir Lionel gave a similar speech to the one he'd made earlier.

David walked across the room to where Pete Nocona was standing.

"Pete, I thought we would lose New York when the Jasmine message went out and we didn't know where the device was. The surveillance team you set up saved the day."

"Thanks, David. I'll pass that along. You know, my dad used to say that sometimes it's better to be lucky than good. Maybe we were a bit of both today although I've never liked the word luck. I always tell my people that if they insist on using that word around me, then I insist on defining it as *preparation meeting opportunity*. You provided the leadership to get everyone in place to take advantage of whatever opportunities arose."

David's next call was to Nahbi.

"Nahbi, I assume you were able to watch and listen."

"Yes. Your direction to have the aircraft watched certainly paid off."

"Look, I need for you to run some probability analyses for me. I've been thinking that Jhalawan might wonder why he hasn't received a Jasmine message from any of the European cities yet. It's been almost twelve hours since the *Light and Knowledge* message went out. Even though he allowed 48 hours for the agents to put the devices in place, he and Malik are too smart not to notice that none of the European cities have transmitted *Jasmine* yet. He might start to worry. Do you think he might get nervous and trigger the London and Paris devices without waiting for the *Jasmine* signals? I realize that you don't have a lot of objective data to work with but your probability analysis is the best we've got at this point."

"Yes, I'll create a logic matrix using what we do know and filling in the voids with my best guesses. I'll get back to you within an hour."

David then asked to speak to Sir Lionel and Gordon in private.

“I am concerned that Jhalawan may get nervous because he hasn’t received any *Jasmine* messages from Europe almost twelve hours after his *Light and Knowledge* message went out. I’ve asked Nahbi to run a probability analysis. I’ll have his input within an hour.”

“I’ve been wondering if perhaps we should send a fake *Jasmine* message for Frankfurt just so Jhalawan will see some progress. But, if we do, he might try to detonate the Frankfurt device. If he did, he’d quickly realize that nothing happened. In that event, I think he’d probably send detonate signals to the other devices immediately.”

“There’s something else bothering me. I think there’s a risk that he’s already sent a detonate message to New York City since he did receive a *Jasmine* reply from Jamel’s cell phone. If he did try to trigger the New York device, and he doesn’t see media coverage of the detonation, I’m afraid he might realize that we’re making progress in locating and disarming the devices. If he thinks that, I feel certain he’ll trigger the other devices. That could happen at any time.”

“We don’t know who his other agents are. We don’t know what expectations Jhalawan may have regarding how long it should take each agent to put his device in place. I’m very concerned that we could still lose London and Paris if we don’t make the right decisions here. I would welcome any thoughts the two of you may have.”

The old spy-master took several moments to consider what David had said. When he finally spoke, his wisdom and decades of experience were evident in his reply.

“It really comes down to two questions. First, have we done a better job of maintaining secrecy or has Ahmed Malik done a better job of gathering the pertinent information Jhalawan needs to make his decisions? I think we must assume that Ahmed Malik knows quite a lot about Task Force 3 and he certainly knows that TF3 won the first round with the interception of the Belle Maria. But, that doesn’t mean that he’s privy to everything we’re doing. I’m fairly

confident that Malik doesn't yet know anything that would cause him to advise Jhalawan to detonate immediately."

"Second, do we think Jhalawan wants to detonate the devices as they are ready or will he wait until all are in place so he can have a massive display of destruction? What are your thoughts Gordon?"

"I think there may be a clue in what Akil El-Sayed has written in criticism of Osama bin Laden for not striking a mortal blow. Jhalawan sent Ambassador Al-Zeid to probe El-Sayed's thinking on the subject. Jhalawan is a man with a very big ego. I think he will prefer a single, massive blow. He is a master tactician but he is also a warrior. To use a boxing analogy, I think he will prefer a knock-out blow to winning on points. Unless he becomes aware of our progress, I think he'll wait until he's received *Jasmine* messages for all of the devices. My advice is to sit tight. Don't send any fake *Jasmine* messages, at least not yet. The situation could change but for now I think we ought to keep doing what we're doing. We don't want to outsmart ourselves."

"I think Gordon's right," Sir Lionel said. "I'd say hold off on sending any false *Jasmine* messages."

"Thank you both. I'll see what Nahbi comes up with."

Forty-five minutes later, Nahbi called.

"David, the decision matrix is inconclusive because so many critical data points are unknown. I cannot assign a realistic probability to the question of whether General Jhalawan might detonate each device when he receives the *Jasmine* message or whether he will wait until all weapons are in place. What does Sir Lionel think?"

"He and Gordon think Jhalawan will wait until they are all in place."

"What are your instincts telling you?"

"I think they're right. Lacking any better decision rationale, I've decided to take the risk and wait."

Tuesday, June 24

London, Canary Wharf
10:20 AM

One of the security cameras being monitored by MI6 showed a delivery truck backing up to the loading dock at the back of the One Canada Square building at Canary Wharf. The sign on the side of the truck identified it as belonging to the Croydon Industrial Lighting Company. A moment later, the driver got out and climbed the stairs at the end of the loading dock. He pressed a button on the intercom box mounted at the end of the platform. He waited until the rollup door began to open before raising the door at the back of his truck. He disappeared inside the truck and then emerged with a wooden crate on a motorized pallet dolly. He closed the truck's cargo door and then guided the pallet jack into the building. A moment later, the building's rollup door closed. Thirty seconds later the officer watching the loading dock area finally keyed his microphone.

The officer on duty at the front desk was a London Metropolitan Police Service veteran named Ted Freeman. He had been with the MPS Counter Terrorism Command, SO15, since it was formed by the merger of the Special Branch and the Anti-Terrorist Branch. He was one of London's top anti-terrorist specialists.

When Freeman heard the tell-tale clicks, he asked for more information. The officer outside described what he'd just seen and admitted he'd hesitated because the wooden crate looked too big to be what they were watching for.

Freeman went immediately to the service delivery area but couldn't find the delivery truck driver. He then noticed that the freight elevator had stopped at the pyramid on top of the building where the maintenance plant was located.

"This is Freeman. I need a backup in the service delivery area immediately"

Forty-five seconds later, another officer joined him. Freeman told him to remain in the delivery area in case the delivery truck driver came back down.

Unsure of what he'd find when he reached the maintenance area, and unwilling to be an easy target when the service elevator door opened, Freeman took the regular passenger elevator to the floor just below the pyramid and used the stairs to get to the maintenance plant area. When he entered the maintenance plant area, he saw the delivery truck driver standing beside a building maintenance employee who was signing some paperwork on a clipboard.

"Good morning," he said to the two men as he walked toward them. "The security system didn't have a record of a scheduled delivery this morning so I've come up to make sure everything is OK."

"No problem," the maintenance employee said. "This is a crate of high-intensity bulbs for the aircraft warning lighting on top of the pyramid. Replacing them is very labor-intensive and dangerous so we replace them all at once when they reach 50% of their rated life."

"If you don't mind, could I verify the contents of the crate?"

"Well, sure. I guess there's no harm in that. I've got to open the crate anyway."

The delivery man reached inside his pocket and took out a cell phone. Freeman instantly drew his pistol and told the driver to freeze. The driver hesitated for a moment but didn't press the send key on the phone.

"Lay the phone down on the floor and put your hands up."

The driver did as he was told. Freeman called for backup and then handcuffed the driver and made him lie face down on the floor.

When he looked around to see where the maintenance employee was, Freeman saw that he was pointing a pistol at him.

"Drop your weapon. Now!" the maintenance employee barked.

Freeman did as he'd been told.

"Lay down on the floor."

At just that moment, the door from the staircase opened and two security officers entered. The maintenance employee opened fire instantly, hitting one of the officers in the shoulder. The other security officer fired a classic double tap at the maintenance employee's chest. He was dead when he hit the floor.

Freeman keyed his microphone at once. "Officer down! We need a medical team in the maintenance area inside the pyramid at the top of One Canada Square STAT! One bad guy fatality. Standby for ID of the contents of a suspicious crate."

After putting a handkerchief on the shoulder wound to stop the bleeding and verifying that their fellow officer was stable, Ted Freeman and the other officer opened the crate. Inside were large light bulbs in cardboard boxes cushioned in cellulose packing material. When they removed several of the boxes, they saw the shiny CO_2 tank that had been concealed on the bottom layer.

Freeman keyed his microphone. "We have the package under control. Mobilize the EOD team to the maintenance plant in the pyramid at the top of One Canada Square."

Twelve minutes later, the EOD team arrived and began getting ready to disarm the weapon. The EMTs showed up three minutes later to take the wounded officer to the hospital.

There was a heavy steel table in a work area at one side of the maintenance plant area. It was a perfect.

Thirty-one minutes later, the EOD team leader pulled the fissile core out of the CO_2 tank.

"Bravo X-Ray," he said into his microphone. "Who's buying tonight?"

Sir Lionel congratulated the team and told the EOD team leader to take his men out for a nice dinner and to send him the bill. David never heard how big the bill was and Sir Lionel never said.

London, MI6 HQ
12:30 PM

The TF3 team assembled in their conference area at David's request. Nahbi was hooked in via the teleconferencing link and both Sir Lionel and Gordon had joined them. David didn't leave them wondering what was on his mind for long.

"We got lucky. It never dawned on us that the Muslim Brotherhood might have an agent inside the building too. We've been going on the assumption that there might be several outside observers and just one delivery agent. Only quick thinking and fast

action by the embedded law enforcement officers saved London today. Had Ted Freeman not recognized the delivery truck driver's intent when he went for his cell phone, or if the other two officers hadn't reacted instantly to the maintenance employee's shot, the device would almost certainly have been detonated. From the relative safety of our basement bunker here in the MI6 building, we would have survived. Several million Londoners wouldn't have."

There were sober looks on everyone's face as the full impact of David's words sank in.

"There's still one more weapon somewhere in Paris. I want an immediate, top-to-bottom review of everything we have in place."

"Nahbi, I'd like for you to review the potential target buildings again. Do whatever probability analysis you need to do. I want to be sure that we haven't overlooked any building that might be the target destination for this last weapon."

"Phil, I want you and Al to review our surveillance postings. Coordinate with Nahbi in case he adds any buildings to our surveillance list. Work with the Paris police to beef it up if there's any doubt about the sufficiency of our surveillance postings.

"Gordon, I'd like for you and your staff to check our communication links and the backup channels. If there are any holes, let's get them plugged."

"Tiera, I want you and Gabe to contact the human resources departments for the building managers. Tell them we're looking for anyone who might have a suspicious background or links to any subversive or known terrorist organizations. This will be time consuming so get right on it. You'll probably have to keep the pressure on the HR departments so they don't brush it off as routine or unimportant."

"We don't need to get back together to debrief these action items unless something really important comes up as you're doing your reviews and coordination. Send a text message or call me if you come across something you think I need to know."

As the team left the conference area to get started on their assignments, David walked over to Sir Lionel.

"Sir, if you wouldn't mind, I'd like for you to have your assistant set up a conference call linking you with Roger Benson, Levi Reznik, and the Director of the DGSE in Paris. Please ask their thoughts about anything they think we should be doing that's not already either in place or underway. I'd like to take advantage of their experience and intuition. I have a nagging feeling that we've overlooked something but I can't put my finger on it."

Paris, Montparnasse Tower
2:15 PM

The manager of the Le Ciel de Paris restaurant stepped out of the elevator from the underground parking garage onto the ground floor and walked to the security desk in the lobby.

"Bonjour, Henri. How is your family?"

"Very well, sir. Thank you for asking."

"Henri, I need a two-wheeled dolly to carry some file boxes from my car to my office. Is there one available?"

"I'll call the building maintenance foreman on the radio. He'll know."

"Jacob, this is Henri. Do we have a two-wheeled dolly that Monsieur Nabil can use for a few minutes?"

"Yes, there's one in the ground-floor janitor's closet. Just be sure to put it back when he's done."

"Merci."

Aziz Nabil thanked the guard before taking the elevator back to the underground parking garage. When he got to his car, he stood the dolly upright behind the back of the SUV and placed a cardboard file box with a ten-inch diameter hole cut in its top on the dolly's base shelf. He looked around to be sure no one was watching and then slid a heavy polished tank out of the back of the SUV onto the tail gate. He positioned his body so he could tip the tank while still letting the tail gate support most of the weight. When he was ready, he took a deep breath and carefully lowered the tank into the hole on the top of the file box.

He then put two other cardboard boxes with holes in both their bottoms and their tops over the tank. The fourth box had a hole in

the bottom but not its top. He then lifted a heavy box containing file folders from the SUV and sat it on top of the stack already on the dolly. He adjusted the position of the boxes to stagger them slightly from one another to make it obvious that they were not connected to further camouflage the fact that the boxes concealed the tank. When he was satisfied with how it looked, he closed the hatchback door and locked the SUV."

He waved to the security guard when he got off of the elevator at the ground floor. He pressed the call button for the high-speed elevator that would take him to the restaurant.

"Do you need any help Monsieur Nabil?"

"Non merci."

The doors opened and he rolled the dolly into the elevator car. He pressed the button for the 56th floor and the doors closed. Forty-two seconds later, the doors opened in the entry foyer of the restaurant. He knew the kitchen staff was already at work baking and preparing salads and desserts for the evening but he didn't meet anyone on the way to his office. He closed the door and locked it behind him. He then tilted the dolly slightly and slid the stack of boxes off onto the floor in the corner.

He sat down at his desk and took his cell phone from his coat pocket. He already had the text message ready to go. All he had to do was press the send key. He looked around one last time and then hit the button to transmit the message. He locked his office door as he left.

Two minutes later, he returned the dolly to the security guard at the front desk and thanked him for his help. He then took the elevator back to the garage and left the building.

London, MI6 HQ
2:40 PM

David saw that the incoming call was from Admiral Green at NSA.

"Hello Admiral. Do you have something for us?"

"Yes. Eight minutes ago, we intercepted a *Jasmine* text message addressed to the cell phone number in Pakistan. The message

originated in the 14th Arrondissement in Paris which suggests it probably came from the Montparnasse Tower."

"That's not good news. I've been monitoring the surveillance team signals. None of them have seen anything suspicious. This means that someone got the weapon into the building without it being recognized. Thanks for the heads up. I'll be in touch."

David then called the senior law enforcement office embedded in the building security force at the Montparnasse Tower.

"This is David Logan at MI6. It looks like the device is already in the building. The *Jasmine* message went out ten minutes ago. Have any of your officers seen anything at all that might conceivably have been the weapon?"

"No. There are dozens of deliveries to this building every day but nothing that's come in from the service delivery area has been in the least suspicious."

"Has anything come in through the main entrance that might be what we're looking for?"

"No," the officer said slowly as though he was thinking about something. "About fifteen to twenty minutes ago, the manager of the restaurant took some file boxes up to his office. It was a stack of those cardboard boxes used to store file folders. I saw the stack of boxes on the dolly but didn't think anything of it. But, in light of what you just told me, it is certainly possible that the device could have been concealed in the stack of boxes. The manager left the building about ten minutes after he took the boxes up."

"OK. Get one of your other officers to cover the main entrance. Take the regular security guard with you. Be sure he has his master keys with him and go search the restaurant, starting with the manager's office. I'll stay on the line. Hurry, we may not have much time."

Eleven minutes later, the officer reported that he'd found the CO_2 tank hidden inside the stack of cardboard file boxes in the manager's office.

David heard the EOD team leader tell his men to move out over the network as he waved to the TF3 team and headed for the video monitoring room. By the time he got there, the screen showed the

EOD team walking quickly across the entry foyer of the building. Two minutes later, the EOD team leader switched his headband camera on so they could see what was happening.

The EOD team swept everything off of the manager's desk and laid a flexible sheet of fabric woven from fine aluminum wires over it. A few moments later, the grounding wires were in place and the device was lifted onto the desk. Watching from the basement of the MI6 building, David and the rest of the TF3 team saw the cylinder braced to keep it from rolling and then saw the EOD team leader remove the antenna from its spring clip retainer. Sir Lionel and Gordon arrived just as the top of the cylinder was being removed.

The EOD team leader pulled the assembly consisting of the detonator, the control module, and the cell phone from the tank and braced them on the table. They heard him say that he was ready to begin making the changes to the toggle switches. They all saw him put the tip of a small flat-blade screwdriver against Toggle number 1 of the Red DIP switch, one of the toggles that was *not* supposed to be moved. Before his backup teammate could say anything to stop him, they all heard the EOD team leader shout *Allāhu Akbar* a tiny fraction of a second before the screen went blank.

David stared at the blank screen for several seconds and then dropped to his knees. Tears ran down his cheeks as he asked God to comfort those who had just lost their loved ones. Tiera came and knelt beside him and laid her cheek on his shoulder. One by one, every other person in the room knelt too.

Epilogue

It was indeed *Autre Jour d'Infamie* — another day of infamy. In a few terrible moments, an area of thirty square miles at the center of the City of Light was destroyed.

The people and buildings in the immediate vicinity of the Montparnasse Tower were vaporized by temperatures that reached several million degrees Fahrenheit within one millionth of a second following detonation. The blast crater was several hundred meters in diameter. The shock wave heated the air so much that it became intensely luminous and the resulting fireball was visible from miles away.

Early estimates from French civil defense authorities put the immediate death toll at two to three million people. Many more would die later from radiation sickness, burns, and tissue damage caused by the massive burst of neutron radiation.

Remarkably, the Eifel Tower was still standing although so severely damaged that it would have to be demolished.

Located less than two miles from the blast center, the 850-year-old Cathedral Notre Dame de Paris was totally destroyed.

The centuries-old Louvre museum was even closer to the blast center than Notre Dame. Most of the old palace that was above ground level was destroyed. French officials hoped that some of the priceless works of art in the below-ground galleries might eventually be recovered but Leonardo di Vinci's 500-year-old *Mona Lisa* and the 2,000-year-old Greek sculptures *Venus de Milo* and *Winged Victory of Samothrace* were gone forever.

Three miles from the blast center, the Arc de Triomphe de l'Étoile was badly damaged but still standing.

Most of the banks and financial institutions in the center of the city were either destroyed or so badly damaged that they would eventually be demolished.

While most of mankind mourned the cold-blooded murder of so many innocent people, millions of Muslims rejoiced and celebrated

just as they had after the attacks on the World Trade Center and the Pentagon.

In Gaza, crowds fired guns into the air and chanted anti-Israeli and anti-American slogans.

All across Northern Africa, crowds marched in celebration. In Egypt, more than a million people marched through the streets of Cairo chanting and displaying anti-American banners. Old grievances in Algeria made it easy to celebrate the death of so many of the hated French colonialists.

Throughout the Middle East, from Iraq and Iran to Oman and Yemen, huge crowds marched to celebrate Islam's glorious victory. Similar demonstrations and celebrations took place in Turkey, the Philippines, and throughout Indonesia.

Millions of poor Muslims had been manipulated, exploited, and brainwashed by radical Islamic clerics for decades while the west largely ignored the poison that was spreading.

On one horrible afternoon in late June, the world finally understood.

LIST OF CHARACTERS

Main Characters

David Logan	Former Army combat intelligence officer; Cambridge Ph.D. in Semitic Languages; Teira Aquilina's boyfriend
Teira Aquilina	Daughter of wealthy Malta banker; Cambridge Ph.D. in Computer Science; David Logan's girlfriend
Nahbi	American, British, and Israeli intelligence agencies doubt his astonishing claims despite his extraordinary capabilities
Lt. Gen. Jhalawan	Director of Pakistan's Inter-Services Intelligence Service (ISI)
Ahmed Malik	Head of ultra-secret ISI S-Wing

British Secret Intelligence Service (MI6)

Sir Lionel Smythe	Director of MI6
Gordon McFarland	Advanced Technologies Specialist
Philip Shaw	MI6 Field Agent

Central Intelligence Agency (CIA)

Albert Warren Oliver, III	Director of the CIA
Roger Benson	CIA Deputy Director, National Clandestine Service
Peter Nocona	Section Chief of the CIA Counter Terrorism Center
Alfonso Flores	CIA Field Agent

National Security Agency (NSA)

Stephen Green	Rear Admiral, U.S. Navy (Ret) Director of NSA
Evelyn Moore	NSA Chief of Station, London

Israeli Mossad

Levi Reznik	Sr. Intelligence Officer and Katsa
Gavriella Adler	Leader of Kidon team
Daniyel Shaltiel	Kidon team
Nathan Lavi	Kidon team
Avi Ben-Shimon	Kidon team

Russian Foreign Intelligence Service (SVR)

Raisa Kovalenko	Senior intelligence agent
Boris Rogozin	Intelligence agent
Sergei Kosygin	Director of SVR

German Federal Intelligence Services (BND)

Ralf Kohler	Field Agent

Chinese Ministry of State Security (MSS)

Tengfei Chén	A Chinese double agent for the Russian SVR

Malta Police Force (MPF)

Rico Massa	Anti-terrorism Officer
Margherita Palma	Director of the MPF Forensic Science Laboratory

INTERPOL

Grégoire Deveaux	Director of INTERPOL's anti-terrorism section in Lyon, France

Terrorists and Associates

Akil El-Sayed	Al Qaeda leader after Osama bin laden
Hassan Al-Zeid	Egyptian Ambassador to Pakistan; Member of Muslim Brotherhood
Yousef Abu Shakra	Ambassador Al-Zeid's driver and bodyguard; Muslim Brotherhood
Hakeem Ghanem	Ghanem Equipment Company owner; Muslim Brotherhood
Ibrahim Al-Jabiri	General Manager of Ghanem Equipment Company; Muslim Brotherhood
Franco Rinaldi	Nephew of Hakeem Ghanem; Muslim Brotherhood
Fredo Rinaldi	Nephew of Hakeem Ghanem; Muslim Brotherhood
Dr. Bashir Ghilzai	Pakistani Nuclear scientist
Tariq Zardari	Young nuclear engineer; Protégé of Dr. Ghilzai
Mohammed Ansari	Sergeant in Pakistan Armed Forces
Ibrahim Hasni	Corporal in Pakistan Armed Forces
Sulaiman el-Masri	Russian oligarch living in the United Kingdom
Jamel el-Masri	Playboy son of Sulaiman el-Masri; Muslim Brotherhood

Other Supporting Characters

Abramo Sartori	Italian yacht broker in Venice
Donatella Sartori	Abramo Sartori's wife
Sarah Clark	David Logan's older sister
Jim Clark	Sarah Clark's husband
Matthias Aquilina	Teira's father
Maria Aquilina	Teira's mother
Nicholas Aquilina	Teira's younger brother
Elena Scarlati	Teira's best friend
Jamila Al-Zeid	Beautiful young wife of Ambassador Hassan Al-Zeid
Teresa Giachetti	Italian prostitute (Lucciole or Firefly)

Lia Pedrazzini	Italian prostitute (Lucciole or Firefly)
Signor Enrico Favaloro	Sicilian Mafia boss
Carlos Vento	Sicilian Mafia assassin
CDR Reginald Burton	Commanding Officer, HMS Sutherland
Sir Theodore Macfarland	Governor and Commander-in-Chief of Gibraltar British Overseas Territory
RADM Lloyd Hooker	Commander of Task Force 60
Mark Hays	Navy Lieutenant and member of SEAL Team Eight
CWO3 Russell Clark	Pilot and Commanding Officer, Navy P-3 Orion based at NAS Sigonella
Ted Freeman	Sergeant in the London Metropolitan Police Service
Abner Myerson	Lieutenant Colonel commanding the Israeli submarine Tekumah

65482808R00245

Made in the USA
Charleston, SC
22 December 2016

SORTIE
LABO
BUREAU
ffière
Cocher
Affort

4

PAS FACILE DE SE FAIRE UN TABLEAU !

Au cours de la nuit dernière, la galerie d'art d'Aimé Voulard a été cambriolée et la toile la plus chère, une peinture de Paolo Pixaco, a été dérobée. En découvrant ce matin le vol, le galeriste sollicite aussitôt l'aide de Maroni.
– Le voleur a su neutraliser le système d'alarme mais il n'a pas vu ma caméra de sécurité. L'appareil tourne autour d'un axe central et prend un cliché toutes les 30 secondes. Ainsi, rien ne lui échappe de ce qui se passe dans la galerie. Regardez vous-même !
Le galeriste étale sur son bureau sept photos prises pendant la nuit. Maroni les classe par ordre chronologique et les étudie avec soin.
– Trois des quatre personnes que l'on voit sur ces photos n'ont rien à voir avec le vol, conclut-il. C'est la quatrième qui a fait le coup.
– Sans aucun doute, renchérit Aimé Voulard. D'ailleurs, sa silhouette me fait penser à José-Jean Porte, un marchand d'art peu scrupuleux, pour ne pas dire crapuleux. Il m'envie mon Pixaco, il a d'ailleurs déjà cherché à me le racheter pour une somme ridicule. J'ai refusé. C'est un bon motif pour venir me le voler, vous ne trouvez pas ?
Le commissaire préfère se faire sa propre opinion. Sur sa demande, Aimé l'emmène chez le marchand d'art. Un simple coup d'œil suffit à Maroni qui murmure en souriant :
– L'affaire est claire. Il ne reste plus qu'à arrêter le coupable.

QUESTION

José-Jean Porte est-il vraiment le voleur du Pixaco ?

. . . .

Vendu
J.-J. PORTE

5

UNE ERREUR DE MONTAGE

– Lentement l'objet étrange achevait son vol fantomatique pour venir atterrir à une petite trentaine de mètres de moi.
L'assistance est pendue aux lèvres de Charles Hattan, le soi-disant grand spécialiste des objets volants non identifiés. Ses conférences sur les ovnis attirent les foules tout en suscitant la colère des scientifiques. Pour eux, l'homme n'est qu'un fieffé escroc qui abuse de la crédulité de son public.
– En voilà la preuve ! s'exclame le conférencier en faisant apparaître sur l'écran l'image de l'ovni.
Ébahis, les spectateurs retiennent leur souffle. Parmi eux se trouve ce soir le commissaire. Non pas parce qu'il croit aux extraterrestres mais pour mettre un terme aux affabulations de Charles Hattan qui rapportent gros à ce dernier. Maroni cherche à prouver que, loin d'être authentiques, les photos montrées par le pseudo-spécialiste sont en vérité d'habiles montages. Des montages si bien faits que notre commissaire a failli s'y laisser prendre. Or, tout à coup, un détail lui saute aux yeux.
– L'affaire est claire ! Charles Hattan, c'est la fin de votre carrière !

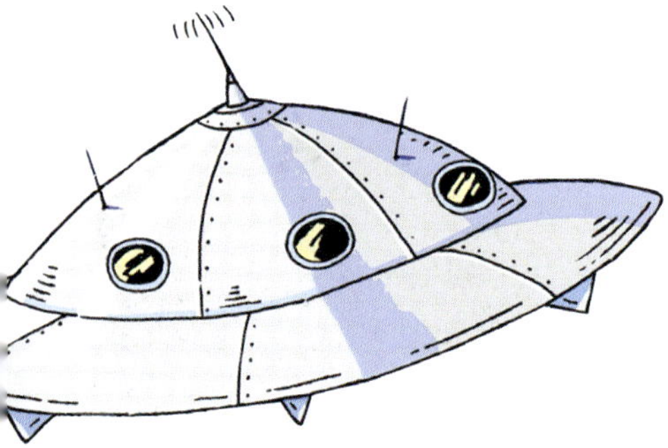

QUESTION

Qu'est-ce qui prouve que la photo a bien été falsifiée ?

....

Charles
Hattan

6

MAUVAIS RÉGLAGE OU BIEN SABOTAGE ?

Sept heures du matin. Éric Raque, directeur de l'entreprise Machinox, convoque ses deux chauffeurs, Aurèle et Larbi, dans son bureau.
– Il faut absolument que le chargement soit chez Amotech avant 17 heures. Sinon nous perdons notre meilleur client. Ce serait grave !
Les deux hommes démarrent, avec Larbi au volant. Avant l'entrée sur l'autoroute, ils s'arrêtent à une station-service. Larbi lance la clé du réservoir au pompiste et court à la boutique pour payer. Aurèle somnole sur son siège. Peu après, ils reprennent la route. Au bout de quelques kilomètres, le moteur se met à tousser, puis le camion s'arrête net.
– Alors là, ça me dépasse, s'emporte Larbi, le camion est passé au garage pour la révision générale la semaine dernière seulement.
Il appelle Éric Raque. Le directeur est au bord de la crise de nerfs.
– C'est du sabotage ! Ne bougez pas, je vous envoie un expert.
Arrivé sur les lieux, Maroni inspecte le réservoir du camion.
– Quelqu'un a versé du sucre dedans, probablement pendant que vous étiez à la station-service. Vous n'avez rien remarqué ?
– Moi non, dit Larbi, j'ai couru payer le gazoil. Et toi, Aurèle ?
Son collègue hésite un instant, puis il déclare :
– J'ai baissé ma vitre pour faire entrer un peu d'air frais. En effet, il me semble avoir vu le pompiste penché sur le réservoir.
– L'affaire est claire, conclut le commissaire sans autre commentaire.

QUESTION

Qui, d'après Maroni, a fait le coup ?

7

NOM D'UN CHIEN !

Le commissaire est embêté. Sa tante Huguette est à l'hôpital et lui a confié ses souris dansantes japonaises. En plus, il doit les faire vacciner contre la grippe. Maroni aime bien sa tante, les souris un peu moins. À 8 heures 45, il s'assied avec sa cage dans la salle d'attente d'Ella Descros, la vétérinaire. Deux autres personnes s'y trouvent déjà, chacune avec un chien obèse à force d'avoir été trop copieusement nourri. La vétérinaire ouvre la porte de son cabinet et salue ses clients familiers :

– Bonjour, madame Lossamoile, bonjour, monsieur Dugras !

C'est alors que son regard tombe sur le placard vitré où sont rangés les médicaments. Son sourire s'estompe, son visage se rembrunit.

– Nom d'un chien ! s'écrie-t-elle, courroucée. Où sont passés les comprimés Mincetoutou ? J'en avais mis une douzaine de boîtes dans le placard en arrivant ce matin. Ils sont chers, ces comprimés.

– Je ne vous le fais pas dire, soupire Mme Lossamoile.

– Je dirais même qu'ils sont hors de prix, renchérit M. Dugras.

Pour le commissaire, l'affaire est claire. C'est la personne arrivée en premier au cabinet qui a volé les boîtes en question.

QUESTION

Qui a empoché les comprimés Mincetoutou ?

SORTIE
Animalia

8

MINE DE RIEN…

Maroni se réjouit. Un chocolat chaud et un bon livre, rien de tel pour se détendre ! Mais voilà que le téléphone sonne. C'est le chef de la police.
– Une urgence, Maroni ! Jimmy Lesbouts vient de se faire la malle. Il s'est enfui en direction de la vieille mine de charbon. Tous nos chiens sont déjà engagés dans une autre poursuite. Alors…
– Alors vous avez pensé à ma Truffette ? C'est bon, chef, on y va.
La petite chienne du commissaire bondit hors de son panier. Un mollet de mauvais garçon, ça vaut bien toutes les croquettes du monde !
Le fugitif a perdu en route sa casquette de prisonnier. Truffette la renifle, puis elle se met sur la trace de Jimmy Lesbouts. La piste mène effectivement à la mine désaffectée. Maroni réussit, non sans mal, à forcer la porte en fer rouillée. Dans la pénombre, un escalier taillé dans la roche plonge dans les profondeurs. Au bout des marches moussues s'ouvre une vaste salle d'où partent les entrées des différentes galeries de la mine. L'eau suinte des murs, formant des rigoles et des mares au sol.
– Un vrai labyrinthe, ces galeries, murmure Maroni. Jimmy Lesbouts doit s'être caché dans l'une d'elles. Vas-y, Truffette, trouve-le-moi !
La truffe frétillante, la petite chienne se met à courir d'une entrée de galerie à l'autre. Pour revenir enfin, la queue basse, de sa chasse infructueuse. Maroni sourit et la prend tendrement dans ses bras.
– Ne t'en fais pas, Truffette ! Grâce à ton flair, l'affaire est claire. Tu as éliminé toutes les galeries où Jimmy Lesbouts ne se trouve pas.

QUESTION

Dans quelle galerie le fugitif se tient-il caché ?

. . . .

Accès interdit
1
2
3
4

9

BIGRE DE BOUGRE DE CORNE D'AUROCHS !

Alerte au château de Roquenbol ! Le comte Waldemar O'Canar vient d'apprendre par le gardien Guy Laffauchey le vol du joyau de sa collection d'armes : le sabre d'or ayant appartenu à son aïeul, Geoffroy de Vaulaille. Une échelle posée contre le mur et une vitre cassée semblent indiquer de quelle façon le voleur s'est introduit dans la salle d'exposition. Waldemar O'Canar pousse un juron à faire trembler les poutres vermoulues du plafond. Il avait enfin trouvé un acheteur pour le sabre d'or, la pièce la plus précieuse de sa collection. La vente est prévue pour cet après-midi. L'argent du sabre d'or doit servir à restaurer le château quelque peu décrépit. Le comte est aux abois : le sabre disparu, pas de nouveau toit en vue. Il lance un appel au secours et Maroni accourt. En présence du comte et du gardien, le commissaire inspecte soigneusement le lieu du délit. Guy Laffauchey s'empresse de lui venir en aide :

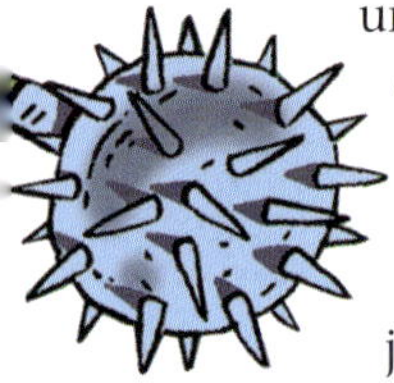

– D'après moi, le voleur est monté par l'échelle. Il a cassé la vitre, puis il est entré par la fenêtre. Ça s'est forcément passé cette nuit car quand j'ai fait ma ronde hier soir, tout était encore en ordre.

– Ça ne me surprend pas, réplique le commissaire. Pour moi, l'affaire est claire. Le voleur connaissait parfaitement les lieux, et il savait aussi à quel moment il pouvait frapper sans se faire prendre. Monsieur le comte, le coupable, c'est votre gardien, Guy Laffauchey.

QUESTION

Quel détail a troublé le commissaire ?

. . . .

10

QUI A SUCRÉ LE GÂTEAU DE TANTE HUGUETTE ?

C'est le soixante-quinzième anniversaire d'Huguette Parlafnette, la tante gourmande du commissaire. Depuis peu, elle habite une chambre à la maison de retraite Sanssouci. Maroni lui a fait livrer tôt ce matin un magnifique gâteau : un rêve de chocolat, de chantilly et de cerises confites. Huguette est aux anges. À 8 heures, elle se rend chez son amie Lucie à l'étage en dessous pour lui raconter sa bonne surprise. En retournant dans sa chambre dix minutes plus tard, elle manque de défaillir : le gâteau n'y est plus ! Huguette soupçonne aussitôt l'un ou l'autre de ses deux voisins d'en face avec lesquels elle ne s'entend pas très bien. Elle appelle son neveu.
– Ou bien c'est Adam Longue de la chambre 3 qui me l'a volé, ou bien c'est Jean Raivay de la chambre 5. Viens vite, je t'en prie !
Maroni soupire, il est en plein travail, mais finalement, c'est l'affection pour sa tante qui l'emporte. Arrivé à la maison de retraite, il interroge les deux hommes. Où étaient-ils à 8 heures ? Adam Longue dit avoir été en train de faire sa valise pour prendre le train l'après-midi et rendre visite à sa sœur. Quant à Jean Raivay, il affirme avoir allumé sa radio comme tous les matins à 8 heures pile pour écouter les informations.
Depuis le couloir, Maroni jette un coup d'œil dans les deux chambres.
– L'affaire est claire, conclut-il en se tournant vers Raivay. Désolé de vous déplaire, mais votre histoire ne tient pas debout.
À 8 heures, vous n'étiez pas devant votre poste de radio, mais vous vous apprêtiez à aller voler le gâteau de ma tante !

QUESTION

Comment le commissaire en est-il arrivé à cette conclusion ?

3
5
ÂGE D'OR
STAR

11

QUELQU'UN VA SE FAIRE TIRER L'OREILLE

Chez Morgane, la fête d'Halloween bat son plein. Monstres, sorcières, fantômes et autres personnages étranges s'amusent follement. En entrant dans le salon avec un plateau de sorbets à la citrouille, Morgane pousse un cri. Quelqu'un a défiguré le portrait de son arrière-grand-père en lui ajoutant avec un gros feutre une énorme moustache noire.

– Qui a fait ça ? demande-t-elle en rassemblant son sang-froid.

Silence penaud. Écœurée, elle appelle Maroni, un ami de la famille.

– Je serai là dans un petit quart d'heure, lui dit-il. En attendant, veille à ce que personne ne quitte la maison !

À son arrivée, Maroni scrute le tableau malmené ainsi que ses environs. Puis il commence à interroger les invités.

– Plus de mystère, l'affaire est claire, déclare-t-il soudain. Je sais qui a barbouillé le tableau.

QUESTION

Qui a menti au commissaire ?

....

12

RIEN QUE DU VENT !

Toute contente, Ella Dupot se présente chez le marchand de journaux. Le billet de loterie qu'elle a acheté hier est le numéro gagnant du gros lot. Seulement, impossible de retrouver le précieux billet ! Pourtant, Ella se souvient parfaitement de l'avoir mis dans son sac ce matin.

À quelque distance, elle remarque Michou Rave. Il semble absorbé par ses pensées. « Bizarre, se dit Ella, il était à côté de moi au kiosque tout à l'heure. Je ne me rappelle pas l'avoir vu acheter quelque chose. »

Elle va vers lui et lui demande si, par hasard, il n'aurait pas trouvé un billet de loterie. Michou feint la surprise, puis il s'exclame :

– En effet, le voilà ! Je ne savais pas que c'était le vôtre. Le vent l'a déposé à mes pieds. J'allais justement le rapporter au kiosque.

Ella ne croit pas un mot de ce qu'il lui dit. Maroni, qui passe à ce moment-là, entend la conversation. Pour lui, l'affaire est claire : Rave n'a pas pu trouver le billet par terre.

QUESTION

Qu'est-ce qui prouve
que le commissaire a raison ?

Mince alors ! Où est mon billet de loterie ?
UEC UN EURO
OUS GAGNEZ
GROS !
LA LOTERIE,
N'EST PAS QUE
R LES COCHONS !
UTOMOBILE
a tendance
st au vélo !
L'Étendard
C'est reparti !
L'Univers
Une pluie d'étoiles
«Le Monde est un vill
ZORRA
LE RETOUR
MANOLINO REVIENT
À L'ATTAQUE
BÉATRICE :
NON AU PRINCE
CHARMANT !
Magouilles
immobilières
concert
public
CUISINE
Hommage
au fromage !
Mon pays
Votre
beauté
GYMAX
MYSTÈRE
REVU
CHETS
HIPS
QUANTS

13

DE QUOI PERDRE LA BOULE !

Ce samedi matin, la célèbre voyante Véra Kivivra reçoit successivement la visite de trois personnes qui se font du souci pour leur avenir. Or, sa boule de cristal semble possédée par un esprit malin. Ce que Véra y voit n'est pas fait pour réjouir ses clients. Rien qui réconforte la jalouse Éva Pabien, l'étudiant Nicolas Sèche et le retraité Albert Ébasc. Pire encore ! La poisse s'attache même à la voyante, l'empêchant de lire dans sa boule de cristal que l'un des trois clients déçus reviendrait pour se venger…

Maroni se dépêche d'interroger les trois clients. Qu'ont-ils fait la veille ? L'affaire est claire, Maroni en a fait toute la lumière.

QUESTION

Qui a volé la boule de cristal ?

. . . .

14

ET HOP ! LA BERGÈRE EST EMBARQUÉE !

Cathy Mini est folle de figurines en porcelaine de Saxe. Seulement voilà, ces petites choses anciennes coûtent très cher et Cathy n'en a pas les moyens. Une fois de plus, en visitant une salle des ventes l'autre jour, elle n'a pas pu résister. Subrepticement, elle a glissé dans son sac une ravissante bergère et ses moutons blancs. Depuis, elle est introuvable. Maroni connaît bien le mauvais penchant de Cathy pour les bibelots de valeur. À plusieurs reprises déjà, il l'a poursuivie mais, à chaque fois, elle a réussi à lui filer entre les doigts. C'est alors que le commissaire apprend par une source anonyme que Cathy se cacherait dans la caravane de son cousin.

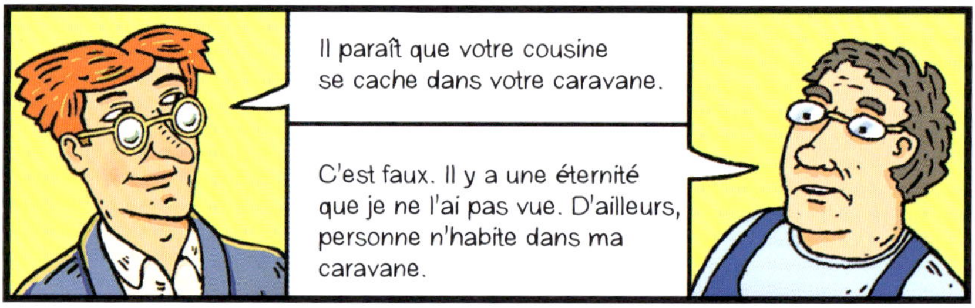

Et le cousin ajoute qu'en raison de sa mauvaise santé, lui-même n'est pas retourné dans sa caravane depuis l'été précédent. Maroni insiste pour la voir, le cousin l'emmène au camping « Les Coucous » où elle est garée.

– Allez-y, regardez partout ! dit le cousin avec un sourire jovial. Vous voyez bien que personne n'habite ici. Toutes les choses sont à la place où je les ai laissées l'été dernier.

– Hmm, murmure Maroni, désolé de penser le contraire. Pour moi, l'affaire est claire. Quelqu'un est venu ici très récemment.

QUESTION

Qu'est-ce qui prouve que le commissaire a raison ?

....

15

LA PÊCHE AUX POISSONS PY KHÊ

En arrivant chez Tristan Guille, Maroni n'y va pas par quatre chemins.
– Vous pêchez en eau trouble, monsieur, j'en ai l'intime conviction. Sachez que je ne sortirai pas d'ici sans avoir récupéré les deux poissons Py Khê que vous avez dérobés hier à l'exposition « Faune et flore des mers du Sud ». Il s'agit de spécimens très rares, interdits à la vente. On m'a fourni une description du suspect. C'est votre portrait tout craché !
– Vous croyez quand même pas que je vais gober ça, ricane Guille. Les poissons sont ma passion, monsieur le commissaire, je l'avoue. Mais comme vous pouvez le voir, tous mes aquariums sont pleins et je nage dans le bonheur. D'ailleurs, les poissons Py Khê ne supportent pas notre climat.
Maroni sourit. Tristan Guille vient de mordre à l'hameçon sans s'en être aperçu car des poissons exotiques enfermés dans un bocal sont insensibles au temps qu'il fait dehors. Les deux poissons Py Khê se trouvent donc bien dans l'un des aquariums. Ils sont parfaitement identiques, ce qui permettra de les repérer facilement. À moins que Tristan Guille ne les ait séparés par mesure de précaution.
– L'affaire est claire comme de l'eau de roche, déclare Maroni après un regard circulaire. Allez, dépêchez-vous de les repêcher !

QUESTION

Où Maroni a-t-il repéré les poissons Py Khê bicolores ?

....

16

UN PÈRE NOËL DOUBLÉ

Noël approche. Pour se faire de la publicité, le magasin de jouets Obokado a eu l'idée d'un démarchage à domicile par un de ses employés déguisé en père Noël. Le père Noël publicitaire, qui a annoncé sa visite, apporte aux enfants un petit cadeau surprise et… un catalogue de jouets. Ce soir, il est venu chez Léa et Léo. Ils l'attendaient en compagnie de leurs parents et de leur grand-père qui habite à l'étage au-dessus. Après sa visite, le grand-père a raccompagné le père Noël jusqu'à la porte d'entrée qu'il a fermée à clé pour la nuit. En regagnant son appartement, une mauvaise surprise l'attend : pendant son absence, un voleur s'est introduit chez lui et lui a dérobé sa montre en or !

Le grand-père appelle Maroni sur son portable et il lui explique :

– Léa et sa maman sont rentrées de la patinoire à 18 heures 30. Peu après et juste avant que la neige ne commence à tomber, Léo est rentré avec son papa qui était allé le chercher à l'école de musique. Le père Noël de chez Obokado est arrivé comme prévu à 20 heures.

Par une heureuse coïncidence, le commissaire, qui est en train de rentrer chez lui, se trouve justement dans les parages. Devant la maison de Léa et de Léo, il aperçoit deux pères Noël qui se disputent en se traitant l'un l'autre d'imposteur, de voleur, de moins que rien. Pour le commissaire, l'affaire est claire. Il met les menottes au voleur du grand-père.

QUESTION

Qu'est-ce qui trahit le coupable ?

17

17

Y A PAS PHOTO !

Le temps que Bibi Bling-Bling referme le coffre à bijoux dans l'arrière-boutique, quelqu'un a brisé la vitrine de sa bijouterie pour repartir avec un collier de diamants exposé. Alors que le bijoutier en colère téléphone à Maroni, un homme déboule en trombe dans son magasin.
– J'ai vu le type se sauver ! s'égosille-t-il. Mon nom est Dylan Tille, je suis photographe de mode. Avec mon équipe, j'étais en train de faire des prises de vue au coin de la rue quand tout à coup…
Bling-Bling lui demande d'attendre l'arrivée du commissaire.
– Nous avions presque fini avec les photos, raconte Dylan Tille à Maroni, quand nous avons entendu un bris de verre. Quelques instants après, j'ai vu un type avec une veste à carreaux tourner le coin en courant. Il est passé devant mon objectif au moment où je déclenchais. Il a réussi à s'enfuir mais j'ai pris sa photo !
– Vous pouvez me la remettre ? demande Maroni.
– Demain, quand j'aurai développé la pellicule au laboratoire.
Le lendemain, avec un large sourire, Dylan Tille remet à Maroni un tirage de la photo de l'homme à la veste à carreaux et les négatifs de la pellicule.
Maroni étudie le tout soigneusement puis il sourit à son tour :
– Vous êtes une équipe bien rodée à ce que je vois, mais votre mise en scène ne tient pas la route. Pour moi, l'affaire est claire, vous avez voulu distraire mon attention en inventant un coupable. C'est vous qui détenez le collier de diamants de Bibi Bling-Bling.

QUESTION

Maroni ne se trompe pas. Qu'est-ce qui le prouve ?

AGENCE DE
VOYAGES
AGENCE DE
VOYAGES
B. BLING-BLING
BIJOUTIER

SAFETY FILM 5063
3
3A
4
4A
5
5A
SAFETY FILM 5063
23A
24
24A

18

C'EST CLAIR ET NET

Alex Tenseur est hors de lui. Hier soir, pendant qu'il descendait la poubelle, quelqu'un a dû s'introduire chez lui pour lui voler son billet d'entrée au spectacle de body-building qui commençait à 21 heures. Alex soupçonne son voisin Justin Flache qui, lui, n'avait pas pu avoir de place. Justin est un passionné de la photo de nuit. Hier soir vers 20 heures, Alex l'a d'ailleurs vu monter l'escalier menant au toit, muni de son appareil et son trépied. Il décide d'appeler son ami Maroni au secours. Tous les deux se rendent chez Justin Flache. Quand Alex l'accuse ouvertement du vol du billet, le voisin se met en colère :

– Mais c'est inouï ! lui lance-t-il. Tu m'as vu toi-même monter sur le toit hier soir. Il y avait un ciel de rêve, entièrement dégagé. J'en ai profité pour faire quelques belles vues d'étoiles. Regardez, par exemple, cette photo de la Grande Ourse. Vous voyez comme elle est nette ? Pour la réussir, il m'a fallu un temps de pose de plus de trois heures. J'étais donc sur le toit jusqu'à onze heures passées. Je ne pouvais pas être au Palais des Sports en même temps !

Le commissaire ne se laisse pas faire. Pour lui, Flache ment éhontément, et c'est la photo qui le prouve !

– L'affaire et claire et plus nette encore que ce cliché, monsieur. Je crois bien que c'est vous qui avez pris le billet d'entrée.

QUESTION

Comment Maroni est-il arrivé à cette conclusion ?

CHAMPIONNAT
BODY-BUILDING
PALAIS DES SPORTS
12 mars 2010
Rangée 32 - Place 14

19

QUI A MARCHÉ SUR LES PLATES-BANDES ?

Il pleut à grosses gouttes depuis ce matin, et Philibert Poucevert se fait du souci pour ses parterres de fleurs. Quand le soleil revient en fin d'après-midi, le retraité sort dans son jardin. Il le trouve dans un piteux état. Par endroits, les fleurs sont écrasées et le gazon est abîmé. Dans le sol détrempé, il croit déceler des empreintes de pied. Pour Poucevert, l'affaire est claire : ce n'est pas la pluie qui a ravagé son jardin ! Il demande au commissaire de venir de toute urgence. Arrivé sur les lieux, Maroni contemple les dégâts, puis il se tourne vers Poucevert d'un air faussement ébahi :

– On dirait bien que des extraterrestres sont passés par là.

– Des extraterrestres ? Mais vous vous moquez de moi, monsieur le commissaire ! rouspète le retraité. Ceux qui ont fait ça, ce sont sûrement les gamins que vous voyez arriver là. Tous les jours, ils viennent jouer dans le pré là-bas.

Quand les garçons passent devant lui, Maroni indique le jardin dévasté :

– C'est vous qui avez fait ça ?

– Nous ? Mais pas du tout ! répondent-ils, la bouche en cœur. On a joué au foot dans le pré tout l'après-midi.

– Arrêtez, les garçons ! Vous me prenez pour un imbécile ?

QUESTION

Qu'est-ce qui trahit les massacreurs de plates-bandes ?

. . . .

20

DE QUOI DORMIR TRANQUILLEMENT SUR SES DEUX OREILLES

Isidore Miron-Zeureux, directeur de la célèbre entreprise Révondoux, s'arrache les cheveux. Une fois de plus, l'un des oreillers de la collection « Nuits au paradis » a quitté la chaîne de fabrication sans laisser de trace. Isidore y laisse des plumes car ces petites merveilles, promesses d'un sommeil sans pareil, coûtent une fortune : duvet d'oie surchoix, housse en soie du Cachemire, fermeture éclair en plaqué or.

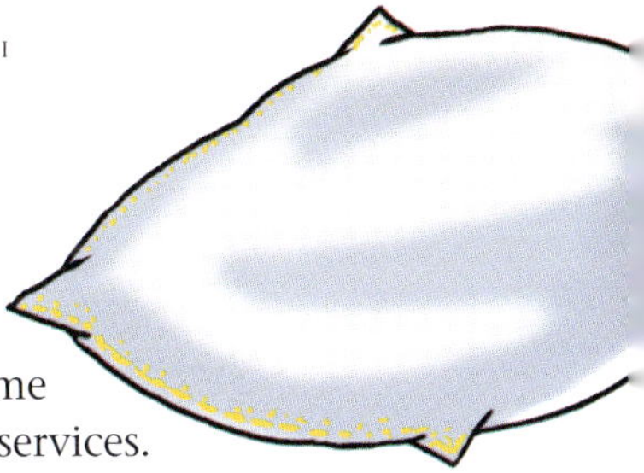

Maroni est introduit par le directeur dans l'usine comme simple visiteur. Le commissaire parcourt les différents services. Il se fait expliquer le travail que l'on y fait, tout en examinant discrètement les employés. À la fin de la journée, il rejoint Isidore Miron-Zeureux dans son bureau qui l'y attend avec impatience.

– Pour moi, l'affaire est désormais claire, dit le commissaire. J'ai deux nouvelles pour vous. L'une est mauvaise mais l'autre est bonne.
– Commencez par la mauvaise, Maroni, je vous en supplie !
– Le voleur a encore frappé aujourd'hui.
– Ça, pour une mauvaise nouvelle, c'en est une. Et la bonne ?
– Il ne frappera plus parce que je l'ai reconnu.

QUESTION

Qui est le voleur des oreillers « Nuits au paradis » ?

. . . .

21

DE QUOI SE FAIRE DES CHEVEUX !

Bal costumé à l'Hôtel Maxime ! Théo Palace, le directeur, a mis des vêtements de femme et une perruque verte. Le réceptionniste se précipite sur lui avec une enveloppe qu'il vient de trouver sur le comptoir. Elle contient une lettre anonyme accompagnée d'une photo. Théo Palace lit :

La photo ci-jointe a été prise tout à l'heure au Bar Biay. L'homme assis à la gauche d'Yvan Lamèche se nomme Bibi Goudis, celui à sa droite est un certain Tiffe. Lamèche veut revendre à l'un ou l'autre la formule secrète d'une lotion capillaire qu'il a volée aux laboratoires Opoal. À la vue d'un policier entrant dans le bar, Tiffe et Goudis sont restés tranquillement assis. Lamèche, qui avait encore la formule sur lui, a réussi à sortir par la porte arrière. Il s'est rapidement procuré un déguisement, et il se trouve maintenant mêlé à la foule dans votre salle de bal. Une bonne occasion pour le faire arrêter ! Signé : *Un ami qui doit rester dans l'ombre.*

– Nom d'une boule de cristal ! lâche Théo Palace à voix basse, je ne suis pas voyant. Comment savoir sous quel déguisement se cache l'énergumène ?

Heureusement son cher ami Maroni figure parmi ses invités ! Un coup d'œil sur la photo, un regard circulaire dans la salle, et le commissaire lève le mystère.

QUESTION

Qui est l'intrus et où se trouve-t-il ?

22

UNE COURSE POUR LA MONTRE

Betty Ketak n'est pas près d'oublier le jour où elle a dû constater que l'un de ses deux employés… Mais commençons par le commencement !
Donc, ce matin-là, lorsque Betty franchit le seuil de son horlogerie-bijouterie, ses deux employés, Nicolas Vence et Ethan Retarre, l'attendent déjà dans la boutique. Ils doivent réparer la précieuse montre-bracelet qu'un client a apportée la veille. Betty ouvre le coffre et blêmit : la montre n'y est plus ! Elle appelle Maroni à la rescousse. Le commissaire vérifie la porte d'entrée et les fenêtres du magasin : pas de marques d'effraction. Sur le coffre non plus : il n'a pas été forcé. Cela revient à dire que le voleur est l'un des deux employés, plus exactement celui qui est arrivé le premier à la boutique. Les deux s'offusquent et, la main sur le cœur, chacun prétend être arrivé après son collègue. Maroni remarque que la caméra de surveillance a été malmenée. Quelqu'un a tenté d'effacer toutes les images prises depuis l'ouverture de la boutique. Cependant, il en reste quelques-unes. Maroni les imprime pêle-mêle.

Il obtient un puzzle d'autant plus déroutant que la plupart des horloges du magasin ne sont pas en fonctionnement. Malgré tout, le commissaire finit par y voir clair, et il passe, clic-clac, les menottes au voleur.

QUESTION

Qui a mis dans l'embarras l'horlogère Betty Ketak ?

. . . .

23

UN RÉVEIL DE PRINCESSE

Miranda s'habille à toute vitesse. Dans le hall de l'hôtel, elle croise le commissaire, également en vacances, qui la salue d'un sourire.

– Bonne chance pour l'élection ! lui dit-il. Votre amie vient tout juste de partir pour la plage.

– Amanda ? Sans moi ? Mais comment ça ? Hier soir, quand elle est venue dans ma chambre, elle m'avait pourtant promis de passer me chercher. Maintenant, c'est trop tard, je ne serai pas princesse.

– Trop tard ? s'étonne Maroni, mais vous n'y êtes pas ! Regardez ma montre. Il est à peine 8 heures moins 20. Pour moi, l'affaire est claire. Miranda est venue vous voir hier soir dans l'intention de vous jouer un mauvais tour. C'est raté. Allez, courez ! Je suis sûr que vous ferez la plus charmante des princesses des sables.

QUESTION

Quel méchant tour la jalouse Amanda a-t-elle voulu jouer à Miranda ?

. . . .

24

BEAUCOUP DE BRUIT POUR RIEN

Maroni s'apprête à sonner chez le professeur Abel Halure lorsqu'il entend aboyer un chien derrière la porte.

– Tais-toi, Hercule ! tonne la voix du professeur. Bonjour, monsieur le commissaire ! Merci d'être venu aussi vite.

Halure fait entrer Maroni dans sa bibliothèque dont les murs sont recouverts de vitrines renfermant des livres anciens et des parchemins.

– Je venais de rentrer avec Hercule de notre promenade du soir, dit le professeur, lorsqu'en passant devant ma bibliothèque, j'ai entendu un bris de verre. Je me suis précipité sur la porte et j'ai vu un inconnu s'enfuir par le balcon en emportant le plus précieux des parchemins de ma collection.

La femme et le fils d'Halure les ayant rejoints, Maroni leur demande si, de leur côté, ils ont remarqué quelque chose de suspect.

– Nous étions dans la pièce à côté, répond l'épouse, quand soudain, nous avons entendu un bris de verre. Puis, ce fut de nouveau le silence. Lorsque nous sommes accourus, mon mari se tenait devant la vitrine brisée, en état de choc.

– Le parchemin était-il assuré ? demande Maroni.

– Oui, heureusement, soupire le professeur qui a l'air soulagé.

– Alors, pour moi, l'affaire est claire, dit le commissaire. C'est vous-même qui avez brisé le verre de la vitrine pour empocher l'argent de l'assurance.

QUESTION

Qu'est-ce qui a mis la puce à l'oreille de Maroni ?

25

LA VICTOIRE EN SE GRATTANT

C'est à peine croyable ! Dans la nuit précédant le match Belgique-France, un supporteur mal intentionné des Bleus s'est introduit dans le vestiaire des Belges. Muni de poudre à gratter, le saboteur en a enduit les maillots de l'équipe. But de la manœuvre : déconcentrer les joueurs, leur faire perdre le nord et, de ce fait, la partie. Or, le lendemain sur le terrain, c'est exactement le contraire qui se produit ! Excités par l'effet de la poudre, les Belges l'emportent par 5 à 0 !
Leur entraîneur ne s'en tient pas là. Il charge le commissaire d'élucider l'affaire des maillots gratteurs. Maroni examine les images prises par la caméra de surveillance placée dans le vestiaire. Bien qu'elles soient assez floues, il est rapidement sûr de son coup : l'une d'elles montre le sinistre individu qui avait voulu faire plier l'équipe belge.

QUESTION

Sur quelle image apparaît le coupable ?

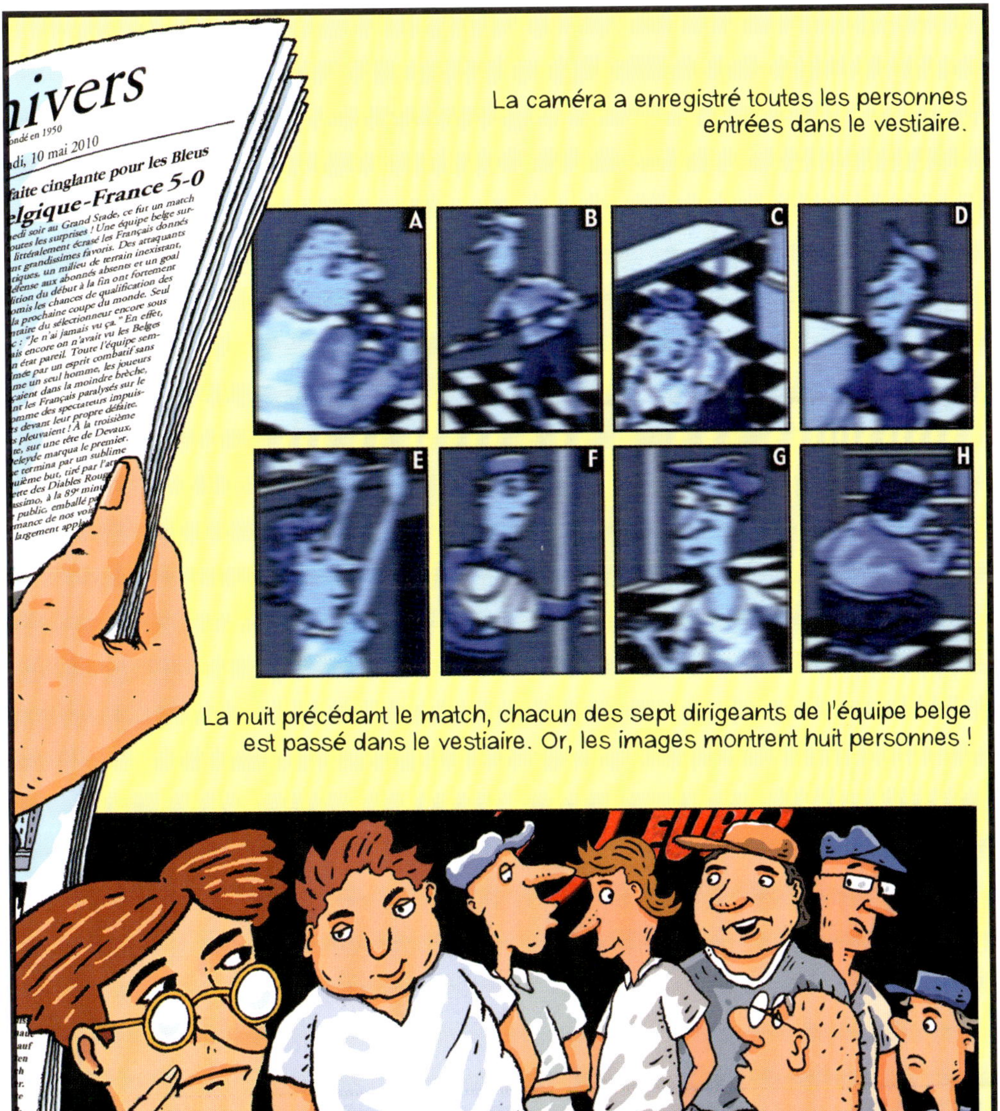
La caméra a enregistré toutes les personnes entrées dans le vestiaire.
A
B
C
D
E
F
G
H
La nuit précédant le match, chacun des sept dirigeants de l'équipe belge est passé dans le vestiaire. Or, les images montrent huit personnes !

26

SOURIS BLANCHES ET CARNET NOIR

Une fois par mois, le grand Gougloff invite chez lui ses collègues magiciens Malini et Bizzaro pour qu'ils puissent échanger leurs dernières trouvailles. Cette fois-ci, ô surprise ! même son redoutable rival, Don Miracolo, fait une brève apparition. Il présente son nouveau tour de magie, qui laisse les autres époustouflés.
À 21 heures, Don Miracolo prend congé. Il doit se préparer pour son spectacle au Ritz qui commence à 22 heures. En partant, il donne une tape amicale sur l'épaule de Gougloff, qui s'apprête à faire découvrir à ses invités sa toute dernière merveille jamais encore dévoilée.
Sur le plateau qu'apporte Gougloff se trouve une boîte minuscule. Après quelques gestes enchanteurs, le magicien en retire vivement le couvercle. Aussitôt cinquante souris blanches jaillissent de la boîte. Malini et Bizzaro sont charmés ! Satisfait, Gougloff arbore un large sourire qui se fige soudain. Son petit carnet noir de magicien, sur lequel il note ses tours et leur mise en œuvre, a mystérieusement disparu. L'un de ses confrères le lui aurait-il volé ? Maroni interroge d'abord Malini et Bizzaro, puis il court au Ritz. Don Miracolo monte sur ses grands chevaux et s'échauffe :
– Comment osez-vous me soupçonner ? Je suis parti de chez Gougloff à 21 heures, peu avant que ce dernier ne montre son tour de souris.
Plus de mystère pour le commissaire : l'affaire est dévoilée.

QUESTION

Qui a volé le carnet du grand Gougloff ?

27

MARONI N'EST PAS TOMBÉ DE LA DERNIÈRE PLUIE

Une pluie torrentielle vient se s'abattre sur la ville. Armand Dragore, le directeur du jardin botanique, est très inquiet. Dès les dernières gouttes tombées, il chausse ses bottes en caoutchouc et part inspecter ses plantes dont certaines sont particulièrement fragiles. Arrivé dans la section réservée aux plantes menacées d'extinction, Dragore se décolore. L'un des deux magnifiques exemplaires de *Calicia mirabilis* a été déterré. Qui a eu le toupet de voler cette fleur si rare ? En y regardant de plus près, le directeur aperçoit des traces de pied qui mènent au trou creusé par le voleur. Il appelle Maroni sur son portable. C'est alors que son assistant, Philippe Hissenly, accourt depuis la grande serre.

– Quel malheur, monsieur le directeur ! J'ai découvert le vol tout à l'heure en passant par hasard après la pluie. Je n'en ai pas cru mes yeux, c'est pourquoi je me suis approché. Vous voyez bien, ce sont mes traces de pied. J'ai voulu vous avertir, je vous ai cherché partout. Finalement, c'est Luc Actusse, notre stagiaire botaniste, qui m'a dit que vous étiez en train d'inspecter le terrain. C'est une sale histoire. Je me demande bien qui a pu faire ça.

– Pas moi, rétorque le commissaire qui, en un éclair, a tout compris. Le voleur, c'est vous, Philippe Hissenly. Rendez la *Calicia mirabilis* !

QUESTION

Qu'est-ce qui trahit le coupable ?

SERRE

28

TIRÉ PAR LES CHEVEUX

Victor Durail en a ras sa casquette de cheminot ! Une fois de plus, sa motrice a été recouverte de graffitis. Il soupçonne Hugues Ribouille, pour l'avoir vu rôder autour du dépôt, mais le garçon clame son innocence :
– C'est pas moi qui ai fait ça mais j'ai vu deux types se sauver à mobylette. Je les ai remarqués parce qu'ils étaient tout en rouge, les vestes, les casques et même les mobylettes.
Victor Durail n'en démord pas, il appelle le commissaire. Quand Maroni arrive, il s'adresse tout d'abord à Hugues :
– Qu'est-ce que tu es venu faire ici aussi tard le soir ? Pas étonnant qu'on ait pu te prendre pour l'auteur de cette merveille.
Hugues Ribouille répète qu'il est innocent et il raconte de nouveau l'histoire des deux inconnus qui se seraient enfuis sur leurs mobylettes.
– Tu peux les décrire ? demande Maroni.
– L'un était grand, l'autre plus petit. Ils portaient des vestes en cuir et des jeans rouges. Le plus grand des deux avait des lunettes de soleil et des cheveux marron coupés très court, l'autre portait des bottes avec des bouts pointus.
– Ça suffit ! coupe le commissaire, cette histoire va te coûter cher. Moi, franchement, si j'avais ton talent, je l'emploierais plus intelligemment.

QUESTION

Comment Hugues s'est-il trahi ?

. . . .

BT JO 857

29

EH NON, CE N'EST PAS ENCORE DANS LA POCHE !

Le professeur Laurent Jade vient de recevoir le prix Navel pour ses travaux sur la lyophilisation des agrumes. Hélas ! sa joie est de courte durée. En rentrant d'un cours donné à ses étudiants, il découvre avec effroi que le dossier renfermant son nouveau projet ultrasecret a été sorti du placard. Il le retrouve posé sur son bureau. Quelqu'un a dû profiter de son absence pour en recopier en toute hâte les passages essentiels. À la main, car la photocopieuse est en panne depuis hier soir.
La mort dans l'âme, le professeur convoque ses quatre collaborateurs. Ils sont les seuls à détenir chacun une clé pour accéder à son cabinet de travail. Qui parmi eux a trahi sa confiance ? Tous les quatre nient avoir mis les pieds dans le cabinet pendant son absence. Appelé à la rescousse, le commissaire ne tarde pas à percer le mystère. Dans sa précipitation, la personne espionne a commis une faute qui lui sera fatale.

QUESTION

Qui des quatre collaborateurs a voulu voler les secrets du professeur ?

Prix Navel
CONFIDENTIEL
LYO/AGR
BBA1
1 - 10

30

LE VERT N'EST PAS UNE COULEUR PRIMAIRE

C'est carnaval. À l'auberge Mistigri, la fête bat son plein. Tout le monde s'amuse, les confettis, les serpentins fusent mais Larry Bambelle, le patron, n'a pas l'air d'être dans son assiette.

– C'est quoi exactement cette affaire de jambon pour laquelle vous m'avez fait venir ? lui demande Maroni.

– Je vous explique, monsieur le commissaire. Tout à l'heure, j'ai voulu procéder au tirage de notre tombola. Seulement voilà, le premier prix, un superbe jambon de pays de douze kilos, avait disparu. Or, dix minutes auparavant, il était encore dans la réserve.

– Un vol de jambon ? (Maroni ne peut s'empêcher de sourire.) Quelqu'un a-t-il remarqué quelque chose ?

Le patron désigne la serveuse Rosie, une jeune femme maquillée en chat qui porte des lunettes en forme de cœur. Elle raconte :

– Tout à l'heure, quand j'ai ouvert la fenêtre pour aérer un peu, j'ai vu deux hommes ranger un gros paquet enveloppé de papier journal à l'arrière d'une voiture verte.

Maroni et Bambelle se précipitent vers la fenêtre et scrutent le parking.

– Trop tard ! soupire le patron, je ne vois pas de voiture verte.

– Moi non plus, glousse soudain le commissaire, mais votre affaire me semble résolue. Les deux énergumènes sont probablement retournés à la fête. En tout cas, leur voiture est toujours là.

QUESTION

Comment Maroni est-il arrivé à cette conclusion ?

P

31

UNE AFFAIRE FUMEUSE

Dans sa boutique d'articles pour fumeurs, la soirée s'annonce longue pour Mélanie Cautine. En effet, elle doit faire l'inventaire des marchandises qui sont entreposées au sous-sol. Pendant qu'elle y fait le compte de son stock, un bruit suspect lui parvient d'en haut, et un courant d'air fait soudain claquer la porte d'accès à la cave. Elle remonte l'escalier sur la pointe des pieds, elle rouvre prudemment la porte et pousse un juron fumant. La porte de la boutique qu'elle avait sans doute oublié de boucler est grande ouverte. Sur le comptoir, plus de trace des boîtes de coûteux cigares havanes qu'on lui avait livrés le soir même.

Mélanie se précipite dans la rue sombre. Tout est silencieux. C'est alors qu'au rez-de-chaussée d'un immeuble de bureaux tout proche, la lumière s'éteint dans la loge du gardien, un certain Vincent Drier. Que faire ? Dans sa colère, Mélanie téléphone au commissaire en le priant d'excuser l'heure tardive de son appel. Maroni la rassure, remet ses chaussures et la rejoint aussitôt. Ils sonnent chez Vincent Drier qui se dit prêt à les renseigner.

– Je viens seulement de rentrer, vous savez. Non, je n'ai rien remarqué de suspect… Ou peut-être bien que si. Sur le mur d'en face, j'ai aperçu l'ombre d'un homme courant vers le débarcadère.

– Merci de vos lumières, réplique le commissaire, mais votre témoignage est faux, et je n'aime pas qu'on me mène en bateau.

QUESTION

Qu'est-ce qui donne raison à Maroni ?

. . . .

ETTES
NTERDIT
20H–7H
DÉBARCADÈRE

32

LA CRÈME NE PREND PAS

Peu avant Pâques, Maroni est promu commissaire divisionnaire. Pour fêter l'événement, il a invité ses collègues les plus proches à une réception à la cafétéria de la préfecture de police. Gourmand dans l'âme, Maroni a commandé trois énormes gâteaux à la crème pour le dessert. Trois serveurs déguisés en lapins les déposent devant le commissaire. Maroni, pelle de tarte à la main, s'apprête à servir leur part aux convives quand, à l'improviste, la lumière s'éteint. Dans l'obscurité, on entend un bruit mat, suivi d'un cri étouffé. La lumière se rallume aussi soudainement, découvrant un commissaire copieusement barbouillé de crème chantilly. Maroni garde son sang-froid. Pendant que les trois serveurs prennent les commandes de boissons, il mène une enquête rapide. Elle lui donne la solution. Alain Sue, un cambrioleur récidiviste, qu'il avait arrêté quelques années auparavant, travaille à la cafétéria depuis sa sortie de prison. Sous son masque de lapin, Sue a voulu se venger du commissaire. Pour Maroni, l'affaire est désormais claire. En regardant bien les trois serveurs, il a distingué le vengeur barbouilleur.

QUESTION

Qui a jeté le gâteau à la crème à la tête du commissaire ?

. . . .

33

UN REPAS QUI NE PASSERA PAS

Comme tous les midis, il y a foule à « La Fine Bouche ». Lucas Rotte, l'un des serveurs, se remémore où il doit apporter les différentes commandes :
Table 3 : plat du jour n° 2 avec un verre de vin rouge.
Table 8 : plat du jour n° 3 avec une bouteille de bière.
Table 11 : plat du jour n° 2 avec une eau minérale.
Table 14 : plat du jour n° 1 avec une eau minérale.
Or, il y a une chose que tout le monde ignore : Lucas Rotte est un aigrefin gratiné. Pendant son service, il dérobe avec dextérité tantôt un portefeuille bien rempli, tantôt un bijou à son goût. Aimable et avenant comme il est, personne n'a jamais osé le suspecter. De plus, Lucas Rotte a fait le nécessaire pour ne pas se faire prendre. Son complice, Théophile Oseille, vient déjeuner tous les jours à « La Fine Bouche », et Lucas Rotte lui sert son butin tout chaud. Comme ce midi. Le serveur indélicat vient tout juste de voler à une cliente son précieux collier de perles. À l'une des quatre tables mentionnées ci-dessus, Théophile Oseille attend pour empocher la marchandise.
Or, les deux larrons ignorent que, soucieux de la réputation de son restaurant, le gérant a demandé à Maroni de mener une enquête.
– J'en ferai mon affaire, lui dit le commissaire après avoir percé le stratagème des deux malotrus qu'il emmène menottés au trou.

QUESTION

Comment et à quelle table Lucas Rotte a-t-il transmis son butin ?

....

PLATS DU JOUR
1. Risotto aux crevettes
2. Tournedos pommes frites
3. Bouchée à la reine, petits pois
4. Gratin d'aubergines à la provençale
14
2
3
MENU
4
11
5
6
MENU
16
18
20
MENU
21

34

CARRÉMENT TIMBRÉ !

Norbert a invité Emma, Louis et Jean pour leur faire une surprise. Comme lui, ses amis sont des collectionneurs passionnés de timbres rares.

– J'ai acheté, dans une brocante, pour trois fois rien, une Jeanne d'Or, leur confie-t-il fièrement. Venez, je vais vous la faire voir !

Intrigués, ses amis le suivent dans sa chambre. Norbert ouvre l'armoire et en retire trois enveloppes : une jaune, une blanche, une grise, toutes remplies de timbres. Il les ouvre toutes pour sortir finalement de l'enveloppe grise la Jeanne d'Or, son nouveau trésor.

– Mais tu es fou de la garder dans ton armoire ! s'exclame Emma.

– Exact, renchérit Louis, n'importe qui peut te la voler !

Jean est de leur avis. Pour s'assurer du prix de la Jeanne d'Or, il retourne seul dans le séjour où il consulte le catalogue des timbres sur Internet. Pendant ce temps, Norbert remet négligemment la Jeanne d'Or dans l'enveloppe blanche et range les trois enveloppes dans l'armoire. Ensuite, il part dans la cuisine pour retirer du four le poulet qu'il a préparé pour ses amis.

En retournant dans sa chambre après le départ de ses invités, Norbert a un haut-le-cœur : l'armoire est ouverte, les trois enveloppes gisent par terre, la Jeanne d'Or a disparu. À Maroni, son parrain, l'affaire paraît claire :

– Norbert, tu t'es laissé faire par un faux ami et je te dirai qui.

QUESTION

À qui Maroni fait-il allusion ?

35

BRUITS DE COULOIR

Laure Taugraffe, la maîtresse du CM1, est en colère. Pendant qu'elle était de surveillance dans la cour, quelqu'un a fouillé dans le tiroir de son bureau. Sans doute pour recopier les réponses au test de grammaire qu'elle fera passer demain aux élèves. Dans le couloir, elle tombe nez à nez avec le commissaire qui vient de parler aux élèves du CE2 du travail de la police. Non loin de là, Didi, Riri et Mimi, trois élèves de Mme Taugraffe, sont en train de discuter à voix basse.

Quand Maroni les questionne, chacun d'eux essaie de tirer son épingle du jeu.
– À votre place, je ne serais pas fier, gronde le commissaire après les avoir entendus.

QUESTION

Qui a recopié les solutions ?

....

36

LA VÉNUS VENUE DU GRAND NORD

La neige tombe à gros flocons. Assis dans son bureau, Maroni parcourt quelques dossiers en cours avant de terminer sa journée de travail. Le téléphone sonne, le commissaire bougonne et décroche en maugréant.

Gêné par la neige, Maroni doit rouler au pas. Il met plus d'une heure pour arriver à destination. Le directeur le reçoit, tout en émoi :

– Vous voilà enfin ! Merci ! Quelle ignominie ! Et quel culot !

Jean Stock a du mal à trouver ses mots, mais Maroni veut des détails.

– Actuellement, dit le directeur, nous présentons une exposition sublime sur le thème de l'hiver. Plusieurs musées étrangers nous ont prêté leurs chefs-d'œuvre. Comme tous les soirs, à 18 heures, j'ai fait le point de la journée avec mes collègues étrangers par le biais d'une vidéo-conférence. C'est alors que j'ai vu par la fenêtre deux hommes emportant « La Vénus de l'igloo » pour la jeter dans une camionnette bleue. J'en aurais pleuré !
Pour le commissaire, l'affaire est claire et nette : il n'y a pas eu de camionnette. Le directeur malhonnête a intégré en cachette la Vénus dans sa propre collection privée. L'heure est venue de le pousser aux aveux.

QUESTION

Pourquoi Jean Stock finit-il par flancher ?

....

37

L'HOMME DE L'OMBRE

L'appel au secours arrive à 19 heures. À l'appareil, le professeur Amédée Paon.
– Venez vite, monsieur le commissaire ! C'est très grave.
Maroni le rejoint au Westend, un salon de thé du centre-ville. Paon lui présente une certaine Ella Buse à qui il passe la parole. Elle raconte :
– Je devais remettre à M. Paon les plans secrets d'une nouvelle invention afin qu'il puisse les examiner. Nous ne nous étions encore jamais rencontrés. Nous avions pris rendez-vous pour 18 heures 45. Je suis arrivée avec cinq minutes d'avance. En m'apercevant, un monsieur s'est dirigé vers moi. Il s'est présenté comme étant le professeur Amédée Paon. Je lui ai remis l'enveloppe scellée, il m'a remerciée, et il est reparti aussitôt en direction de la bouche de métro de la ligne 7, à droite de la cathédrale. Je n'ai pas pu voir s'il a pris le passage menant au métro car j'étais aveuglée par le soleil couchant. Quelques instants plus tard, le vrai M. Paon est arrivé.
– Quelle calamité ! s'exclame ce dernier. Je me demande comment l'inconnu a pu savoir l'heure et le lieu de mon rendez-vous avec Mme Buse. Qu'en dites-vous, monsieur le commissaire ?
– L'affaire est claire, l'inconnu n'existe pas. Mme Buse l'a inventé pour pouvoir détourner les plans et les revendre à son profit.

QUESTION

Qu'est-ce qui prouve qu'Ella Buse s'est jouée d'Amédée Paon ?

WESTEND
TOUT PROPRE !
SERVICE
DE NETT
7 OUEST
7 EST
COI
WESTEND MENU
WESTEND MENU

38

L'AFFAIRE EST DANS LE SAC !

Le père Noël est soulagé ! Tous les cadeaux pour les enfants sont enfin emballés et enfermés dans un grand sac bien lourd. Sans l'aide de ses cinq assistants, il n'y serait probablement pas arrivé à temps. Pendant qu'il vérifie les patins de son traîneau garé derrière sa maisonnette, les cinq repartent chez eux, Gratien en premier, suivi peu à peu par les autres. Quand le père Noël revient, il n'y a plus personne – et plus de sac non plus ! Il fait appel à son ami Maroni qui, malgré l'heure tardive, va aussitôt interroger les cinq suspects chez eux. Ils nient tous. C'est en arrivant devant chez le père Noël que l'affaire devient enfin claire pour le commissaire.

QUESTION

Lequel des cinq a volé le sac rempli de cadeaux ?

39

CAFÉ AMER

Rino Zérox est furibond ! Pour fêter le cinquantième anniversaire de l'entreprise familiale spécialisée dans les fournitures de bureau, il a fait fabriquer trois cents trombones en or afin de les offrir à ses clients. Entreposés hier soir dans un tiroir de son bureau, ils ne s'y trouvent plus ce matin. Zérox fait appel à Maroni qui vient aussitôt interroger les six personnes présentes. C'est forcément la personne arrivée la première sur les lieux qui a commis le vol. Le commissaire les écoute toutes attentivement.
Mme Casse : « Je suis arrivée vers 9 heures 40 après mon rendez-vous chez le médecin. J'ai croisé Mme Chamoix dans l'escalier. Mes collègues étaient déjà tous à leur place. »
Mme Chamoix, la femme de ménage : « J'ai commencé par nettoyer l'escalier. Les employés étaient tous là, à part Mme Casse qui est arrivée en courant. Elle a failli se prendre les pieds dans mon balai. »
Mme Mine : « À mon arrivée, j'ai trouvé M. Boux et M. Poil réunis autour de la machine à café. Mme Leyratte était déjà plongée dans ses dossiers. »
M. Poil, agent technique de Presso Service : « Je suis arrivé à 9 heures pile pour réviser la machine à café. J'ai proposé un café à Mme Leyratte, qui m'avait ouvert la porte. Elle n'en a pas voulu. Quand M. Boux est arrivé, je lui ai préparé un bon expresso. »
Mme Leyratte : « Moi, le café, le matin, je n'en prends jamais. Ça me donne des palpitations. »
M. Boux : « Je suis arrivé à 9 heures 05. J'avais passé une mauvaise nuit. Le café de M. Poil m'a requinqué. »
– Mon cher Zérox, le résultat de mon enquête est hélas amer, conclut le commissaire. Je sais à présent qui vous a sucré vos trombones.

QUESTION

Qui est le coupable ?

....

ZÉROX
QUALITÉ PRO !
ZÉROX & CO
ZÉROX
P
B. CASSE
O. POIL
PRESSO
PRESSO SERVICE
R. MINE
PRESSO SERVICE
I. BOUX
C. LEYRATTE

40

MARONI VOIT ROUGE

Alerte en ville ! Catou Fochay est de retour ! La voleuse ne manque pas d'astuce pour soutirer en souriant leur argent aux passants crédules. L'une de ses victimes avertit Maroni, qui se met aussitôt à la recherche de Catou. Or la voleuse semble s'être envolée. Par un coup de téléphone anonyme, le commissaire apprend qu'elle se cache probablement chez son vieil ami Jean Saylon, un retraité qui habite dans un faubourg de la ville. Maroni se présente chez Saylon qui le fait entrer dans son appartement.

– Si vous cherchez Catou Fochay, vous n'êtes pas à la bonne adresse ici. Il y a une éternité que je ne l'ai pas vue.

– Vous habitez seul ? lui demande Maroni.

– Non, je sous-loue une pièce à un étudiant. Ça m'arrange, vous comprenez, monsieur le commissaire. Impossible de m'en sortir autrement avec ce que je reçois comme retraite. Allez, je vais vous faire un petit café pour que vous ne soyez pas venu pour rien.

Pendant que Saylon prépare le café en sifflotant, Maroni laisse courir son regard qui s'accroche à un tout petit détail. Alors tout s'éclaire pour le commissaire : Jean Saylon ment comme un arracheur de dents ! C'est bel et bien une femme qu'il loge chez lui et puisqu'il le dément, il s'agit sans doute de Catou Fochay.

QUESTION

Qu'est-ce qui a attiré l'attention de Maroni ?

PLUK
PIZZA
réparateur frigo jeudi matin
La nature
ASTRO
Mystères
MISTER X
Liste des courses :
collant
shampoing
GAZETTE

SOLUTIONS

1. Qui a fait boire la tasse à Guy Bolle ?
William Stramgramme ment. Si Guy Bolle avait bu son infusion à 10 heures 30, la tasse ne serait plus chaude. C'est donc lui qui y a mis le somnifère peu avant le passage de Jean Revienpa.

2. Le vol de Guignol
Sur l'un des bouts de verre gisant par terre se trouve un peigne. Quand Gérard Écherre est sorti pour prendre son café, Dédé Pic a cassé la vitre. En se penchant pour voler le Guignol, il a perdu son peigne.

3. Il faut regarder les choses en face
Comment Yves Affort aurait-il pu voir depuis la porte du bureau le pansement sur la joue gauche du technicien s'enfuyant du laboratoire par la porte du fond ? C'est lui en personne qui a sectionné le câble d'alimentation.

4. Pas facile de se faire un tableau !
En classant les photos par ordre chronologique, on constate que le 4 mai à 23 heures 57 quelqu'un traverse la galerie. Neuf minutes plus tard, on voit la même personne quitter la salle précipitamment en emportant un portrait. On retrouve ce tableau chez José-Jean Porte adossé au mur derrière son bureau.

5. Une erreur de montage
La pleine lune apparaît en haut à droite sur l'image. L'ombre de l'ovni ne se trouve donc pas du bon côté.

6. Mauvais réglage ou bien sabotage ?
Le témoignage d'Aurèle est faux. De son siège, il n'a pas pu voir le réservoir du camion qui se trouve du côté opposé. C'est lui qui a mis du sucre dans le réservoir pendant l'absence de Larbi.

7. Nom d'un chien !
Le manteau de M. Dugras est pendu par-dessus celui de Mme Lossamoile, ce qui prouve que Dugras est arrivé après elle. C'est donc Mme Lossamoile qui a empoché les comprimés Mincetoutou.

8. Mine de rien...
Jimmy Lesbouts s'est enfui par la troisième galerie. L'énorme flaque d'eau à son entrée a empêché Truffette de suivre sa trace.

9. Bigre de bougre de corne d'aurochs !
La fenêtre s'ouvre vers l'extérieur ! Grimpé en haut de l'échelle, le « cambrioleur » évoqué par le gardien n'aurait donc pas pu l'ouvrir. C'est Guy Laffauchey lui-même qui a mis en scène le cambriolage. D'abord il est monté à l'échelle pour casser la vitre de l'extérieur. Puis il a retiré l'échelle pour pouvoir ouvrir la fenêtre de l'intérieur et, finalement, il a remis l'échelle pour faire croire à un cambriolage.

10. Qui a sucré le gâteau de tante Huguette ?
Comme le montre l'horloge de l'église, le réveil de Jean Raivay retarde d'un quart d'heure. Quand il a allumé sa radio, les informations étaient déjà passées. Il n'a donc pas d'alibi pour les dix minutes pendant lesquelles Huguette était absente de sa chambre.

11. Quelqu'un va se faire tirer l'oreille
Sélina prétend ne pas être entrée dans le salon. Or il lui manque une boucle d'oreille. Elle se trouve sur le canapé, juste en dessous du tableau barbouillé.

12. Rien que du vent !
Le vent n'a pas pu déposer le billet de loterie aux pieds de Michou Rave car il souffle dans le sens contraire, comme le montre le drapeau à l'arrière-plan.

13. De quoi perdre la boule !
Le journal dans les mains de Véra Kivivra porte la date de lundi. Le vol a donc eu lieu la veille. Or, le dimanche, les bibliothèques sont fermées.

14. Et hop ! la bergère est embarquée !
La fleur dans le pot à côté de la radio a été arrosée récemment, ce qui prouve bien que quelqu'un habite dans la caravane. Ça ne peut être que Cathy Mini.

15. La pêche aux poissons Py Khê
Les deux poissons Py Khê sont rouges avec une queue bleue. L'un nage dans le grand bocal sur la table en marbre, l'autre se trouve très à l'étroit dans un bocal de l'étagère à droite du thermomètre.

16. Un père Noël doublé
Le voleur est le père Noël de droite. Il s'était introduit dans la maison avant que la neige ne se soit mise à tomber. C'est pourquoi on voit uniquement ses traces de pieds menant de la maison à la rue et non pas, comme chez l'autre père Noël, des traces qui font l'aller-retour.

17. Y a pas photo !
Dylan Tille prétend avoir été en plein travail avec son équipe quand le voleur est passé devant son objectif. Or, la photo qui montre le suspect se trouve au début de la pellicule, les photos de mode viennent seulement après. Cela signifie qu'elles ont été prises uniquement pour faire croire à une session de prises de vue qui, en vérité, n'a pas eu lieu.

18. C'est clair et net
Avec un temps de pose de plus de trois heures, la photo montrerait les étoiles non pas comme des points fixes mais – à cause de la rotation de la Terre – sous forme de traînées lumineuses dans le ciel.

19. Qui a marché sur les plates-bandes ?
Si les garçons avaient vraiment joué au foot, leur ballon serait aussi sale qu'eux.

20. De quoi dormir tranquillement sur ses deux oreilles
Dans sa blouse blanche, l'employé à la moustache apparaît plutôt mince. Dans son manteau, à la sortie de l'usine, il montre curieusement un certain embonpoint.

21. De quoi se faire des cheveux !
Sur la photo, Yvan Lamèche se trouve au milieu. Dans la salle de bal, affublé d'un long nez en forme de carotte, il se tient près de l'escalier. On le reconnaît au petit doigt manquant de la main droite.

22. Une course pour la montre
Quand Ethan Retarre pousse la porte de la boutique ce matin-là – le 13 du mois –, la corbeille n'est plus vide. En revanche, sur la photo montrant l'arrivée de son collègue, elle l'est encore. C'est donc Nicolas Vence qui est arrivé le premier et a volé la précieuse montre-bracelet.

23. Un réveil de princesse
La veille, Amanda a secrètement tourné le réveil de Miranda de 90 degrés. En le regardant ce matin, Miranda a donc cru qu'il était 11 heures moins le quart alors qu'il n'était que 7 heures et demie !

24. Beaucoup de bruit pour rien
Si un étranger avait essayé de s'introduire dans la maison, Hercule aurait aboyé – comme il l'a fait à l'arrivée de Maroni. Or, l'épouse et le fils du professeur ont seulement entendu un bruit de verre. Cela revient à dire qu'Abel Halure a mis en scène lui-même le faux cambriolage.

25. La victoire en se grattant
Maroni doit rechercher l'homme qui apparaît sur la photo D.

26. Souris blanches et carnet noir
Comme il le dit lui-même, Don Miracolo a pris congé de ses confrères magiciens avant que le grand Gougloff ne fasse sortir les souris de la boîte. Il n'a donc pas vu le nouveau tour mais il l'a lu dans le carnet noir qu'il a dérobé.

27. Maroni n'est pas tombé de la dernière pluie
Les flaques, les feuilles et les rameaux qui recouvrent partiellement les traces de pied prouvent que Philippe Hissenliy s'est affairé autour de la *Calicia mirabilis* avant la tempête.

28. Tiré par les cheveux

Comment Hugues Ribouille peut-il savoir que l'un des deux inconnus avait les cheveux marron coupés court puisque, toujours d'après lui, tous les deux portaient des casques ?

29. Eh non, ce n'est pas encore dans la poche !

C'est Juju Theux qui a recopié les formules secrètes de Laurent Jade. La preuve : la grande photo sur le mur de droite montre le professeur dans son bureau exhibant fièrement son prix Navel. Dans le pot à crayons, on distingue un stylo noir et jaune – le même qui apparaît dans la poche de la blouse de Juju Theux qui a oublié de le replacer dans le pot après s'en être servi.

30. Le vert n'est pas une couleur primaire

La voiture bleue des voleurs de jambon se trouve toujours sur le parking. Elle n'a pas bougé depuis que Rosie l'a vue en vert à travers ses lunettes aux verres teintés. Jaune + bleu = vert, c'est clair !

31. Une affaire fumeuse

La seule lumière dans la rue provient du réverbère qui se trouve tout en haut. Elle ne peut donc pas projeter l'ombre d'un homme sur le mur en contrebas. C'est Vincent Drier qui l'a inventée pour détourner les soupçons.

32. La crème ne prend pas

Le commissaire reçoit la tarte à la crème sur partie droite du visage, c'est donc un gaucher qui l'a lancée. Alain Sue est le lapin du milieu.

33. Un repas qui ne passera pas

Théophile Oseille est assis à la table 11. Lucas Rotte lui apporte le collier dissimulé dans l'assiette par les pommes frites.

34. Carrément timbré !

Contrairement à Louis et Emma, Jean n'était pas dans la chambre quand Norbert a remis les timbres dans les enveloppes. Ne sachant pas que Norbert a rangé la Jeanne d'Or dans l'enveloppe blanche, Jean a ouvert les trois pour la retrouver.

35. Bruits de couloir
Mimi a menti. La porte de la salle de classe s'ouvre vers l'extérieur. Pour la garder fermée, quelqu'un se trouvant à l'intérieur ne se serait sûrement pas appuyé dessus, bien au contraire !

36. La Vénus venue du Grand Nord
Quand Maroni arrive au musée, Jean Stock déclare que le vol de la Vénus s'est produit pendant la vidéo-conférence de 18 heures. Or au moment où il prévient le commissaire du vol du tableau, il est seulement 17 heures 20 comme l'indique la pendule sur le bureau de Maroni.

37. L'homme de l'ombre
Ella Buse prétend que, aveuglée par le soleil couchant, elle n'a pas vu par où s'enfuyait l'inconnu. Or les ombres des passants prouvent bien que le soleil se trouvait du côté opposé.

38. L'affaire est dans le sac !
Saturnin est trahi par les traces que ses bottes ont imprimées dans la neige. Fluet comme il est, il ne se serait jamais enfoncé aussi profondément – sans le sac rempli de cadeaux qu'il portait sur son dos.

39. Café amer
L'une des photos sur son bureau montre Mme Leyratte à côté d'une voiture rouge – la même qui est garée maintenant au fond de l'impasse, derrière la camionnette de M. Poil. C'est donc Mme Leyratte qui est arrivée la première ce matin. D'ailleurs M. Poil dit bien que c'est elle qui lui a ouvert la porte.

40. Maroni voit rouge
Jean Saylon ment. Sur la table de la cuisine, Maroni a aperçu une liste de courses avec deux écritures différentes. La première est celle de Sayon. Et la seconde ? Ce n'est sûrement pas un étudiant qui penserait à s'acheter du vernis à ongles et du rouge à lèvres !

TABLE

DU MÊME AUTEUR

www.actes-sud-junior

Reproduit et achevé d'imprimer
en avril 2012
par CPI Aubin Imprimeur à Ligugé
pour le compte des éditions
ACTES SUD
Le Méjan
Place Nina-Berberova
13200 Arles

Dépôt légal
1re édition : mai 2010
N° impr. 1204.0458
(Imprimé en France)